NEGOTIATING CIVIL WAR

Civil war has been a fact of political life throughout recorded history. Unlike inter-state wars, however, international law has not traditionally regulated such conflicts. How then can we explain the post-1945 emergence and evolution of international treaty rules regulating the conduct of internal armed conflict: the 'civil war regime'? *Negotiating Civil War* combines insights derived from Realist, Rationalist, Liberal and Constructivist approaches to International Relations to answer this question, revisiting the negotiation of the 1949 Geneva Conventions, the 1977 Additional Protocols and the 1998 Rome Statute of the International Criminal Court to provide a rigorous, critical account of the making of the civil war regime. Sophisticated and persuasive, *Negotiating Civil War* illustrates the complex interplay of material, ideational, social and strategic factors in shaping these rules with important lessons for the making and unmaking of international law in a rapidly shifting international political, economic and security environment.

HENRY LOVAT is Lord Kelvin Adam Smith Research Fellow at the University of Glasgow.

NEGOTIATING CIVIL WAR

The Politics of International Regime Design

HENRY LOVAT

University of Glasgow

CAMBRIDGE
UNIVERSITY PRESS

CAMBRIDGE
UNIVERSITY PRESS

University Printing House, Cambridge CB2 8BS, United Kingdom

One Liberty Plaza, 20th Floor, New York, NY 10006, USA

477 Williamstown Road, Port Melbourne, VIC 3207, Australia

314–321, 3rd Floor, Plot 3, Splendor Forum, Jasola District Centre, New Delhi – 110025, India

79 Anson Road, #06–04/06, Singapore 079906

Cambridge University Press is part of the University of Cambridge.

It furthers the University's mission by disseminating knowledge in the pursuit of education, learning, and research at the highest international levels of excellence.

www.cambridge.org
Information on this title: www.cambridge.org/9781108497275
DOI: 10.1017/9781108667302

First published 2020

A catalogue record for this publication is available from the British Library.

Library of Congress Cataloging-in-Publication Data
Names: Lovat, Henry Mark, author.
Title: Negotiating civil war / Henry Mark Lovat.
Description: Cambridge, United Kingdom ; New York, NY : Cambridge University Press, 2019. | Includes bibliographical references and index.
Identifiers: LCCN 2019027965 (print) | LCCN 2019027966 (ebook) | ISBN 9781108497275 (hardback) | ISBN 9781108739702 (epub)
Subjects: LCSH: Civil war. | War (International law)
Classification: LCC KZ6397 .L68 2019 (print) | LCC KZ6397 (ebook) | DDC 341.6–dc23
LC record available at https://lccn.loc.gov/2019027965
LC ebook record available at https://lccn.loc.gov/2019027966

ISBN 978-1-108-49727-5 Hardback

This book is dedicated to Bernice Lipton, Keren Maschler, and Ella Lovat.

'פיה פתחה בחכמה ותורת חסד על לשונה'

אשת חיל, Proverbs 31: 26

CONTENTS

FIGURES

ACKNOWLEDGEMENTS

Negotiating Civil War began life as a doctoral dissertation at the Hebrew University of Jerusalem, and I am grateful to Moshe Hirsch and Arie Kacowicz for their guidance, support and patience throughout that project. I am also indebted to Tal Dingott Alkopher, Michael Gross and Yuval Shany for help in designing that study and for helpful and constructive comments throughout. Yuval's invitation to participate in his ERC-funded research project on the Effectiveness of International Courts also provided an immensely valuable avenue of further intellectual exploration as well as assisting in defraying the costs of prolonged study: I am also grateful to him for his continued support and advice as the doctoral project evolved into this book.

Research was funded principally by scholarships from the Leonard Davis Institute for International Relations and the Israeli Ministry of Immigrant Absorption, whose support I am pleased to acknowledge. This project could also not have been completed without the facilities of the Mount Scopus Library, the British Library, the UK National Archives, the US National Archives and Records Administration, and the Institute of Advanced Legal Studies in London. I am also grateful for the support of colleagues at the UK Government Legal Department, Council of Europe, University of Glasgow, HM Treasury and the British Business Bank.

This project has benefited from assistance, encouragement and insights from too many to name. It would be remiss, though, not to thank: Emanuel Adler, Martha Baker, Kristin Bakke, Matthias Behnke, Alex Belle, David Bicknell, Andrea Birdsall, David Birnbaum, Thorbjörn Björnsson, Adam Bower, Mark Brawley, Jutta Brunnée, Marie-Claire Cordonier Segger, Shai Dothan, Cian O'Driscoll, Kim Fontaine-Skronski, Mark Furse, Charles Garraway, Markus Gehring, Robin Geiss, Rotem Giladi, James Gow, Brian Greenhill, Sigall Horowitz, Talbot Imlay, Haim Itzhaki, Peter Jackson, Rachel Kerr, Karen Knop, Fiona Leverick, Juergen Lichem, Iain MacLeod, Paul McKell and FCO colleagues, Saskia Millmann, Gilad Noam, Victor Peskin, Ingo Rohlfing, Sivan Shlomo, Ty Solomon, Mia Spiro, Christian Tams, Rina Tzalik and Maria Varaki. I also remain hugely indebted to the late Norman Geras and Harry Lesser of the University of Manchester. Thanks to the Levitt, Levstein and Taylor clans for warmth and hospitality over the years.

It is a pleasure to acknowledge and thank Tom Randall, Finola O'Sullivan, Becky Jackaman, Gemma Smith and colleagues at Cambridge University Press for shepherding *Negotiating Civil War* immaculately through the publication process, Gayathri Tamilselvan for project management and CUP's anonymous reviewers for their valuable, constructive comments – though the usual disclaimer, of course, applies.

Last, thanks to my extended nuclear family – Keren and Ella, Mervyn and Linda, Bernice and Derek, Toby and Adam, Lucy and Ben, Itzhak and Anna and family – for their (often critical) support.

Introduction

> 'Civil war has gradually become the most widespread, the most destructive, and the most characteristic form of organized human violence.'[1]

> 'What in any case remains indisputable is that humanitarian multilateral treaties, however else they may be regarded, are political products.'[2]

The Puzzling Civil War Regime

Insurrection and violent rebellion against rulers have been facts of political life throughout recorded history.[3] In contrast to the treatment of inter-state wars, however,[4] international law has traditionally not regulated the conduct of internal armed conflict.[5] Rather, governments have long preferred to retain the broadest possible discretion in responding to challenges to their domestic monopolies over the legitimate use of force.

The post-1945 emergence of multilateral treaty provisions – and entire instruments – regulating the conduct of internal armed conflict thus constitutes a puzzling international legal innovation. This 'civil war regime', moreover, forms an increasingly critical element of the international legal order, as civil conflicts continue to outnumber inter-state wars – according to the International Committee of the Red Cross

[1] Armitage, *Civil Wars: A History in Ideas*, 5.

[2] Best, *War and Law since 1945*, 407.

[3] Herodotus, for example, (himself writing against the background of the First Peloponnesian War) provides an extensive discussion of the Ionian rebellion against Persian rule in 499–493 BC (Herodotus, *The Histories, Revised*). Comparable antique conflicts include the Babylonian revolt against Assyria (626–616 BC); the Warring States period in Chinese history (475–221 BC); the Carthaginian Civil War (309–308 BC); and the various Roman Republican and Imperial civil conflicts.

[4] The conduct of international armed conflict has long been subject to widely understood and recognised rules, which can be traced back to the mediaeval period. See generally e.g. Neff, *War and the Law of Nations: A General History*.

[5] The phrases 'internal armed conflict' and 'non-international armed conflict' are used interchangeably with 'civil war' in the present volume, save where the context indicates otherwise.

(ICRC), having 'more than doubled (in number) between 2001 and 2016, from fewer than 30 to more than 70' – as well as causing more fatalities than the latter.[6] These conflicts have also become more complex over time, with increasing numbers of parties involved: indeed, as of 2016, only a minority of non-international armed conflicts were between two parties.[7] It is perhaps unsurprising that civil war has been termed the 'dominant mode of organized violence' since the end of the Cold War.[8]

The central elements of the international civil war regime (notionally) regulating such conflicts comprise Common Article 3 of the Geneva Conventions of 1949, Article 1(4) of Additional Protocol I and Additional Protocol II of 1977 to these Conventions, and Article 8 of the 1998 Rome Statute of the International Criminal Court. Each of these provisions and instruments has sought to constrain, progressively more closely, the range of acceptable conduct on the part of governments and non-state actors in internal armed conflict, in effect granting asymmetric benefits to the latter by restricting governments' latitude in prosecuting civil wars. The development of these measures forms the central puzzle motivating this book.

Overview

Negotiating Civil War addresses this puzzle over the course of six substantive chapters. Chapter 1 ('Theorising the Civil War Regime') establishes the theoretical orientation of the book, mapping approaches typically taken by International Relations (IR) scholars to regime development and using these to develop a pluralist theoretical framework tailored to analysis of the multilateral negotiations that produced the civil war regime. This framework is then applied in three case studies (Chapters 3, 4 and 5), examining the negotiation of internal armed conflict-regulating treaty provisions in diplomatic conferences in 1949,

[6] ICRC, '*The Roots of Restraint in War*', 13. See data and discussions in von Einsiedel, 'Civil War Trends and the Changing Nature of Armed Conflict'; Melander, Pettersson, and Themnér, 'Organized Violence, 1989–2015'; Leitenberg, 'Deaths in Wars and Conflicts between 1945 and 2000, Cornell University Peace Studies Program'.

[7] ICRC, '*The Roots of Restraint in War*', 13. ('[O]nly one-third of conflicts today are between two belligerent parties: 44 per cent have between three and nine opposing forces, and 22 per cent have more than ten. Some conflicts have hundreds: by the end of the war in Libya in October 2011, 236 separate armed groups were registered in the city of Misrata alone, and the Carter Center counted over 1,000 armed groups fighting in Syria in 2014.')

[8] Checkel, 'Transnational Dynamics of Civil War', 3.

1974–7 and 1998, respectively. The findings from the case studies are brought together in Chapter 6 ('Explaining the Civil War Regime').

The theoretical framework at the heart of the book, set out in Chapter 1, incorporates five hypotheses reflecting central 'Realist', 'Rationalist', 'Constructivist' and 'Liberal' insights into regime design, enabling *Negotiating Civil War* to benefit from the capacity of these traditions to shed light on important, distinct aspects of treaty negotiation. The hypotheses highlight the potential role in shaping civil war-regulating treaty outputs of: great power preferences; rational assessments by governments of anticipated costs and benefits of drafting proposals; the characteristics of 'norm entrepreneurs' seeking to promote civil war regulation; the strength, coherence and consistency with shared values and principles of the arguments deployed in negotiations; and the extent to which key state participants in negotiations represent more or less democratic polities. Chapter 1 also sets out indicators for the operation of each of these propositions, as well as presenting in 'straw person' diagrammatic form an ex ante view of how the causal factors underlying these hypotheses might interact and together have contributed to shaping treaty drafting outcomes.

Chapter 2 ('Historical Precursors and Regime Origins') provides context for the study as a whole, situating the development of the civil war regime within the evolution of the international law of armed conflict.[9] The chapter considers classical, mediaeval and Enlightenment manifestations of the legal distinction between international and internal armed conflict; the rise and fall of the doctrines of belligerency and insurgency; the development of the US Lieber Code and the establishment and early activities of the International Committee of the Red Cross, before surveying the development of the law of armed conflict from the late nineteenth century until the Second World War. The chapter then considers the development of the civil war regime between 1949 and 1998 and subsequently, highlighting the key elements of the regime and setting these in the broader international legal context, including the development of international human rights law and international criminal law.

The first part of Chapter 3 ('Negotiating Common Article 3 (1949)') describes the background to and the negotiation of Common Article 3 of the 1949 Geneva Conventions. The second part of the chapter analyses

[9] The older term 'law of armed conflict' and the more modern 'international humanitarian law' are used interchangeably in the present volume, depending on the context. It bears observing, however, that the shift in terminology can itself be considered a political move. See e.g. Wilson, 'The Myth of International Humanitarian Law'; Alexander, 'A Short History of International Humanitarian Law'.

these negotiations, examining debates and negotiating processes and outcomes from the perspectives of key actors (principally US, UK, Soviet, French and ICRC delegations) with accompanying observations on positions taken by other delegations. The chapter then considers the implications of the negotiating history for the five hypotheses, finding that the drafting reflects a balance between competing perceived costs and benefits, arrived at largely through processes of principled contestation and moral and technical persuasion, conducted against the (material) backdrop of the nascent Cold War and decolonisation, as well as a broader humanitarian international normative Zeitgeist. The conclusion includes a brief discussion of the manner in which governments, international institutions and civil society (including the ICRC) have utilised Common Article 3 since 1949.

Chapter 4 ('The Additional Protocols of 1977') opens with an overview of the discussions on internal armed conflict at the four sessions of the diplomatic conference convened between 1974 and 1977 (the CDDH) which led to the conclusion of the first two Additional Protocols to the 1949 Conventions. The chapter then considers the civil war-regulating outcomes of the CDDH – Article 1(4) of Protocol I, which requires 'wars of national liberation' to be treated as international rather than internal armed conflicts, and Protocol II in terms of scope and content – from the perspective of the principal actors in the negotiations. In this instance, these were the USA, the UK, Canada, the Nordic states (particularly Norway), Australia, Egypt, India, Pakistan, the Soviet Union and the ICRC. On this occasion, the provisions on internal armed conflict notably reflected the preferences of materially less powerful states: the 1974 negotiation of Article 1(4) also illustrates the limited efficacy of moral persuasion, technical authority and principled argument in the absence of a normative consensus across delegations. The 1977 negotiations over Protocol II, in contrast, highlight the ability of weaker powers to deploy moral and technical authority alongside principled argument to bring about drafting outcomes. The concluding section of the chapter again includes a discussion of the post-negotiation 'afterlives' of Article 1(4) and Protocol II, including consideration of how the challenges involved in crafting these measures have shaped their subsequent (often limited) impact.

Chapter 5 ('War Crimes and Internal Armed Conflict in the Rome Statute (1998)') examines the 1998 negotiation of the civil war-regulating paragraphs of Article 8(2) of the Rome Statute of the International Criminal Court. The chapter provides some historical background before setting out the key turning points in the negotiation of these clauses. As in preceding chapters, the negotiations are considered from the perspectives of key actors: in this case, the 'Like-Minded Group', the permanent five members of the UN Security Council (particularly the USA, the UK and France), the Non-Aligned Movement, and prominent civil society participants (including Amnesty International, Human Rights Watch, and the International Federation for Human Rights (FIDH)). The chapter underlines that while like-minded and NGO moral authority and technical expertise played a large part in persuading wavering delegations, the internal armed conflict provisions of Article 8(2) closely reflect the preferences of the Western 'P3' as well as the post-Cold War liberal Zeitgeist. The conclusion again includes a brief discussion of post-negotiation use of the internal armed conflict provisions of the Rome Statute at the ICC and elsewhere.

Chapter 6 ('Explaining the Civil War Regime') draws together the case study findings. The first section of the chapter assesses the collective implications of the case studies for the hypotheses set out in Chapter 1, and revisits Chapter 1's diagrammatic representation of interaction amongst causal factors in light of the case studies. This is followed by a reconsideration, building on the revised diagrammatic representation, of how these factors interacted in shaping key drafting outcomes in the 1949 Conventions, the 1977 Additional Protocols and the 1998 Rome Statute.

Closing observations are set out in the Conclusion. This reviews the major points discussed in the book, sets these in their broader context and identifies implications of *Negotiating Civil War* for the practice and study of the civil war regime, and of international law and politics more broadly.

Findings

Chapters 1–3 set out specific conclusions in respect of each of the case studies. More broadly, however, *Negotiating Civil War* underlines the differentiated impact on regime design of perceived moral authority and technical expertise, and the critical importance of nesting arguments in the dominant Zeitgeist of multilateral treaty negotiations. In particular, the book highlights that the perceived moral authority of state and civil society norm entrepreneurs and the ability of these actors to rhetorically frame coherent arguments in terms of widely shared principles and values have been key factors in the development of the civil war regime.

Technical expertise unallied with moral authority, however, has had less impact on proceedings.

The study also illustrates that materially weaker states cannot be taken for granted in multilateral treaty negotiations. The preferences of great powers have had a constraining effect on treaty drafting outcomes, but these preferences are themselves often endogenous, with outcomes more dependent on the ability of morally authoritative participants to nest arguments effectively in the normative context of negotiations. Materially less powerful states have also had a significant impact on proceedings as norm entrepreneurs and – acting in combination – have been capable of forcing great powers to compromise on even strongly held preferences.

The impact of domestic governance type on drafting preferences and outcomes is more ambiguous. Governments of states undergoing democratic transitions following internal unrest have in many instances been particularly ready to embrace a robust, demanding regime. Governments of authoritarian states have also been relatively unconcerned about the adoption of demanding treaty wording, however, whereas governments of liberal democracies facing domestic unrest (including in colonial possessions) have been more exercised by this prospect.

The civil war regime has been extensively examined from a range of perspectives. To date, however, analysis of the political factors and dynamics that shaped these measures has been limited in important respects. *Negotiating Civil War* accordingly fills important gaps in current understandings of this regime, providing a nuanced, theoretically informed analysis of the emergence of the civil war regime through multilateral treaty negotiations in 1949, 1974–7 and 1998.

The book also underlines more generally the rich understanding of international regime design that can be obtained by applying together insights drawn from multiple 'mainstream' IR research traditions, with the selection of such traditions and insights underpinned by – in the case of *Negotiating Civil War* – an epistemologically positivist orientation to social scientific enquiry. It also provides a valuable worked example of practice-oriented scholarship, suggesting that in comparable future instances, treaty negotiators – including in technically adept delegations – would be well-advised to pay close attention to the prevailing normative Zeitgeist of negotiations, and to endeavour to frame arguments accordingly to enhance their effectiveness.

Situating *Negotiating Civil War*

Negotiating Civil War broaches new ground in providing fresh, theoretically structured insight into the origins and development of the civil war regime. In so doing, it builds on and enriches existing research on civil war regulation, a literature that has to date – albeit with important exceptions – largely been dominated by doctrinal and historical studies.[10] *Negotiating Civil War* also contributes to a growing body of interdisciplinary literature seeking to better understand the emergence and development of international law,[11] including through the application of IR theory to the design and operation of international legal rules

[10] Recent doctrinal texts include: Zamir, *Classification of Conflicts in International Humanitarian Law: The Legal Impact of Foreign Intervention in Civil Wars*; Dinstein, *Non-International Armed Conflicts in International Law*; Sivakumaran, *The Law of Non-International Armed Conflict*; Watkin and Norris, *Non-International Armed Conflict in the Twenty-First Century*; Cullen, *The Concept of Non-International Armed Conflict in International Humanitarian Law*; La Haye, *War Crimes in Internal Armed Conflicts.* Focused historical studies include: Perna, *The Formation of the Treaty Law of Non-International Armed Conflicts*; Moir, *The Law of Internal Armed Conflict*; Abi-Saab, 'Non-International Armed Conflicts'; Suter, *An International Law of Guerrilla Warfare: The Global Politics of Law-Making.* Also related historical discussions in: Armitage, *Civil Wars: A History in Ideas*; Forsythe, *The Humanitarians: The International Committee of the Red Cross*; Neff, *War and the Law of Nations: A General History*; Moorehead, *Dunant's Dream: War, Switzerland and the History of the Red Cross*; Best, *War and Law since 1945*; and more recently van Dijk, 'Human Rights in War: On the Entangled Foundations of the 1949 Geneva Conventions'. As to exceptions to these trends, see in particular the work of Giovanni Mantilla ('Forum Isolation: Social Opprobrium and the Origins of the International Law of Internal Conflict'; 'The Origins and Evolution of the 1949 Geneva Conventions and the 1977 Additional Protocols'; 'Conforming Instrumentalists: Why the USA and the United Kingdom Joined the 1949 Geneva Conventions'; 'Under (Social) Pressure: The Historical Regulation of Internal Armed Conflicts through International Law'). Also: Abbott, 'International Relations Theory, International Law, and the Regime Governing Atrocities in Internal Conflicts'; Dunoff and Trachtman, 'The Law and Economics of Humanitarian Law Violations in Internal Conflict'; Finnemore, *National Interests in International Society.*

[11] The current interest amongst scholars of International Relations in international law can be traced back to the post-Cold War 'legalisation' of international politics. This engagement was given particular impetus by a 2000 special issue of International Organization (Goldstein et al., *Legalization and World Politics*), but also encompasses earlier work such as Risse, Ropp and Sikkink, *The Power of Human Rights*; Keck and Sikkink, *Activists beyond Borders*; Finnemore, *National Interests in International Society.* Subsequent work in this vein, drawing on a variety of IR theoretical traditions, includes: Koremenos, *The Continent of International Law: Explaining Agreement Design*; Pouliot, *International Pecking Orders: The Politics and Practice of Multilateral Diplomacy*; Cho, *The Social Foundations of World Trade: Norms, Community, and Constitution*; Dill, *Legitimate Targets?: Social Construction, International Law and US Bombing*; Morrow, *Order within Anarchy: The Laws of War as an International Institution*; Risse, Ropp, and Sikkink, *The*

and institutions,[12] so enhancing understanding (albeit modestly) of how the world 'hangs together'.[13]

Negotiating Civil War also goes beyond existing studies in a number of important respects. Perhaps most critically, it demonstrates the capacity of a set of theoretical insights derived from multiple research traditions to shed light on the range of strategic, social, material and ideational factors that have shaped regime design. The book's empirical scope also embraces civil war-regulating measures beyond the traditional parameters of the law of armed conflict, including detailed examination of the drafting of critical elements of the Rome Statute of the International Criminal Court. The case studies also draw on a range of archival and previously unpublished sources.

With the 1949 Geneva Conventions now past their seventieth anniversary, civil wars are more prevalent and deadlier than ever before. With this in mind, it is hoped that the present volume will not only aid understanding of how states have collectively sought to grapple with internal armed conflict through the medium of treaty law in the period since 1945, but will also helpfully inform efforts by state and non-state actors to implement the existing international 'law on the books' regulating civil war, as well as future endeavours to develop more effective international legal regimes in this and other fields.

Persistent Power of Human Rights: From Commitment to Compliance; Barnett and Finnemore, *Rules for the World*; Slaughter, *A New World Order*.

12 The design and operation of international criminal courts has formed a particular focus of research. See: Rudolph, *Power and Principle: The Politics of International Criminal Courts*; Bosco, *Rough Justice: The International Criminal Court's Battle to Fix the World, One Prosecution at a Time*; Schiff, *Building the International Criminal Court*; Bass, *Stay the Hand of Vengeance: The Politics of War Crimes Tribunals*. More generally, the application of IR (and more broadly social science) methods to the development and operation of international legal institutions is one of the hallmarks of an increasingly prominent empirical approach to international law. Volumes in this vein have examined international adjudication (Alter, *The New Terrain of International Law: Courts, Politics, Rights*; Hillebrecht, *Domestic Politics and International Human Rights Tribunals: The Problem of Compliance*; Shany, 'Assessing the Effectiveness of International Courts: A Goal-Based Approach') and human rights (Hafner-Burton, *Making Human Rights a Reality*; Sikkink, *The Justice Cascade: How Human Rights Prosecutions Are Changing World Politics*; Simmons, *Mobilizing for Human Rights: International Law in Domestic Politics*).

13 To paraphrase Ruggie, 'What Makes the World Hang Together?'

1

Theorising the Civil War Regime

Introduction

The international legal rules regulating civil war present an abiding conundrum: why have governments collectively designed standards regulating the conduct of armed conflict within their borders, when such rules are likely to primarily benefit armed non-governmental opponents? To explain the shape of this 'civil war regime', *Negotiating Civil War* adopts a pluralist theoretical approach, adapting insights from a number of International Relations (IR) research traditions to build a theoretical lens for the empirical analysis that follows in Chapters 3, 4 and 5. This lens is developed and presented in the present chapter.[1]

As with other academic disciplines, International Relations has no shortage of grand theoretical traditions – variously termed 'paradigms', 'theoretical approaches' or 'research traditions' – any number of which are capable of generating insights into the development of civil war-regulating multilateral treaty provisions.[2] Whereas a series of 'paradigm wars' overshadowed much previous IR scholarship, there is now growing

[1] As noted above, the terms 'internal armed conflict' and 'non-international armed conflict' are used interchangeably with 'civil war' in *Negotiating Civil War*, save where the context indicates otherwise.

[2] Patrick Thaddeus Jackson is clearly correct to observe that what are commonly referred to as IR 'paradigms' are nothing of the sort. It is probably more accurate to refer to 'theoretical perspectives', 'theoretical approaches' or 'research traditions' (this last defined by Laudan as 'a set of ontological and methodological "do's" and "don'ts"' (*Progress and Its Problems*, 80). Nevertheless, in pragmatic recognition of traditional IR nomenclature, these terms will be used interchangeably in the present volume. (See discussions in Jackson, *The Conduct of Inquiry in International Relations: Philosophy of Science and Its Implications for the Study of World Politics*, 57–9; Sil and Katzenstein, *Beyond Paradigms: Analytic Eclecticism in the Study of World Politics*, 5–9.)

recognition of the value of conducting problem-oriented, theoretically pluralist research cutting across paradigmatic boundaries.[3]

The present volume is situated within this pluralist vein, recognising that mono-paradigmatic approaches to empirical puzzles typically suffer from various deficiencies, but also acknowledging that theoretical traditions persist precisely because they encapsulate important insights about complex realities. This approach holds out the benefit, moreover, of harnessing together multiple such traditions to provide a sophisticated understanding of civil war regime development.

With this last in mind, this chapter establishes the theoretical and methodological basis for *Negotiating Civil War*. It first maps traditional and more recent IR approaches to regime development and then contrasts these with the epistemologically positivist 'analytically eclectic' pluralist approach taken in the present volume, highlighting the rationale for and the principal benefits (and costs and challenges) of drawing on realist, rationalist, liberal and constructivist insights in combination to explain the development of the civil war regime.

Five hypotheses are then derived from and situated in their respective bodies of theory, and their underlying explanatory factors and associated causal mechanisms are detailed. These propositions highlight, respectively, potential relationships between treaty outcomes and: great power preferences; the perceived costs and benefits to negotiating governments of drafting outcomes; the characteristics of key norm entrepreneurs; the quality of arguments presented during negotiations; and the extent to which the national delegations participating in treaty negotiations represent more or less democratic regimes. Together the hypotheses provide

[3] The predominant dynamic of debate during IR's 'paradigm wars' is nicely encapsulated in Friedrichs and Kratochwil's evocation of a 'gladiator style of analysis, where one perspective goes forth and slays all others' (Friedrichs and Kratochwil, 'On Acting and Knowing: How Pragmatism Can Advance International Relations Research and Methodology', 721; citing Checkel 'Why Comply? Social Learning and European Identity Change', p. 581). On how such debates have historically structured (and limited) IR, see e.g. Wæver, 'The Rise and Fall of the Inter-Paradigm Debate'; Haas et al., 'Symposium: Beyond Paradigms and Research Programs'; Lake, 'Theory Is Dead, Long Live Theory: The End of the Great Debates and the Rise of Eclecticism in International Relations'; Hamilton, 'A Genealogy of Metatheory in IR: How "Ontology" Emerged from the Inter-Paradigm Debate'. On theoretical pluralism in IR, see discussion below and more generally: Jackson, *The Conduct of Inquiry in International Relations: Philosophy of Science and Its Implications for the Study of World Politics*; Wight, Dunne, and Hansen, 'Special Issue: The End of International Relations Theory?; Neack, 'Forum: Pluralism in IR Theory'; Levine and McCourt, 'Why Does Pluralism Matter When We Study Politics? A View from Contemporary International Relations'.

a theoretical lens tailored to facilitate analysis of the negotiation of the civil war regime, allowing for the consideration of a range of material, ideational, social and strategic factors potentially relevant to regime design. The chapter then sets out potential interactions amongst the hypothesised factors in shaping treaty-drafting outcomes in a 'straw person' arrow diagram, before concluding with a brief methodological discussion.[4]

1.1 Traditional Approaches to Regime Development

IR scholarship encompasses multiple theoretical traditions capable of speaking to international regime development.[5] While the contours of these are not always entirely clear, moreover, realist, rationalist, liberal and social constructivist approaches arguably constitute the principal mainstream 'camps . . . that give international relations its distinctive sociological structure'.[6]

Of these, realism remains by some way the most venerable school of thought, work in this vein typically emphasising material drivers of international politics and, in particular, 'that states respond to material needs, incentives and power'.[7] Although latter-day realism may take a multiplicity of forms, including classical, offensive, defensive, neo-, neo-classical and post-classical variants, Waltz's insight that the structure of international

[4] This is revisited in Chapter 6, following the case studies.

[5] A regime is understood for present purposes as a set of 'implicit or explicit principles, norms, rules, and decision-making procedures around which actors' expectations converge in a given area of international relations' (Krasner, 'Structural Causes and Regime Consequences: Regimes as Intervening Variables', 186).

[6] Kristensen, 'International Relations at the End: A Sociological Autopsy', 245. Kristensen refers to realist, liberal institutionalist, and constructivist 'isms': these categories may be debated (and indeed, the second is reconfigured and disaggregated for present purposes, reflecting the prominence of 'liberal' theorising in international law scholarship). The broader point, however, remains: as a discipline IR continues to be structured around 'isms' of various stripes. (Keohane, for example, has referred to: Realism, 'Choice-Based Institutionalism', and 'Sociological Institutionalism, including Constructivism' ('Observations on the Promise and Pitfalls of Historical Institutionalism in International Relations', 322).)

[7] Hurd, 'Constructivism', 299. In a similar vein, Kristensen describes realism as typified by 'share(d) broad ontological assumptions (e.g. a focus on power politics among rational states under anarchy) and a relatively unified empirical focus on security and conflict' ('International Relations at the End: A Sociological Autopsy', 252). While these definitions are helpful for present purposes, realism persistently eludes definitive definition, to a degree perhaps unique amongst IR research traditions. An idea of the associated challenges may be gleaned from Donnelly, *Realism and International Relations*, 7–8.

politics is explicable by the systemic distribution of material capabilities continues to function as a key point of reference for work in this tradition.[8] From this perspective, international treaty agreements might be expected to reflect the preferences of the most materially powerful states in the international system.

Neo-liberal institutionalism provides the most established alternative to realism.[9] In similar fashion to much realist work, this approach is avowedly rationalist in orientation.[10] Where realism privileges material drivers of international politics, however, neo-liberal institutionalism and similarly non-realist 'rationalist' approaches are distinguished by a focus on 'instrumentalism . . . the theory that states pursue individual advantage by calculating costs and benefits'.[11]

Arguably, the key such 'rationalist' insight, encapsulated most famously in Keohane's work, is that governments collectively establish institutions to facilitate cooperation under conditions of anarchy by reducing uncertainty via enhanced information provision. Reflecting Keohane's functionalist logic, from this perspective governments may be expected to support a given set of treaty provisions to the extent they promote the realisation of significant common goods by reducing uncertainty. Equally, however, where fewer or less significant common goods stand to be realised, governments are less likely to be inclined to cooperate, especially where significant costs may also be incurred.[12]

Constructivists share with rationalists an interest in explaining aspects of international politics, such as the development of apparently demanding international regimes, which realist perspectives generally

[8] See Waltz, *Theory of International Politics*.

[9] See e.g. Keohane, *After Hegemony*; Axelrod and Keohane, 'Achieving Cooperation under Anarchy'; Keohane and Martin, 'Institutional Theory as a Research Program'; Keohane and Milner, *Internationalization and Domestic Politics*.

[10] Indeed, some view Waltzian neo-realism and neo-liberal institutionalism as forming a common rationalist research programme (the 'neo-neo synthesis'). See Wæver, 'The Rise and Fall of the Inter-Paradigm Debate'. See also Keohane's distinction between rationalist and 'reflectivist' approaches to IR ('International Institutions').

[11] Hurd, 'Constructivism', 299. Again, this characterisation is debatable. It is perhaps helpful to conceive of 'neo-liberal institutionalism' as at the heart of a broader set of rationalist literature that is to varying degrees 'liberal' and/or focused on the development of and impact on international politics of international 'institutions'. As Arthur Stein notes: 'those who use the label (of neoliberal institutionalism) never address whether the "liberal" qualification means that there is an "illiberal institutionalism", or whether it is possible to talk of institutions and not be a liberal' ('Neoliberal Institutionalism', 202).

[12] See generally Keohane, *After Hegemony*; Martin, 'An Institutionalist View: International Relations and State Strategies'; Keohane and Martin, 'Institutional Theory as a Research Program'.

fail to accommodate satisfactorily.[13] They differ, however, in their characterisation of international norms. For rationalists, state interests and preferences are largely assumed: for constructivists, international norms are capable of constituting state identities and interests. In the words of Risse and Sikkink: 'norms become relevant and causally consequential during the process by which actors define and refine their collective identities and interests'.[14]

As a theoretical orientation, constructivism is an exceedingly broad church.[15] A so-called 'conventional' constructivist approach to regime development, however, might be expected to focus on how support for a given set of treaty provisions can be explained by reference to social interaction amongst state and non-state actors, through which government preferences (and potentially interests) are reconfigured.[16]

A further school of thought might be termed the 'new liberal' approach to international relations. Work in this vein highlights the manner in which domestic politics is capable of informing foreign policy behaviour and that, owing to their internal institutional structures and value-commitments, liberal – primarily Western – democracies are more likely

[13] See e.g. discussions in Wendt, 'Anarchy Is What States Make of It: The Social Construction of Power Politics'; Hopf, 'The Promise of Constructivism in International Relations Theory'; Checkel, 'Review: The Constructivist Turn in International Relations Theory'; Finnemore, *National Interests in International Society*.

[14] Risse and Sikkink, 'The Socialization of International Human Rights Norms into Domestic Practices: Introduction', 9. Norms are perhaps most helpfully understood as sets of 'collective expectations for the proper behavior of actors within a given identity' (Katzenstein, 'Introduction: Alternative Perspectives on National Security', 5).

[15] Indeed, the identification of constructivism as 'just another –ism' may be objectionable to some. Adler has noted that constructivism is better conceived as a multi-layered understanding of the mutual constitution of social science and social reality, involving 'metaphysics, social theory and IR theory and research strategies', with debates taking place across all three areas ('Constructivism in International Relations: Sources, Contributions and Debates', 114).

[16] Hopf defines 'conventional constructivism' (as distinct from 'critical constructivism') as 'a collection of principles distilled from critical social theory but without the latter's more consistent theoretical or epistemological follow-through' ('The Promise of Constructivism in International Relations Theory', 181). In contrast, Finnemore and Sikkink observe in respect of 'critical constructivists' that '[t]heir purpose is not to build or test new causal theory but to denaturalize dominant constructions, in part by revealing their connection to existing power relations' ('Taking Stock: The Constructivist Research Program in International Relations and Comparative Politics', 398).

than non-democratic states to promote liberal values and associated norms of behaviour globally.[17]

IR is an increasingly pluralist discipline, and scholars within it have drawn freely on insights developed in other disciplines, particularly economics and sociology. International law scholarship has similarly drawn on disciplines including IR for insight into the development and operation of international legal regimes in what has been termed an 'empirical turn'.[18] Nevertheless, mainstream IR approaches alone are capable of generating a range of valuable insights into regime development.

1.2 The Shortcomings of (Paradigmatic) Isolationism

Notwithstanding this capacity, considered in isolation each of these traditions also harbours significant weaknesses.

Perhaps most famously, realist theory has long been criticised as indeterminate in the absence of auxiliary assumptions: Waltz's work, e.g. fails to indicate clearly when states will 'bandwagon' or 'balance'.[19] Neo-realism, moreover, is reliant on implicit assumptions about state identities and preferences.[20] Similarly, just as classical realists struggled to define the nature and content of the national interest, latter-day 'neo-classical realists' have been taken to task for ad hoc borrowing from other theoretical approaches.[21]

[17] See Moravcsik, 'Liberalism and International Relations Theory'; Slaughter, 'International Law in a World of Liberal States'; Moravcsik, 'Taking Preferences Seriously: A Liberal Theory of International Politics'; Moravcsik, 'The Origins of Human Rights Regimes: Democratic Delegation in Postwar Europe'; Slaughter, 'Building Global Democracy'; Moravcsik, 'Liberal International Relations Theory: A Scientific Assessment'; Slaughter, *A New World Order*; Moravcsik, 'The New Liberalism'. On democratic peace theory more broadly see Doyle, 'Kant, Liberal Legacies, and Foreign Affairs'; Russett et al., 'The Democratic Peace'; Small and Singer, 'The War-Proneness of Democratic Regimes, 1816–1965'.

[18] See Shaffer and Ginsburg, 'The Empirical Turn in International Legal Scholarship'. International law theory has also reflected (and been reflected in) IR theory – see e.g. Brunnée and Toope, *Legitimacy and Legality in International Law: An Interactional Account*; Brunnée and Toope, 'International Law and Constructivism'; Franck, *The Power of Legitimacy among Nations*. See also Koh, 'Internalization through Socialization'; Koh, 'The 1998 Frankel Lecture: Bringing International Law Home'; Chayes and Chayes, *The New Sovereignty: Compliance with International Regulatory Agreements*.

[19] Walt, *Origins of Alliances*.

[20] Wendt, 'The Agent-Structure Problem in International Relations Theory'.

[21] See discussions in e.g. Morgenthau, 'Another "Great Debate": The National Interest of the United States'; Wolfers, '"National Security" as an Ambiguous Symbol'; Legro and Moravcsik, 'Is Anybody Still a Realist?'

In similar fashion, institutionalist-minded scholars continue to struggle to explain satisfactorily why some cooperative arrangements are suboptimally efficient, Keohane and Martin conceding that this approach can make it difficult to disentangle 'the effects of institutions from the effects of underlying structure'.[22] Neo-liberal institutionalism and neorealism are also handicapped by the shared assumption that states can be modelled as rational unitary actors, making it difficult to accommodate domestic or transnational sources of state preferences.[23]

Constructivist approaches can also suffer from comparable handicaps. For one, the constructivist emphasis on discursive processes of identity and preference formation risks underestimating the role of material forces and strategic calculation in these same processes. In a similar vein, not every interaction amongst states will have a perceptible bearing on state identities: as Katzenstein and Okawara observe, collective identities tend to shift only over extended periods of time, so that often 'identity is . . . less directly at stake than are trust and reputation'.[24]

In turn, liberal scholars' focus on domestic sources of state behaviour risks overlooking the manner in which government preferences are informed transnationally by the preferences of actors in other states, or structurally by the cumulative preferences of other governments.[25] Moreover, while this perspective may provide valuable insights into the reasons why the governments of liberal democracies may support international legalisation, it does not necessarily provide a great deal of guidance into the circumstances in which non-liberal or less liberal democratic states are likely to support intrusive, demanding international regimes.[26] As with other IR 'isms', uncertainty persists as to the more (or less) essential attributes of liberal democratic governance.[27]

These traditions are not alone in suffering from weaknesses. The ontologically and methodologically pluralist English School, for example, is poorly suited to the derivation of explanatory statements

[22] Keohane and Martin, 'Institutional Theory as a Research Program', 105. See also Katzenstein and Okawara, 'Japan, Asian-Pacific Security, and the Case for Analytical Eclecticism', 172.

[23] Moravcsik, 'Taking Preferences Seriously: A Liberal Theory of International Politics'.

[24] Katzenstein and Okawara, 'Japan, Asian-Pacific Security, and the Case for Analytical Eclecticism', 174.

[25] Ibid., 170.

[26] See variously Hathaway, 'Do Human Rights Treaties Make a Difference?'; Hathaway, 'The Cost of Commitment'; Hathaway, 'Why Do Countries Commit to Human Rights Treaties?'

[27] See Alvarez, 'Do Liberal States Behave Better? A Critique of Slaughter's Liberal Theory'.

or 'if-then' hypotheses in relation to empirical phenomena.[28] Similarly, international law theories that are less reliant on empirical evidence for support and/or designed for normative ends can prove challenging to adapt for (if not altogether impervious to) empirical analysis.[29]

1.3 Pluralism in International Relations

In light of these difficulties, it is not surprising that IR has seen a turn towards theoretical pluralism. In part, this reflects growing recognition of the 'multi-paradigmatic' nature of IR and appreciation that 'no single knowledge system, discipline, theory, or method can claim singular access to truth'.[30] At the same time, this turn is also emblematic of what has been termed the 'end of International Relations Theory',[31] with the passing of the era of inter-paradigm 'great debates' and a shift to middle-range, problem-solving scholarship – recognising that 'the complex links between power, interest, and norms defy analytical capture by any one paradigm'.[32]

Reflecting this turn, *Negotiating Civil War* examines the extent to which a rounded understanding of civil war regime development can be obtained by harnessing together insights derived from four traditional theoretical approaches to IR. In doing so, the book adheres most closely to an 'eclectic' approach to pluralism.

This approach is most closely associated with the work of Rudra Sil and Peter Katzenstein, who advocate the adoption of an 'analytically eclectic' form of theorising about international politics, applying insights

[28] See Copeland, 'A Realist Critique of the English School'; also Friedner Parrat, 'Bridging the Divide: What the English School Does, and Why'.

[29] On some of the difficulties that have historically dogged interdisciplinary IL/IR research see Beck, 'International Law and International Relations'.

[30] Levine and McCourt, 'Why Does Pluralism Matter When We Study Politics? A View from Contemporary International Relations', 92. See also Neack, 'Forum: Pluralism in IR Theory'. As Kratochwil puts it: 'a lot could be gained if we were to begin our research with a problem or question instead of looking for the perfect hammer and searching for nails to pound' ('The Monologue of 'Science', 128).

[31] See Wight, Dunne, and Hansen, 'Special Issue: The End of International Relations Theory?'

[32] Katzenstein and Okawara, 'Japan, Asian-Pacific Security, and the Case for Analytical Eclecticism', 154. Also Lake, 'Why "Isms" Are Evil: Theory, Epistemology, and Academic Sects as Impediments to Understanding and Progress'.

drawn from multiple theoretical perspectives in 'tool-kit' fashion to better understand real-world problems.[33] Put differently, analytic eclecticism 'seeks to extricate, translate, and selectively integrate analytic elements – concepts, logics, mechanisms, and interpretations – of the theories or narratives that have developed within separate paradigms but that address related aspects of substantive problems that have both scholarly and practical significance'.[34]

Viewed against the backdrop of the weaknesses in the various approaches noted above, an analytically eclectic form of pluralism has much to commend it. Sil and Katzenstein's pragmatic, practically oriented focus promises to better reflect 'the complexity and messiness of particular real-world situations'.[35] Moreover, by facilitating the generation of 'complex causal stories' about phenomena, such scholarship should outperform mono-paradigmatic approaches analytically, 'captur(ing) the interactions among different types of causal mechanisms normally analyzed in isolation from each other'.[36]

That said, analytic eclecticism is far from the only means of combining insights drawn from multiple research traditions in empirical analyses. Friedrichs and Kratochwil, for example, present 'abduction' as an alternative to analytic eclecticism, involving reasoning from an 'intermediate level' between induction from facts and deduction from theory.[37] Similarly, Moravcsik argues that it should be possible to draw insights together sequentially from multiple paradigms into a single 'synthetic' model, which could then be tested by examining each element and their linking assumptions.[38]

33 Katzenstein and Okawara, 'Japan, Asian-Pacific Security, and the Case for Analytical Eclecticism', 177. Dunoff and Pollack, 'IL/IR Book Discussion: Beyond the "Isms War"?'

34 Sil and Katzenstein, *Beyond Paradigms: Analytic Eclecticism in the Study of World Politics*, 10 (cited in Levine and McCourt, 'Why Does Pluralism Matter When We Study Politics? A View from Contemporary International Relations', 95). For similar sentiments see Fearon and Wendt, 'Rationalism v. Constructivism: A Skeptical View'; Lake, 'Theory Is Dead, Long Live Theory: The End of the Great Debates and the Rise of Eclecticism in International Relations'.

35 Sil and Katzenstein, 'Analytic Eclecticism in the Study of World Politics: Reconfiguring Problems and Mechanisms across Research Traditions', 412. On pragmatism and IR more generally see e.g. discussions in Hellmann et al., 'Pragmatism and International Relations'; Pratt, 'Pragmatism as Ontology, Not (Just) Epistemology: Exploring the Full Horizon of Pragmatism as an Approach to IR Theory'.

36 Sil and Katzenstein, 'Analytic Eclecticism in the Study of World Politics: Reconfiguring Problems and Mechanisms across Research Traditions', 412.

37 Friedrichs and Kratochwil, 'On Acting and Knowing: How Pragmatism Can Advance International Relations Research and Methodology', 709.

38 See Moravcsik, 'Theory Synthesis in International Relations: Real Not Metaphysical', 131–3.

Neither approach is clearly preferable to the eclecticism advocated by Sil and Katzenstein: rather, each is in its own way problematic. Friedrichs and Kratochwil appear to suggest, for example, that 'abductive' scholars should use concepts and postulates developed idiosyncratically for individual analyses. It is difficult to see how such an approach would obviously facilitate accumulation of knowledge amongst scholars, however (even in the fragmented universe of IR theory). In contrast, an eclectic approach is on relatively stronger ground in directing scholars towards insights drawn from existing paradigms. Moravcsik's synthetic approach also seems insufficiently flexible: as put by Checkel, in this vision 'each theory works in isolation from the other . . . The possibilities of intellectual-theoretical cross fertilization are minimal if not nil'.[39]

Typological theorising provides a further potential approach, aimed at generating 'structured pluralism' by combining sets of causal mechanisms into a series of 'typologies'.[40] Andrew Bennett, perhaps the foremost advocate of this approach, provides a taxonomy of theories on social mechanisms to provide 'a bridge to the vast literature couched in terms of the isms . . . without reifying theories about mechanisms into Kuhnian paradigms or Lakatosian research programs'. This taxonomy is to be used to 'develop . . . theories about how combinations of mechanisms interact in shaping outcomes for specified cases or populations', facilitating cumulative theorising and 're-energising' engagement between IR and other social scientific fields.[41]

It is not clear, though, that typological theorising is necessarily preferable to analytic eclecticism. Bennett's taxonomy, for example, breaks down traditional IR 'isms' and debates into associated bundles of causal mechanisms. As Craig Parsons has observed, however, breaking down research traditions in this way risks losing sight of the contrasting natures of the different theoretical approaches that underpin analysis. As he notes: 'if we want a combined argument to deepen our understandings rather than just pulverising them, we must first contrast our multiple narrative threads to each other to highlight their distinct content as best

39 Checkel, 'Theoretical Pluralism in IR: Possibilities and Limits', 226.

40 As developed by George and Bennett, 'types' are 'specific conjunctions or configurations of (independent) variables . . . A fully specified typological theory provides hypotheses on all of the mathematically possible types relating to a phenomenon' (*Case Studies and Theory Development in the Social Sciences*, 235). See also Elman, 'Explanatory Typologies in Qualitative Studies of International Politics'; Bennett, 'The Mother of All Isms: Causal Mechanisms and Structured Pluralism in International Relations Theory'.

41 Bennett, 'The Mother of All Isms: Causal Mechanisms and Structured Pluralism in International Relations Theory', 472, 474–5.

we can'.[42] Moreover, building and defending a comprehensive taxonomy of social mechanisms as a precursor to combinatory analysis arguably adds unnecessary complexity into the explanatory exercise.[43]

This is not to say that the above approaches do not have important advantages in different circumstances. To the extent that the traditional IR 'isms' are recognised in the present study as distinct sources of insights relating to civil war regime development, however, eclecticism remains preferable to Bennett's vision of typological theory, as well as to Moravcsik's 'synthetic' and Friedrichs and Kratochwil's 'abductive' approaches to theoretical pluralism.[44] Indeed, since the publication of Sil and Katzenstein's eponymous volume[45], eclecticism has come to form perhaps the most prominent form of pluralist theorising about international politics, in Reus-Smit's words 'quite rapidly becom(ing) part of mainstream debates about the kind of knowledge the field ought to pursue and how such knowledge is best attained'.[46]

That said, analytic eclecticism remains an evolving endeavour, with researchers continuing to refine understandings and approaches to (as well as debate advantages and costs of) eclectic theorising in different contexts.[47] Parsons, for example, underlines the need for the inclusion in eclectic analyses of insights from multiple research traditions to be carefully considered and structured.[48] Grieco similarly notes the limited

[42] Parsons, 'Before Eclecticism: Competing Alternatives in Constructivist Research', 531. See also Parsons, *How to Map Arguments in Political Science*, 43: 'There is no solid middle ground without poles, no useful eclecticism without distinct things to mix.'

[43] Constructing and managing the 'property space' of a typological theory, in particular, may be challenging given the range of mathematically possible types for anything more than a minimal set of independent variables, and the risk of creating 'an infinite number of types, as it can always be argued that each case is idiosyncratic' (George and Bennett, *Case Studies and Theory Development in the Social Sciences*, 242). Typological theorising also risks reifying typologies. (See Elman, 'Explanatory Typologies in Qualitative Analysis'.)

[44] Similar observations may be added in respect of Grieco's plea for 'collaborative challenges', which comes uncomfortably close to a call for a return to the 'good old, bad old days' of Friedrichs and Kratochwil's 'gladiator style of analysis' (Grieco, 'The Schools of Thought Problem in International Relations').

[45] Sil and Katzenstein, *Beyond Paradigms: Analytic Eclecticism in the Study of World Politics.*

[46] Reus-Smit, 'Beyond Metatheory?', 591. David Lake has similarly termed analytic eclecticism 'the only real alternative to the status quo' ('Why "Isms" Are Evil: Theory, Epistemology, and Academic Sects as Impediments to Understanding and Progress', 472).

[47] In terms of operationalising eclecticism, see e.g. Cornut, 'Analytic Eclecticism in Practice'; Pohl and Willigen, 'Analytic Eclecticism and EU Foreign Policy (In)Action'; Hayes et al., 'Systemism, Analytic Eclecticism, and the Democratic Peace'; Makinda, 'Terrorism in International Society: An Eclectic Perspective'.

[48] Parsons, 'Before Eclecticism: Competing Alternatives in Constructivist Research'.

utility of overly complex 'kitchen-sink' accounts of international politics.[49] The following discussion considers how these and other issues may be addressed in constructing an eclectic framework for the analysis of civil war regime development.

1.3.1 Metatheory and Eclecticism

In Scott Hamilton's words, IR's metatheoretical debates have 'fostered a growing atmosphere of ambivalence and detachment' that rather than 'increase IR's theoretical scope and power ... instead magnifies a widening gulf between IR theory and real-world political problems and practices .... (consigning) IR to a Sisyphean, self-referential, and increasingly detached and self-indulgent "philosophy of science debate"'.[50] To the extent that eclectic theorising attempts to reorient scholarship towards complex, real-life problems it is a welcome corrective.[51] This should not be understood, however, as implying that risks of theoretical and analytic incoherence can be ignored. Rather, it becomes all the more important to set out and explain the metatheoretical positions and compromises that underlie analysis.[52]

Perhaps most critical are issues of epistemology: setting aside ontology and acknowledging that reality may not be constituted by ideas or

[49] Grieco, 'The Schools of Thought Problem in International Relations'.

[50] Hamilton, 'A Genealogy of Metatheory in IR: How "Ontology" Emerged from the Inter-Paradigm Debate', 137.

[51] As Reus-Smit observes: 'in recent years much of the heat seems to have gone out of these [metatheoretical] divisions ... many positivists have retreated from strong claims about truth with a capital "T", and conventional constructivists no longer insist that study of intersubjective phenomena has any particular epistemological or methodological implications' ('The Contours of Analytical Eclecticism', 5).

[52] Lake warns, for example of an 'intellectual tower of Babel' ('Why "Isms" Are Evil: Theory, Epistemology, and Academic Sects as Impediments to Understanding and Progressl', 472). That said, though, as Sil and Katzenstein note in response: '[f]or real-world problems characterized by extensive endogeneity and the ubiquity of complex interaction effects ... a modular conception of theory and a standardized lexicon [as proposed by Lake] would simply create a new intellectual hierarchy and reproduce a new set of blinders' ('De-Centering, Not Discarding, the "Isms: Some Friendly Amendments', 483). Sil and Katzenstein suggest instead ensuring that 'concepts and analytic principles are properly understood in their original conceptual frameworks, and [adjusting or translating] these terms by considering how they are operationalised in the relevant empirical contexts by proponents of various paradigms' (*Beyond Paradigms: Analytic Eclecticism in the Study of World Politics*, 15). Even such a context-sensitive approach has limits, however.

material factors 'all the way down' does little to resolve the difficulties posed by attempting to adopt both positivist and interpretivist theories of knowledge simultaneously. Put bluntly, the hermeneutic focus of the latter is prima facie antithetical to the prioritisation of identifying causal relationships amongst phenomena in the former.[53]

Given this difficulty, one means of minimising incoherence in pluralist work is to restrict bridge-building to insights that are consistent with a positivist epistemology – i.e. the view that it is possible to identify causal relationships amongst factors and outcomes in international politics. This need not preclude the adoption of a wide range of insights in eclectic analysis, but adopting such an epistemologically conservative approach would exclude insights derived from post-positivist (including some constructivist) approaches.[54]

The principal downside of this approach is a risk of potentially valuable insights being excluded from consideration on grounds having little to do with their empirical purchase. Restricting bridge-building to insights capable of being applied within a positivist epistemological framework is nevertheless arguably the more sensible choice, not least given the operational challenges involved in combining radically interpretive and positivist elements within a single study.[55] To the extent that mainstream IR remains a largely positivist endeavour, moreover, an epistemologically positivist orientation is also more likely to enhance the development of a cumulative body of knowledge about international affairs.[56]

It bears underlining that even this conservative framework is capable of embracing a wide range of insights implicating both material and social/ideational drivers of international politics. The present study accordingly adopts a positivist epistemological (and corresponding

[53] See Marsh, Ercan and Furlong, 'A Skin Not a Sweater: Ontology and Epistemology in Political Science', 184. It bears noting that even work within paradigms is not immune to such criticism: see e.g. discussions of constructivist and rationalist approaches, respectively, in Price and Reus-Smit, 'Dangerous Liaisons?: Critical International Theory and Constructivism'; Kratochwil and Ruggie, 'International Organization: A State of the Art on an Art of the State'.

[54] Checkel, 'Theoretical Pluralism in IR: Possibilities and Limits', 235.

[55] Jackson describes Hopf's 2012 study of early Cold War Soviet political culture and foreign policy, for example, as 'an attempt to force what we might call careful textual ethnography . . . into a methodological straightjacket that does not fit it especially well'. See also Steele, 'Book Review: *Reconstructing the Cold War: The Early Years, 1945–1958*'.

[56] See generally discussion in Checkel, 'Theoretical Pluralism in IR: Possibilities and Limits'.

methodological) orientation, but without privileging either material or ideational conditions – i.e. adopting an 'ontologically agnostic' approach – with a view to facilitating evidence-guided analysis of the empirical record. That said, there remains a risk of '(almost) everything goes' theorising resulting from the adoption of an eclectic approach – even within epistemological boundaries – if insights are not identified and adapted with care. The following section accordingly considers how best to delimit the range of theoretical traditions from which such insights are derived for present purposes.

1.3.2 Selecting Relevant Research Traditions and Insights

Identifying which insights to select from which research traditions in constructing an eclectic framework for analysis of civil war regime development presents a number of challenges. Perhaps foremost amongst these is that an ideal selection exercise would require an omniscient investigator with ex ante mastery of the universe of potentially applicable theories and of the empirical record.[57] In the absence of such mastery, decisions as to which traditions to include or exclude are necessarily made on the basis of partial information, making it all the more critical for such decisions to be explicitly reasoned.

A related difficulty is that identifying the central claims of paradigms is not a straightforward exercise and may in some instances be a fool's errand.[58] Accordingly, in the absence of a clear guiding rationale, it may be difficult to know where to look to identify potentially most-relevant insights. A further challenge, reflecting the risk of 'everything but the kitchen-sink' theorising, is that of identifying reasonable outer bounds for the sources of potentially relevant insights, to avoid assembling a *Rashomon*-style set of insights where no more can be said than that 'everything, somehow, matters'.[59]

Given these challenges, for present purposes hypotheses are derived only from those mainstream IR traditions which appear to be potentially

[57] Friedrichs and Kratochwil, 'On Acting and Knowing: How Pragmatism Can Advance International Relations Research and Methodology', 709.

[58] See Legro and Moravcsik, 'Is Anybody Still a Realist?'; Feaver et al., 'Brother, Can You Spare a Paradigm?'

[59] Sil and Katzenstein recognise this challenge. They provide minimal guidance, however, beyond recognising the value of retaining reference to originating research traditions (Sil and Katzenstein, 'Analytic Eclecticism in the Study of World Politics: Reconfiguring Problems and Mechanisms across Research Traditions', 414).

most relevant, and are restricted to the most salient insights that can be derived from each tradition. To reduce scope for theoretical pottage, moreover, mainstream IR's traditional preference for parsimony is retained: all else being equal, simpler insights are preferred to more complex ones, with the whole framed within the epistemological limits imposed by the decision to adopt a positivist approach. This enables insights to be drawn from mainstream approaches ranging from realism to conventional constructivism, but excludes more radical constructivist/post-structuralist approaches, the English School and avowedly critical approaches to IR.

This scoping decision ultimately reflects pragmatic considerations. At the most basic level, limiting analysis to insights derived from realist, rationalist, positivist constructivist and liberal theoretical approaches recognises that these persist as 'mainstream' traditions in large part because they encapsulate important, distinct insights into international affairs. In addition, while each approach presents a wide range of theoretical facets, it is equally possible to identify a subset of particularly relevant insights that can be derived from each of these schools of thought, tailored to the subject under examination. These can then be applied together to provide more comprehensive analysis of the drivers and dynamics of civil war regime development than would be gleaned from adopting any single such perspective in isolation.

It is only fair to note that this approach is not uncontroversial. In particular, the proposed combinatory approach is metatheoretically conservative, begging the question of whether a different set of insights could be assembled from a broader variety of sources that would result in further-reaching, more comprehensive understanding of civil war regime development. Even if this were the case, though, adopting a more eclectic 'pick and mix' approach to insight selection might not result in more robust or defensible results. Indeed, any decision about theoretical framing is unlikely to escape criticism. This, in turn, underlines the importance of carefully considering and setting out as clearly as possible the rationale underlying the selection of theoretical insights. Even here, however, pragmatism may be inescapable, in eclecticism as in other pluralist approaches.

Typological theorising, for example, provides a structured means of identifying and organising theoretical traditions and insights to combine in analysis, by reference to the 'property space' of insights derived from multiple IR theoretical approaches. As noted by Elman and Bennett, though, typological property spaces are rarely 'fully specified': rather, the mathematically possible range of combinatory options of causal factors may need to be winnowed to be manageable, using tools such as 'logical compression to eliminate any empirically empty cells that are theoretically unlikely ever to include actual cases'.[60] In the final analysis, even in the context of typological theorising, researchers may have little option but to simply 'decide to focus on a more narrowly circumscribed set of specific cells or subtypes',[61] Elman referring to 'pragmatic compression' enabling researchers to 'focus on cells that cover hypotheses of interest'.[62]

In a similar endeavour, Jérémie Cornut suggests using a 'logic of questions' to identify the 'contrast space' of a research question. However, this approach also leaves unresolved the difficulty that even very varied theoretical perspectives may be drawn on to inform any number of potentially relevant insights. As Cornut acknowledges, the selection of insights will ultimately depend on the standards and expectations of the community to which the enquiry is directed rather than on any intrinsic qualities of the research traditions or propositions in question.[63]

In short, neither technique provides a 'magic bullet' to guide selection among potentially relevant theoretical approaches to be combined in analysis, or to identify which insights should be derived from these as the basis for theorising about civil war regime development. In contrast, the 'conservative eclectic' approach adopted in the present volume, which harnesses together a small number of key insights derived from mainstream, positivist IR theoretical traditions – to paraphrase Sil and Katzenstein, de-centring but not discarding the 'isms'[64] – serves as a preferable pragmatic starting point. It explicitly restricts the ex ante 'property space' of causal drivers to a limited number of postulates

[60] Bennett and Elman, 'Case Study Methods', 508.

[61] Bennett and Elman, 508.

[62] Elman, 'Explanatory Typologies in Qualitative Studies of International Politics', 307. As Bennett and George put it: 'The investigator can and should exercise judgment as to the extent to which to construct from the cases more and more refined, narrowly circumscribed types' (George and Bennett, *Case Studies and Theory Development in the Social Sciences*, 242).

[63] See Cornut, 'Analytic Eclecticism in Practice: A Method for Combining International Relations Theories'. Cornut draws here on Alan Garfinkel's observation that '[t]he demarcation of the contrast space clarifies the potential complementarity of different explanations because 'the various relations among explanations correlate with various relations among their contrast spaces' (Cornut, 60, quoting Garfinkel, *Forms of Explanation: Rethinking the Questions in Social Theory*, 27–8).

[64] Sil and Katzenstein, 'De-Centering, Not Discarding, the 'Isms: Some Friendly Amendments'.

derived from a limited range of theoretical approaches.[65] To the extent that this approach risks failing to identify potentially important additional causal factors, moreover, the fine-grained analysis permitted by in-depth case studies facilitates the identification of further insights that may emerge inductively from the empirical analysis.[66]

1.4 A Pluralist Approach to Civil War Regime Development

Negotiating Civil War seeks to explain why governments have collectively designed a set of increasingly demanding treaty rules limiting the range of acceptable conduct in internal armed conflicts. Mainstream bodies of IR theory – realist, rationalist, constructivist and liberal – furnish a range of insights potentially relevant to this question.

1.4.1 Realist Insights

Realist scholarship has not displayed a conspicuous interest in questions of international legal regime development. Rather, it is fair to say that realists of various stripes have focused on the importance and limitations of state power in determining the course of international politics, albeit with growing recognition of the role of a range of 'intervening variables' in accounting for state behaviour. Realist scholarship in the post-1945 period, moreover, has been dominated by Kenneth Waltz's minimalist 'neo-realist' vision, in which the course and shape of international politics are determined by relative power differentials amongst states.[67]

[65] George and Bennett, in discussing limitations and of typological theorising, similarly note advantages of a conservative approach to theoretical selection (*Case Studies and Theory Development in the Social Sciences*, 261–2). See also Checkel, 'Mechanisms, Process and the Study of International Institutions', 92.

[66] Reflecting this scope for induction as well as the deductive derivation of hypotheses from research traditions, the present volume is perhaps best characterised as an exercise in 'abduction' as adapted by Martha Finnemore, drawing on John Ruggie and Charles Peirce: 'neither deduction nor induction but a dialectical combination of the two ... supplement(ing) ... deductive arguments with inductively derived insights' (Finnemore, *The Purpose of Intervention: Changing Beliefs about the Use of Force*, 13).

[67] Waltz, *Theory of International Politics*. As Jackson observes, Waltz's work is arguably rather more sophisticated than set out here (*The Conduct of Inquiry in International Relations: Philosophy of Science and Its Implications for the Study of World Politics*, chapter 5). Indeed, Waltz himself acknowledges in an earlier volume, referring to his identification of individual, state, and system-level 'images' of state foreign policy drivers, that: 'some combination of our three images, rather than any one of them, may be required for an accurate understanding of international relations' (Waltz, *Man, the State and War*, 14, see also 229–30). This notwithstanding, however, the position noted

Indeed, while Waltzian neo-realism has been the subject of sustained critique, it continues to serve as a totemic reference point both for critics of realism and amongst self-professed realists.[68]

Perhaps the most telling critique of Waltzian neo-realism, however, is that it is indeterminate – that it fails to explain important aspects of state behaviour and of international politics more generally.[69] Given this, some self-described realists have sought to establish a distinct form of 'neo-classical' realism, augmenting Waltz's insights by taking into account additional considerations – most commonly domestic political factors – in explaining the course of international politics.[70]

Two difficulties have plagued efforts to develop such 'neo-classical' approaches to date, however. The first is that, like analytic eclecticism, neo-classical realism remains more of a 'tool-box' than a theory, with proponents selecting varied sets of auxiliary explanatory factors in explaining state behaviour in different contexts.[71] A second, related challenge is that there is little that is distinctively 'realist' about neo-classical realism: as put by Legro and Moravcsik, much of the explanatory power of the work of Wohlforth and others is derived from the inclusion in analyses of insights derived from other theoretical approaches to IR.[72] In a further difficulty, while neo-classical realism may be capable of generating more comprehensive, compelling accounts of state behaviour than neo-realism, it is also a more challenging approach from which to

above is probably a fair statement of the manner in which Waltz's central insights have been adopted in mainstream IR usage.

68 Walt, for example, has sought to refine Waltz's approach by identifying conditions under which states might 'bandwagon' with stronger states rather than balance against them (Walt, *Origins of Alliances*). In similar fashion, John Mearsheimer has been a prominent advocate of 'offensive' realism, arguing that the anarchic context of international politics, coupled with uncertainty, is likely to lead states to pursue untrammeled power (Mearsheimer, *The Tragedy of Great Power Politics*).

69 The failure to predict the end of the Cold War is perhaps the most prominent example. (See e.g. discussion in Lebow, 'The Long Peace, the End of the Cold War, and the Failure of Realism'.)

70 See e.g. Rose, 'Neoclassical Realism and Theories of Foreign Policy'; Schweller, *Unanswered Threats: Political Constraints on the Balance of Power*; Brooks and Wohlforth, *World out of Balance: International Relations and the Challenge of American Primacy*; Lobell, Ripsman, and Taliaferro, *Neoclassical Realism, the State, and Foreign Policy*; Ripsman, Taliaferro and Lobell, *Neoclassical Realist Theory of International Politics*. Other 'post-Waltzian' variants include, for example, Stephen Brooks' 'Postclassical Realism' ('Dueling Realisms').

71 Smith, 'Can Neoclassical Realism Become a Genuine Theory of International Relations?', 745.

72 Legro and Moravcsik, 'Is Anybody Still a Realist?'

derive parsimonious 'if-then' hypotheses, reflecting the context-specific character of much neo-classical research.

That said, notwithstanding realism's traditional eschewing of interest in international law, it is possible to identify a number of distinctively realist insights into the design and operation of international legal regimes, reflecting the centrality to this school of thought of 'material needs, incentives and power'.[73] Stephen Krasner famously observed in 1983 that 'regimes, for Waltz, can only be one small step removed from the underlying power capabilities that sustain them', and that from this perspective:

> regimes, if they can be said to exist at all, have little or no impact. They are merely epiphenomenal. The underlying causal schematic is one that sees a direct connection between changes in basic causal factors (whether economic or political) and changes in behavior and outcomes. Regimes are excluded completely, or their impact on outcomes and related behavior is regarded as trivial.[74]

This in time has come to be understood as reflecting a widespread realist view of international law as politically 'epiphenomenal', with John Mearsheimer advancing the claim that international institutions matter 'only on the margins' and have 'minimal influence on state behavior'.[75]

This view of the implications of international law for international politics is, however, contested both by realists and critics. Schweller and Priess, for example, have argued that realism is capable of embracing a more sophisticated understanding of international institutions (and by extension, law) than admitted by Mearsheimer.[76] Richard Steinberg has similarly taken to task scholars concerned to 'rescue' international law from realism for mischaracterising neo-realism's view of international law's 'epiphenomenonality'.[77]

Even if the realist case for international law's (ir)relevance to state behaviour can be overstated, moreover, there are also important commonalities amongst realist approaches to international law, particularly as regards the creation of legal regimes. As Schweller and Priess put it:

[73] See note 7.

[74] Krasner, 'Structural Causes and Regime Consequences: Regimes as Intervening Variables', 190.

[75] Mearsheimer, 'The False Promise of International Institutions', 7.

[76] Schweller and Priess, 'A Tale of Two Realisms: Expanding the Institutions Debate'.

[77] Steinberg, 'Wanted – Dead or Alive'.

> [r]ealists do not deny the veracity of the neoliberal claim that international regimes may be created through negotiated processes ... In explaining these kinds of orders, however, realists of all stripes characterize them, not in terms of cooperation to promote the general welfare of states ... but rather as a form of *collusion* among powerful oligopolistic actors to serve their perceived interests at the expense of the 'others'.[78]

Krasner similarly emphasises that the scope of cooperative international legal agreements is likely to be limited by great power preferences, harking back to realism's Melian foundations, while Morgenthau expected governments to use international law as a tool to advance national interests.[79]

In other words, regardless of the extent to which international law might be politically 'epiphenomenal', there is also longstanding, widespread support in realist thought for the view that international legal regimes will inevitably reflect the preferences of more rather than less powerful states.[80]

The insight that the views of some states will matter more in negotiations than those of others is, of course, not limited to realism. Institutionalist-minded scholars have long recognised the centrality of power and national interests to regime creation.[81] Similarly, recent constructivist work has drawn attention to the workings of international 'pecking orders' in multilateral contexts.[82] Arguably, however, this

[78] Schweller and Priess, 'A Tale of Two Realisms: Expanding the Institutions Debate', 8.

[79] Krasner, 'Structural Causes and Regime Consequences: Regimes as Intervening Variables'; Morgenthau, *Politics among Nations: The Struggle for Power and Peace*, 268–9.

[80] This is not to say, of course, that realist-minded political leaders will necessarily openly seek to rely on material power preponderance alone in dealings with other states (à la Melian dialogue). Rather, as noted by Wohlforth, '[i]f power influences the course of international politics, it must do so largely through the *perceptions* of the people who make decisions on behalf of states' (*The Elusive Balance: Power and Perceptions during the Cold War*, 2 (emphasis added)). The implication of much realist theory, however, is that material power differentials alone will inevitably inform relationships and decisions. Such differentials may, moreover, be understood for present purposes to be relatively clear throughout the period examined, given the status of China, France, the UK and USA and the Soviet Union/Russia as the sole permanent members of the UN Security Council in the post-1945 period, US and Soviet superpower status during the Cold War and US dominance immediately following the Cold War (Krauthammer, 'The Unipolar Moment').

[81] See Krasner, 'Structural Causes and Regime Consequences: Regimes as Intervening Variables', 198–200.

[82] Pouliot, *International Pecking Orders: The Politics and Practice of Multilateral Diplomacy*. For related international law debates see e.g. Koskenniemi, *From Apology to Utopia: The Structure of International Legal Argument*; Krisch, 'International Law in Times of Hegemony: Unequal Power and the Shaping of the International Legal Order'.

widespread recognition of the extent to which international law can be said to be in thrall to great powers merely serves to underline the continuing relevance of the central realist insight that 'international politics is still synonymous with power politics, as it has been for all of recorded history'.[83]

With the above in mind, while latter-day realism may embrace a range of domestic and international drivers of state behaviour,[84] arguably the most distinctive and salient insight that may be derived from this school of thought for present purposes is that – regardless of other considerations – great power preferences are likely to be a key determinant of the shape of the civil war regime. Put simply, the preferences of materially powerful states are likely to be especially influential in regime design, not least as other governments will be inclined to weigh more carefully the implications of great power preferences over those of non-great powers in charting a collective course forward. As such, the following 'realist' proposition may be derived:

Hypothesis 1: The preferences of great powers are likely to be especially significant in shaping the civil war regime. (The Realist hypothesis)

1.4.2 Rationalist Insights

Where realism is distinguished by its focus on material drivers of international politics, rationalism can be associated with reasoned assessment by governments of the costs and benefits associated with different policy options in any given set of circumstances.[85] Neo-liberal institutionalism, moreover – the most enduring form of rationalist theory – primarily problematises international cooperation. Central to this approach is Keohane's functionalist argument that the establishment of international regimes reflects the pursuit by rationally self-interested states of shared benefits, enabled by 'reducing uncertainty, minimizing transactions costs, creating focal points, and raising expectations of compliance'.[86]

83 Mearsheimer, 'Structural Realism', 65.

84 There is, for example, a growing literature exploring the extent to which factors – such as perceived status – that have long been eschewed by Waltzian neo-realism can be harnessed alongside more traditional realist insights in making sense of international political life. See e.g. Paul, Larson, and Wohlforth (eds.), *Status in World Politics*.

85 While clearly shorthand, distinguishing these approaches in this manner helpfully enables distinct sets of insights to be derived from the component elements in the 'neo-neo synthesis'.

86 Simmons, 'International Law and International Relations', 193.

Such functionalist logic lies at the heart of the rationalist endeavour, underpinning the expectation that international legal regimes can be explained primarily as solutions to collective action problems.

Work in this vein identifies a variety of factors as potentially affecting the likelihood of such arrangements arising and their ultimate shape.[87] Barbara Koremenos, for example, has illustrated how rational design insights can be applied to areas of cooperation that cannot neatly be plotted onto a traditional 2x2 game-theoretical matrix. To the extent the civil war regime constitutes a rational solution to such a cooperation problem, the underlying logic would be (to paraphrase Koremenos) that states will be willing to tolerate the associated costs in order to retain the benefits to be gained.[88]

Others have argued that the costs to a given government of commitment to a regime can serve as a means to convey information about compliance intentions.[89] Guzman, for example, has made the case that regime development will reflect 'state concern about both reputational and direct sanctions triggered by violations of the law'.[90] In similar fashion, James Morrow has argued that IHL treaties are designed to inform 'strategic expectations' of behaviour in armed conflict, facilitating observance 'by specifying when reciprocal sanctions are appropriate, by controlling the response to violations outside the control of state parties, and by screening out states that are unwilling to abide by a treaty through their refusal to ratify it'.[91]

Reflecting the focus of much such work on regimes as solutions to collective action problems, a rationalist approach to civil war regulation may be expected to highlight the manner in which sets of international and domestic costs and benefits – which may be reputational, political, military, economic or otherwise – are likely to shape government

[87] See discussion in Simmons, 'International Law and International Relations'. Also: Fearon, 'Bargaining, Enforcement, and International Cooperation'; Koremenos, Lipson and Snidal, 'The Rational Design of International Institutions'; Goldsmith et al., 'Rational Choice and International Law (Volume Supplement)'; Goldsmith and Posner, *The Limits of International Law*; Morrow, *Order within Anarchy: The Laws of War as an International Institution*.

[88] Koremenos, *The Continent of International Law: Explaining Agreement Design*, 13 at note 20.

[89] See e.g. Martin, 'The President and International Commitments: Treaties as Signaling Devices'; Simmons and Danner, 'Credible Commitments and the International Criminal Court'.

[90] Guzman, 'A Compliance-Based Theory of International Law', 1827.

[91] Morrow, 'The Laws of War, Common Conjectures, and Legal Systems in International Politics', S41.

preferences for regime design. In other words, a functionalist logic should apply, with design outcomes reflecting perceived costs and benefits amongst negotiation participants.

Collective and individual costs and benefits to governments of a potentially demanding, intrusive civil war regime, however, may in many instances be relatively remote, especially compared to those relating to the regulation of interstate conflict. In particular, where a demanding interstate regime can be viewed as undergirded by expectations of reciprocity amongst states parties to a treaty, such benefits are largely absent in the context of civil wars, where governments face opposition from domestic actors rather than one another.[92]

In some instances, there may be direct, individual benefits or costs, for example in terms of promoting power equilibria in civil wars elsewhere. Benefits from a demanding civil war regime for most governments in most states, however, are likely to be indirect, potentially including an enhanced reputation as a 'good international citizen', or marginally reduced likelihood of either being expected to place armed forces in harm's way as peacekeepers in other states' civil wars or of suffering from cross-border spillovers of violence.[93] These may be of non-negligible importance in some instances, but even where significant – e.g. in respect of governments with an interest in promoting a particular set of power relationships in particular civil conflicts – governments may also have compelling reasons to prefer a weaker regime (e.g. be facing possible domestic unrest themselves).

In short, in many instances it is likely to be functionally rational for governments – particularly those that perceive themselves to be at risk or potential risk of encountering such situations – to place a high value on the ability to effectively combat domestic insurgencies, and accordingly to minimise the domestic 'reach' of the law of armed conflict. The costs of a demanding, intrusive civil war regime may also be particularly acute when there is a risk of external intervention with the capacity to 'internationalise' an otherwise purely domestic affair, or where there is a risk of such rules lending legitimacy – whether domestically or internationally –

[92] On reciprocity, see Morrow, *Order within Anarchy: The Laws of War as an International Institution*. There may, of course, be reciprocal incentives on governments and non-state actors to comply with relevant regimes: these are likely to be rather more asymmetric in civil wars than in interstate conflicts, however.

[93] Dunoff and Trachtman, 'The Law and Economics of Humanitarian Law Violations in Internal Conflict'.

to rebel groups.[94] The value of reputational and non-spillover benefits is also likely to be limited for many governments, including those facing insurgencies, but also those with any more than minimal risk of encountering domestic unrest. More generally, all else being equal, it may be assumed that governments will be reluctant to permit interference in domestic affairs in any event – i.e. that, in the absence of particularly compelling benefits, they will prefer less rather than more restrictive or intrusive provisions.[95]

To be fair, even where collective or cross-border benefits may be remote and potential domestic costs of a demanding regime high, negotiating such a regime may be particularly valuable to some governments. Ropp and Sikkink's research on the 'power of human rights' in Chile and Guatemala suggests, for example, that governments may be more prepared to endorse civil war-regime provisions when a period of civil unrest has recently ended, especially where ending such unrest is associated with domestic human rights improvements.[96] Such support may be motivated by a desire to reassure concerned domestic or external constituencies, or – per Moravcsik – to 'lock-in' successor governments to norm-compliance in future internal armed conflicts.[97]

In the absence of such particular concerns, however – i.e. to paraphrase Henkin, for most states most of the time – a rationalist approach to civil war regulation as a collective action problem may be expected to result in only a weak, minimally demanding regime, reflecting aggregate costs and benefits amongst participating governments.[98] As such, while reputational and legitimacy benefits and a reduced likelihood of civil war

[94] On some of the issues associated with the regulation of 'internationalised' civil wars, see e.g. Akande, 'Classification of Armed Conflicts: Relevant Legal Concepts'; Ferraro, 'The ICRC's Legal Position on the Notion of Armed Conflict Involving Foreign Intervention and on Determining the IHL Applicable to This Type of Conflict'.

[95] Indeed, given the potentially higher stakes for governments in civil wars, incentives to avoid commitment to demanding international legal rules in internal armed conflicts under IHL may be considerably stronger than those obtaining in respect of commonly studied human rights contexts. (See discussions in Simmons, 'Why Commit? Explaining State Acceptance of International Human Rights Obligations'; Hathaway, 'Why Do Countries Commit to Human Rights Treaties?'; Risse, Ropp, and Sikkink, *The Persistent Power of Human Rights: From Commitment to Compliance.*)

[96] Ropp and Sikkink, 'International Norms and Domestic Politics in Chile and Guatemala', 203.

[97] See Simmons and Danner, 'Credible Commitments and the International Criminal Court'; Moravcsik, 'The Origins of Human Rights Regimes: Democratic Delegation in Postwar Europe', 248–9.

[98] Henkin, *How Nations Behave: Law and Foreign Policy*, 47.

spillover may encourage (or indeed be sufficient for some) governments to support demanding civil war regulation, from this perspective the prospects for a demanding regime appear limited. Accordingly, perhaps the central rationalist insight that can be derived for present purposes is the following:

Hypothesis 2: The more intrusive or restrictive any proposed set of civil war-regulating treaty provisions, the less likely they are to be supported by governments in the course of treaty negotiations, especially where governments are engaged in or foresee a possibility of a civil war or insurgency. The end of a civil war or insurgency may, however, make a government more likely to support such provisions. (The Rationalist hypothesis)

1.4.3 Constructivist Insights

Constructivism is arguably the broadest of the research traditions surveyed, embracing an evolving range of more and less critical variants.[99] Pluralist approaches, moreover, are well established in constructivist scholarship, with broad recognition that state behaviour is informed by both normative and strategic considerations.[100] The very richness and variety of constructivist thought, as well as constructivism's status as a metatheoretical orientation to IR – a counterpart to realism and institutionalism's shared 'rationalism' – can make it challenging to derive a limited number of insights for analysis.

Like realist and rationalist thought, however, it is possible to identify a number of prominent, persistent strands of constructivist thought that are likely to be particularly salient to the present context. These reflect the

[99] For overviews of constructivism and recent developments see e.g. Reus-Smit, 'Constructivism'; Hurd, 'Constructivism'; Adler, 'Constructivism in International Relations: Sources, Contributions and Debates'; Bates, 'Sophisticated Constructivism in Human Rights Compliance Theory'; McCourt, 'Practice Theory and Relationalism as the New Constructivism'; Subotic, 'Constructivism as Professional Practice in the US Academy'; Nexon et al., 'Seizing Constructivist Ground? Practice and Relational Theories: Symposium'.

[100] Perhaps the foremost example of such scholarship is Risse, Ropp and Sikkink's *The Power of Human Rights*, where the authors seek to produce 'a multi-causal model that mapped very closely into the real world of human rights, where even the most casual observer will appreciate that change comes from both arm-twisting and threats *and* the normative power of the ideals of human dignity' (Checkel, 'Theoretical Pluralism in IR: Possibilities and Limits', 228).

focus of much constructivist thought on international norms, often understood as reflected in multilateral treaty rules, and the means by which such norms are generated, garner government support and evolve over time. Two established sets of insights are considered here, reflecting what have been termed 'sociological institutionalist' and 'Habermasian communicative action'-inspired approaches to IR.[101] The former is associated primarily with the work of prominent 'conventional' American constructivists, focusing on 'norm entrepreneurship' and on how norm entrepreneurs use a 'logic of appropriateness' to influence state behaviour and the course of international politics more generally.[102] While work in this vein has embraced a range of empirical contexts, a significant body of such work focuses on the role of norm entrepreneurship in the creation of international legal regimes and on relationships between international norms and international law more generally.[103]

In contrast, work in the latter vein is dominated by a group of mainly European scholars, examining the operation and impact of a 'logic of argument' in debate and normative contestation in international fora. Again, while related insights have been applied in a range of contexts, the

[101] See Reus-Smit, 'Imagining Society: Constructivism and the English School', 493–4. Reus-Smit also identifies a further variant of constructivism, 'draw[ing]inspiration from Foucauldian arguments about knowledge and power ... employ[ing] a distinctive "genealogical" method' (494). Genealogy, in this approach, is 'strategically aimed at that which looks unproblematic and is held to be timeless; its task is to explain how these present traits, in all their vigour and truth, were formed out of the past' (Bartelson, *A Genealogy of Sovereignty*, 73; cited in 'Imagining Society: Constructivism and the English School', 494). Viewed in this fashion, this approach is arguably particularly well-suited to more critically oriented research, though as Vucetic observes, Foucauldian genealogical method 'can (also) be seen as a research strategy for making standard social science truth claims similar to the mainstream qualitative research tools' ('Genealogy as a Research Tool in International Relations', 1311–12). While potentially valuable, however, a genealogical approach to the civil war regime would also likely require quite a different epistemological and methodological orientation to that adopted in *Negotiating Civil War*: as such, this endeavour will be left to others.

[102] See March and Olsen, 'The Institutional Dynamics of International Political Orders'; March and Olsen, 'The Logic of Appropriateness'.

[103] See e.g. Finnemore, *National Interests in International Society*; Price, 'Reversing the Gun Sights: Transnational Civil Society Targets Land Mines'; Risse, Ropp, and Sikkink, *The Power of Human Rights*; Finnemore, 'Are Legal Norms Distinctive?'; Price, 'Emerging Customary Norms and Anti-Personnel Landmines'; Fehl, 'Explaining the International Criminal Court: A Practice Test for Rationalist and Constructivist Approaches'; Hillebrecht, *Domestic Politics and International Human Rights Tribunals: The Problem of Compliance*; Bower, *Norms without the Great Powers: International Law and Changing Social Standards in World Politics* Rudolph, 'Constructing an Atrocities Regime: The Politics of War Crimes Tribunals'.

design of international legal regimes, including multilateral treaties, has formed a distinct focus.[104]

These approaches should not, it is to be stressed, be understood as reflective of the entirety of constructivist IR thought about regime design, which remains an incredibly fecund, pluralist enterprise.[105] Rather, they reflect two prominent, longstanding streams of constructivist thought that speak to multilateral treaty design.

1.4.3.1 Agent Characteristics Matter

A significant body of conventional constructivist research has focused on the role of norm entrepreneurs, including non-governmental organisations (NGOs) such as the International Committee of the Red Cross (ICRC), and international organisations (IOs) such as the United Nations High Commissioner for Refugees, in 'teaching' governments about normatively appropriate behaviour.[106] The 'constructivist moment' in much of this work lies 'in the process of persuasion, which

[104] See e.g. Risse, '"Let's Argue!": Communicative Action in World Politics'; Müller, 'Arguing, Bargaining and All That: Communicative Action, Rationalist Theory and the Logic of Appropriateness in International Relations'; Deitelhoff, 'The Discursive Process of Legalization: Charting Islands of Persuasion in the ICC Case'; Müller and Wunderlich, 'Not Lost in Contestation: How Norm Entrepreneurs Frame Norm Development in the Nuclear Nonproliferation Regime'.

[105] There is, for example, a growing body of literature focused on what has been termed 'new constructivism', including the recent 'practice turn'. (See e.g. Walter, 'The Road (Not) Taken? How the Indexicality of Practice Could Make or Break the 'New Constructivism'; Nexon et al., 'Seizing Constructivist Ground?'; McCourt, 'Practice Theory and Relationalism as the New Constructivism'; Bueger and Gadinger, 'The Play of International Practice'; Pouliot and Cornut, 'Practice Theory and the Study of Diplomacy: A Research Agenda'; Pouliot, *International Security in Practice*.)

[106] See e.g. Finnemore, *National Interests in International Society*; Price, 'Reversing the Gun Sights: Transnational Civil Society Targets Land Mines'; Klotz, 'Norms Reconstituting Interests: Global Racial Equality and US Sanctions against South Africa'; Sikkink, 'Human Rights, Principled Issue-Networks, and Sovereignty in Latin America'; Risse, Ropp and Sikkink, *The Power of Human Rights*; Barnett and Finnemore, *Rules for the World: International Organizations in Global Politics*. More generally, norm entrepreneurship is an increasingly pervasive, central concept in much constructivist-derived and pluralist work. See more recently e.g. Bratberg, 'Ideas, Tradition and Norm Entrepreneurs: Retracing Guiding Principles of Foreign Policy in Blair and Chirac's Speeches on Iraq'; Lantis and Wunderlich, 'Resiliency Dynamics of Norm Clusters: Norm Contestation and International Cooperation'; Bloomfield, 'Norm Antipreneurs and Theorising Resistance to Normative Change'; Mills and Bloomfield, 'African Resistance to the International Criminal Court: Halting the Advance of the Anti-Impunity Norm'; Müller and Wunderlich, 'Not Lost in Contestation: How Norm Entrepreneurs Frame Norm Development in the Nuclear Nonproliferation Regime'.

contradicts the rationalist assumption that states act on the basis of fixed preferences'.[107]

Persuasion, it bears noting, is a contested term. In some accounts this 'quintessential constructivist mechanism' is used to refer to a broad range of discursive means through which 'pro-normative' behaviour can be elicited, including peer pressure, legitimation, conformity and self-esteem.[108] More recently, however, persuasion has been recast in some studies as referring solely to 'changing minds, opinions, and attitudes about causality and affect (identity) in the absence of overtly material or mental coercion' – i.e. as operating to inculcate 'internalised' understandings of appropriate behaviour – as contrasted with microprocesses of 'social influence', including 'backpatting, opprobrium or shaming, social liking, status maximization', typified by 'conformity without private acceptance'.[109]

While this opening up of social micro-mechanisms is to be welcomed, 'persuasion' is given its prior, broader meaning in the present context. This reflects the focus of the present discussion on the attributes that are likely to make norm entrepreneurs more or less effective 'teachers' of appropriate behaviour,[110] recognising that such agents are capable of deploying various forms and combinations of social (and material) pressure to elicit pro-normative behavioural change.[111]

[107] Fehl, 'Explaining the International Criminal Court: A "Practice Test" for Rationalist and Constructivist Approaches', 366.

[108] Bates, 'Sophisticated Constructivism in Human Rights Compliance Theory', 1179–80. See also Finnemore and Sikkink, 'International Norm Dynamics and Political Change'.

[109] Johnston, *Social States: China in International Institutions, 1980–2000*, 20, 25, 155, 165; referencing Festinger, 'An Analysis of Compliant Behavior'. See e.g. Giovanni Mantilla's examination of the role of 'forum isolation' in the crafting of Common Article 3 of the 1949 Geneva Conventions ('Forum Isolation: Social Opprobrium and the Origins of the International Law of Internal Conflict'). Also Efrat, 'Professional Socialization and International Norms: Physicians against Organ Trafficking'; Petrova, 'Rhetorical Entrapment and Normative Enticement: How the United Kingdom Turned from Spoiler into Champion of the Cluster Munition Ban'; Mantilla, 'Conforming Instrumentalists: Why the USA and the United Kingdom Joined the 1949 Geneva Conventions'; Solomon and Steele, 'Micro-Moves in International Relations Theory'.

[110] See Figure 1.1 at Johnston, *Social States: China in International Institutions, 1980–2000*, 18.

[111] Accordingly, while reference is made to both 'persuasion' and mechanisms of 'social influence' in this study, these are considered together (generally under the heading of the former) for present purposes. This approach acknowledges that a variety of distinctions may be drawn amongst such mechanisms, but enables a focus on the entrepreneurs seeking to 'teach' targeted governments about appropriate behaviour, which process may implicate varying types and combinations of social mechanisms, deployed both intentionally and unintentionally.

The constructivist focus on norm entrepreneurship is also not unproblematic, and in particular has been associated with a progressive 'Whig' reading of history.[112] Nevertheless, entrepreneurship remains a key concept in constructivist research, 'inject[ing] agency into IR theory'.[113] In Finnemore and Sikkink's seminal formulation, such actors are 'critical for norm emergence because they call attention to issues or even "create" issues by using language that names, interprets and dramatizes them'.[114] While the success or failure of entrepreneurship in any given context will depend on a range of factors, agent attributes and capacities, as well as position ('how actors are connected to others'), and interlocutor perceptions of these, are all likely to play an important part.[115]

In light of this, it may be helpful to distinguish between what might be termed the *decisional* and *discursive* power of such actors.[116] The former involves leveraging expert, policy-relevant technical knowledge and access to decision-makers to affect policy decisions. The latter, in contrast, involves leveraging perceived moral authority to affect policy positions.[117] If persuasiveness is indeed related to the capacity to deploy

112 There is in particular a risk of overlooking instances of 'failed' norm entrepreneurship, reflecting the potential difficulty of identifying (would-be) entrepreneurship in the absence of resultant change. Indeed, studies of 'failed' norm entrepreneurship appear to be remarkably rare (though see e.g. Jose, 'Not Completely the New Normal: How Human Rights Watch Tried to Suppress the Targeted Killing Norm'). That said, neither constructivism nor IR generally is alone in facing this challenge: as Karen Alter puts it, 'intellectual histories are looking in the rear-view mirror, explaining the origin of "successful" ideas often without exploring why successful ideas won out over equally plausible alternatives that were also backed by powerful individual and states' (Alter, 'The Empire of International Law?', 186). This is similarly a challenge facing *Negotiating Civil War*: indeed, since it is a historical examination, the 'rear-view mirror' problem is inescapable. Nevertheless, through examining three distinct treaty-drafting instances in detail, the study highlights the extent to which outcomes in each case were highly contingent, dependent on a range of factors besides norm entrepreneurship.

113 Goddard, 'Brokering Change: Networks and Entrepreneurs in International Politics', 253. See also Young, 'Political Leadership and Regime Formation: On the Development of Institutions in International Society'.

114 Finnemore and Sikkink, 'International Norm Dynamics and Political Change', 897. As stated more recently '[t]he dispute between norm entrepreneurs is the engine driving norm dynamics' (Müller and Wunderlich, 'Not Lost in Contestation: How Norm Entrepreneurs Frame Norm Development in the Nuclear Nonproliferation Regime', 351).

115 See Goddard, 'Brokering Change: Networks and Entrepreneurs in International Politics', 256–7.

116 See Arts, 'Non-State Actors in Global Governance'.

117 This distinction and the attribution of expertise-based authority and power to communities of non-state actors echoes work on epistemic communities. See e.g. Haas, 'Introduction: Epistemic Communities and International Policy Coordination'; Adler

these forms of power, then civil war regime norm entrepreneurs are likely to be most effective in eliciting pro-normative behavioural change when they possess both a high degree of relevant technical expertise (e.g. in the international legal regulation of war) and perceived moral authority in the eyes of key interlocutors (i.e. particularly 'target' governments).[118] These attributes, moreover, while each tending to reinforce the effectiveness of entrepreneurship, may be present to varying degrees in any instance: an organisation may be technically expert in a given field, for example, but widely viewed as morally bankrupt. The converse is similarly plausible. In contrast, entrepreneurship might be expected to have greatest prospects of success where the proponents of a given position possess both significant decisional and discursive power.

Civil society campaign strategies often focus on building coalitions of states committed to eliciting pro-normative behaviour from other governments: indeed, governments may already have been socialised or domestically driven to support certain norms.[119] There is growing appreciation, moreover, that alongside individuals, non-governmental and international organisations, governments can also act as norm entrepreneurs.[120] Indeed, non-material forms of state power, as with

and Haas, 'Conclusion: Epistemic Communities, World Order, and the Creation of a Reflective Research Program'. Re. varying concepts of power in international politics more generally see e.g. discussions in: Barnett and Duvall, *Power in Global Governance*; Barnett and Duvall, 'Power in International Politics'.

118 Finnemore, *National Interests in International Society*; Forsythe, *Human Rights in International Relations.*

119 Alderson, 'Making Sense of State Socialization'; Finnemore and Sikkink, 'International Norm Dynamics and Political Change'. See also Perna, *The Formation of the Treaty Law of Non-International Armed Conflicts*, 134; Klotz, 'Norms Reconstituting Interests: Global Racial Equality and US Sanctions against South Africa'. Simmons has also noted a correlation between the physical proximity of a 'target' state to other states that have ratified human rights treaties. She does not, however, provide a clear causal explanation for this apparent relationship. See Simmons, *Mobilizing for Human Rights: International Law in Domestic Politics*, 110–11.

120 As noted by Wunderlich (2013), '[o]nly in the last decade has research shifted its attention to states as norm entrepreneurs; prior to that, states were predominately depicted as norm receivers' (Wunderlich, 'Theoretical Approaches in Norm Dynamics', 33; cited in Jose, 'Not Completely the New Normal: How Human Rights Watch Tried to Suppress the Targeted Killing Norm', 241. See also e.g. Ingebritsen, 'Norm Entrepreneurs: Scandinavia's Role in World Politics'; Björkdahl, 'Swedish Norm Entrepreneurship in the UN'; Heller, Kahl and Pisoiu, 'The "Dark" Side of Normative Argumentation – The Case of Counterterrorism Policy'; Wunderlich, 'A "Rogue" Gone Norm Entrepreneurial? Iran within the Nuclear Nonproliferation Regime'; Müller and Wunderlich, 'Not Lost in Contestation: How Norm Entrepreneurs Frame Norm Development in the Nuclear Nonproliferation Regime'.

the power of NGOs and IOs, are 'constituted by non-material factors, most notably legitimacy, and legitimacy is in turn conditioned by established or emergent norms of rightful agency and action'.[121] Put differently, governments may also wield discursive 'soft power' to varying degrees as well as more coercive material 'hard power'.[122]

In similar fashion to civil society organisations, the ability of governments to exercise moral authority may vary. Governments may be more effective agents of norm propagation, for example, where they are perceived by interlocutors as having 'clean hands'. Post-Abu Ghraib, for instance, the USA may no longer be a particularly credible promoter of anti-torture norms, in contrast to governments of states with stronger reputations for human rights observance, such as Sweden or Canada, or governments of states that are perceived by other governments (whether entirely accurately or not) as credible 'honest brokers' interested in advancing common interests rather than promoting a narrowly partisan agenda.[123]

States are also likely to vary in their capacity to deploy technical expertise in relation to civil war regulation: while states with well-developed academic and bureaucratic communities are likely to be able to field strong national delegations, states with weaker specialised communities are likely to have a smaller pool of national expertise to draw on. Governments of some states may equally be more at home and familiar with the mores, customs, and procedures of any given multilateral context.[124]

Importantly, however, while wealthier and more economically developed states may generally be at an advantage in terms of decisional power, this attribute need not correlate directly with material power differentials. Indeed, the most materially powerful states may perceive less value in ensuring the development of technical expertise in given areas (e.g. international human rights law) than economically developed but materially less-powerful 'middle' powers. Switzerland, for example, is

[121] Reus-Smit, 'Constructivism', 209.

[122] In Joseph Nye's original formulation, soft power was conceptualised as 'the ability to get what you want through attraction rather than through coercion', arising from 'the values an organization or country expresses in its culture, in the examples it sets by its internal practices and policies, and in the way it handles its relations with others' (*Soft Power: The Means to Success in World Politics*, 8).

[123] See e.g. discussion in Nye, *Soft Power:The Means to Success in World Politics*. The point has also been recognised in respect of the USA: see e.g. Khalaf, 'Autocrats of the World Benefit from Donald Trump's Win'.

[124] See generally Pouliot, *International Pecking Orders: The Politics and Practice of Multilateral Diplomacy*.

arguably an international leader in the field of international humanitarian law and associated diplomatic practice, yet would not be counted among the conventional 'great powers'. Moreover, while this attribute may often advantage the governments of economically developed states, it does not accrue from material power alone (cf. Hypothesis 1, earlier).

These insights lead to the following proposition:

Hypothesis 3: The greater their perceived moral authority and their ability to leverage subject area expertise, the more likely governments and non-state actors are to be able to elicit the support of other governments for demanding civil war-regulating provisions in the course of treaty negotiations. (The Agent Characteristics hypothesis)

1.4.3.2 Quality of Argument Matters

A second strand of constructivist research demonstrates how a 'logic of argument' may prevail in negotiation contexts, where 'in contrast to the strategic calculation of bargaining … arguing could be described as a coordination of actions based on mutual (complex) learning where only the power of the better argument prevails'.[125] Scholars working in this vein have made the case that where arguments in favour of or opposing a given proposal for collective action are subject to (at least) peer scrutiny and draw on a common 'lifeworld' – 'a shared culture, a common system of norms and rules perceived as legitimate, and the social identity of actors being able to communicate and to act'[126] – a 'logic of argument' may play a significant part in determining negotiation outcomes, with governments being expected 'to justify a course of action with commonly accepted reasons'.[127]

125 Albert, Kessler and Stetter, 'On Order and Conflict: International Relations and the "Communicative Turn"', 51. The classic statement of this position is in Risse, '"Let's Argue!": Communicative Action in World Politics'. See also Deitelhoff, 'The Discursive Process of Legalization: Charting Islands of Persuasion in the ICC Case'; Deitelhoff and Müller, 'Theoretical Paradise – Empirically Lost? Arguing with Habermas'.

126 Risse, 'Global Governance and Communicative Action', 296. As Risse goes on to state: 'The common lifeworld provides arguing actors with a repertoire of collective understandings to which they can refer when making truth claims'. International law, and related international legal discourse, may be considered to constitute such a lifeworld. (See Habermas, *The Divided West*, 115, 119. See also discussions in Deitelhoff, 'The Discursive Process of Legalization: Charting Islands of Persuasion in the ICC Case'; Wheatley, *The Democratic Legitimacy of International Law*, 140–1.) This line of argument also holds out the prospect of a lifeworld being constructed (though 'constituted' may be a more appropriate term) through communicative action.

127 Deitelhoff, 'The Discursive Process of Legalization: Charting Islands of Persuasion in the ICC Case', 35.

Should this logic operate, positions in favour of which strong principled arguments can be marshalled (i.e. the 'better argument') will be favoured over courses of action which are more difficult for governments to justify in socially acceptable terms. This is in contrast to the standard bargaining model of strategic interaction based on pre-determined preferences posited by rationalist scholars. The negotiation of the Rome Statute of the International Criminal Court has been cited as an example of such a logic in operation. Nicole Deitelhoff points to 'islands of persuasion' in the treaty negotiations as civil society and government advocates of certain positions gradually embedded preferred values in the normative frame of reference of discussions, requiring other delegations to justify positions in terms of these commonly accepted values.[128]

While Deitelhoff and others have provided a range of instances in which such a 'logic of argument' can be said to have operated, this concept and its operationalisation are not unproblematic. Johnston has observed that the operation of a 'logic of argument' is itself dependent on prior internalisation of 'basic assumptions about the deep structure of . . . interaction: who are legitimate players and what is a legitimate value to be bargained over?'[129] An associated challenge is that of identifying the characteristics of a 'convincing' argument, as well as the conditions under which a 'logic of argument' is likely to operate.[130]

As Risse concedes, 'Habermas's theory is rather silent on the question of how much of a common lifeworld people need to share in order to communicate in a reasonable manner'.[131] However, to the extent that a 'logic of argument' requires debate to be conducted within a lifeworld that 'provides arguing actors with a repertoire of collective understandings to which they can refer when making truth claims', the international legal and diplomatic context within which multilateral regime design negotiation takes place, particularly in the context of international humanitarian law, makes this environment a strong candidate to fulfil these

[128] See generally Deitelhoff, 'The Discursive Process of Legalization: Charting Islands of Persuasion in the ICC Case'.

[129] Johnston, *Social States: China in International Institutions, 1980–2000*, 18. Johnston appears to suggest that studies of communicative action and the operation of a Habermasian lifeworld in IR are closely associated with an 'almost exclusive' focus on persuasion (i.e. internalisation of some set of preferred values). Even if this is the case, however, it is not necessary for arguments to be internalised to be effective: rather a lifeworld may be conceived of as structurally limiting the range of socially acceptable arguments (and thereby outcomes) in a given context.

[130] Ibid., 19.

[131] Risse, '"Let's Argue!": Communicative Action in World Politics', 14.

conditions.[132] In general, interaction amongst actors at multilateral treaty-making conferences is tightly structured formally by procedural rules, and socially through mores and customs that have developed over time. Alongside the prevalence of debate closely informed by (and, indeed, amongst) legal specialists, and arguments predicated on existing law and practice, this provides a dense set of such 'collective understandings'.[133]

This is particularly likely where international humanitarian law forms the subject matter, given the enduring, public acceptance by governments of underlying precepts and principles. In consequence, such a context provides an environment potentially conducive to the operation of a 'logic of argument'.[134] This is especially so where proceedings are open to the public and/or non-state organisations or conceivably even where proceedings are recorded and thus capable of introducing a 'shadow of transparency'. Indeed, such law-making contexts have formed a prominent focus of empirical research in this vein.[135]

While some degree of shared lifeworld may be key to the operation of a 'logic of argument', it is important to note that for such a logic to operate there is no requirement for the proponents of different views in a debate to be motivated by 'genuine truth seeking', as might be the case

132 Habermas, *The Divided West*, 115, 119. See also discussions in Deitelhoff, 'The Discursive Process of Legalization: Charting Islands of Persuasion in the ICC Case'; Wheatley, *The Democratic Legitimacy of International Law*, 140–1.

133 As put by Ulbert, Risse and Muller: 'diplomacy has found ways to substitute for the lack of a lifeworld rooted in domestic cultures and directs our attention to the type of normative reference systems negotiators use while exchanging arguments' ('Arguing and Bargaining in Multilateral Negotiations', 4). Similarly, Faizullaev: 'Diplomatic negotiations depend highly on internationally adopted social norms and are grounded on specific normative interactions accepted by the international community' ('Diplomatic Interactions and Negotiations', 278). More broadly, Reus-Smit refers to contractual international law and multilateralism as 'the two principal fundamental institutions of contemporary international society' ('The Constitutional Structure of International Society and the Nature of Fundamental Institutions', 572).

134 See Risse, 'Arguing about Arguing: A Comment', 342–3. Elsewhere, '"arguing in a public sphere" appears to be particularly conducive to processes of persuasion, if the speakers do not know for sure the preferences of their audience and if the consent of the audiences is required, be it at the domestic level (as in a "two-level arguing process") or be it in front of a transnational public sphere in which negotiators see the need to legitimize their positions' (Ulbert and Risse, 'Deliberately Changing the Discourse: What Does Make Arguing Effective?', 359).

135 Ulbert, Risse, and Müller, 'Arguing and Bargaining in Multilateral Negotiations'; Deitelhoff, 'The Discursive Process of Legalization: Charting Islands of Persuasion in the ICC Case'.

in an idealised context.[136] Rather, even though actors may have differing interests, motivations and preferences, the particular social context in which debate is conducted will (or may not) tend towards the operation of a 'logic of argument'. In the case of civil war treaty regime negotiations, for example, the context may render arguments predicated on naked self-interest discursively 'out of bounds', with arguments instead appealing to (real or notionally) shared principles and values more closely associated with the 'humanitarian' subject matter and the legal and diplomatic context of debate.

Moreover, the 'better argument' need not necessarily be internalised by the actors concerned in order to bring about pro-normative outcomes. Rather, agents may seek to use a variety of techniques and devices to promote the adoption of pro-normative arguments and associated drafting language. Negotiators may, for example, try to discursively graft a position onto or nest a position within the broader international normative order to reinforce their argument or to weaken an opponent's.[137] Alternatively, a negotiator may make an argument premised on a norm that a target government has already endorsed. The social unacceptability of abjuring this endorsement enables the rhetorical entrapment of the latter,[138] enhancing the likelihood of a government 'abid(ing), eventually, by the better argument'.[139] In short, the operation of a 'logic of argument' is consistent with the deployment by pro- (and counter-)normative agents of multiple argumentative techniques. For

136 Müller, 'Arguing, Bargaining and All That: Communicative Action, Rationalist Theory and the Logic of Appropriateness in International Relations'.

137 Price, 'Reversing the Gun Sights: Transnational Civil Society Targets Land Mines', 617; Raymond, 'Problems and Prospects in the Study of International Norms'; Reus-Smit, 'Society, Power and Ethics', 286. Legro refers in similar fashion to the degree of 'concordance' of a norm (Legro, 'Which Norms Matter? Revisiting the "Failure" of Internationalism', 35).

138 See Petrova, 'Rhetorical Entrapment and Normative Enticement: How the United Kingdom Turned from Spoiler into Champion of the Cluster Munition Ban'; Schimmelfennig, 'The Community Trap: Liberal Norms, Rhetorical Action, and the Eastern Enlargement of the European Union'. In the words of Schimmelfennig: '[a]ctors who can justify their interests on the grounds of the community's standard of legitimacy are therefore able to shame their opponents into norm-conforming behavior and to modify the collective outcome that would have resulted from constellations of interests and power alone' (48). Krebs and Jackson similarly illustrate the extent to which rhetoric can serve 'coercive' as well as 'persuasive' (narrowly understood) purposes ('Twisting Tongues and Twisting Arms: The Power of Political Rhetoric').

139 Deitelhoff and Müller, 'Theoretical Paradise – Empirically Lost? Arguing with Habermas', 172; Risse and Sikkink, 'The Socialization of International Human Rights Norms into Domestic Practices: Introduction', 28.

such a logic to operate effectively, however, we would expect the arguments and positions expressed to centre around principles and values that negotiation participants have collectively endorsed (whether more or less internalised by relevant individuals or governments) and understand as integral to the relevant lifeworld. In consequence, the following proposition may be derived:

Hypothesis 4: Governments will be more likely to support the adoption of civil war-regulating provisions in treaty negotiations when strong, coherent arguments premised on widely shared values and principles are made in support. (The Logic of Argument hypothesis)

1.4.4 Liberal Insights and Regime Type

It is also possible to identify a distinct liberal theoretical approach to regime design. Slaughter, for example, argues that, due to the nature of state–society relations in liberal states, liberal democracies are more likely to make use of international law as a means of regulating conduct than other states.[140] Moreover, as Beth Simmons has shown, domestic factors can also limit international legal relations.[141]

Broadly speaking, liberal research can be understood as suggesting that democracies are more likely than non-democracies to endorse and/or promote a demanding international civil war regime.[142] The role of democracies, particularly so-called 'middle powers', in the campaigns to ban land mines, to establish the ICC and to end apartheid in South Africa may be cited as instances in which the governments of democratic states have played prominent roles in promoting such novel humanitarian international regimes.[143]

140 Slaughter, 'International Law in a World of Liberal States'. Slaughter draws here on the earlier work of Moravcsik. (See Moravcsik, 'Liberalism and International Relations Theory: A Scientific Assessment'.) In similar vein, Doyle refers to the 'liberal peace' (Doyle, 'Three Pillars of the Liberal Peace').

141 Simmons, *Mobilizing for Human Rights: International Law in Domestic Politics.*

142 Interestingly, liberal scholars appear to have paid little attention to less liberal – sometimes termed 'illiberal' – democracies. (See e.g. Slaughter's definition of a 'liberal democracy' in 'International Law in a World of Liberal States', 511.)

143 See variously: Klotz, 'Norms Reconstituting Interests: Global Racial Equality and US Sanctions against South Africa'; Price, 'Reversing the Gun Sights: Transnational Civil Society Targets Land Mines'; Deitelhoff, 'The Discursive Process of Legalization'; Bower, *Norms without the Great Powers: International Law and Changing Social Standards in World Politics.*

It could be argued that this reference should be restricted to *liberal* democracies, but given the uncertain (and sometimes elastic) understandings of different scholars towards the essential components of this form of governance, a broader approach is adopted for present purposes.[144] Indeed, the classification of colonial states such as France, the Netherlands or the UK as 'liberal' (let alone democratic) in respect of their overseas possessions could also be questioned - though given the concentration of decision-making power in broadly 'liberal' metropolitan centres in such cases, save where particular circumstances might suggest otherwise, such states will also be considered 'liberal democracies' for the purposes of the present study.

This broad ambit should not be understood as implying that only democracies will endorse a demanding legal regime. Indeed, Oona Hathaway has found that less democratic states are likely to be relatively more willing to commit to human rights treaties where there are low prospects of enforcement, whereas even in the absence of effective enforcement prospects, democracies with weaker human rights records are likely to be more reluctant to make the same commitment.[145] Nevertheless, this observation underlines that democracies – even those with reason to hesitate before signing up to a given regime – would appear to be more ready to engage in the creation of demanding, potentially intrusive international legal regimes than non-democracies, including with respect to the conduct of civil wars.

There are a number of possible explanations for this tendency. First, the (relative) readiness of democratic states to promote humanitarian norms may reflect domestic institutions and/or shared values. The governments of democracies may, for example, benefit domestically from signalling an intention to refrain from socially costly internal behaviour, or from minimising the risks of 'spillover' from civil conflicts elsewhere.[146] Bass has argued, too, that 'humanitarianism begins at home', inter alia via a cultural commitment to 'legalism' in liberal democracies.[147] Decision-makers in

[144] See related discussion in Chapter 6, Section 6.1.5.

[145] See Hathaway, 'Why Do Countries Commit to Human Rights Treaties?' See generally Keith, 'Human Rights Instruments', 359–61. Re. 'bad-ass' behaviour by authoritarian governments, see also Vreeland, 'Dictatorships, Torture, and Human Rights Treaties: The Bad Ass Theory'; Voeten, 'The Bad Ass Theory of Why Dictators Sign the Convention against Torture'.

[146] Moravcsik, 'Liberal International Relations Theory: A Scientific Assessment'; Moravcsik, 'The New Liberalism'.

[147] Bass, *Stay the Hand of Vengeance*; Bass, *Freedom's Battle: The Origins of Humanitarian Intervention.*

democracies with long-established means of peacefully settling internal disputes may also perceive a relatively low likelihood of encountering violent civil unrest, and therefore may not be overly concerned about tying their own hands in the future.[148] Governments of 'new', non-established democracies may also be anxious to lock in commitments to rule-of-law-associated regimes domestically, potentially including civil war-related regulatory frameworks as well as human rights treaty rules.[149] Finally, decision-makers in democracies are likely to be more accessible to norm advocates than those in more authoritarian states, enhancing the prospects of norm entrepreneurship.

Furthermore, Risse and Ropp suggest that the governments of non-democratic states may be less likely than those of democracies to support international humanitarian treaty provisions without significant external pressure.[150] Even when the governments of such states do show support, though, Hathaway's research suggests that this may evince only nominal commitment to underlying principles. In contrast, while democracies may also hesitate to lend support to a given set of provisions, where there is endorsement this may be more likely to signal principled commitment than might be the case with respect to a non-democracy.[151]

In light of the above, the following proposition may be derived:

Hypothesis 5: Democracies are more likely to support intrusive, restrictive civil war-regulating provisions than non-democracies. (The Regime Type hypothesis)

1.5 Hypothesised Factors: Indicators and Interactions

1.5.1 Drivers, Mechanisms and Indicators

The preceding discussion has set out five hypotheses, incorporating factors and insights drawn from multiple research traditions, which may have a bearing on government attitudes to civil war regulation and, in turn, on the outcome of associated treaty negotiations. While oriented towards answering a single empirical puzzle, however, these

[148] Though this may not be the case in all instances, for example with respect to overseas possessions of colonial states.

[149] Moravcsik, 'The Origins of Human Rights Regimes: Democratic Delegation in Postwar Europe'.

[150] Risse and Ropp, 'International Human Rights Norms and Domestic Change', 260. See also Keck and Sikkink, *Activists beyond Borders*.

[151] For discussion, see Hathaway, 'Do Human Rights Treaties Make a Difference?'

hypotheses are predicated on and reflect multiple decision-making logics, drivers, and associated causal mechanisms. This begs the question(s) of what these underlying drivers are, through which causal mechanisms they are likely to operate and interact in affecting negotiation outcomes, and what evidence might enable us to determine whether and how a given hypothesised factor contributed to bringing about outcomes in any given treaty negotiation instance.[152]

The key explanatory factor underpinning the Realist hypothesis, for example, is the persistence and recognition of material power differentials amongst states, with the implication that, all else being equal, more powerful states, particularly great powers, will generally succeed in imposing their views on less powerful states. In terms of operative mechanisms, such power differentials may feed into government positions directly, with more powerful states utilising their material power to implicitly or expressly coerce governments of weaker states to align their views with their own. Equally, however – and perhaps more likely in a publicly reported, diplomatic context where a premium is placed on decision-making by consensus – great powers may influence outcomes indirectly, with negotiations conducted 'in the shadow' of leading power preferences and participants and organisers likely to prefer to design a regime with more rather than less great power support.[153]

In terms of determining the operation of such influence, first-hand statements and recognition by weaker powers of the influence of great power preferences on their own positions and on negotiation outcomes would provide ideal evidence. Public (and even private) statements to this effect may be uncommon, however, as it may not be in the interests of either great or less great powers to recognise this impact – and indeed, even where made explicit, such evidence may also be inaccessible. In consequence, while such

[152] This discussion is indebted to Jérémie Cornut's observation, drawing on Alan Garfinkel, that '[t]he demarcation of the contrast space clarifies the potential complementarity of different explanations because "the various relations among explanations correlate with various relations among their contrast spaces"' (Cornut, 'Analytic Eclecticism in Practice: A Method for Combining International Relations Theories', 60, quoting Garfinkel, *Forms of Explanation: Rethinking the Questions in Social Theory*, 27–8). See also discussion of process tracing below re. the characterisation of evidence as 'causal process observations'.

[153] As observed by Courtney Smith in 1999, '[p]ressure towards consensus now dominates almost all multilateral efforts at global problem solving' ('The Politics of Global Consensus Building: A Comparative Analysis', 173). In Pouliot's words, '"joining the consensus" is an imperative of diplomacy' ('Diplomats as Permanent Representatives: The Practical Logics of the Multilateral Pecking Order', 551).

recognition will be extremely helpful if available, it will also be important to consider the extent to which outcomes and courses of events reflect the preferences of the most powerful states in the international system and observers' views of how and why this may or may not have been the case.[154]

In similar fashion, the principal causal driver underpinning the Rationalist hypothesis is the anticipated tendency of government preferences at any given point to reflect a reasoned balance of costs and benefits, likely in many (if not most) instances to militate against a demanding civil war regime. While governments are likely to arrive at negotiations with a predetermined set and ranking of preferences, this functionally derived calculus may also shift during negotiations as circumstances change: previously second-best (or lower-ranked) outcomes, for example, may come to be seen as preferred compared with other possible outcomes. To the extent that similar rationalist logic informs the overall conduct of negotiations, negotiation outcomes as a whole may also be expected to reflect a balance of costs and benefits (and preferences) across delegations.

It should be relatively straightforward to assess, by reference to public negotiation records, the extent to which key delegations are more or less supportive of demanding and/or intrusive regulation of civil war, and to track the evolution of these positions over time. The ideal evidence that positions result from a process of rational calculation, however, would be direct recognition from governments and delegations of such a process underlying the adoption of a given perspective, preferably including a ranking and explication of preferences at any given point in terms of costs and benefits. Similarly, insofar as negotiation outcomes overall can be understood as reflecting a broader balance of costs and benefits across delegations, straightforward evidence of this would be provided by explicit recognition of the operation of this functional logic by participants and negotiation managers.

As with the Realist hypothesis, the scope to provide unambiguous evidence of this hypothesis in operation via these processes may be limited by difficulties in accessing relevant data, as well as by potential reluctance on the part of participants and observers to publicly recognise the operation of such functionalist logic.[155] Given this, as in the former

[154] This combination of more specific causal process observations and what might be termed 'circumstantial' evidence of causal mechanism operation in the context of 'explaining outcome' process tracing is discussed further below.

[155] Norm entrepreneurs, for example, may prefer to highlight the role of normative arguments on outcomes, even where strong strategic drivers of outcomes are also evident.

case, it is likely to be necessary also to examine corroborative evidence relating to government preferences, courses of conduct and negotiation outcomes in considering whether or not and how such functionalist logic might have informed both individual delegation preferences and the overall course of negotiations.

Domestic governance complexion provides the key explanatory factor underlying the Regime Type hypothesis, in that different forms of governance may result in varied dispositions towards a progressive civil war regime. In this instance, drivers may be cultural (reflecting domestic institutions and values) and/or reflect particular constellations and manifestations of domestic political commitments, interests and preferences. In terms of transmission mechanisms, such cultural and domestic political drivers would be expected to manifest in government and delegation preference-setting processes (transmitted to delegations via instructions and reflected in private delegation and government communications) and in behaviour and expressed preferences during the course of negotiations.

The optimal evidence to illustrate the Regime Type hypothesis in operation would once again be explicit participant recognition of the role of these factors in determining delegation positions and the translation of these into outcomes. Where this is lacking, however, corroborative, indirect evidence of this hypothesis and associated mechanisms in operation may again inform understanding of the salience of regime type to government preferences and negotiation outcomes more generally.

For its part, the Agent Characteristics hypothesis is predicated on the operation of norm entrepreneurship, and on the discursive processes through which norm entrepreneurs inform domestic policy preferences and negotiation outcomes by deploying technical expertise and moral authority to elicit pro-normative behaviour. This would ideally be evidenced by identifying and tracking the influence of such expertise and authority on targets of norm entrepreneurship – as recorded by entrepreneurs and their targets. The Logic of Argument hypothesis in turn relies on negotiations being conducted in an environment conducive to reasoned argument. The key causal mechanism here is the manner in which such an environment discursively limits the range of arguments and positions participants put forward, and which will be acceptable to other participants, in the course of negotiations. To evidence this logic in operation, we would ideally identify instances where participants recognise the discursive bounds and framework of negotiations, and the importance of framing arguments in terms of values and principles understood by them and others as consistent with this context. In both instances, however, in the absence of direct evidence, contextual, corroborative evidence is again likely to prove valuable.

1.5.2 Mapping Interaction

There is likely to be close interplay between the operation of the causal drivers and mechanisms associated with these hypotheses in affecting negotiation outcomes. With this in mind, it may be helpful to consider some of the likely relationships amongst these underlying drivers, government preferences and negotiation outcomes, and how these might be portrayed in 'straw person' arrow diagrammatic form. Understanding of these relationships and interactions will then be revisited and refined on the basis of the case study chapters that follow.

The interaction between and relative priority of causal factors reflecting different theoretical approaches have, of course, been extensively debated amongst proponents of different perspectives. Reflecting the eclectic approach set out above, however, it is critical to note that the present exercise does not seek to establish either covering law-type relationships amongst these factors or their relative primacy. Rather, the object is to provide an overview of ex ante most likely relationships amongst the identified causal factors in shaping civil war regime treaty provisions, without asserting any primacy amongst these. With this last in mind, Figure 1 identifies a range of such potential interactions.[156]

While necessarily oversimplifying a complex reality, Figure 1 reflects a set of potentially likely relationships of causal drivers to outcomes.

In respect of plotting the interaction of Realist material power differentials with other hypothesised factors, for example, neither the course of negotiations nor their outcome will themselves change the relative material power of states. To the extent these may affect the operation of other hypothesised factors without being themselves susceptible to change, great power preferences may be expected to influence drafting outcomes independently of other hypothesised factors.[157] Rationalist considerations are

[156] The arrows in this diagram can be considered to 'show the path of influence or causality predicted by the theory' (Clark, *Political Science Research Methods: Exploring America at a Crossroads*, 59).

[157] It may be more accurate to refer to such factors as acting 'exogenously' – i.e. as factors 'whose value is determined by factors or variables outside the causal system under study' (Little, 'Exogenous Variable'). Bennett and Checkel, however, describe 'exogenous' variables as 'those excluded from a model because they are either not powerful or

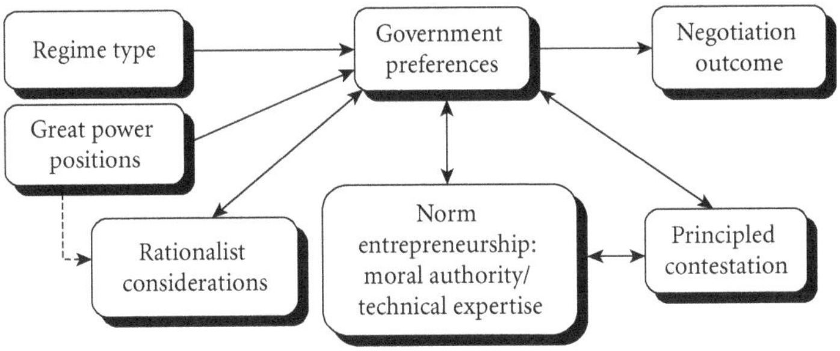

Figure 1: Mapping Interaction (Version 1)

similarly positioned to reflect the expectation that governments' preferences will reflect an ex ante cost/benefit analysis, taking into account that this calculus is likely to include consideration of great power preferences (indicated by the dotted line) and may also shift during the process of negotiations (indicated by the arrow running in both directions).

The bi-directional arrows linking norm entrepreneurship, principled contestation and government preferences are similarly designed to capture the potentially close interplay between the operation of the Agent Characteristics hypothesis and the Logic of Argument hypothesis, insofar as technical expertise and moral weight are more likely to be relevant in open, structured negotiations where these factors can most effectively inform principled, reasoned arguments. Conversely, moral suasion and principled argument are less likely to be salient where negotiations are conducted behind closed doors.

It bears reiterating that the operation of the five hypotheses and their underlying drivers and associated causal mechanisms is likely to be far more complex, iterative, and generally endogenous in practice than portrayed above.[158] Figure 1 should therefore be understood as setting out only one possible set of interactions between hypotheses, drivers and outcomes. Nevertheless, for present purposes it will suffice as a simplified portrayal of a set of baseline expectations for the multi-causal analysis of civil war regime development that follows.

frequent enough, or too complex or unpredictable, to be brought into the theory' (Bennett and Checkel, 'Process Tracing: From Philosophical Roots to Best Practice', 7). Accordingly, to avoid confusion, 'independently' is preferred to 'exogenously' in the present discussion.

[158] Regime type, for example, may conceivably affect both susceptibility to norm entrepreneurship and the effectiveness of a state as a norm entrepreneur.

1.6 Methodology

Negotiating Civil War takes the form of a structured, focused comparison of three cases,[159] analysing the development of the civil war regime,[160] understood for present purposes as manifested in the international humanitarian law treaty rules of conduct for combatants in internal armed conflict – the 'dependent variable' of the study.[161] Each of the case studies considers an example of the same phenomenon: the negotiation of a set of civil war-regulating multilateral treaty provisions, covering the most significant such measures to be agreed to date,[162] and so are sufficiently similar to enable the same 'standardized, general' questions to be asked in each instance.[163]

The explanatory hypotheses selected draw on the most prominent research traditions in IR theory. The risk of overlooking critical drivers of and causal paths to outcomes that may be associated with the adoption of a narrower theoretical perspective is accordingly reduced by including each of the 'major theoretical categories of social explanation ... explanations based on actors' material power, institutional constraints and opportunities, and social norms or legitimacy'.[164] Asking the same questions in each instance and examining the phenomenon from the perspective of the same five hypotheses, while remaining sensitive to inductive findings from

159 George and Bennett, *Case Studies and Theory Development in the Social Sciences*, 67–72.

160 The term 'civil war', which is used interchangeably throughout with 'internal armed conflict', should be understood here as referring to armed conflicts amongst 'agents of (or claimants to) a state and organized, nonstate groups' (Fearon and Laitin, 'Ethnicity, Insurgency, and Civil War', 76). This is not, however, an attempt to define civil war for anything other than present purposes – as Armitage observes, civil war remains an 'essentially contested concept' (*Civil Wars: A History in Ideas*, 226).

161 George and Bennett, *Case Studies and Theory Development in the Social Sciences*, 67. A regime is understood as referring to a set of 'implicit or explicit principles, norms, rules, and decision-making procedures around which actors' expectations converge in a given area of international relations' (Krasner, 'Structural Causes and Regime Consequences: Regimes as Intervening Variables', 186).

162 It is worth adding that no multilateral attempt was made to explicitly regulate civil war by treaty before 1949. Accordingly, the universe of possible case studies is in any event effectively limited to the post-war period (Mahoney and Goertz, 'The Possibility Principle: Choosing Negative Cases in Qualitative Research').

163 George and Bennett, *Case Studies and Theory Development in the Social Sciences*, 69. To the extent that the operation of the various hypothesised factors and associated mechanisms is the focus of *Negotiating Civil War*, the selection of 'typical cases' is also consistent with the approach to case selection proposed by Beach and Pedersen ('Selecting Appropriate Cases When Tracing Causal Mechanisms').

164 See Bennett and Checkel, 'Process Tracing: From Philosophical Roots to Best Practice', 21, 23.

the case studies regarding additional factors that should be taken into account, also facilitates distinguishing more from less salient case-specific background conditions, as well as enabling the fine-tuning (or, if merited, reconsideration) of the hypotheses themselves.[165]

The principal research method adopted is process-tracing: 'the analysis of evidence on processes, sequences, and conjunctures of events within a case for the purpose of either developing or testing hypotheses about causal mechanisms that might causally explain the case'.[166] Understanding of and approaches to process tracing in IR have become increasingly sophisticated in recent years, highlighting potential costs and risks as well as benefits of this method, as well as providing valuable practical guidance for the conduct of process tracing.[167]

Process tracing allows the illustration of causation through tracing the mechanisms connecting causal factors to outcomes, allowing hypotheses to be tested on the basis of only a few cases.[168] There is broad recognition,

[165] See ibid., 29: 'One of the great advantages of process tracing is that it puts researchers at risk of stumbling upon many potential causal factors, evident in the details and sequences of a case, which they had not anticipated'.

[166] Ibid., 7. This is a recent reformulation: perhaps the more 'classic' definition refers to process tracing as attempting 'to trace the links between possible causes and observed outcomes . . . [examining] histories, archival documents, interview transcripts, and other sources to see whether the causal process a theory hypothesises or implies in a case is in fact evident' (George and Bennett, *Case Studies and Theory Development in the Social Sciences*, 6). Process tracing remains a contested concept, however: in a recent study Trampusch and Palier identify 20 definitions of this methodology, and 18 types of process tracing ('Between X and Y: How Process Tracing Contributes to Opening the Black Box of Causality').

[167] As Trampusch and Palier note, 'while process tracing was originally defined as a method to analyse decision-making processes, now it is predominantly defined as a method aiming to identify or test hypotheses on causal mechanisms in order to compensate for weaknesses in correlational analysis' ('Between X and Y: How Process Tracing Contributes to Opening the Black Box of Causality', 441). See e.g. Rohlfing, *Case Studies and Causal Inference*; Beach and Pedersen, *Process-Tracing Methods: Foundations and Guidelines*; Kittel et al., 'Symposium: Reassessing the Methodology of Process Tracing'; Elman et al., 'Symposium on Process Tracing'; Bennett and Checkel, *Process Tracing: From Metaphor to Analytic Tool*; Beach and Pedersen, *Causal Case Study Methods: Foundations and Guidelines for Comparing, Matching, and Tracing*. That said, as Checkel notes 'many contemporary constructivist studies . . . continue to invoke process tracing more as a metaphor than as an analytic tool' ('Methods in Constructivist Approaches', 156).

In terms of practical guidance, Bennett and Checkel set out, for example, ten 'best practices': 'Process Tracing: From Philosophical Roots to Best Practice', 20–31. See also various checklists in Beach and Pedersen, *Process-Tracing Methods: Foundations and Guidelines*.

[168] George and Bennett, *Case Studies and Theory Development in the Social Sciences*, 215. Process-tracing exercises can be designed to assess the degrees of certitude of in-case

however, that such mechanisms are in effect unobservable.[169] In consequence, it is necessary to search for their 'empirical fingerprints' in what have been termed 'causal process observations': 'an insight or piece of data that provides information about context, process, or mechanism, and that contributes distinctively to causal inference'.[170] These observations can then be used to trace the processes connecting underlying causal factors to outcomes.[171]

Care needs to be taken, moreover, in the identification of such observations and of accompanying 'diagnostic evidence', to ensure that these reliably reflect the operation of the mechanism(s) in question.[172] To this end, Section 1.5 considered a range of such indicators and evidence for the operation of the present set of hypothesised factors and associated causal mechanisms.

The nature (and definition) of causal mechanisms remains a subject of debate – in particular, there is arguably a growing tendency amongst practitioners of process tracing to seek to identify increasingly 'micro' causal mechanisms, with a view to theory development or testing.[173] This tendency

inferences via 'hoop' tests (enabling the elimination of hypotheses that fail to operate as anticipated); 'smoking gun' tests (capable of confirming the operation of a hypothesis); and 'straw in the wind' tests (providing 'some evidence in favor of or against a hypothesis, but (which is) not decisive') (Mahoney, 'The Logic of Process Tracing Tests in the Social Sciences', 572).

169 Bennett and Checkel, 'Process Tracing: From Philosophical Roots to Best Practice', 12. See also further references below re. causal mechanisms.

170 Collier, Brady, and Seawright, 'Introduction to the Second Edition: A Sea Change in Political Methodology', 2 at note 3.

171 George and Bennett, *Case Studies and Theory Development in the Social Sciences*, 215. The characterisation of such observations is, moreover, tied up with the characterisation of causal mechanisms. As Beach and Pedersen observe in the context of an argument for a narrower conception of causal mechanisms, albeit critically: '[causal process observations] ranged from information about the context within which a process played out, over circumstantial evidence that suggested that a process might be in play, to more direct evidence of the actual operation of the process' ('How Do I Know Mechanistic Evidence When I See It? A Four-Step Procedure for Tracing Causal Mechanisms in Case Study Research', 7).

172 Bennett and Checkel refer to 'diagnostic evidence' as 'observable events that intercede between hypothesized causes and observed effects' (Bennett and Checkel, 'Process Tracing: From Philosophical Roots to Best Practice', 7).

173 Derek Beach, for example, argues that Bennett and Checkel employ a (sub-optimal) 'minimalist' understanding of mechanisms, as these are 'not unpacked theoretically in any detail, meaning that our mechanistic evidence is somewhat superficial because we have not empirically traced the workings of each part of the mechanism' ('Process-Tracing Methods in Social Science'). A recent debate regarding the nature of causal mechanisms, illustrating the implications of different views, can be found in Jacobs et al., 'Symposium: Causal Mechanisms and Process Tracing'.

has in turn given rise to debate as to the optimal level of granularity at which mechanisms should be specified and evidenced in different contexts. Ultimately, however, the position adopted in this regard by Beach and Pedersen – that '[t]he choice of level for our theorization of causal mechanisms in process-tracing depends on the pragmatic concern of the level at which the empirical manifestations of a given causal mechanism are best studied' – provides perhaps the most sensible approach in the present context, charting a via media between overly macro- and micro-conceptualisations of causal mechanisms.[174] This view sits well with the theoretically eclectic, 'problem-solving' approach adopted in *Negotiating Civil War*, itself characteristic of what Beach and Pedersen describe as 'explaining outcome' process tracing. In the latter context, 'the term causal mechanism is used in a much broader sense ... (recognising that) to craft a minimally sufficient explanation we almost always need to combine mechanisms into an eclectic conglomerate mechanism to account for a historical outcome ... The result is case-specific combinations of

[174] Beach and Pedersen, *Process-Tracing Methods: Foundations and Guidelines*, 43 and see generally discussion at 40–3. Bennett and Checkel, in contrast, take the view that: '[e]xplanation via reference to causal mechanisms ... involves a commitment in principle to being consistent with the lowest level of analysis and finest degree of detail observable' (Bennett and Checkel, 'Process Tracing: From Philosophical Roots to Best Practice', 12). This position is also reflected in George and Bennett, *Case Studies and Theory Development in the Social Sciences*, 142. At the same time though, Checkel also recognises that a focus on micro-mechanisms risks overlooking macro drivers of outcomes (Checkel, 'Mechanisms, Process and the Study of International Institutions', 93). Adopting a more balanced view, Beach and Pedersen note that a focus on micro-mechanisms is unnecessarily restrictive, as 'many of the most interesting social phenomena we want to study, such as democratization, cannot meaningfully be reduced solely to the actor level but in certain situations can be better analyzed empirically at the macrolevel ... There are social mechanisms whose observable implications can best be theorized and measured at the macrolevel' (*Causal Case Study Methods*, 41–2). In particular, they highlight the limited utility of theorising at a micro (individual) level, where insufficient data might be available and where such insights may add little by way of verifiable structural implications. They also flag the risk of an infinite regress in the pursuit of ever more micro neurological, 'biochemical and so on' causal mechanisms, leading to a situation in which 'no causal claims can be established without absurd amounts of information' (Beach and Pedersen, *Process-Tracing Methods: Foundations and Guidelines*, 43 citing: Stinchcombe, 'The Conditions of Fruitfulness of Theorizing About Mechanisms in Social Science'; Kincaid, *Philosophical Foundations of the Social Sciences: Analyzing Controversies in Social Research*; Steel, 'Social Mechanisms and Causal Inference'). They therefore conclude that: '[i]f the strongest tests of a given mechanism are possible at the macrolevel, then it should be theorized and studied empirically at this level, whereas if the empirical manifestations are better observed at the microlevel, then we should conceptualize and operationalize our study at this level' (*Causal Case Study Methods*, 43).

mechanisms in eclectic conglomerates'.[175] As Beach and Pedersen observe, explaining outcomes in this manner is likely to involve an approach in which '[t]heorized mechanisms are . . . seen as heuristic instruments whose function is to help build the best possible explanation of a particular outcome'.[176]

Bearing this last in mind, the focus in *Negotiating Civil War* is on identifying diagnostic evidence at a level of granularity consistent with the various hypotheses – that is to say, primarily at state/government level. Individual-level psychological analysis, for example, is not obviously required to test the operation of any of the hypothesised factors.[177] In short, the level of detail sought in respect of each hypothesis in the case studies reflects the content (in terms of causal drivers and mechanisms) of each proposition.

In terms of identifying periods for investigation, the case studies each focus on periods during which the regulation of civil war was on the international 'legislative agenda' as part of broader initiatives to reform or revise elements of the law of armed conflict more generally. Accordingly, the 'lower temporal bound' of the individual cases comprises the commencement by relevant actors of these reform/revision processes. Context is, however, provided by a more wide-ranging introductory discussion of the development of the civil war regime (Chapter 2), highlighting background conditions and processes to each case.[178]

[175] Beach and Pedersen, 'What Is Process-Tracing Actually Tracing? The Three Variants of Process Tracing Methods and Their Uses and Limitations', 22. With respect to identifying a 'minimally sufficient' explanation for a case, '[t]here is no foolproof answer to this question; instead, the decision that we have a minimally sufficient explanation is based on an assessment of whether all of the relevant facets of the outcome have been accounted for adequately' (Beach and Pedersen, *Process-Tracing Methods: Foundations and Guidelines*, 20).

[176] Beach and Pedersen, *Process-Tracing Methods: Foundations and Guidelines*, 19, citing generally Humphreys 'The Heuristic Explanation of Explanatory Theories in International Relations' and Jackson, *The Conduct of Inquiry in International Relations*.

[177] And in any case, as Checkel notes: '[i]t makes little sense to spend time attempting to process trace what cannot be measured empirically' (Checkel, 'Transnational Dynamics of Civil War', 22).

[178] This approach is broadly in line with that suggested by Bennett and Checkel: 'the time at which a key actor or agent enters the scene or gains some material, ideational or informational capacity' ('Process Tracing: From Philosophical Roots to Best Practice, 27). More generally, though not theorised here, such broader initiatives might be expected to follow 'exogenous shocks' and associated 'critical junctures'. In the words of Soifer: '[t]he distinct feature of a historical juncture with the potential to be critical is the loosening of the constraints of structure to allow for agency or contingency to shape divergence from the past, or divergence across cases' ('The Causal Logic of Critical

This approach is in some respects less than ideal. The 'conglomerate' approach to mechanisms in particular risks glossing over potentially more fine-grained causal relationships.[179] That said, an important, compensatory advantage of this approach is that it can 'point to potential systematic factors that can be investigated further by future studies, or that can act as building blocks for future attempts to build generalizable causal mechanisms that can explain outcomes across the population of relevant cases'.[180]

Identifying, obtaining and utilising evidence of the operation of even relatively coarse-grained mechanisms is not necessarily straightforward, however. Locating and accessing reliable, unbiased data in particular remains a key challenge. Indeed, even where detailed first-hand information on government decision-making is available this may be insufficient as evidence of genuine preferences. In particular, statements of preferences and associated reasons given by actors – especially in strategic contexts and where recorded with potential public exposure in mind – may not reveal genuine preferences and reasons for conduct.[181]

A related issue is that 'absence of evidence does not equate to evidence of absence'. In other words, an absence of observations in relation to a given set of factors or mechanisms may not be sufficient to conclude that the latter were not relevant to outcomes – it may simply not be possible to access the requisite evidence. Similarly, factor/mechanism operation may ultimately be evidenced in ways other than anticipated.[182]

The most obvious means of dealing with potentially unreliable data is to seek to triangulate amongst a broad range of primary and independent

Junctures', 1573). See more generally: Capoccia, 'Critical Junctures'; Pierson, *Politics in Time: History, Institutions, and Social Analysis*; Widmaier, Blyth and Seabrooke, 'Exogenous Shocks or Endogenous Constructions? The Meanings of Wars and Crises'; Risse-Kappen, 'Ideas Do Not Float Freely: Transnational Coalitions, Domestic Structures, and the End of the Cold War'.

179 Though, as noted above, even amongst researchers concerned with focusing on micro-mechanisms of causation, the optimal conception (and level of analysis) of such mechanisms remain heavily debated. See Beach and Pedersen, 'How Do I Know Mechanistic Evidence When I See It? A Four-Step Procedure for Tracing Causal Mechanisms in Case Study Research, 1–2.

180 Beach and Pedersen, 'What Is Process-Tracing Actually Tracing? The Three Variants of Process Tracing Methods and Their Uses and Limitations', 28.

181 See Bennett and Checkel, 'Process Tracing: From Philosophical Roots to Best Practice', 32 ('the only option is to infer preferences from an actor's earlier rhetoric and actions and use them to explain subsequent behaviour, while also investigating the possibility that preferences may change over time through learning or other processes').

182 Ibid., 19.

secondary sources. Even this may be insufficient, though, as secondary sources may reflect not only biases implicit in primary sources, but also the agendas of secondary authors themselves.[183]

Reliability and availability of evidence thus present significant challenges in the present examination, which requires partially reconstructing relevant domestic, inter-, and transnational discourses in each case study.[184] Indeed, the numbers of parties to the various sets of negotiations alone pose challenges with regard to data availability and accessibility. A wide variety of archival and secondary material is available with respect to British, French, and American conduct in the run-up to and during the negotiation of the 1949 Conventions and the 1977 Additional Protocols, for example. There is, however, a relative paucity of primary source material available with respect to non-Western delegations, particularly Soviet, Egyptian, and Indian decision-makers, in these instances. Similar difficulties are encountered in researching the drafting of the 1998 Rome Statute.

Given accessibility limitations, issues of reliability are mitigated in the case studies by reference to a broad range of sources, and by taking into consideration the potential biases and interests of authors, particularly in respect of first-hand, written records of decisions and events. Similarly, care is taken throughout to bear in mind that an absence of data points to support or oppose a given proposition cannot alone be understood as implying anything about the operation or non-operation of underlying drivers and causal mechanisms. Nevertheless, it is worth underlining that, reflecting these challenges, the findings remain in an important sense provisional, illustrating no more than part of the 'repertoire of causal paths' leading to the civil war regime as it stands today.[185]

Before concluding, it is worth underlining and explaining why this volume focuses on international legal regulation of internal armed conflict by treaty only.[186] Some may in particular be discomfited by the

[183] See Ibid., 27–8.

[184] Thies, 'A Pragmatic Guide to Qualitative Historical Analysis in the Study of International Relations'.

[185] Bennett and George, 'Process Tracing in Case Study Research, Paper Presented at the MacArthur Foundation Workshop on Case Study Methods', 6. In Mahoney's terms (see note 168), *Negotiating Civil War* is perhaps best conceived as an exercise to assess the plausibility of explaining outcomes in terms of hypothesised causes, individually and collectively, through a series of 'straw in the wind' tests.

[186] On the relationship between customary international law and regimes from an IR perspective, see Byers, *Custom, Power and the Power of Rules: International Relations and Customary International Law.*

absence of focused examination of customary international law. The focus on treaty provisions should not, however, be understood as diminishing the significance or salience of customary international law regarding internal armed conflict. The latter constitutes an important aspect of the normative framework delineating internal armed conflict and the associated standards of conduct for combatants.[187] Arising as it does through state practice and *opinio juris* rather than explicit negotiation, though, custom is ill-suited to examination in the present volume. Moreover, discussion of custom risks becoming bogged down by the relative indeterminacy of customary international law generally and in the area of internal armed conflict in particular, as compared to more or less clearly drafted treaty negotiation outputs.[188] Lastly, of course, to the extent that customary international law has a bearing on government preferences and negotiation outcomes, this should be evident in any event in discussions over treaty design.

Conclusion

Negotiating Civil War applies a pluralist set of theoretically derived hypotheses to the design of the civil war regime. The present chapter sets out the theoretical and methodological basis for the examination, suggesting that regime design is likely to be closely related to:

- the extent of great power support or opposition to any provisions (the Realist hypothesis)
- the extent to which proposals present potential costs and/or benefits domestically and internationally to negotiating governments (the Rationalist hypothesis)
- the decisional and discursive power of norm entrepreneurs (the Agent Characteristics hypothesis)
- the quality of the arguments that can be made in negotiations in favour of or against a set of provisions (the Logic of Argument hypothesis)

[187] See e.g. sections in Moir, *The Law of Internal Armed Conflict*; Dinstein, *Non-International Armed Conflicts in International Law*.

[188] As Monica Hakimi puts it: 'CIL finding is deeply entangled with CIL making' ('Custom's Method and Process: Lessons from Humanitarian Law', 148–9). On tension between states and non-state actors in finding (and making) custom, see also Shereshevsky, 'Back in the Game: The Reengagement of States in International Humanitarian Law Making'. In contrast, as William Schabas has observed, treaties are 'the clearest formulation of legal obligations that states are prepared to assume' (*Unimaginable Atrocities: Justice, Politics, and Rights at the War Crimes Tribunals*, 178).

- the extent to which a state is more or less democratic (the Regime Type hypothesis).

Taken together, these propositions reflect a set of insights derived from the major research traditions in International Relations. This is not to say, of course, that even in combination the underlying factors and associated causal mechanisms will necessarily be capable of providing a compelling account of the development of the civil war regime. Reflecting a process-tracing methodology that remains open to inductive as well as deductively derived insights, however, the case studies should also facilitate the identification of additional, non-ex ante hypothesised causal factors and mechanisms that have played a part in bringing about the various components of the civil war regime over time.

With this last in mind, Chapters 3, 4 and 5 examine the extent to which and the manner in which the propositions set out above are borne out in three instances: the negotiation, respectively, of Common Article 3 of the 1949 Geneva Conventions; key elements of the two 1977 Additional Protocols to these Conventions; and the provisions of Article 8 of the 1998 Rome Statute of the International Criminal Court relating to non-international armed conflicts. Before focusing more closely on these individual episodes, however, Chapter 2 provides essential background, situating these case studies in historical perspective.

2

Historical Precursors and Regime Origins

Introduction

In contrast to international armed conflict, it is only relatively recently that a set of international legal rules has been developed to regulate internal armed conflicts. These rules did not arise ex nihilo in 1949, however, and were closely informed by earlier debates and experience. The present chapter provides an overview of these antecedents and of the origins and developments of the latter-day civil war regime, setting the scene for the case studies that follow in Chapters 3, 4 and 5.

2.1 Rebellion and Civil War Prior to 1949

2.1.1 Antiquity and the Mediaeval Period

The history of war underlines the extent to which civil and international conflicts have long been considered distinct phenomena. Archaic Greek societies, for example, drew a distinction between *stasis* – conflict amongst members of a political community – and *polemos* – conflict with outsiders.[1] In similar fashion, while the term 'civil war' first appears (as *bellum civile*) in descriptions of the Roman wars of the late republican period in the first century BC,[2] Cicero's view was that only a political entity possessing 'a Commonwealth, a Senate-house, a treasury [and]

[1] See Aristotle, *Politics: Books V and VI*, trans. David Keyt, 63–5. Also discussion in Neff, *War and the Law of Nations: A General History*, 19; Price, *Thucydides and Internal War*, 67–72; Dawson and Dawson, *The Origins of Western Warfare: Militarism and Morality in the Ancient World*, 45–107; Bederman, *International Law in Antiquity*, 245–7.

[2] See Caesar, *The Civil War* (Latin: '*Commentarii de Bello Civili*').

a consensus of like-minded citizens' could constitute a 'true enemy' (*hostes*) for the purposes of war.[3]

Early Islamic thought adopted a slightly more nuanced view, distinguishing two sources of internal strife: *muharib* – essentially, criminal bands – and *bughat* – opponents motivated by some form of ideology other than private gain. Traditional law enforcement measures applied to the former, whereas the latter benefited from a measure of protection from imprisonment, enslavement, ransom or expropriation.[4]

Mediaeval 'just war' doctrine, however, recognised no such fine distinctions. As a just war could only be waged when sufficient *auctoritas* – proper authority – was present on both sides of a conflict, for example when opponents each had independent sovereign rulers, in the absence of such authority rebels could neither constitute a proper enemy for doctrinal purposes, nor declare a just war. In consequence, there were few notional limits on the ability of mediaeval European rulers to suppress rebellions.[5]

Aquinas did concede that domestic rebellion could be considered just if waged against a government not committed to just causes. This was with the caveat, however, that the damage inflicted by a rebellion on the population as a whole could not outweigh that inflicted by the perpetuation of unjust government – a challenging requirement given that he placed no such limitation on a government's ability to respond to insurrection.[6] Theological antipathy towards rebellion proved, moreover, difficult to shake off. Luther, for example, writing in the early sixteenth century, claimed that 'a rebel is not worth rational arguments' and that 'it is God's will that the king be honoured and the rebels destroyed'.[7]

[3] Cicero, *The Philippics*, ed. and trans. David R. Shackleton-Bailey, 143, cited in Neff, *War and the Law of Nations: A General History*, 18. For a detailed account of Greek and Roman conceptions of civil war, see Chapters 1–2 in Armitage, *Civil Wars: A History in Ideas*.

[4] See variously: Neff, *War and the Law of Nations: A General History*, 44; El Fadl, 'Ahkam Al-Bughat: Irregular Warfare and the Law of Rebellion in Islam', 149–76; El Fadl, *Rebellion and Violence in Islamic Law*; Michael Bonner, *Jihad in Islamic History: Doctrines and Practice*, 10–12; Van Creveld, *The Transformation of War*, 140; Bartels, 'Timelines, Borderlines and Conflicts', 43.

[5] See discussion in Bartels, 'Timelines, Borderlines and Conflicts', 42–4. See also Perna, *The Formation of the Treaty Law of Non-International Armed Conflicts*, 1–5; Sunderland, *Rebel Barons: Resisting Royal Power in Medieval Culture*, 39 (and generally 35–42).

[6] Aquinas, *Summa Theologica*, Vol. II, Quest. 42, Art. 2, cited in Perna, *The Formation of the Treaty Law of Non-International Armed Conflicts*, 3.

[7] Luther, 'An Open Letter on the Harsh Book against the Peasants', in Marrin (ed.) *War and the Christian Conscience: From Augustine to Martin Luther King, Jr.*, 101–2, cited in

2.1.2 From Reformation to Enlightenment

While holding firm to the essentials of just war doctrine, Reformation theologians such as Calvin and Knox were challenged by circumstances to develop novel interpretations of scripture to justify rebellions against rulers. Calvin responded by relaxing the prohibition on the commencement of wars by non-rulers, taking the view that in extremis it would be permissible for 'lesser magistrates' (though still not private citizens) to rebel against an 'apostate' ruler.[8] Knox added that such a ruler had no right to better treatment by rebels than the former would have accorded the latter.[9]

During the seventeenth and eighteenth centuries, theologians began to take a back seat to jurists drawing on theories of natural law to develop a social-contract-based view of relations between rulers and citizens. From this perspective, the state was primarily a vehicle for the protection and promotion of citizens' rights: rebellion could thereby be justified if necessary to vindicate these rights. At the same time, though, rebels would still be required to respect the rights of governments and their supporters, suggesting that the conduct of non-inter-state conflict should be subject to some limitations.

The seventeenth century also saw the crystallisation of the concept of sovereignty, most famously in the 1648 Peace of Westphalia. Associated understandings included: that sovereign powers had (at least notional) monopolies over the legitimate use of force within their territories; that only sovereign states were proper subjects of international law; and the consequent (albeit again notional) exclusion of external constraints on sovereign conduct in the domestic sphere.

This tendency strengthened scholarly views of international and internal war as distinct phenomena. Grotius, for example, held that

Bartels, 'Timelines, Borderlines and Conflicts', 43; Perna, *The Formation of the Treaty Law of Non-International Armed Conflicts*, 6–7.

8 Tuininga, *Calvin's Political Theology and the Public Engagement of the Church: Christ's Two Kingdoms*, 350–2. See also Perna, *The Formation of the Treaty Law of Non-International Armed Conflicts*, 7.

9 See Knox, 'The Debate at the General Assembly, June 1564', in Mason (ed.) *On Rebellion*, 195. See also Knox, 'The Right of Revolution in Scotland', in Marrin (ed.) *War and the Christian Conscience: From Augustine to Martin Luther King, Jr.*, 108–11, cited in Perna, *The Formation of the Treaty Law of Non-International Armed Conflicts*, 8, note 31; also discussion generally in ibid., 7–9.

'public war' – that is, subject to the 'restraints imposed by the law of war' – could be waged between sovereigns only, echoing Gentili's position that civil wars fell outside the purview of international regulation.[10]

Writing in the eighteenth century, Vattel similarly adopted the basic position that violence within a society generally falls outside the ambit of international regulation. Unlike Gentili and Grotius, however, Vattel commended clement treatment of rebels by sovereigns on grounds of prudence, noting that the use of more extreme measures may simply harden hearts.[11] In a more radical move, he went on to argue that 'when a party is formed within the state which ceases to obey the sovereign and is strong enough to make a stand against him, or when a republic is divided into two opposing factions, and both sides take up arms', the rules of conduct applicable in *international* conflicts should apply. The reasoning here is that such conflicts give 'rise to two independent parties, who regard each other as enemies and acknowledge no common judge. Of necessity, therefore, these two parties must be regarded as forming ... two distinct Nations.'[12]

In doctrinal terms, Vattel's work sets the stage for the latter-day application of international law to non-international armed conflict. Vattel's focus on the magnitude and form of a conflict as the locus for its classification, moreover, was echoed in the manner in which governments broached the applicability of international law in civil wars in the nineteenth century and subsequently – both in respect of recognition and conduct of third states vis à vis the parties to a civil war, and in relation to the conduct of hostilities in such conflicts.

[10] See Grotius, *The Rights of War and Peace: Including the Law of Nature and of Nations*, trans. Archibald Colin Campbell, 55–7. See also discussion in Perna, *The Formation of the Treaty Law of Non-International Armed Conflicts*, 17–18; Gentili, *Three Books on the Law of War*, ed. J. B. Scott, 22, cited in Perna, *The Formation of the Treaty Law of Non-International Armed Conflicts*, 19, note 74. See also Bartels, 'Timelines, Borderlines and Conflicts', 45–6. On Grotius' attitude to civil war more generally, see discussion in Armitage, *Civil Wars: A History in Ideas*, 104–5.

[11] Vattel, *The Law of Nations or the Principles of Natural Law, Applied to the Conduct and Affairs of Nations and Sovereigns*, ed. J. B. Scott, 336–7, cited in Perna, *The Formation of the Treaty Law of Non-International Armed Conflicts*, 21–2.

[12] Vattel, *Law of Nations*, 338, cited in Perna, *The Formation of the Treaty Law of Non-International Armed Conflicts*, 23. See also discussion in Neff, *War and the Law of Nations: A General History*, 254; Armitage, *Civil Wars: A History in Ideas*, 128–34.

2.1.3 The Regulation of Internal Armed Conflict in the Nineteenth Century

2.1.3.1 Belligerency, Insurgency and Recognition

The most prominent international legal device developed to regulate civil conflicts in the nineteenth century was the doctrine of belligerency. This represented an attempt to ease the difficulties faced by third-party states in maintaining relations – in particular trading relations – with domestic factions engaged in fighting against a government.[13]

The doctrine of belligerency allowed the governments of third-party states to recognise rebels as 'belligerents' possessing the same obligations and rights in relation to a recognising state as the governments with whom they were engaged in combat. The effect of this was to render a civil war – notionally – an international war from the perspective of recognising states. For example, during the Dutch war of independence from Spain – the 'Eighty Years' War' – spanning the sixteenth and seventeenth centuries, the governments of England and France considered the Dutch forces as properly required to conduct themselves as if engaged in an inter-state war, consistent with the position taken by the Dutch themselves.[14]

At times, moreover, although such decisions remained voluntary, governments engaged in civil wars also had an interest in recognising the belligerency of rebels. In 1775, for example, the British government authorised American colonial rebels to be treated as 'open enemies', later (in 1777) invoking the international law of neutrality to 'caution foreign states to refrain from providing aid to the insurgents'.[15] A similar course of action was adopted by Great Britain during the

[13] The literature on the doctrine of belligerency is extensive. For an overview of legal perspectives, and for the provenance of the distinctions between rebellion, insurgency and belligerency, see e.g. Anthony Cullen, *The Concept of Non-International Armed Conflict in International Humanitarian Law*, 7–23. Also: Bartels, 'Timelines, Borderlines and Conflicts', 48–52; Lindsay Moir, *The Law of Internal Armed Conflict*, 4–18; Moir, 'The Historical Development of the Application of Humanitarian Law in Non-International Armed Conflicts to 1949', 338–9; La Haye, *War Crimes in Internal Armed Conflicts*, 35. Older works addressing belligerency and recognition, and providing some idea of the contexts in which these discussions took place, include, inter alia, Oglesby, *Internal War and the Search for Normative Order*; Higgins, 'International Law and Civil Conflict', in Luard (ed.) *The International Regulation of Civil Wars*; Falk, 'Introduction', in Falk (ed.) *The International Law of Civil War*, 11–16.

[14] See discussion in Neff, *War and the Law of Nations: A General History*, 253.

[15] See Prohibitory Act 1775 (6 Geo.3 c.5), Treason Act 1777 (17 Geo.3 c.9), Neff, *War and the Law of Nations: A General History*, 255.

Boer War.[16] A key policy consideration in each case was that a maritime blockade could be announced and maintained on rebel-held ports only by asserting a right to interfere with (including search and/or seizure of) foreign shipping – ordinarily available only where belligerency was recognised.'[17]

One of the major difficulties with this doctrine in terms of legal certainty was that the applicability of the doctrine of belligerency remained in the hands of governments, whether of a state involved in a civil war or of third states. The somewhat counterintuitive consequence of this approach was that practices such as declarations of neutrality by third parties came to determine which body of legal rules should apply between the participants with respect to such third parties. The lack of clarity as to the conditions in which belligerency was more or less likely to be recognised was compounded by inconsistent state practice.

Over time, international legal scholars did attempt to provide some doctrinal coherency. Some sought to impose restrictions on the discretion of third-party governments, for example, such that belligerency was only to be recognised either when the government against which a rebellion was being pursued recognised its opponents' belligerency or when rebels held territory, possessed a governmental structure and required organised troops to observe the laws of armed conflict. There was also an attempt on the part of some practitioners to render belligerent recognition automatic in certain circumstances.[18] No consensus developed in this regard, however, and in practice states followed their own counsel as to whether to recognise belligerency.

As may be evident from the above discussion, the doctrine of belligerency was conceptually and practically problematic. The question of what constituted an act of recognition, for example, remained vexed throughout the doctrine's currency. Moreover, as recognition was in any case only ever bi-

[16] Sadoul, *De la guerre civile en droit des gens: reconnaissance de belligérance.*, 165–70, cited in Neff, *War and the Law of Nations: A General History*, 264. For further discussion (and examples), see e.g. Mantilla, 'Under (Social) Pressure: The Historical Regulation of Internal Armed Conflicts through International Law', 58; Sivakumaran, *The Law of Non-International Armed Conflict*, 17–20.

[17] See discussion in e.g. Wright, 'International Law and the American Civil War'; Heintschel von Heinegg, 'Blockade'.

[18] See variously discussions in Neff, *War and the Law of Nations: A General History*, 264–8; Moir, *The Law of Internal Armed Conflict*, 11–18. As Moir puts it, those scholars who evinced enthusiasm for the automatic application of the rules and principles of international law of armed conflict 'tended to be American … and hugely influenced by the Civil War of 1861–1865' (p. 11, see also notes 40–1 on pp. 11–12, citing e.g. Woolsey, *Introduction to the Study of International Law*, 168; Taylor, *Treatise on International Public Law*, 454).

(or at most tri-) lateral, applying between sets of parties and third states, the doctrine provided little guidance as to which, if any, rules were generally applicable in any given context. Rather, the doctrine provided actors with discretion to apply whichever set of rules they considered appropriate or convenient in any given context. Recognition of belligerency also implicitly placed governments and rebels on an even legal footing, making it a politically awkward tool from the perspective of recognising governments.[19]

Given these (and other) challenges, it is perhaps unsurprising that the doctrine of belligerency fell into disuse over time. An alternative was provided by the slightly more flexible idea of recognition of 'insurgency'. This doctrine permitted third states to recognise the de facto authority of insurgents in areas they controlled, (notionally) without infringing on the rights of the 'rightful' government, enabling third-state governments in effect to retain the economic benefits of recognition of belligerency without the 'blunderbuss' effects of that doctrine.[20] In practice, the primary implication was that a central government could not simply close rebel-held ports by decree – rather it would be forced to enforce a blockade to actively prevent access by third-state shipping.[21]

This doctrine found particular favour with the governments of trade-hungry third states. Governments dealing with rebellions, however, were rather less enamoured of it and – again – recognition of insurgency by a third-party government did not necessarily have any bearing on the law applicable between governments and rebels.[22] In short, in terms of assisting the parties to a conflict to determine the appropriate sets of international legal rules bearing on their conduct vis à vis one another, the doctrine of insurgency was no more helpful than its predecessor.

[19] Neff, *War and the Law of Nations: A General History*, 268. At the same time, of course, recognition could also convey support for and/or legitimise belligerents. (See also Mantilla, 'Under (Social) Pressure: The Historical Regulation of Internal Armed Conflicts through International Law', 57.)

[20] Neff observes that 'recognition of belligerency was something of a legal blunderbuss. It caused the *entire* range of duties of the law of neutrality to fall onto the recognising state in a single, inconveniently large bundle . . . In addition, recognition of belligerency was likely to cause great offence to the government of the disordered state . . .' (*War and the Law of Nations: A General History*, 268).

[21] Ibid., 268–72.

[22] See for further discussion Ibid., 268–75. Cullen, following recent international tribunal jurisprudence, makes the claim that 'international law has now evolved to require the application of the law of armed conflict in all situations of insurgency' (Cullen, *The Concept of Non-International Armed Conflict in International Humanitarian Law*, 13). As he himself notes, however, even if this is the case, the implications for combatants remain uncertain.

2.1.3.2 The Lieber Code

Debates in respect of belligerency and insurgency were largely focused on protecting the rights and interests of third parties to a civil conflict, rather than on regulating the conduct of combatants with respect to one another. Some clarity in this latter regard was nevertheless provided by the drafting and 1863 publication of what has become known as the 'Lieber Code'.

By way of background, in 1862 the US Supreme Court took the view that the Union had recognised the belligerent status of the Confederate states, a majority of the Court holding in its *Prize Cases* decision that 'war in the legal sense' had begun in April 1861.[23] Subsequently, the US War Department appointed Francis Lieber, a Berlin-born Columbia College professor, to a board charged with providing 'a Code of Regulations for the government of armies in the field, as authorized by the laws and usages of war' to provide some clarity to the Union military as to the applicable rules and principles.[24] The code was largely drafted by Lieber, though when the original draft did not include a set of provisions dealing with civil war, an additional section was added at the insistence of Henry Halleck, at that point the General-in-Chief of the Union armies as well as a prominent international lawyer.[25] The Code, consisting of 157 articles, was subsequently published in April 1863 as 'General Orders No. 100', with the title: 'Instructions for the Government of the Armies of the United States in the Field'.

The various sections of the Code address, broadly speaking: the imposition and exercise of martial law in occupied territory; the protection of property and non-combatants; the treatment of prisoners of war; the giving of quarter; the treatment of spies and traitors; exchanges of

[23] 67 US 635 (1863). See discussion in Quincy Wright, 'The American Civil War', in Falk (ed.) *The International Law of Civil War*, 42. See also Bartels, 'Timelines, Borderlines and Conflicts', 52; Moir, *The Law of Internal Armed Conflict*, 16. It bears observing that the implications of this decision remained contentious during the American Civil War, not least as the court had observed that the exercise of 'belligerent rights' did not preclude the exercise of 'sovereign rights'. See discussion in Witt, *Lincoln's Code: The Laws of War in American History*, 144–51. Also Neff, *Justice in Blue and Gray: A Legal History of the Civil War*, chapter 7.

[24] Quoted in Davis, 'Doctor Francis Lieber's Instructions for the Government of Armies in the Field', 19. Also quoted in Root, 'Francis Lieber', 19, cited in Giladi, 'Humanity in the Service of Order: Intellectual Roots of the Occupation Category', note 86.

[25] Halleck to Lieber, Feb. 28, Apr. 8, 1863, cited in Childress, 'Francis Lieber's Interpretation of the Laws of War: General Orders No. 100 in the Context of His Life and Thought',: 38–9, note 14; Giladi, 'Humanity in the Service of Order: Intellectual Roots of the Occupation Category', n. 92.

prisoners and the use of flags of truce and distinctive markings for purposes of protection (e.g. of hospitals); the granting of parole; the conclusion of armistices; the prohibition of assassination; and – in Section 'X' – rules applicable in internal armed conflict. Certain provisions also echo later principles of what has become known as international humanitarian law, including the principle of distinction (Articles 22, 35, 115); the protection and humane treatment of civilians and persons hors de combat (Articles 23, 56, 79, 80); the principle of military necessity (Articles 14, 16, 68); and the protection of specific categories of persons and institutions (Articles 50, 53, 116).[26]

As regards internal armed conflict, Lieber distinguished 'insurrection' from 'civil war' and 'rebellion' but was careful to frame the applicability of any 'rules of regular war' towards rebels as 'in no way . . . imply(ing) a partial or complete acknowledgement of their government'.[27] Rather, such rules were to be applied in place of ordinary civil law only owing to considerations of humanity. In Lieber's view, moreover, the protections granted to rebels did not have to equal those granted to participants in inter-state conflicts: to wit, (per Art. 154) 'treating . . . the rebellious enemy according to the law and usages of war has never prevented the legitimate government from trying the leaders of the rebellion or chief rebels for high treason'. That said, Lieber nevertheless imposed some limitations on those combating a rebellion – perhaps seeking to render such wars 'purgatory' rather than 'hell' – as 'common justice and plain expediency require that the military commander protect the manifestly loyal citizens, in revolted territories, against the hardships of the war as much as the common misfortune of all war admits' (Art. 156).[28]

The broader significance of the Lieber Code is underlined by its subsequent service as a model for other states' militaries.[29] For present

[26] On origins of the term 'international humanitarian law', see Alexander, 'A Short History of International Humanitarian Law', 109–38.

[27] See Arts. 152, 153 and 157. See more broadly discussion in Armitage, *Civil Wars: A History in Ideas*, 161–90.

[28] It bears noting, however, that this treatment need not extend to 'disloyal citizens' (see Art. 155). The phrase 'war is hell' is commonly attributed to General Sherman. He was unable to recall having used this phrase, though he apparently did so to a group of military academy graduates. (See Kennedy and Bailey, *The American Spirit: United States History as Seen by Contemporaries*, 509; Vetter, *Sherman: Merchant of Terror, Advocate of Peace*, 140.)

[29] Abi-Saab refers to the Dutch, French, Russian and Turkish codes as being influenced by Lieber's Code (Abi-Saab, 'Humanitarian Law and Internal Conflicts: The Evolution of Legal Concern', in Delissen and Tanja (eds.) *Humanitarian Law of Armed Conflict:*

purposes, however, it is primarily significant as an attempt to formalise and codify the laws of war, including provision for internal armed conflict, at least to a degree reflecting 'law in practice', rather than a purely scholarly (or scholastic) view of how the law ought to look.[30] As Perna observes, the Code also evinces 'humanitarian concern with regard to conflicts (i.e. civil wars) which, for a long time, international law had considered to be outside its scope'.[31]

That said, the Code is not an entirely satisfactory document, especially in relation to civil conflicts.[32] For one, while there appears to be an academic consensus that the laws of war were 'generally observed' by both sides in the American Civil War, it is not clear how or which of the 'laws of war' contained in the Code were specifically intended to be applied in civil war contexts.[33] Moreover, Lieber's view that the applicability of international legal standards in civil wars was at the discretion of the 'recognising' government was not uncontroversial, even at the time. The British position, for example, was that, by virtue of the scope and duration of the conflict, the American Civil War was properly considered a 'civil war' on objective grounds, entitling prisoners to prisoner of war status.[34] Indeed, Stephen Neff cites Halleck's opinion that '*within* the territory of the state where the conflict occurred, the rebels had a legal right to treatment on a par with belligerents once

Challenges Ahead: Essays in Honour of Frits Kalshoven 210, cited in Giladi, 'Humanity in the Service of Order: Intellectual Roots of the Occupation Category', note 94).

30 See discussion at Perna, *The Formation of the Treaty Law of Non-International Armed Conflicts*, 31–2 citing (at note 11); Root, 'Francis Lieber', 11. ('[A] practical presentation of what the laws and usages of war were, and not a technical discussion of what the writer thought they ought to be.')

31 Perna, *The Formation of the Treaty Law of Non-International Armed Conflicts*, 33.

32 Indeed, notwithstanding Perna's observation, Richard Baxter agreed with Percy Bordwell, an earlier commentator, that the Code was 'diffuse and academic' (Baxter, 'The First Modern Codification of the Law of War – Francis Lieber and General Orders No. 100 (II)', 249–50 citing (at note 162) Bordwell, *The Law of War between Belligerents: A History and Commentary*, 74).

33 See Wright, 'The American Civil War', 56, cited by Moir, *The Law of Internal Armed Conflict*, 12, note 44; Bartels, 'Timelines, Borderlines and Conflicts', 53, note 116.

34 Lord John Russell to Lord Lyons, 24 January 1862: 'An insurrection extending over nine States in space, and ten months in duration, can only be considered as a civil war; and persons taken prisoners on either side should only be considered as prisoners of war' (quoted in Halleck and Baker, *Halleck's International Law: Or, Rules Regulating the Intercourse of States in Peace and War*, 3rd edn., 121). See also discussion in Bartels, 'Timelines, Borderlines and Conflicts', 53.

they controlled a portion of territory and began acting as a de facto government within it'.[35]

2.1.3.3 The International Red Cross

Though certainly groundbreaking, not least because it was state-sponsored, the Lieber Code did not provide significantly greater clarity as to the international legal rules that should properly apply in internal armed conflicts. Thus, at the beginning of the twentieth century, Oppenheim could still state that, for the purposes of international law, civil wars were not real wars unless the contending parties recognised one another as belligerents.[36]

The establishment and initial activities of the International Committee of the Red Cross (ICRC) and of the Red Cross movement generally can be viewed in a similar light. The history of the ICRC has been recounted in depth elsewhere.[37] In brief, though, this body was originally established as the

[35] Neff, *War and the Law of Nations: A General History*, 273. It bears noting, however, that Halleck also distinguishes 'civil wars' from 'mere rebellions'. The former term, he observes, 'is more usually applied to those contests which are waged between rival families or factions, for party ascendancy in a state, rather than for its dismemberment, or for a radical change in its government'. Accordingly, while he notes that in civil wars '[e]ach party ... is usually entitled to the rights of war as against the other, and, also with respect to neutrals', he also adds that '[m]ere rebellions, however, are considered as exceptions to this rule, as every government treats those who rebel against its authority according to its own municipal laws, and without regard to the general rules of war which international jurisprudence establishes between sovereign states ... every neutral state, in such a contest, must determine for itself when it will consider a party in a rebellion, insurrection, revolution, or civil war, entitled to the rights of a belligerent in its international relations' (Halleck, *International Law: Or, Rules Regulating the Intercourse of States in Peace and War,* 333). Elsewhere though, he notes that: '[w]ars of insurrection, of rebellion, and of revolution, come under the general head of civil wars, and are governed by the same rules so far as regards international law and the laws of war ... It may be stated, as a general rule, that *the laws of war*, as understood and defined by the law of nations, govern in the *commercia belli*, or belligerent intercourse of the contending parties in civil wars'. Halleck adds, though, that: 'the adoption of rules of regular warfare towards rebels does not imply any recognition of their government ... nor of themselves as legitimate belligerents .... Treating them as prisoners of war when captured ... has never prevented the legitimate government from trying and punishing them for high treason' (Halleck, *Elements of International Law and Laws of War*, 152–3).

[36] Oppenheim, *International Law: A Treatise*, Vol. II, 65, cited in Bartels, 'Timelines, Borderlines and Conflicts', 47–8.

[37] See e.g. Boissier, *From Solferino to Tsushima: History of the International Committee of the Red Cross*; Durand, *From Sarajevo to Hiroshima: History of the International Committee of the Red Cross*; Finnemore, *National Interests in International Society*, 69–88; Hutchinson, *Champions of Charity: War and the Rise of the Red Cross*; Forsythe, *The Humanitarians: The International Committee of the Red Cross.*

'International Committee for Relief to the Wounded' in 1863 by Henry Dunant, Gustave Moynier and three others to protect and assist victims of war, with the ambition of setting up 'in peacetime "relief societies for wounded soldiers and . . . a corps of voluntary nurses to armies in the field"'.[38]

The Committee – the prototypical international humanitarian law norm entrepreneur – rapidly produced a draft international Convention to regulate the organisation of national relief societies.[39] A subsequent conference was held in Geneva in August 1864, which resulted in the conclusion of the first multilateral treaty specifically regulating humanitarian aspects of armed conflict, focused on the protection of persons hors de combat. Interestingly, (non-democratic) Prussia was amongst the keenest supporters of the volunteer relief activities proposed in the 1863 discussions, whereas France and the UK were both initially opposed, ostensibly because they preferred to rely on professional military medical relief services. While there were only twelve initial signatories, moreover – the UK, Saxony and Sweden having attended in 1864 but not signed the treaty – by 1868 the Convention had achieved broad acceptance amongst European and key non-European states, in no small part owing to ICRC advocacy.[40]

Civil conflicts were not on the initial legislative agenda of the ICRC. The 1864 Convention, however, set a precedent for the development of international humanitarian law by means of multilateral treaties – a significant development given that previous statements of applicable international law were 'based solely on customary usage and, to a lesser extent, on legal opinions'.[41] The establishment of the ICRC and its initial activities also set a pattern for civil society–government relations in the context of future Red Cross movement conferences and diplomatic conferences, as well as in the development of international humanitarian law generally, which has seen civil society work alongside government 'norm entrepreneurs' in developing the law of armed conflict, with the ICRC traditionally in the vanguard of such efforts.

The 1864 Convention's silence notwithstanding, Red Cross bodies – primarily national societies – did provide services in civil wars during this early period, by one count assisting in nineteen civil conflicts by 1914.[42]

[38] Quoted in Boissier, *From Solferino to Tsushima*, 54. The ICRC remains an exclusively Swiss association, with a close relationship with the Swiss government.

[39] See Finnemore, *National Interests in International Society*, 77.

[40] See generally ibid., 69–88.

[41] Ibid., 80.

[42] Moorehead, *Dunant's Dream: War, Switzerland and the History of the Red Cross*, 125–6, 231. Bugnion cites only two instances prior to 1912 where the ICRC 'went beyond

There is little to suggest that these activities directly paved the way for the drafting of Common Article 3 in 1949, however.[43] Like the Lieber Code, therefore, the 1864 Convention and early activities of the ICRC are perhaps most significant for present purposes in so far as they are indicative of a trend towards greater international legal regulation in the field of armed conflict. It was to be some time before internal armed conflict came to be considered by governments generally as an appropriate field for such formal regulation.

2.1.4 Civil War Regulation from the Late Nineteenth Century until the Second World War

2.1.4.1 1899, 1907 and the Martens Clause

The conclusions of the Hague Peace Conferences held in 1899 and 1907, inspired by pacifist calls for the abolition of war by various sectors of civil society (though motivated by the Russian government's fear of being outspent in a European arms race), do not evince a great deal of enthusiasm on the part of governments to extend international legal regulation to encompass the conduct of civil wars.[44] Nevertheless, The Hague Conventions of 1899 and 1907 did suggest that governments were increasingly ready to allow significant, codified restrictions to be placed on the conduct of international armed conflict.[45]

a declaration of the humanitarian principles to be applied' – the Third Carlist War (1872–6) and the Macedonian uprising against the Ottoman Empire (1903–4) (Bugnion, *The International Committee of the Red Cross and the Protection of War Victims*, 247–8). More generally, numbers of such interventions vary by categorisation (and account), however. Of the 44 ICRC and national Red Cross society interventions in 'internal conflicts' between 1868 and 1949 cited by Mantilla, for example, only 14 are categorised as 'civil wars' (Mantilla, 'Under (Social) Pressure: The Historical Regulation of Internal Armed Conflicts through International Law' 71).

43 Indeed, in this early period the ICRC elected not to seek to regulate the conduct of internal armed conflict. See Abi-Saab, *Droit humanitaire et conflits internes: origines et évolution de la réglementation internationale*, 31.

44 A similarly conservative demeanour dominated in respect of the same subject in discussions in the Institut de Droit International in 1898 and 1900. (See Mantilla, 'Under (Social) Pressure: The Historical Regulation of Internal Armed Conflicts through International Law', 85–8 drawing on Abi-Saab, *Droit humanitaire et conflits internes: origines et évolution de la réglementation internationale*.) On the relationship between the 'peace societies' and the Red Cross movement, see Durand, 'Gustave Moynier and the Peace Societies'. For general background on the Hague conferences and their achievements and failures, see Tuchman, *The Proud Tower: A Portrait of the World before the War, 1890–1914*, 229–88.

45 There are a few earlier examples of coordinated international attempts to regulate armed conflict, including instances pre-dating the first Geneva Convention, such as the 1856

While the extent to which humanitarian concerns motivated participants at the Hague meetings is debatable, these meetings did point the way for 'considerations of humanity' to become a guiding motif in the regulation of armed conflict. One of the more notable achievements of the first conference in this regard was the inclusion in the preambles of various of the treaties of what has become known as the 'Martens Clause', included in the 1899 text at the suggestion of Fyodor Martens, a Russian delegate, to overcome an impasse over whether to preserve a right of resistance for the inhabitants of occupied territories.[46] In its original form the clause provides that

> until a more complete code of the laws of war is issued, the High Contracting Parties think it right to declare that in cases not included in the Regulations adopted by them, populations and belligerents remain under the protection and empire of the principles of international law, as they result from the usages established between civilized nations, from the laws of humanity and the requirements of the public conscience.[47]

The legal implications of the Martens Clause remain ambiguous.[48] Nevertheless, as with the 1864 Convention, the Martens Clause proved a significant step by suggesting that principles relating to the conduct of war could be derived directly from 'laws of humanity', further embedding a humanitarian ethos within the latter-day law of armed conflict.

Paris Declaration on Maritime Law (cited in Moir, *The Law of Internal Armed Conflict*, 19) and the 1868 St. Petersburg Declaration (see Best, *War and Law since 1945*, 18). As Tuchman puts it, civic awareness may have played a significant role in the limited successes achieved in 1899 and 1907: 'Feeling themselves the cynosure of the world's hope, the delegates began to feel the stirring of a desire not to disappoint it' (Tuchman, *The Proud Tower*, 258).

46 See for background Giladi, 'The Enactment of Irony: Reflections on the Origins of the Martens Clause', 847–69.

47 The clause was first included in the preamble to Hague Convention (II) (1899) With Respect to the Laws and Customs of War on Land. It was subsequently included in the preamble to Hague Convention (IV) (1907) Respecting the Laws and Customs of War on Land. The clause was also included in varying forms of wording in each of the four 1949 Geneva Conventions (respectively, as Articles 63, 62, 142 and 158), in Additional Protocol 1 (Article 1(2)) and in Additional Protocol II (preamble).

48 See e.g. discussion in Ticehurst, 'The Martens Clause and the Laws of Armed Conflict', 125–34. Also Meron, 'The Martens Clause, Principles of Humanity, and Dictates of Public Conscience', 78–89; Cassese, 'The Martens Clause: Half a Loaf or Simply Pie in the Sky?', 187–216. The clause has been understood as having ongoing relevance to non-international armed conflicts, though this is certainly a very modern reading. (See e.g. Oeter, 'Civil War, Humanitarian Law and the United Nations', in Frowein and Wolfrum (eds.), *Max Planck Yearbook of United Nations Law*, Vol. 1, 195–229; Allen, Cherniack and Andreopoulos, 'Refining War: Civil Wars and Humanitarian Controls', 747.)

2.1.4.2 1907–1945: '*Silent enim leges inter arma*' (In Battle, Indeed, the Laws Are Silent)[49]

In the period between 1907 and 1945, despite the demands of non-state groups – principally Red Cross movement bodies – and the backdrop of a number of severe civil wars, states collectively failed to develop authoritative rules or principles governing internal armed conflict. This absence is striking given the progress made during this time in building up a positive body of rules regulating inter-state conflict.

War at sea, for example, was revisited in the 1909 London Declaration Concerning the Laws of Naval War. The use of poison gas was prohibited by an agreement (the Geneva Protocol) concluded in 1925, while the 1864 Geneva Convention protecting the wounded and sick was revised in 1929 and supplemented by an additional Convention regarding the treatment of prisoners of war. The Washington Treaty of 1922 between the USA, Great Britain, France, Italy and Japan, alongside the London Treaties of 1930 and 1936, constituted novel attempts to cap naval expenditure, as supplements to the limits placed on German naval capacity after the First World War. The Kellogg–Briand Pact of 1928 represented an even more ambitious attempt to 'outlaw aggressive war', while the 1935 Roerich Pact signalled the extension of international legal regulation to cultural property.

The period leading up to 1939 thus witnessed a significant expansion in international legal regulation of war. To an extent this is not surprising: the era was not especially peaceful – and, indeed, encompassed the First World War. Further rumblings of the 'legalisation' of international relations were also heralded by the establishment and operation of the League of Nations. Several of the more severe conflicts to take place during this period were, however, non-international in nature, most notably the Russian Civil War (1917–1923) and the Spanish Civil War (1936–1939).

The latter conflicts are significant for any number of reasons. In the international legal context, though, perhaps the first aspect that should be noted is that in neither case was there any question of the participants according one another belligerent rights, reinforcing the desuetude of the doctrine of belligerency.[50] Indeed, neither of these conflicts was fought

[49] Cicero, *Pro Milone*, trans. N. H. Watts, 16.

[50] Bugnion, '*Jus ad bellum, jus in bello* and Non-International Armed Conflicts', 181. Lauterpacht took the view that the Spanish Civil War was, rather, a case of recognition of insurgency by third states (Lauterpacht, *Recognition in International Law*, 270–1, cited in Moir, *The Law of Internal Armed Conflict*, 20 at note 77).

with any obvious regard for the laws or customs of law.[51] In the Spanish case, even though a number of third states swiftly recognised the insurgent nationalists as the legitimate government of Spain (e.g. Germany, Italy and Portugal), as Moir observes, this did not necessarily entail recognition of belligerency.[52] Furthermore, other states, in particular the USA and Great Britain, withheld recognition of belligerency, although the fact of insurgency appears to have been recognised.[53] In contrast, there appears to be have been little discussion of any question of recognition of belligerency or insurgency in the context of the Russian Civil War – the Allied powers, at least, being preoccupied with preventing Germany from obtaining access to Russian resources.[54]

In both instances – as in the Finnish Civil War (1918), the Spartacist Uprising in Germany (1919), the Hungarian Revolution (1919) and the Upper Silesian Conflict (1921) – Red Cross bodies quietly intervened to provide protection to persons hors de combat, reflecting a growing consensus within the Red Cross movement.[55] The American Red Cross society, for example, raised the question of the role of national Red Cross societies in civil wars at the 9th International Conference of the Red Cross, held in 1912.[56] Following the collapse of the Russian Red

[51] See Bugnion, '*Jus ad bellum, jus in bello* and Non-International Armed Conflicts', 181.

[52] Moir, *The Law of Internal Armed Conflict*, 20.

[53] See O'Rourke, 'Recognition of Belligerency and the Spanish War', 404. Also generally discussion in Moir, *The Law of Internal Armed Conflict*, 20.

[54] See Somin, *Stillborn Crusade: The Tragic Failure of Western Intervention in the Russian Civil War, 1918–1920*, 30; Bacino, *Reconstructing Russia: U.S. Policy in Revolutionary Russia, 1917–1922*.

[55] See discussions variously in: Abplanalp, 'The International Conferences of the Red Cross as a Factor for the Development of International Humanitarian Law and the Cohesion of the International Red Cross and Red Crescent Movement', 536–9; Bartels, 'Timelines, Borderlines and Conflicts', 54–6 including citations to Hannikainen, Hanski and Rosas, *Implementing Humanitarian Law Applicable in Armed Conflicts: The Case of Finland*, 27–31. See also Durand, *From Sarajevo to Hiroshima*, 195–246 passim. The ICRC fared poorly in an attempt to intervene in the Irish Free State in 1923. As put by the then-Minister of Foreign Affairs, Desmond Fitzgerald: 'Refuse [to] discuss measures considered necessary by my Government to repress rebellion in Ireland. They are internal in character' (Fitzgerald to Gustave Ador (ICRC), 26 January 1923 (original in French), quoted in Durand, 227). A similar response was received from the Spanish and French authorities when it was proposed that the ICRC should intervene in the Rif War in 1924. (See discussion in Ibid., 239–43.) Interestingly, the record of the ICRC in the Russian Civil War was more mixed. (See Lowe, 'Humanitarianism and National Sovereignty: Red Cross Intervention on Behalf of Political Prisoners in Soviet Russia, 1921–3', 652–74.)

[56] Owing to opposition from state participants (in particular from Russia) the matter was dropped during this conference. See account in Bugnion, *The International Committee of the Red Cross and the Protection of War Victims*, 248–50. Also Mantilla, 'Under (Social)

Cross in the aftermath of the October Revolution, moreover,the new Soviet authorities were at least initially welcoming of ICRC assistance in re-establishing a domestic Red Cross society, and in monitoring and seeking to ameliorate the conditions of wartime detainees.[57]

These experiences – in the words of François Bugnion – showed 'the importance of Red Cross intervention in civil wars and the need to establish a basis for it'.[58] In consequence, and prompted by high-level lobbying from a member of the former (Imperial) Russian Red Cross Society, a resolution was adopted at the 10th International Conference in 1921, 'entrust(ing) the International Committee of the Red Cross with the mandate to engage in relief in the event of civil war'.[59]

From this point on, then – at least from the perspective of the Red Cross movement – 'as a matter of principle ... the Red Cross was competent to assist victims of insurrections and civil wars', with the ICRC allocated a role alongside national societies. Indeed, as one commentator has put it, 'the inclusion of this item on the agenda of the 10th Conference was intended to prompt consideration of how, and not whether, such intervention should take place'.[60]

Pressure: The Historical Regulation of Internal Armed Conflicts through International Law', 91–3.

[57] See accounts in Bugnion, *The International Committee of the Red Cross and the Protection of War Victims*, 250–8; Lowe, 'Humanitarianism and National Sovereignty: Red Cross Intervention on Behalf of Political Prisoners in Soviet Russia, 1921–3'. As Bugnion notes, ICRC operations in prisons were 'the first time that the International Committee had tried to intervene on behalf of people detained in connection with an internal conflict' (*The International Committee of the Red Cross and the Protection of War Victims*, 255).

[58] Bugnion, *The International Committee of the Red Cross and the Protection of War Victims*, 257. Bugnion, in common with a number of commentators, has a long-running and close association with the ICRC, in his case as a former delegate and chief of mission, and until 2006 as Director for International Law and Cooperation. Accordingly, while instructive, his views of the ICRC are not necessarily the most critically observed.

[59] Para. 3, Resolution XIV of the Tenth International Conference of the Red Cross (quoted in Bugnion, 262). See generally Abplanalp, 'The International Conferences of the Red Cross as a Factor for the Development of International Humanitarian Law and the Cohesion of the International Red Cross and Red Crescent Movement', 535–40; Bugnion, *The International Committee of the Red Cross and the Protection of War Victims*, 258–62. For background, see Mantilla, 'Under (Social) Pressure: The Historical Regulation of Internal Armed Conflicts through International Law', 99–100.

[60] Abplanalp, 'The International Conferences of the Red Cross as a Factor for the Development of International Humanitarian Law and the Cohesion of the International Red Cross and Red Crescent Movement', 536. See, in a similar vein, Bugnion's observation that: '[t]he authority of the Red Cross to assist the victims of uprisings and civil wars was henceforth accepted as a matter of principle. In including this

If the Russian Civil War provided the ICRC with an institutional opening and mandate, the Spanish Civil War – in the ICRC view – underlined the limitations of that mandate in the absence of treaty provisions covering internal armed conflict. The ICRC was at the forefront of Red Cross activities in Spain during the conflict, and sought to base its activities on the negotiation of reciprocal, voluntary declarations by the warring parties to observe elements of the laws of armed conflict, particularly in respect of the treatment of detainees and respect for medical facilities and personnel displaying the Red Cross emblem.[61] Over time, however, the range of its activities expanded to encompass various aspects of civilian protection more generally, including providing material relief and intervening with the warring parties to minimise – albeit with limited effectiveness – the extent to which the civilian population was subjected to unnecessary risk of harm (particularly from the then-new technique of aerial bombing).[62]

From the Committee's perspective, two key conclusions were drawn from these experiences. Firstly, civil wars were not inimical to the provision of humanitarian relief and there was scope for a Red Cross role in such conflicts. Second, the Spanish experience highlighted to the Committee the limitations of ad hoc accommodations with parties in civil war contexts, necessitated (in its view) by a legal framework that did not regulate the conduct of hostilities in internal armed conflict.[63]

In advance of the 16th Red Cross Conference in London in 1938, the ICRC prepared a report including a proposal to empower the ICRC to act 'spontaneously and on its own authority' to provide humanitarian assistance in internal armed conflicts, albeit only with the express consent of the 'interested parties', and with the caveat that any '[s]uch action . . . shall in no case be considered as the recognition of a state of war or of belligerence, nor as help furnished to one or other of the

item on the agenda of the Tenth Conference, the sole intention was to determine precisely when and how such an intervention should take place . . .', and the national society reports for the 1921 meeting that: '[t]he authority of the Red Cross to assist victims of civil wars or disturbances was taken for granted; it was not a right which the Red Cross claimed for itself, but a prerogative whose possession by the Red Cross was acknowledged . . .. It therefore followed that no legal or political consideration could inhibit Red Cross work for the victims of internal strife' (*The International Committee of the Red Cross and the Protection of War Victims*, 258–9).

[61] Bugnion, *The International Committee of the Red Cross and the Protection of War Victims*, 269–70.

[62] Ibid., 275–81.

[63] Ibid., 282–3.

hostile parties'.[64] During the conference, though, it became clear that support for this position was far from unanimous: not only were the then-two Spanish national societies divided on this issue, the neighbouring French and Portuguese delegations (whose governments were exercised for different reasons about the prospect of legitimising external intervention in Spain) preferred not to press the matter.[65] The result was the adoption of a watered-down resolution, paying tribute to the ICRC's work in civil wars and indicating the conference's reliance on the ICRC 'to continue its activity in this connection', but ultimately falling some way short of ICRC preferences.[66] This period also witnessed a number of intergovernmental and other initiatives designed to provide some protection to non-combatants in the Spanish Civil War, principally the adoption in 1938 of a League of Nations resolution for the 'Protection of Civilian Populations against Bombing from the Air in Case of War'. However, as Bugnion notes, as the conflict wore on international attention became increasingly diverted, with '[t]he Sino-Japanese conflict, the annexation of Austria and the Sudeten crisis . . . (setting) the stage for new cataclysmic upheavals of which the Spanish Civil War was only the prelude'.[67]

With that in mind, it is perhaps unsurprising that verbal statements of principle were the principal indication until after the Second World War that there was any significant support amongst governments for adapting

[64] Ibid., 283–4, citing Yung, 'Le rôle et l'action de la Croix-Rouge en temps de guerre civile', 112.

[65] Bugnion, *The International Committee of the Red Cross and the Protection of War Victims*, 285–6. The Blum and Daladier governments in France aligned France with British policy in respect of the Spanish Civil War – the latter being officially non-interventionist, though with sympathy for the Nationalist rebels – against a background of pronounced domestic divisions. (See Pike, *France Divided: The French and the Civil War in Spain*; also Friedlander, 'Great Power Politics and Spain's Civil War: The First Phase', 72–92; Warner, 'France and Non-Intervention in Spain, July–August 1936', 203–20.) The Salazar government in Portugal was supportive of Spanish Nationalist forces under Franco, and indeed acted as a conduit for German aid to the latter, but was also particularly concerned to avoid the prospect of external oversight of the Spanish–Portuguese border. (See variously: Plummer, 'France and Portugal in the Spanish Civil War – Domestic and International Policies'; Edwards, *The British Government and the Spanish Civil War, 1936–1939*; Kay, *Salazar and Modern Portugal*.) On the development of various national policies to the outbreak of war in Spain see esp. Jackson, *Spanish Republic and the Civil War, 1931–1939*, 247–61.

[66] See Resolution XIV, *Report of the Sixteenth International Red Cross Conference, London, 1938*, 104. .

[67] Bugnion, *The International Committee of the Red Cross and the Protection of War Victims*, 283.

the international law of armed conflict for application in civil wars. Equally though, while the Spanish Civil War undoubtedly brought the shortcomings of the regime into focus in such conflicts, the ICRC focused its own legislative efforts during the inter-war period primarily on international armed conflict, principally on the treatment of prisoners of war in the 1929 Convention.

2.2 The Regulation of Internal Armed Conflict: 1945–1998

The post-1945 world presented a different prospect to the years running up to 1939. One of the immediate responses to the depredations of the Second World War was a renewed (if short-lived) enthusiasm on the part of the victorious powers for international law and legalisation, with the establishment of the United Nations and of the International Court of Justice in place of the pre-war League of Nations and Permanent Court of International Justice. The legal difficulties thrown up at Nuremberg in prosecuting German leaders for pre-war treatment of their own citizens, as well as the development of international human rights discourse – particularly the 1948 adoption of the Universal Declaration of Human Rights and the 1948 Convention on the Prevention and Punishment of the Crime of Genocide – also held out greater promise for closer international legal regulation of civil wars as the conduct of governments in their domestic realms became increasingly subject to international scrutiny.[68]

2.2.1 Common Article 3 and the 1949 Geneva Conventions

The drafting and adoption of Common Article 3 to the Geneva Conventions of 1949 is considered in detail in Chapter 3. In brief, however, the effort to include internal armed conflict in the ambit of these instruments was largely Red Cross-driven, with the ICRC preparing a set of draft provisions regulating civil wars for the 1948 International Red Cross Conference, on the basis of which Common Article 3 was negotiated and included in the four Geneva Conventions of 1949.

Common Article 3 represented a significant departure from the prewar consensus in that the clause requires 'parties' to a conflict – use of the latter term in place of the more usual 'high contracting parties' indicating

[68] See Armitage, *Civil Wars: A History in Ideas*, 203–9 for a helpful overview.

the intention to bind both state and non-state actors – to observe a minimal set of 'fundamental humanitarian restraints'. These include ensuring humane treatment of individual combatants no longer engaged in fighting, as well as of civilians who may have been involved in, but who are no longer engaged in, acts of violence. 'Humane treatment' is not defined: rather Article 3(1) details conduct which will not qualify as 'humane' and which is absolutely prohibited. This includes 'murder of all kinds, mutilation, cruel treatment and torture' and 'outrages on personal dignity, in particular, humiliating and degrading treatment'. The taking of hostages is also prohibited, and while Common Article 3 does not prohibit the imposition of the death penalty on 'protected persons', it requires that this only be imposed following 'previous judgment pronounced by a regularly constituted court, affording all the judicial guarantees which are recognised as indispensable by civilized peoples' (Article 3(1)(d)). To minimise the risk of an offer of assistance by a body such as the ICRC being construed as unauthorised intervention in a state's internal affairs, Common Article 3 also permits an 'impartial humanitarian body', to 'offer its services' to the participants in any such conflict.

The guarantees provided in Common Article 3 form the basis of the modern civil war regime – having come to be viewed by the International Court of Justice as reflecting 'elementary considerations of humanity'.[69] From this point on, given the broad, swift ratification by states generally of the four 1949 Conventions, a regime as such – that is, a set of 'implicit or explicit principles, norms, rules, and decision-making procedures around which actors' expectations converge' – can be considered to have come into existence in this field.[70] As civil wars multiplied in number and severity in the post-1949 period, moreover, other institutions and actors joined the ICRC in considering ways in which the protection afforded to civilians and other non-combatants in such conflicts could be enhanced.[71]

[69] *Military and Paramilitary Activities in and against Nicaragua (Nicaragua v. United States of America). Merits, Judgment. I.C.J. Reports 1986*, 14, para. 218. For commentary seeFleck, 'The Law of Non-International Armed Conflicts', in Fleck (ed.) *The Handbook of International Humanitarian Law*, 605–34.

[70] Around 65 states had ratified by 1957, including the five permanent members of the UN Security Council.

[71] Reference may be made variously to civil wars during this period in Greece, Lebanon, Laos, Congo, Yemen and Cyprus as well as to the Algerian Revolution and various components of the armed conflict in Vietnam. For legal analyses of these conflicts see

2.2.2 *The Additional Protocols of 1977*

One indication that the civil war regime would not start and end at Common Article 3 was the conclusion in 1954 of the Hague Convention for the Protection of Cultural Property. Article 1 of this instrument provides that: 'in the event of an armed conflict not of an international character occurring within the territory of one of the High Contracting Parties, each party to the conflict shall be bound to apply, as a minimum, the provisions of the present Convention which relate to respect for cultural property'. Little further formal progress was made in the subsequent sixteen years, however, until the ICRC was spurred into action by discussions in UN contexts in the late 1960s, in particular at the 1968 Tehran Conference on Human Rights. In the wake of the latter, the ICRC convened meetings of Red Cross and government experts in 1971 and 1972, producing a pair of draft protocols to the 1949 Conventions which were later presented by the ICRC for discussion at the 'Diplomatic Conference on the Reaffirmation and Development of International Humanitarian Law' (the CDDH),[72] which convened in 1974 and which ran for four sessions until 1977.

This conference, considered more closely in Chapter 4, produced two protocols to the 1949 treaties. Additional Protocol I expands on the 1949 Conventions with respect to the conduct of inter-state armed conflicts as traditionally conceived and of 'wars of national liberation' – a sub-category of internal armed conflict promoted primarily by the governments of the Non-Aligned Movement as being properly 'international' in nature. An abbreviated Additional Protocol II places additional limits on the conduct of non-international conflicts not covered by Protocol I. It bears noting that neither instrument has been quite as widely ratified by states as the 1949 Conventions – at the time of writing, Protocol I has 174 states parties, and Protocol II 168, contrasting with the 196 parties to the 1949 treaties, with the USA joining Eritrea, India, Indonesia, Iran, Israel, Malaysia, Myanmar, Nepal, Pakistan, Somalia, Sri Lanka, Thailand and Turkey in refusing to ratify either protocol.[73]

e.g. contributions to Falk (ed.), *The International Law of Civil War*; Luard (ed.), *The International Regulation of Civil Wars*.

[72] The acronym derives from the French ('Conférence diplomatique sur la réaffirmation et le développement du droit international humanitaire applicable dans les conflits armés').

[73] International Committee of the Red Cross, 'State Parties to the Following International Humanitarian Law and Other Related Treaties as of 7-Aug-2019'.

The ambit of Additional Protocol II is also somewhat narrower than that of Common Article 3, first by the exclusion of 'wars of national liberation', and second by the protocol's application being restricted to 'armed conflicts ... which take place in the territory of a High Contracting Party between its armed forces and dissident armed forces or other organised armed groups which, under responsible command, exercise such control over a part of its territory as to enable them to carry out sustained and concerted military operations and to implement this Protocol'. Conflicts amongst non-state armed groups (i.e. rather than between state and non-state forces) are thus excluded from the protocol's protection. Article 1 also adds a minimum threshold, not present in respect of Common Article 3, stating that the Protocol is not applicable 'to situations of internal disturbances and tensions, such as riots, isolated and sporadic acts of violence and other acts of a similar nature'.

Notwithstanding Additional Protocol II's narrow scope, in substantive terms it goes beyond Common Article 3. For example, Article 4 (which deals generally with 'fundamental guarantees' and is adapted from Article 4 of Geneva Convention IV) contains articles adding to the Common Article 3 protections a further prohibition on the giving of orders 'that there shall be no survivors', and adding to the list of prohibited acts 'collective punishment'; 'acts of terrorism'; 'slavery and the slave trade'; 'pillage'; 'enforced prostitution'; 'indecent assault'; and 'threats to commit any of the foregoing acts', Article 4 also provides protection for children affected by civil wars, including obligations to provide children with education; to facilitate family reunion; to refrain from recruiting children under the age of 15 and obligating governments to remove children temporarily from areas affected by hostilities.

Article 5 of Additional Protocol II also sets out new ground, containing a series of restrictions on the treatment of persons 'deprived of their liberty for reasons related to the armed conflict'. Some of these set minimum standards (e.g. that protected persons shall 'to the same extent as the local civilian population, be provided with food and drinking water and be afforded safeguards as regards health and hygiene and protection against the rigors of the climate and the dangers of the armed conflict'), while other provisions require observance by those responsible for detention 'within the limits of their capabilities'. Article 6 sets out basic fair trial guarantees for criminal offences related to armed conflicts – principally that '[n]o sentence shall be passed and no penalty shall be executed on a person found guilty of an offence except pursuant to a conviction pronounced by a court offering the essential guarantees of independence and impartiality'. These guarantees align broadly with the protections afforded by key human rights treaties, making specific provision for equality of arms, the principle of legality, a presumption of innocence and limiting the imposition of the death penalty to persons who were 18 years old or over at the time of the offence. Additionally, Article 6 requires authorities in power at the end of hostilities to 'endeavour to grant the broadest possible amnesty to persons who have participated in the armed conflict, or those deprived of their liberty for reasons related to the armed conflict'. Of the remaining provisions, Articles 7–12 relate to the protection of the wounded, sick and shipwrecked and Articles 13–18 to protection of the civilian population.

In many ways 'progressive development' of the regime governing international armed conflict by way of Additional Protocol I proved more straightforward to achieve than the development of its non-international counterpart, notwithstanding the more extensive form of Protocol I (comprising 91 substantive articles). Article 1(4) of this Protocol, however, which brings 'wars of national liberation' within the scope of that instrument, is perhaps its most interesting aspect for present purposes – and was a particular focus of debate (and for some concern) during the drafting process.

2.2.3 The 1998 Rome Statute of the International Criminal Court

In the years following the conclusion of the 1977 Protocols the international rules applicable in civil wars were significantly enhanced, especially in the post-Cold War period. The 1993 Chemical Weapons Convention,[74] for example, prohibits the use of chemical weapons in both inter-state and non-international armed conflict, without distinction. Other treaties from this period with a notional bearing on the conduct of civil wars include the 1997 Ottawa Anti-Personnel Mine Convention,[75] the 1999 Second Hague Protocol on the Protection of Cultural Property in Armed Conflict[76] and the 2001 amendment to the 1980 Conventional Weapons Convention.[77]

[74] Convention on the Prohibition of the Development, Production, Stockpiling and Use of Chemical Weapons and on Their Destruction (1974 UNTS 45).

[75] Convention on the Prohibition of the Use, Stockpiling, Production and Transfer of Anti-Personnel Mines and on Their Destruction (2056 UNTS 241).

[76] Second Protocol to the Hague Convention for the Protection of Cultural Property in the Event of Armed Conflict (2253 UNTS 172).

[77] Amendment to Article I of the Convention on Prohibitions or Restrictions on the Use of Certain Conventional Weapons which may be deemed to be Excessively Injurious or to

Indeed, viewed alongside the 1998 Rome Statute, the conclusion of these treaties arguably lends credence to the view that we 'appear to be moving tentatively towards the position whereby the legal distinction between international and non-international armed conflict is becoming outmoded'.[78]

The Rome Statute of the International Criminal Court (ICC) stands out as the 'jewel in the crown' of this post-Cold War trend, primarily owing to its ground-breaking nature in explicitly extending, through its war crimes provisions, the reach of international criminal law to encompass the conduct of civil wars. The Rome Statute is also, after the 1949 Conventions and the 1977 Additional Protocols, one of the most widely ratified treaties regulating the conduct of governments in civil wars, with 122 states parties as at the time of writing.[79]

The traditional position, dating back to 1949, was that states parties to the Geneva Conventions were required to treat as criminal only specified 'grave breaches' of the Conventions committed in wartime.[80] Reflecting the jurisdiction (and decisions) of the ad hoc tribunals established by the Security Council for the Former Yugoslavia and Rwanda, however, Article 8 of the Rome Statute goes significantly beyond this traditional

have Indiscriminate Effects (2260 UNTS 82). See also Protocol on Prohibitions or Restrictions on the Use of Mines, Booby-Traps and Other Devices as Amended on 3 May 1996 (amended Protocol II to the 1980 Convention on Certain Conventional Weapons) (2048 UNTS 9335); 2000 Optional Protocol to the Convention on the Rights of the Child on the involvement of children in armed conflict (2173 UNTS 222). Other instruments in a similar vein since 2001 have included: the 2008 Convention on Cluster Munitions (2688 UNTS 39) and the 2013 Arms Trade Treaty (General Assembly resolution 67/234, The Arms Trade Treaty, A/RES/67/234 B (2 April 2013)).

78 Moir, *The Law of Internal Armed Conflict*, 51.

79 See International Criminal Court, 'States Parties – Chronological List': https://asp.icc-cpi.int/en_menus/asp/states%20parties/Pages/states%20parties%20_%20chronological%20list.aspx [accessed 11 August 2019].

80 Article 49, Convention I; Article 50, Convention II, Article 129, Convention III, Article 146, Convention IV each oblige each state party: 'to enact any legislation necessary to provide effective penal sanctions for persons committing, or ordering to be committed, any of the grave breaches ... defined in the following Article ... (and) to search for persons alleged to have committed, or to have ordered to be committed, such grave breaches, and (each state party) shall bring such persons, regardless of their nationality, before its own courts. It may also, if it prefers, and in accordance with the provisions of its own legislation, hand such persons over for trial to another High Contracting Party concerned, provided such High Contracting Party has made out a prima facie case.' As Roger O'Keefe observes: 'The grave breaches provisions of the 1949 Geneva Conventions ... constituted the first treaty-based embodiment of an unconditional universal jurisdiction applicable to all states parties. They also amounted to the first multilateral recognition by states of universal jurisdiction over war crimes' ('The Grave Breaches Regime and Universal Jurisdiction').

view, including within the ICC's jurisdiction (at Article 8(c)) 'serious violations of article 3 common to the four Geneva Conventions of 12 August 1949' and (at Article 8(e)) 'other serious violations of the laws and customs applicable in armed conflicts not of an international character, within the established framework of international law'.[81]

Sub-paragraphs detail the conduct prohibited: paragraph (c), mirroring paragraph (b), essentially criminalises breaches of Common Article 3, listing, respectively, 'violence to life and person'; 'outrages upon personal dignity'; the 'taking of hostages' and the passing of sentences and carrying out of executions without judicial guarantees. Paragraph (e) performs the same function in relation to other 'laws and customs' (including norms set out in Additional Protocol II), prohibiting pillage, criminalising sexual violence including forced pregnancy, and prohibiting 'killing or wounding treacherously a combatant adversary' and 'destroying or seizing the property of an adversary unless such destruction or seizure be imperatively demanded by the necessities of the conflict'.

These provisions of the Rome Statute are novel and significant in two aspects. First, while the 'blurring of the fundamental differences between international and internal armed conflicts', at least in legal terms, was a process that began some time before, the Rome Statute was the first treaty in which this process was recognised as extending beyond the confines of Common Article 3 and Additional Protocol II.[82]

Second, the very existence of the Rome Statute suggests that many governments are no longer quite so vehemently opposed to the prospect of international intervention (at least in judicial form) in the domestic sphere in times of civil war. The significance of the endorsement of a highly independent court by so many states is underlined by the extent to which great care was taken in previous attempts to criminalise breaches of the law of armed conflict (primarily through the Grave Breaches regime of the 1949 Conventions) to ensure that responsibility for identifying and punishing perpetrators lay with states. In contrast, the Rome Statute endorses what might be termed 'international judicial intervention' in civil wars.[83]

81 See generally discussion at Chapter 5.

82 The 1948 Genocide Convention, for example, draws no such distinction.

83 The Rome Statute also makes provision for crimes against humanity and the crime of genocide to fall within the court's jurisdiction, regardless of whether the relevant conduct is restricted to the territory of a single state.

2.2.4 Other Components of the Civil War Regime

There are a range of other treaties which are also applicable in civil wars, with notional implications for the conduct of governments and rebels in such circumstances. Human rights treaties such as the European Convention on Human Rights (1950), the 1966 International Covenants on Civil and Political Rights and on Economic, Social and Cultural Rights, and the 1988 Convention against Torture provide the leading instances, although such treaties also typically allow states the option of derogating from all but a 'hard core' of provisions should a government be faced with extensive threats to public order.[84]

The current study does not include extensive commentary on human rights or other treaties with a bearing on the conduct of civil wars. This should not be understood, however, as indicating that the content of these treaties is not legally significant, nor that the inclusion of civil wars within their scope is not interesting. Similarly, history did not come to an end in 1998, and efforts have continued on the part of the ICRC and others to more closely circumscribe the conduct of civil wars.[85] Nevertheless,

[84] Article 15 of the European Convention on Human Rights, for example, allows states to enter derogations in respect of almost all provisions in times of 'war or other public emergency threatening the life of the nation'. That said, the applicability of human rights treaties in armed conflicts is another topic altogether. See e.g. discussions in: Droege, 'The Interplay between International Humanitarian Law and International Human Rights Law in Situations of Armed Conflict', 310; Lubell, 'Parallel Application of International Humanitarian Law and International Human Rights Law: An Examination of the Debate', 648; Krieger, 'A Conflict of Norms: The Relationship between Humanitarian Law and Human Rights Law in the ICRC Customary Law Study', 265–91; Moir, *The Law of Internal Armed Conflict*, 193–231; Murray, *Practitioners' Guide to Human Rights Law in Armed Conflict*; Oberleitner, *Human Rights in Armed Conflict: Law, Practice, Policy*.

[85] See e.g. (and perhaps most prominently) the multiple-volume ICRC study into customary international humanitarian law: Henckaerts and Doswald-Beck (eds.), *Customary International Humanitarian Law: Volume I – Rules*; Henckaerts and Doswald-Beck (eds.), *Customary International Humanitarian Law: Volume II – Practice.* Scholarly work has also continued in this vein, including in respect of the role of international human rights law in armed conflict. See e.g. Kreβ and Mégret, 'The Regulation of Non-International Armed Conflicts: Can a Privilege of Belligerency Be Envisioned in the Law of Non-International Armed Conflicts?', 29–66; Murray, *Practitioners' Guide to Human Rights Law in Armed Conflict.* Much of this work focuses on developments in customary law, given limited multilateral treaty activity in this sphere since the 1990s. Though regularly referred to as authoritative statements of law within specialist international law communities, the extent to which such work is (or should be) accepted more broadly – in particular by governments – as authoritative is debatable. See related discussion at Chapter 1, Section 1.6, and in similar vein Hakimi, 'Custom's Method and Process: Lessons from Humanitarian Law', in Bradley (ed.) *Custom's Future: International Law*

Common Article 3, the two Additional Protocols (primarily Additional Protocol II) and Article 8 of the Rome Statute constitute the most significant components of the latter-day civil war regime, the first two by virtue of their wide ambit and focus specifically on internal armed conflict, and the third in consequence of the imposition of international criminal responsibility for conduct in internal armed conflict. As such, the following chapters focus on the negotiation of these instruments and provisions.

Conclusion

Civil wars are not a new phenomenon. Even so, both international legal scholars and governments long proved reluctant to extend the scope of international law to civil wars. Accordingly, there is no obvious reason ex ante to have expected such conflicts to have been brought within the ambit of international humanitarian law as it has developed in the period since the Second World War. Nevertheless, this is what has happened, principally through the inclusion of Common Article 3 in the Geneva Conventions of 1949, the negotiation of the 1977 Additional Protocols and the drafting of Article 8 of the 1998 Rome Statute of the ICC. The following chapters examine the roles played by various factors in bringing about the respective drafting outcomes in each case.

in a Changing World, 148–71; Shereshevsky, 'Back in the Game: The Reengagement of States in International Humanitarian Law Making'.

3

Negotiating Common Article 3 (1949)

'Half a loaf is better than no bread.'[1]

Introduction

Common Article 3 of the 1949 Geneva Conventions regulates the conduct of combatants in internal armed conflicts. At the time of drafting it was considered a remarkably daring innovation, even if with time it has been overshadowed by subsequent legal developments. The provision remains at the heart of the international law of non-international armed conflict, however, and its interpretation and implications continue to be heavily debated amongst scholars and practitioners.

This chapter recounts the background to the inclusion of this provision in the 1949 treaties and provides an overview of the drafting process. The unfolding of these negotiations is then considered from the perspectives of the principal actors involved, focusing on British, French, American, Soviet and ICRC experiences, highlighting conduct reflecting the operation of hypothesised causal factors and mechanisms. The concluding section assesses the extent to which the hypotheses set out in Chapter 1 are capable of helping make sense of the drafting of Common Article 3, and considers the implications of the drafting process for the former.

Taken together, the five hypotheses go a significant way towards explaining the drafting of Common Article 3, illustrating the value of the theoretical perspective set out in Chapter 1. The discussion highlights in particular the critical interaction of great power preferences and the ICRC's strategic humanitarian activism and use of technical expertise within a constrained legal and political environment. Reflecting Western hesitance in the face of Soviet humanitarianism, however, there is only limited support for the expectation that democracies will be more likely

[1] Plinio Bolla, Head, Swiss Delegation, Diplomatic Conference for the Establishment of International Conventions for the Protection of Victims of War, *Final Record of the Diplomatic Conference of Geneva of 1949*, III, Vol. II (Section B), 335.

than non-democratic states to support a demanding civil war regime, while the discussion also suggests a need to take into account the broader international normative environment in which Common Article 3 was drafted - the Zeitgeist of negotiations.

3.1 Historical Background

3.1.1 Origins of the Treaty Revision Process

The process of treaty revision that culminated in 1949 originated with the ICRC, Max Huber writing to governments and national Red Cross and Red Crescent societies in February 1945 to seek co-operation in a review of the law of armed conflict.[2] Government reactions to this invitation varied, largely depending on the wartime relationships between governments, the ICRC and national Red Cross societies. The Roosevelt administration was unsurprised, for example, having developed a close relationship with the American Red Cross during the war, and indeed was already working on a 'revision agenda' with the latter.[3] The UK government, in contrast, had kept the British Red Cross and the ICRC at arm's length during the war, so had not anticipated the invitation.[4]

A further communication from Huber followed in September 1945, after the conclusion of hostilities, inviting the governments of the 'Big Five' – China, France, the Soviet Union, the UK, and the USA – to participate in a meeting of government experts. In the event, however, this meeting was only convened in April 1947, and then without Soviet participation, by which time the League of Red Cross Societies had also become involved in treaty revision.[5]

[2] 'Documentation préliminaire pour la revision et l'établissement de conventions ayant trait à la Croix-Rouge: mémorandum adressé par le comité international de la Croix-Rouge aux gouvernements des États parties à la convention de Genève et aux Sociétés nationales de la Croix-Rouge', 85–9. See Best, *War and Law since 1945*, 80.

[3] Best, *War and Law since 1945*, 80.

[4] See Crossland, *Britain and the International Committee of the Red Cross, 1939–1945*, chapter 3. In late 1944, in a meeting with the Canadian High Commissioner in London, the head of the prisoner of war section in the UK Foreign Office was apparently 'dismissive of the notion that the UK would or should find time' for any such plans on the part of the ICRC, 'anyway for five years' (CAN 619-40c. Letter signed S. Morley Scott to Ministry of External Affairs, 15 September 1944, quoted in: Best, *War and Law since 1945*, 81).

[5] International Committee of the Red Cross, *Report on the Work of the Conference of Government Experts for the Study of the Conventions for the Protection of War Victims (Geneva, April 14–26, 1947)*, 2–5.

The League and ICRC had been engaged in on-off competition for leadership of the Red Cross movement since the establishment of the former in 1919, under American Red Cross stewardship. The Swiss-composed ICRC was traditionally conservative, while the national societies represented in the League collectively tended to be more militant and radical. With the war's end, moreover, Count Folke Bernadotte of the Swedish Red Cross emerged as a vocal critic of the ICRC, as Sweden sought to supplant Switzerland as the leading neutral 'humanitarian' power.[6]

The League's effort to force the ICRC to 'surrender or at any rate to share its prerogatives' commenced with 'a brisk engagement' at a July 1946 meeting of the League Board of Governors in Oxford. In particular, this meeting adopted a Bernadotte-inspired proposal to establish a 'Special Committee to Study the Ways and Means of Reinforcing the Action of the [ICRC]' – conceived as part of an initiative to 'internationalise' the Committee. This was followed by a meeting of national society representatives in Geneva in July–August 1946, which established a special committee of the League Executive to review ICRC papers for the upcoming (17th) International Red Cross Conference – the major periodic international meeting of the Red Cross movement – scheduled to take place in Stockholm in August 1948. This meeting would bring Red Cross societies, the ICRC and governments together en masse for the first time since 1938.[7]

It was against this background of intra-movement tension, as well as growing criticism of the Committee's wartime record,[8] that the ICRC

6 See Best, *War and Law since 1945*, 86–7; Junod, *The Imperiled Red Cross and the Palestine–Eretz-Yisrael Conflict, 1945–1952: The Influence of Institutional Concerns on a Humanitarian Operation*, 13–14, 24–32; Forsythe, *The Humanitarians: The International Committee of the Red Cross*, 35–8; Steinacher, *Humanitarians at War: The Red Cross in the Shadow of the Holocaust*, 19–20, 70–80.

7 Best, *War and Law since 1945*, 91–2. Also Junod, *The Imperiled Red Cross and the Palestine–Eretz-Yisrael Conflict, 1945–1952: The Influence of Institutional Concerns on a Humanitarian Operation*, 24–33; Steinacher, *Humanitarians at War: The Red Cross in the Shadow of the Holocaust*, 95, 224.

8 The ICRC's ambivalent response to the Holocaust formed a central element in such criticism. (See generally Steinacher, *Humanitarians at War: The Red Cross in the Shadow of the Holocaust*.) As Junod notes, the ICRC was also 'cautious about intervening on behalf of civilians in concentration camps, especially Jews, to avoid antagonizing Hitler and endangering the activities it was able to conduct lawfully and effectively to help prisoners of war. It pointed out, moreover, that its headquarters were in a country hemmed in by the Axis countries' (*The Imperiled Red Cross and the Palestine–Eretz-Yisrael Conflict, 1945–1952: The Influence of Institutional Concerns on a Humanitarian Operation*, 19). The Soviet government was also critical of ICRC efforts to protect prisoners of war, with a broader (and arguably

decided to 'promote the reinforcement of international humanitarian law' by revising the 1929 Geneva Conventions, as a central element in a strategy 'to reestablish and reinforce its position', starting with the 1948 meeting in Stockholm.[9]

The ICRC's preference in 1946, reflecting pre-war experiences in Spain as well as drawing on post-war analysis, was for the future law of armed conflict to embrace internal as well as international armed conflict, but to make application in internal conflicts conditional on the readiness of the parties involved to give undertakings to that effect. The Committee accordingly proposed to the July–August 1946 meeting of national Red Cross society representatives that parties to civil wars should be 'invited to declare their readiness to apply the principles of the Convention, subject to reciprocity being observed'.[10]

The national societies took a slightly different approach, though. ICRC caution notwithstanding, there was widespread support in the summer of 1946 for revised treaties to apply in armed conflicts 'within the borders of a State' as in international armed conflicts, unless one of the parties to such a conflict expressly declined to apply such rules.[11] The meeting of

justified) perception amongst Allied governments that the ICRC and Swiss authorities had been overly close to the German authorities during the war (Junod, *The Imperiled Red Cross and the Palestine-Eretz-Yisrael Conflict, 1945–1952: The Influence of Institutional Concerns on a Humanitarian Operation*, 14–15; Crossland, *Britain and the International Committee of the Red Cross, 1939–1945*, 7).

9 The other main element in this strategy was to illustrate the ICRC's value through intervening in Palestine in 1947–1948 (Junod, *The Imperiled Red Cross and the Palestine-Eretz-Yisrael Conflict, 1945–1952: The Influence of Institutional Concerns on a Humanitarian Operation*, 32–3. See also Forsythe, *The Humanitarians: The International Committee of the Red Cross*, chapter 2.) The two 1929 Conventions were the Geneva Convention for the Amelioration of the Condition of the Wounded and Sick in Armies in the Field of 27 July 1929, and the Geneva Convention relative to the Treatment of Prisoners of War of 27 July 1929. These sat alongside Hague Convention (X) for the Adaptation to Maritime Warfare of the Principles of the Geneva Convention of 18 October 1907.

10 International Committee of the Red Cross, *Report on the Work of the Preliminary Conference of National Red Cross Societies for the Study of the Conventions and of Various Problems Relative to the Red Cross, Geneva, July 26–August 3, 1946*, 15. See also: Junod, *The Imperiled Red Cross and the Palestine-Eretz-Yisrael Conflict, 1945–1952: The Influence of Institutional Concerns on a Humanitarian Operation*, 34–5.

11 See Abi-Saab, *Droit humanitaire et conflits internes – origines et évolution de la réglementation internationale*, 43; Perna, *The Formation of the Treaty Law of Non-International Armed Conflicts*, 51. International Committee of the Red Cross, *Report on the Work of the Preliminary Conference of National Red Cross Societies for the Study of the Conventions and of Various Problems Relative to the Red Cross, Geneva, July 26–August 3, 1946*, 15.

government experts that the ICRC convened in April 1947 came to a similar view, though in somewhat milder form, referring merely to the prospect of Convention 'principles' applying in such conflicts, and including (in a move opposed by the ICRC) a reciprocity requirement making the application of these principles dependent on antagonists observing the relevant strictures.[12]

3.1.2 Prelude: Stockholm 1948

The Stockholm Conference took place in August 1948, chaired by Count Bernadotte as President of the Swedish Red Cross.[13] Fifty-two national Red Cross societies participated in the meeting, alongside representatives from 50 governments – though the latter had varying mandates. The UK, for example, merely sent two observers.

Red Cross movement conferences hold an uncertain legal position: governments are under no obligation to participate or to treat their outputs as authoritative. Nevertheless, owing to custom and Red Cross movement arrangements, the Stockholm Conference was a necessary stage through which draft texts had to be processed.[14]

The 'internal armed conflict' text prepared by the ICRC for inclusion in the Stockholm treaty drafts differed from that produced by the government experts, retaining the expert group's reference to Convention principles, but omitting the reference to reciprocity. This text read:

> In all cases of armed conflict which are not of an international character, especially cases of civil war, colonial conflicts, or wars of religion, which may occur in the territory of one or more of the High Contracting Parties, the implementing of the principles of the present Convention shall be obligatory on each of the adversaries. The application of the Convention

[12] International Committee of the Red Cross, *Report on the Work of the Conference of Government Experts for the Study of the Conventions for the Protection of War Victims (Geneva, April 14–26, 1947)*, 8. As Mantilla observes, by this point 'governments knew the idea had wings' ('Forum Isolation: Social Opprobrium and the Origins of the International Law of Internal Conflict', 320).

[13] It bears noting that by this point Bernadotte's enthusiasm for internationalising the ICRC had dissipated, owing in part to developing Cold War tensions and an associated risk of schism in the Red Cross movement, and in part to a growing personal focus on his role as UN mediator in Palestine. (See Steinacher, *Humanitarians at War: The Red Cross in the Shadow of the Holocaust*, 222; Junod, *The Imperiled Red Cross and the Palestine–Eretz-Yisrael Conflict, 1945–1952: The Influence of Institutional Concerns on a Humanitarian Operation*, 27–30.)

[14] Paraphrasing Best, *War and Law since 1945*, 93.

> in these circumstances shall in nowise depend on the legal status of the parties to the conflict and shall have no effect on that status.[15]

This provision received relatively little attention at the Stockholm Conference. Perhaps the strongest objection put forward was that of Michel Pesmazoglou, a Greek government and Red Cross society delegate – at a period when Greece was itself enduring a civil war. He observed that the effect of the proposed wording would be that 'if someone steals a loaf of bread in order to feed his family . . . the unfortunate individual will be put into prison, while he who has resorted to arms against his own country, against his national power, will not be called upon to suffer the consequences of his action'.[16]

Despite Greek misgivings, debate at Stockholm tended towards the League's views. The conference thus saw a return to 'provisions' rather than 'principles' in the drafting, with the ICRC countering an American argument in support of a reciprocity requirement by pointing to the potential scope for government (rather than rebel) non-compliance, albeit eventually conceding the inclusion of such a requirement in the draft 'POW' and 'Civilians' Conventions.[17] Wary of the prospect of over-restrictive interpretation, the Committee, with US and French support, also effected the removal of the wording 'especially cases of civil war, colonial conflicts, or wars of religion' from the text. The reported Stockholm text in the

[15] International Committee of the Red Cross, *Draft Revised or New Conventions for the Protection of War Victims Established by the International Committee of the Red Cross with the Assistance of Government Experts, National Red Cross Societies and Other Humanitarian Associations*, 5. This wording formed part of Article 2 of each of the (entirely new) 'Civilians' Convention, and of the revised draft 'Wounded and Sick', 'Maritime' and 'POW' Conventions. The last sentence was included to assure governments that the regulation and protection of non-state actors under the revised Conventions would not be understood as according belligerent status to the latter. (See International Committee of the Red Cross, *Report on the Work of the Conference of Government Experts for the Study of the Conventions for the Protection of War Victims (Geneva, April 14–26, 1947)*, 9.)

[16] International Committee of the Red Cross, *Seventeenth International Red Cross Conference, Stockholm, August 1948: Report*, 72.

[17] The risk of foreign intervention in a civil conflict under the guise of a 'protecting power' was a particular focus of US concern. (See Abi-Saab 'Non-International Armed Conflicts', 220: permitting '"rebels" to appoint another State as "Protecting Power" would inexorably internationalize the conflict' See also Mantilla, 'Forum Isolation: Social Opprobrium and the Origins of the International Law of Internal Conflict', 322; 'Under (Social) Pressure: The Historical Regulation of Internal Armed Conflicts through International Law', 131.

draft Wounded and Sick and Maritime Conventions accordingly read:

> In all cases of armed conflict not of an international character which may occur in the territory of one or more of the High Contracting Parties, each of the adversaries shall be bound to implement the provisions of the present Convention. The Convention shall be applicable in these circumstances, whatever the legal status of the Parties to the conflict and without prejudice thereto.[18]

It was accordingly in this form – with additional wording catering for reciprocity in the POW and Civilians drafts – that the application of international humanitarian law in internal armed conflicts came before governments, as draft Paragraph 4 of Article 2 of each of the draft Conventions, at the Swiss-convened diplomatic conference which opened in Geneva on 21 April 1949.[19]

3.2 The Diplomatic Conference: Geneva 1949

3.2.1 Plenary and the Joint Committee

The regulation of internal armed conflict rapidly became a key challenge at the Geneva conference. The locus of this debate was initially a 'Joint Committee' of the other conference committees, with ICRC legal expert

[18] See International Committee of the Red Cross, *Seventeenth International Red Cross Conference, Stockholm, August 1948*, 10.

[19] The draft POW and Civilians provisions were worded slightly differently: 'In all cases of armed conflict not of an international character which may occur in the territory of one or more of the High Contracting Parties, each of the Parties to the conflict shall be bound to implement the provisions of the present Convention, subject to the adverse party likewise acting in obedience thereto. The Convention shall be applicable in these circumstances, whatever the legal status of the Parties to the conflict and without prejudice thereto' (International Committee of the Red Cross, *Revised and New Draft Conventions for the Protection of War Victims*, 51–2, 114). Prior to the 1949 conference, the ICRC consulted in December 1948 with a further group of international legal experts, including Hersch Lauterpacht. This group proposed a number of drafting amendments to the approved Stockholm drafts, including the replacement of Stockholm's 'each of the adversaries' in the draft Wounded and Sick Conventions, with the draft POW and Civilians Conventions' 'each of the Parties to the conflict', and the removal of the reciprocity requirement in the draft POW and Civilians wording. The Stockholm drafts, however, remained the formal basis for discussion at Geneva. (See International Committee of the Red Cross, *Remarks and Proposals Submitted by the International Committee of the Red Cross: Document for the Consideration of Governments Invited by the Swiss Federal Council to Attend the Diplomatic Conference at Geneva (April 21, 1949)*, 6, 9, 26, 36–8, 68.)

participation, set up at Australian and UK instigation to consider the common articles of the four proposed Conventions.[20]

Various delegations set out their stalls in initial discussions on 26–27 April. French, Spanish, British, and Greek delegates were uncomfortable with the progressive protection of insurgents, with the UK, Spain, and France emphasising the risks to sovereignty posed by granting insurgents (in effect) belligerent protections. Pesmazoglou of Greece also reiterated his concerns from 1948 regarding the status of detained insurgents, adding that allowing a protecting power to intercede for such detainees risked inciting further rebellion.[21]

The USA formed part of this group, head of delegation Leland Harrison arguing that Convention provisions should apply only in 'war as understood in international law'. The Australian, Canadian, Chinese (nationalist), Italian and Burmese delegations agreed with this formulation – its uncertainty notwithstanding – the Burmese representative stating that 'the proposed Convention should not give legal status to insurgents who sought by undemocratic methods, to overthrow a legally constituted government'.[22]

The USSR – along with allied Eastern European states, last-minute attendees at the meeting – took a diametrically opposed, avowedly anti-colonialist view, notionally in favour of the ICRC draft and opposed to more conservative western views, advancing arguments based inter alia on the UN Charter. The Soviet Union and its satellites were also not alone in this view: Mexico evinced particular concern for 'humanitarian considerations', while a Norwegian delegate indicated that '[i]t was a step forward in international law to say explicitly that, even if war was not recognized, the rules concerning the conduct of war should be applied'. Danish, Romanian, and Hungarian delegates were similarly aligned.[23]

A more conciliatory tone was struck by the Monegasque and Swiss delegates – (French) law professor Paul de Geouffre de La Pradelle and Swiss Supreme Court judge Plinio Bolla – the latter suggesting the setting up of a 'Special Committee' to draft a text reconciling the various views. This was agreed in short order on 29 April by the Joint Committee, with Australia, the USA, France, Greece, Italy, Monaco, Norway, the UK,

[20] See Diplomatic Conference for the Establishment of International Conventions for the Protection of Victims of War, *Final Record of the Diplomatic Conference of Geneva of 1949*, III, Vol. II (Section A), 21–4.

[21] *Final Record*, Vol. II (Section B), 10–11.

[22] Ibid., 12–13, 15.

[23] See *Final Record*, Vol. II (Section B), 11.

Switzerland, and the USSR as initial members, shortly supplemented by Burma and Uruguay.[24]

3.2.2 The Special Committee

A series of amendments to the Stockholm wording were submitted prior to the first meeting of the Special Committee. A radically humanitarian Hungarian proposal was favoured by the Norwegians, while a French proposal to make reference to 'the general humanitarian principles appearing in the Preamble of the Civilians Convention' gathered support from the Italian and Greek delegates.[25] Little headway was initially made, however: the Australians and USA (again) called for the inclusion of threshold conditions that insurgents would have to satisfy before they could receive the benefit of the provision, echoing criteria previously put forward by Lauterpacht for the recognition of belligerency, while the Soviet Union remained wedded to a robust 'humanitarian' position.[26]

An indication of potential scope for compromise emerged on 9 and 11 May, when participants voted ten to one, with one abstention, to include civil wars within the ambit of the revised Conventions, but without using the Stockholm text as the basis for drafting. A smaller working party was then set up to draft a generally acceptable form of wording, comprising American, French, Australian and Norwegian participants, with a Swiss chair.[27]

The working party reported back to the Special Committee on 16 May with wording which closely reflected US and Australian concerns, requiring a demanding set of preconditions, including reciprocal observance, to be satisfied for Convention protections to apply.[28] Perhaps unsurprisingly, this met a lukewarm reception: in particular, French, Italian, US and British delegates criticised the draft (in principle) for being overly generous to rebels and as being (in practice) unworkable. Criticism continued on 18 and 19 May when Soviet and Burmese representatives reiterated their respective positions in favour of the Stockholm draft and

[24] *Final Record*, Vol. II (Section B), 14–16. De Geouffre de La Pradelle later wrote one of the early French-language accounts of the negotiations: *La conférence diplomatique et les nouvelles conventions de Genève du 12 Août 1949*.

[25] See *Final Record*, Vol. II (Section B), 40–1.

[26] *Final Record*, Vol. II (Section B), 41–3. See also Lauterpacht, *Recognition in International Law*, 176.

[27] *Final Record*, Vol. II (Section B), 45–6.

[28] See wording at *Final Record*, Vol. II (Section B), 46–7.

against any wording at all. The ICRC made a forceful contribution to the fifth meeting, Claude Pilloud – head of its Legal Division – stating that 'in his view, the text drawn up by the Working Party could never have been applied in any recent case of civil war. It therefore did not represent a progress'. The working party was subsequently asked by the Special Committee's chair to reconsider its draft.[29]

The working party reported back on 14 June, identifying two possible approaches: to narrow either the scope of the conflicts to which the Conventions would apply, or the range of provisions which would be applicable in civil war contexts. The working party was, however, still largely wedded to the idea that some sort of minimum criteria would have to be satisfied on the part of insurgents before they could benefit from protection under revised Conventions, ensuring that these proposals met with muted enthusiasm from advocates of a more 'humanitarian' position.[30]

Following growing realisation on the part of the French and British of the strength of 'humanitarian' sentiment, on 8 June the former had put forward compromise wording: this was discussed in Committee on 15 June. The French proposal was undeniably humanitarian in tone, but also more open to interpretation than previous drafts, proposing that: 'the humanitarian rules contained in the Preamble of the Convention ... be applied also to a war of a non-international character'.[31] On this occasion, only the Australian, American and Norwegian delegates expressed dissatisfaction. In the eyes of the US delegation, the French proposal did not go far enough, as it 'removed any obligation of the Parties to the Convention to apply it in any circumstances'. The Norwegians similarly viewed the working party's draft as providing more satisfyingly obligatory protection to civilians. In contrast, though, each of the other members was able to produce a reason to endorse the French approach – suggesting that notwithstanding the different positions represented, there was a growing appreciation that compromise was both desirable and (potentially) feasible.[32]

[29] See discussion at *Final Record*, Vol. II (Section B), 47–50.

[30] *Final Record*, Vol. II (Section B), 76–7. An exception was the Civilians Convention, where the working party simply recommended observance of 'the underlying humanitarian principles of the Convention'.

[31] *Final Record*, Vol. II (Section B), 78. See Annex 13 at: *Final Record of the Diplomatic Conference of Geneva of 1949*, Vol. III, 28. On UK and French views at this point, see Mantilla, 'Under (Social) Pressure: The Historical Regulation of Internal Armed Conflicts through International Law', 141.

[32] *Final Record*, Vol. II (Section B), 78–9.

The UK delegation was 'in favour of some formula along the lines of the French amendment', while even the Burmese took the view that 'the French proposal met all situations'. Uruguay and Monaco similarly assented, while the Soviets asked 'the French Delegate to formulate a new draft' for comparison with the Stockholm text. The ICRC similarly lent its support, rebutting US concerns, and noting that the French proposal had practical merit 'in adopting and embodying the humanitarian principles referred to in . . . the Working Party's document'.[33]

At this point, various issues remained to be addressed. For one, the preamble referred to in the French proposal was not yet settled (and was ultimately discarded).[34] The perhaps-unsurprising upshot of this discussion was the formation of a second working party to consider further the French proposal. With a French chair, this had a more diverse make-up than its predecessor, comprising Italy, Monaco, the UK and the USSR.

The second working party reported back to the Special Committee on 24 June, proposing a text which avoided reference to a Conventional preamble, but which rather required parties in internal armed conflicts to apply a minimal set of humanitarian standards. These were again drawn principally from a French proposal, though taking into account British, Burmese and ICRC views. Responses on this occasion were also more positive than on 15 June, although the Soviet delegation was hamstrung (and was to remain so for some time) by an absence of instructions from Moscow. The USA, however, retained misgivings, one delegate noting that: 'it would be unfortunate if the obligation were not laid upon the Contracting States to apply the Conventions in certain instances of civil war'.[35] On 29 June, the US and UK delegations put forward a proposal to limit the applicability of the wording to 'High Contracting Parties', but the ICRC representative forestalled discussion, countering that this 'would tend to distort the meaning of those who had framed this Article, and who wished to bind not only the legal Governments, but also the insurgents'.[36]

Discussions continued in the absence of Soviet instructions, focused primarily on the legal and practical difficulties involved in binding insurgents to treaty observance. The USA, UK and Australia raised

[33] Ibid., 78–9.

[34] On the influence of 'human rights thinking' on the (eventually discarded) preamble, see van Dijk, 'Human Rights in War: On the Entangled Foundations of the 1949 Geneva Conventions', at 576–7.

[35] *Final Record*, Vol. II (Section B), 82–4.

[36] Ibid., 90.

(again) the possibility of requiring insurgents to observe Convention principles themselves in order to benefit from their application, though the UK delegate was also quick to clarify on this occasion that 'any civilized government should feel bound to apply the principles of the Convention even if the insurgents failed to apply them'.[37] Notwithstanding, the ICRC concurred with a Greek legal analysis in this case, effectively putting an end to debate. The ICRC delegate similarly effectively quashed a British proposal for parties to accept ICRC assistance if offered, arguing that ICRC independence 'would be jeopardized if the ICRC were mentioned in any mandatory clause'.[38]

A radically humanitarian counter-proposal was eventually put forward by the Soviet delegation on 8 July. This proposal entailed differing wording for each draft treaty, tailored to reflect their different subject matters. The proposal also removed any references to the legal status of the parties to civil conflicts and to the ICRC's right of initiative, and required the application of the prisoner of war regime as a whole to civil conflicts, thus going significantly beyond the French text.[39] Opposition was led on this occasion by British and French delegates, who noted practical difficulties in implementing the Soviet proposal and the challenges to 'sovereignty' which the Soviet proposal would imply, primarily in relation to the granting of prisoner of war status to captured insurgents and the associated provision of a 'protecting power' for detainees. Only the Danes appeared somewhat sympathetic to the Soviet proposal, with Swiss and Italian delegates speaking in favour of the French proposal and the Australians doggedly maintaining support for the first working party's draft.[40]

The first working party's second draft, the French and the Soviet proposals were considered once again on 8 and 11 July. In these final Special Committee discussions, the Soviet proposal was rejected by a vote of one to nine, while the first working party's second draft was similarly rejected by four votes to seven. The French proposal garnered more support, but ultimately also failed to gather sufficiently clear support to be adopted.[41] The Chair of the Special Committee – at Australian and Soviet prompting – then opted to include all three

[37] Ibid., 94.
[38] Ibid., 95.
[39] See *Final Record*, Vol. II (Section B), 97–8.
[40] *Final Record*, Vol. II (Section B), 98–9.
[41] Ibid., 100–2.

proposals in its final report to the Joint Committee, without providing a collective recommendation.[42]

3.2.3 *Return to the Joint Committee and Plenary*

The Joint Committee considered the Special Committee's report on internal armed conflict on 19 and 20 July. While all three drafts were considered, the revised French proposal was put forward jointly by the French, Greek, Italian, UK, Swiss and Uruguayan delegations, suggesting that it was likely to command the broadest support. This, indeed, turned out to be the case: the Soviet proposal and the revised draft of the first working party gained 9 and 5 votes, respectively, at a first, informal vote, as against 22 for the revised French proposal. The French-inspired draft was subsequently adopted by the Joint Committee by 21 votes to 6, with 14 abstentions.[43] The sole dissenting voice raised publicly at this stage was that of General Oung of Burma, who voiced principled misgivings as to the whole business of regulating such conflicts.[44] This was not the end of the matter, however: the Joint Committee's report to the conference as a whole followed the template set by the Special Committee, noting the Joint Committee's preference for the French proposal, but also setting out the Soviet proposal and the first working party's draft.[45]

The conference considered the various proposals in plenary on 28 and 29 July. The former was the occasion for an impassioned debate between the Soviet Union, the proponents of the somewhat more sovereignty-friendly French proposal, and General Oung, seemingly speaking on behalf of post-colonial and newly independent states. The Soviet delegation argued that adoption of the French proposal would be 'tantamount to denying the necessity of applying, in case of conflicts of a non-international character, a large number of important provisions in the Draft Conventions'.[46] General Oung, on the other hand, made an extended plea for the deletion of the offending article, citing the vagueness of the phrase 'armed conflicts not of an international character', the risk of encouraging rebellion, and the implicit provision of 'a place in international law' to insurgents. Oung also warned that the French proposal would 'seriously endanger' de jure government sovereignty by

[42] Ibid., 102, 106.
[43] Ibid., 33–7.
[44] See also e.g. *Final Record*, Vol. II (Section B), 106, 120.
[45] See *Final Record*, Vol. II (Section B), 129.
[46] *Final Record*, Vol. II (Section B), 326–7.

'taking away from it its own legal machinery (sic) to maintain the security of its population and the prosperity of its State'.[47]

At the final reading on 29 July, further interventions were made along similar lines: Romanian and Czechoslovak delegates, for example, spoke in favour of the Soviet proposal. The Burmese delegate likewise repeated his concerns. It must have been evident to all though, that the French proposal commanded the most support, ICRC member Paul Carry concluding that the 'text is simple and clear and has the merit of ensuring, in the case of civil war, at least the application of the humanitarian rules which are recognized by all civilised peoples'.[48] In a secret ballot, the amended French proposal was subsequently adopted by 34 votes to 12, with one abstention.[49]

3.3 Roles and Perspectives

The following section considers the development of Common Article 3 from the perspectives of key national delegations and the ICRC, and the extent to which the causal factors and mechanisms set out in Chapter 1 can be seen in operation in these experiences.

3.3.1 Western Great Powers

3.3.1.1 The UK

The British government had little love for the ICRC in the aftermath of the Second World War. The relationship between the two had been severely tested by what the British saw as weak ICRC performance during the war (particularly in respect of POW protection) and by the political machinations of ICRC then-President Carl Burckhardt as the war neared its conclusion.[50] The British also had continued concerns about the ICRC's peculiar status as a Swiss NGO with 'quasi-political and diplomatic functions', and were 'completely out of touch with what went on in

[47] See *Final Record*, Vol. II (Section B), 327–30.

[48] *Final Record*, Vol. II (Section B), 337. Carry also decried the Burmese proposal as 'a calamity'.

[49] *Final Record*, Vol. II (Section B), 339. Concerns regarding Common Article 3 nevertheless resulted in the inclusion of provisional reservations by both Argentina and Portugal on signature, though these were not maintained on ratification. (See *Final Record of the Diplomatic Conference of Geneva of 1949, III*, Vol. I, 343, 351.)

[50] See generally Crossland, *Britain and the International Committee of the Red Cross, 1939–1945*, chapters 3–7.

the international Red Cross movement' owing to the unusually distant relationship between Whitehall and the British Red Cross.[51]

The UK consequently attended the 1947 meeting of government experts reluctantly, principally on the basis that 'the UK had better go to the party, if only because most other states would do so'.[52] In a similar vein, the British failed to send delegates to Stockholm in 1948 (two non-voting observers were sent in response to US pressure), owing to unease at being seen to endorse the ICRC's 'political' functions and financial arrangements.[53] It is accordingly unsurprising, in light of the UK's lack of sympathy with the ICRC's agenda for the development of the Geneva regime and general discomfiture with the Red Cross movement, that the UK joined the 1949 conference with a conservative, even neuralgic, demeanour, sceptical of both the ICRC's motives and its capacities in seeking to revise the 1929 Conventions.[54]

The British position with respect to internal armed conflict was of a piece with this attitude, evincing (to put it mildly) 'little enthusiasm for the idea of extending the Conventions to cover internal as well as international conflicts'.[55] The cabinet instruction to seek to avoid the inclusion of such provisions in revised treaties was underpinned by a doctrinal position that 'anything that it is proposed to put in the Convention (should) be based upon international law' – indicative of the type of argument that the UK proposed to make in debate.[56] Moreover, in the event that it was not possible to exclude civil war altogether from the scope of any revised treaties, the UK was initially prepared to concede

[51] Best, *War and Law since 1945*, 90.

[52] Indeed, the UK agreed to Huber's inclusion on the agenda of a possible 'civilians' Convention only after the Foreign Office had overcome Home Office and War Office objections (Best, 'Making the Geneva Conventions of 1949: The View from Whitehall', 8–9).

[53] This did not signal a British preference for the League, however, Whitehall evidently viewing the ICRC as 'more genuinely and reliably neutral than any other body that could be found' (Best, 'Making the Geneva Conventions of 1949: The View from Whitehall', 10, 13).

[54] Per War Office Deputy Under-Secretary David Roseway in 1945: 'to assist the [ICRC] with the benefit of our experience in administering and interpreting the two Conventions . . . [may] be going some way towards recognising their political claims to intervene with governments as regards the treatment of prisoners' (Cited in Best, 'Making the Geneva Conventions of 1949: The View from Whitehall', 7).

[55] Best, *War and Law since 1945*, 89.

[56] See pre-Conference UK Memorandum, quoted in Best, 'Making the Geneva Conventions of 1949: The View from Whitehall', 13.

only that: 'the Conventions can be regarded as applicable only when the Sovereign Power recognises a state of Civil War'.[57]

If reluctance to fall into line with the 'progressive' humanitarian trend at Geneva reflected broader political and doctrinal misgivings, the UK position on internal armed conflict was particularly closely informed by a perception that, as the pre-eminent imperial power, the UK was especially at risk from calls for greater restrictions to be placed on the conduct of 'colonial' wars.[58] To British eyes, such worries were far from fanciful: alongside concerns about the prospect of Communist uprisings in post-war Europe,[59] the UK had only recently withdrawn from a quagmire in Palestine; its forces were engaged in an ongoing conflict in Malaya in 1949; and Northern Ireland and Aden were also raised during preparatory discussions.[60] The British preoccupation with restricting the ambit of revised treaties in internal armed conflict also reflected policymakers' concerns about Britain's continued post-war status as a world power.[61]

Underlying British views and preferences do not appear to have changed significantly during the 1949 conference. As the meeting progressed, however, the UK delegation adopted a more conciliatory position in respect of internal armed conflict, seeking and receiving revised

[57] UK Foreign and Commonwealth Office, 'Mill Irving, Foreign Office Minute: "Revision of the Geneva Conventions"' (1949). See also UK Foreign and Commonwealth Office, 'United Kingdom Delegation Circular No. 10 – Diplomatic Conference on Protection of War Victims (Note on meeting held in the Attorney-General's Room at the House of Commons on Monday, 11th April, 1949)' (1949); UK Foreign and Commonwealth Office, 'United Kingdom Delegation Circular No. 15 – Diplomatic Conference on Protection of War Victims (attaching official record of meeting with the Attorney General of 11 April 1949)' (1949). This position was adopted, moreover, notwithstanding ministers having been made aware early in 1949 that it would be 'almost impossible for the UK to resist' the prospect of civil war regulation at Geneva (UK War Office, 'Army Council Secretariat, Brief for Secretary of State, Cabinet Meeting of Ministers, "Revision of Geneva Conventions: Application of Geneva Conventions to Civil War"' (1949), cited in Hitchcock, 'Human Rights and the Laws of War: The Geneva Conventions of 1949', 104).

[58] UK Foreign and Commonwealth Office, 'Letter from M. Reed, Law Officers' Dept., to Kemball, Foreign Office, "Question of the Application of the Red Cross Conventions to Civil War"' (1949). See also Hitchcock, 'Human Rights and the Laws of War: The Geneva Conventions of 1949', 104–5; Mantilla, 'Conforming Instrumentalists: Why the USA and the United Kingdom Joined the 1949 Geneva Conventions', 502.

[59] UK Foreign and Commonwealth Office, 'Letter from M. Reed, Law Officers' Dept., to Kemball, Foreign Office, "Question of the Application of the Red Cross Conventions to Civil War"'.

[60] See Best, *War and Law since 1945*, 173.

[61] See Reynolds, 'Great Britain', in Reynolds (ed.) *The Origins of the Cold War in Europe*, 86–7.

instructions in late May, enabling the UK to support the French proposal of 15 June.[62]

A number of factors contributed to this shift. First, while the British had anticipated 'trouble with the "idealist" countries such as Mexico and others like France who had been occupied in the recent war', Soviet and satellite participation appears to have challenged British pre-conference planning.[63] In short, while the UK may have assumed it would have been able to wield outsize influence at Geneva as a great power in partnership with the USA, Soviet participation and the accompanying shift in political dynamics at Geneva forced the British to recalibrate their position to take into account Soviet bloc as well as the expected 'idealist' humanitarianism.

The extent and manner of the British shift in position evidently reflected not only a shift in the political balance of power at the conference, but also slow-dawning recognition that British arguments in respect of internal armed conflict were proving ineffective. A key difficulty was that the delegation's instructions placed the British well outside mainstream opinion at the diplomatic conference. This challenge was then compounded by the ill-chosen, legalistic tactics the British adopted to expose the difficulties and contradictions in the Stockholm texts and other 'humanitarian' proposals, compounded by belated British recognition of the value of engaging with the delegations of 'smaller' states.[64]

These difficulties ultimately led to the delegation's effective isolation in a context where there was significant support for a progressive agenda to regime revision.[65] In other words, it was not enough for the UK to have

[62] On UK and French choreography here, see Mantilla, 'Forum Isolation: Social Opprobrium and the Origins of the International Law of Internal Conflict', 337–8; Mantilla, 'Under (Social) Pressure: The Historical Regulation of Internal Armed Conflicts through International Law', 147–50.

[63] UK Foreign and Commonwealth Office, 'Alexander to Kemball (Excerpt)' (1949). Cited in: Nabulsi, *Traditions of War*, 15, at note 41. See also UK Foreign and Commonwealth Office, 'FO Minute by Mr Alexander: Geneva Convention-Protection of War Victims. Draft Letter from Mr. Kemball to Mr. W. H. Gardner, War Office, Enclosing Copy of Sir R. Craigie's Final Report on the Geneva Conference on the Protection of War Victims' (1949), paras. 16, 17 (in appended final report). See also discussion in: Best, *War and Law since 1945*, 87.

[64] See discussion in Nabulsi, *Traditions of War*, 13–14.

[65] See UK Foreign and Commonwealth Office, 'Notes of 11th Meeting of the United Kingdom Delegation' (1949). Also Best, 'Making the Geneva Conventions of 1949: The View from Whitehall', 11–14. ('This is what our masters call "going against the stream".') (UK Foreign and Commonwealth Office, 'Alexander to Kemball (Excerpt)' (1949).) See more generally: Mantilla, 'Forum Isolation: Social Opprobrium and the Origins of the International Law of Internal Conflict', 334–6.

good technical arguments or to present these as a great power: rather, it became apparent that, to be effective, any arguments would have to be expressed in principled terms, consistent with the progressive, humanitarian Zeitgeist of the meeting.[66] The shift in UK position was also evidently affected by the unwelcome prospect of being publicly cast as anti-humanitarian, with criticism of British positions (including with respect to the regulation of civil war) emerging in UK and international media.[67] As Best observes: 'not only Pravda and its echoes but a wide band of merely "liberal" newspapers had already begun to roast the UK for its forbidding and intransigeant stance'.[68]

In terms of causal factors and mechanisms, the UK's status as an (erstwhile) great power availed it relatively little in negotiations over the regulation of internal armed conflict. Indeed, even when aligned with France and with US support after 15 June, the prospects for adoption of the UK's by then preferred drafting option remained uncertain until the final debate in plenary. In short, from the British perspective, reliance on great power status – and, more bluntly, on sheer weight of delegation numbers – was far from sufficient to bring about a more palatable final result in respect of internal armed conflict regulation.[69]

Given this last, it is tempting to view the UK experience in 1949 as indicating potential limitations of the Realist hypothesis. At the same time, though, British policymakers were themselves pre-occupied post-1945 with combating (arguably well-founded) perceptions of the UK as a declining, imperial power. Accordingly, the British experience could equally be viewed as reflecting the weakened status by 1949 of a United

[66] As one senior British official noted: 'is there not probably some modicum of truth in what Sir R. Craigie describes as the "reaction of the conference to our attitude" that the UK is influenced by conservative legalism and is indifferent to, and indeed is opposing, the efforts of others to effect amendments and extensions to international law?' (quoted in Best, 'Making the Geneva Conventions of 1949: The View from Whitehall', 14).

[67] See Mantilla, 'Forum Isolation: Social Opprobrium and the Origins of the International Law of Internal Conflict', 334.

[68] Best, 'Making the Geneva Conventions of 1949: The View from Whitehall', 14–15. See also Best, *War and Law since 1945*, 111.

[69] The UK had by some distance the largest national delegation at the 1949 conference (19 individuals). The next largest were the Netherlands with 14 members, Italy with 13, and the USSR with 12. The US, Swedish, and French delegations each had 9 members. Rounding out the P5, China's delegation had 6 members. Of the 59 delegations participating, the average had between 4 and 5 members. (See Diplomatic Conference for the Establishment of International Conventions for the Protection of Victims of War. *Final Record*, Vol. I, 158–72.)

Kingdom that was no longer able to exert the same degree of influence over global affairs it had in the pre-war period.

The British experience does, however, appear to present a clear illustration of the operation of the Rationalist hypothesis. Indeed, both the initial British preference to remove regulation of civil war from the revised Conventions, and the subsequent recalibration of preferences, supporting the French proposal once it became evident that initial British objectives were exceedingly unlikely to be realised, appear to have been made consistently with this hypothesis, relying in both instances on reasoned weighing up of pros and cons. An important element in this recalibration, moreover, which was absent from the earlier internal Whitehall debates, was recognition that not only were British legalist tactics proving unhelpful to the advancement of the delegation's interests, but also that the dominant 'humanitarian' discourse in Geneva meant that positions predicated – as the UK's was – on the protection of traditionally 'sovereign' prerogatives were likely to receive fairly short shrift in debate.[70] Put differently, the British belatedly realised the importance of framing arguments around the humanitarian principles and values prevalent at Geneva. Sensitivity to negative media portrayals of UK conduct during negotiations also points to the operation of distinctly 'liberal' considerations, reflecting policy-makers' concerns about preserving the UK's liberal-democratic credentials amongst both international and domestic audiences.

The above account suggests that the UK lent support to the French proposal not out of a significant shift in underlying convictions, but rather because initial British tactics in respect of civil war regulation had failed, and the conceivable alternatives were likely to be more demanding of governments in internal armed conflict. Indeed, this support ultimately extended not only to lobbying the US and Commonwealth governments in favour of the French language, but also to resisting last-minute Burmese pressure to push for the deletion of language regulating civil war.[71] In short, as the head of the British

[70] As acknowledged by the head of delegation in contemplating this shift: 'We all feel that it will be necessary to abandon any formula specifically leaving the decision in this matter to the Sovereign Power, and to seek rather some formula which, while not dotting the I's, would in fact leave the last word to the Sovereign Power' (UK Foreign and Commonwealth Office, 'Letter from R. Craigie to H. A. Caccia, enc. "Memorandum on developments in the Conference on the subject of the application of the Conventions to Civil War"' (1949) cited in Mantilla, 'Forum Isolation: Social Opprobrium and the Origins of the International Law of Internal Conflict', 336).

[71] Indeed, once the conference was over, Whitehall appears to have come round rapidly to a broadly supportive position in respect of Common Article 3. As noted post facto by one

delegation put it post facto: '[w]hile the United Kingdom delegation would still have preferred such deletion it was clear that only a "*texte de conciliation*" would command any majority and the Delegation lobbied for the Joint Committee text both to defeat the possible reinstatement of the Stockholm text and also to defeat a new Soviet text . . . [which] would virtually have reinstated the Stockholm text'.[72]

3.3.1.2 The United States

While there was a relatively high degree of co-ordination between the UK and the USA, both in the run-up to and during the 1949 conference, the USA took a less conservative approach than the UK at Geneva.[73] In particular, although the US approach was also in some respects 'legalistic', the USA was significantly more at ease than the UK with the prospect of including internal armed conflict within the ambit of revised Conventions, as well as with ICRC leadership of the revision exercise.[74]

In particular contrast to the UK, the American starting point was that serious internal armed conflicts should be covered in any revised Conventions.[75] This view was tempered, however: the initial US preference was that 'the conventions should be applied to those internal conflicts which constitute war under international law' – understood to require reciprocal application of the Conventions by government and

of the UK delegation lawyers: '[t]he appearance of an article of this kind in an international Convention . . . is an innovation which, it is submitted, is in accordance with the general trend of international law' (Gutteridge, 'The Geneva Conventions of 1949', 301). This echoes a similar sentiment expressed by then Foreign Minister Ernest Bevin in November 1949: 'No doubt any civilized State would wish to conform to these humanitarian provisions in any event and there is therefore little fear that the provisions might jeopardize State security by encouraging subversive elements' (UK Cabinet Office, 'Memorandum by the Secretary of State for Foreign Affairs, Ministerial Committee for the Revision of the Geneva Conventions on War Victims' (1949) at p. 11, para. 21, cited in Mantilla, 'Conforming Instrumentalists: Why the USA and the United Kingdom Joined the 1949 Geneva Conventions', 505).

72 UK Foreign and Commonwealth Office, 'FO Minute by Mr Alexander: Geneva Convention-Protection of War Victims. Draft Letter from Mr. Kemball to Mr. W. H. Gardner, War Office, Enclosing Copy of Sir R. Craigie's Final Report on the Geneva Conference on the Protection of War Victims', 5 (in appended final report).

73 See Best, *War and Law since 1945*, 95.

74 See Barsalou, 'Making Humanitarian Law in the Cold: The Cold War, the United State and the Genesis of the Geneva Conventions of 1949', 16–18. As Steinacher observes, the US government 'was willing to work with any international Red Cross body as long a results were achieved' (*Humanitarians at War: The Red Cross in the Shadow of the Holocaust*, 193). See also: Best, *War and Law since 1945*, 91.

75 Yingling and Ginnane, 'The Geneva Conventions of 1949', 395.

insurgent forces.[76] The Americans were thus dissatisfied with the end result of the Stockholm meeting, though less so than the British.[77]

Nevertheless, while the USA was not necessarily amongst the most progressive voices at Geneva, the Americans remained concerned to ensure that internal armed conflicts of a serious magnitude fell within the ambit of the revised Conventions, adopting a pragmatic approach as to how this was achieved. Thus, in the event, the Americans were willing to depart from the traditional principles of belligerent recognition to support the French proposal, agreeing, for example, to have determinations as to whether a conflict qualified as a 'genuine' civil war made on a factual basis, without requiring recognition of belligerency by a de jure government.[78]

The pragmatism demonstrated by the USA in respect of internal armed conflict echoed the degree of flexibility granted by Washington, DC to the US delegation more generally at Geneva.[79] By adopting this approach, moreover, the US delegation appears to have been more successful than the UK in maintaining productive relationships with other delegations at the conference. This flexibility also reflects the relatively relaxed view taken by the USA of ICRC participation at the conference and stewardship of the revision process, as well as relatively close (compared to the UK) US engagement in the latter.[80]

The pragmatic US attitude may also have been due to developments in great power politics and the nascent Cold War. The USA was very

[76] Yingling and Ginnane, 'The Geneva Conventions of 1949', 395; McCahon, 'Toward Revision of the Geneva Convention', 465. See also Mantilla, 'Conforming Instrumentalists: Why the USA and the United Kingdom Joined the 1949 Geneva Conventions', 494.

[77] Yingling and Ginnane, 'The Geneva Conventions of 1949', 396. According to one contemporaneous US report: 'The drafts of the three revised conventions represent a considerable improvement over the ones which they are intended to replace ... The new texts are ... based on practical and realistic considerations while at the same time retaining the basic humanitarian objectives on which the first Geneva convention was founded' (McCahon, 'Revision and Extension of the Geneva Conventions', 340).

[78] See e.g. discussion at: Diplomatic Conference for the Establishment of International Conventions for the Protection of Victims of War, *Final Record*, Vol. II (Section B), 12.

[79] See discussions in Best, *War and Law since 1945*, 100; Barsalou, 'Making Humanitarian Law in the Cold: The Cold War, the United State and the Genesis of the Geneva Conventions of 1949', 19–21.

[80] As noted above, the American Red Cross had been working with the US Departments of State, War, Navy, Justice and the Interior since 1945 on possible revisions to international humanitarian treaties. See discussion and references in Barsalou, 'Making Humanitarian Law in the Cold: The Cold War, the United State and the Genesis of the Geneva Conventions of 1949', 10–14.

concerned, for example, to ensure Soviet participation in the Geneva Conference, both to lend credibility to the meeting's outputs, and to ensure Soviet support for appropriate protection of POWs – with an eye to future US–Soviet conflict.[81] As Crossland observes, 'unlike the British, the United States' approach to the 1949 conference was shaped by a wider fear of the Soviet Union and the need to draft a Convention that would be acceptable to Moscow, thus adding stability to the post-war order'.[82]

The progressive 'humanitarianism' espoused by many of the delegations present, including the USSR and satellites, but also Scandinavian delegations and Mexico, may also have enabled the US delegation to make a virtue of necessity in embracing an agenda for which there was significant support amongst both allies and opponents.[83] At the same time, however, US policymakers – much more clearly than their British counterparts – viewed participation at Geneva through a broader lens in which 'the laws of war were integrated into a broader scheme aimed at defending Western values and international law against the spread of Communist ideology'.[84]

In short, as with the UK, US preferences and behaviour in respect of the regulation of internal armed conflict appear to have reflected an assessment of the costs and benefits of different options, consistent with the Rationalist hypothesis, with the USA prepared to take a pragmatic view in respect of civil war regulation (and other areas) to facilitate cross-bloc consensus. Reflecting this more pragmatic attitude, moreover, the American delegation showed greater awareness of and sensitivity to the social dynamics of the diplomatic conference than the British, including a readiness to accommodate the preferences of less powerful states and the prevailing humanitarian Zeitgeist, consistent with the expectations of the Logic of Argument hypothesis.[85] The

[81] Best, *War and Law since 1945*, 91; Steinacher, *Humanitarians at War: The Red Cross in the Shadow of the Holocaust*, 193.

[82] Crossland, *Britain and the International Committee of the Red Cross, 1939–1945*, 245 at note 9.

[83] Best, *War and Law since 1945*, 91.

[84] Barsalou, 'Making Humanitarian Law in the Cold: The Cold War, the United State and the Genesis of the Geneva Conventions of 1949', 15. See also Best, *War and Law since 1945*, 111. In contrast, British policymakers were more preoccupied with maintaining British status as a great power – vis à vis both the USA and the Soviet Union. (See Deighton, 'Britain and the Cold War, 1945–1955'.)

[85] As observed by Albert Clattenburg, Chairman of the US delegation to the 1947 meeting of government experts, and later a member of the US delegation at Geneva: '[t]o the weaker nations, to the members of the armed forces, to populations in areas likely to be overrun by hostile troops, the humanitarian conventions represent a sort of insurance policy. They

relatively close relationship between the US government and the American Red Cross and the willingness of the former to work with the ICRC, also appear to have facilitated a relatively constructive, trusting relationship between the US delegation and the ICRC. This bolstered ICRC credibility and authority in American eyes, suggesting that the ICRC was relatively well placed to leverage discursive and decisional power vis à vis the USA (and certainly more so than in respect of the UK), consistent with the Agent Characteristics hypothesis.[86]

Its status as a nascent superpower, however, also clearly benefited the USA in achieving its aims, consistent with the Realist hypothesis, and again in contrast to the British experience. Put simply, like the USSR, the USA was able to rely on its recognised power primacy to ensure a degree of support for its positions – to an extent which outstripped the ability of the UK to enlist even traditionally aligned Commonwealth governments in support of its positions. The Canadian delegation, for example, was more closely aligned with the USA than the UK going into the diplomatic conference.[87] Similarly, Latin American delegations were largely expected to follow the American lead, though such fidelity could not be taken for granted: the US delegation was clearly concerned about 'the development of some unreliability, amounting to a sort of indiscipline' amongst its southern neighbours on occasion.[88] That said, though, Scandinavian states evidently also demonstrated a strong degree of sympathy with Soviet humanitarianism, suggesting that – unlike the Soviet Union in relation to its satellite delegations – the USA could not rely on its allies to follow its lead blindly. Rather, to maintain leadership of the Western bloc at Geneva, the USA was required to balance reliance on its regional material hegemony with rhetorical and discursive flexibility.[89]

hope not to collect on it but it helps allay fears. The negotiation of such agreements has become part of the normal pattern of behaviour of governments' (US Department of State, 'Albert Clattenburg Jr., Chairman of the American Delegation, to the Secretary of State' (1947), cited in Barsalou, 'Making Humanitarian Law in the Cold: The Cold War, the United State and the Genesis of the Geneva Conventions of 1949', 17).

[86] As Steinacher puts it: '[t]rust and cooperation between Red Cross and government officials were thus critical, and the support of the United States for the humanitarian project would prove decisive' (*Humanitarians at War: The Red Cross in the Shadow of the Holocaust,* 191).

[87] Best, *War and Law since 1945*, 95.

[88] Best refers also to the US delegation feeling 'some indignation when they (the Latin Americans) were not with it at important junctures' (*War and Law since 1945,* 96; citing inter alia US Department of State, 'Albert Clattenburg Jr., Chairman of the American Delegation, to the Secretary of State').

[89] Best, *War and Law since 1945*, 96.

3.3.1.3 France

France played a distinctive balancing role at Geneva: clearly part of the Western bloc, but at the same time singularly anxious to ensure Soviet attendance at Geneva and participation in the final agreements. Moreover, while notionally a great power – and with similar post-war status concerns to the British – France also had first-hand experience of occupation during the war and was a newly 'liberated' country – an experience shared with the Soviet Union, nationalist China and Western European allies.[90]

Most generally, the desire to ensure both Soviet and American participation reflected a strong French preference to maintain dialogue with and avoid antagonising the Soviet Union whilst maintaining alignment with the USA.[91] This in turn reflected a post-war French ambition to pursue a role as a mediator between the superpowers, even while being drawn into the North Atlantic alliance. The end result was to render ensuring Soviet participation and endorsement 'a hallmark of the French approach' at Geneva.[92]

At the same time, France also had its own preferences entering into negotiations. France shared with other formerly occupied countries a concern to accord POW protections to captured partisans, reflecting wartime experience and discussions with prominent civil society groups, as well as the presence of former *résistants* in government.[93] In similar fashion to the British, French preferences in respect of internal armed conflict also reflected concerns about colonial embroilments: by 1949

[90] As expressed by French President Vincent Auriol in December 1947: 'Does one believe that France is a pygmy between two colossi? No. The country which listens to the voice of wisdom and humanity is not a pygmy' (quoted in Young, *France, the Cold War and the Western Alliance, 1944–49: French Foreign Policy and Post-War Europe*, 155). Note also though, Georges Bidault's private admission earlier that year that: 'I am only too well aware that France is a defeated country . . . and our dream of restoring her power and glory at this juncture seems far from reality' (Caffery', The Ambassador in France (Caffery) to the Secretary of State', 154, quoted in Hitchcock, *France Restored: Cold War Diplomacy and the Quest for Leadership in Europe, 1944–1954*, 72). See also discussion in Mantilla, 'Forum Isolation: Social Opprobrium and the Origins of the International Law of Internal Conflict', 327–8.

[91] See Soutou, 'France' in Reynolds (ed.), *The Origins of the Cold War in Europe*, 105, 107.

[92] Best, *War and Law since 1945*, 89.

[93] Nabulsi, *Traditions of War*, 14. As Mantilla observes: '[t]he voice of the 'Liberated' resonated strongly in Geneva, not least because former resistors now sat in positions of power, including in the French team studying revisions to the law' (Mantilla, 'The Origins and Evolution of the 1949 Geneva Conventions and the 1977 Additional Protocols', 41).

France had lost possessions in Syria and Lebanon, was fighting a colonial war in Indo-China, and decision-makers were starting to think about 'how to avoid running into similar trouble in North Africa'.[94]

Like the UK, France accordingly had a significant stake in ensuring that treaty provisions regulating internal armed conflict would be workable. In contrast to the British, however, the French appear to have been far more attuned to the 'humanitarian' atmosphere at Geneva, while also conscious of the need for reworked Conventions to be legally sound and practicable, as well as acceptable to the Soviet bloc.[95]

Like the UK, the French saw a host of difficulties associated with including the regulation of internal armed conflict within revised treaties, and accordingly initially sought (albeit more subtly than the British) an 'attenuated' form of wording.[96] Over time, though, the French delegation – in common with, and indeed working alongside, the British, came to appreciate the meagre prospects of these ambitions being realised. In consequence, like the British, the French delegation sought fresh instructions.

Notice of the sought change of policy was subsequently received in early June revised instructions indicating that the delegation should seek 'to apply as broadly as possible [in civil wars] the humanitarian principles which lay at the basis of the Universal Declaration of Human Rights and the Genocide Convention recently approved by the United Nations. These principles are precisely the same as those that appear on the Preamble of the Convention on Civilians and which, it is desired, should

[94] Best, *War and Law since 1945*, 172.

[95] Van Dijk highlights the impact on French legal attitudes of '[t]he experience of total defeat and brutal counterinsurgency as an occupied country, combined with the dominant influence of human rights thinking in debates among the former victims of war on its preparatory commission' ('Human Rights in War: On the Entangled Foundations of the 1949 Geneva Conventions', 570).

[96] Ministère des Affaires étrangères, '"La question de la guerre civile": A. Lamarle, French Head Delegate, to Robert Schuman, Minister of Foreign Affairs in Paris' (1949); cited in Mantilla, 'Forum Isolation: Social Opprobrium and the Origins of the International Law of Internal Conflict', 337. A UK note of a pre-conference conversation with Albert Lamarle of the French delegation records that '[t]he French do not wish to take the lead in the matter [of civil war] but if we propose deletion of the appropriate clause they will support us generally and propose a compromise. M. Lamarle added that if they were defeated on their compromise they would gladly accept complete deletion. The compromise would take the form of adding sufficiently widely drawn exceptions to the clause to make it largely inapplicable' (UK Foreign and Commonwealth Office, 'United Kingdom Delegation Circular No. 11 – Diplomatic Conference on Protection of War Victims (appending "record of conversations held in Paris between the Deputy Leader of the French Delegation and Mr. Strutt and Mr. Alexander")' (1949) 2).

be extended to the other Conventions.' The humanitarian tone suggests that the French specialists recognised much more clearly than their British counterparts the benefits of framing arguments around the prevailing humanitarian Zeitgeist of the negotiations, consistent with the Logic of Argument hypothesis. The revised French instructions also recognised the advantages of this strategy, however, in terms of not 'having to apply the precise text of the Conventions' in internal armed conflicts.[97]

In short, the French position in respect of internal armed conflict can again be viewed as eminently rational, reflecting concerns about perceptions of France as a declining colonial power, and leveraging French technical expertise and moral authority accordingly. At the same time, French positioning in respect of this issue, as elsewhere, appears to have been closely attuned to superpower preferences and so reflective of the Realist hypothesis, with the French distinctly aware of the need to arrive at forms of wording that would satisfy both the USA and the USSR, as well as of the value of couching their proposal in humanitarian terms, aligned with 1948's Universal Declaration.

The French delegation's 'social' advantages over the British at Geneva were arguably also key in enabling the former to exert greater influence over proceedings than the latter. Alone amongst the Western great powers, France had first-hand experience of 'being invaded, occupied, exploited, imprisoned, interned and deported', lending the French delegation a degree of moral authority at Geneva that was not available to the UK or the USA.[98]

The presence of the widely respected French legal academic Paul de Geouffre de La Pradelle in Monaco's delegation may also have enabled Monégasque presence and participation to function as

[97] Ministère des Affaires étrangères, 'Note "Conventions de Genève en cas de guerre civile" sent by Ministry of Foreign Affairs, International Organizations Direction, to French Delegation in Geneva' (1949), quoted in Mantilla, 'Forum Isolation: Social Opprobrium and the Origins of the International Law of Internal Conflict', 338. As van Dijk observes, '[i]n French eyes, there was no necessary contradiction between promoting human rights on the international stage and protecting colonial sovereignty' ('Human Rights in War: On the Entangled Foundations of the 1949 Geneva Conventions', 577).

[98] Best, *War and Law since 1945*, 88. As Mantilla observes: '[t]he power of the Liberated countries lay not only in their ability to find allies/sympathizers and wield numerical majorities (although this seemed to be a necessary condition). The firsthand testimony they brought to the table relied on extraordinary moral authority that was hard for their more powerful peers to brush off completely' ('The Origins and Evolution of the 1949 Geneva Conventions and the 1977 Additional Protocols', 41).

a 'force multiplier' for French influence, adding further technical as well as moral authority.[99] As such, whilst adopting a position that was similarly rational, given background material and social circumstances, it is perhaps unsurprising that the French delegation was better positioned and more able than the UK to act as an effective norm entrepreneur in eliciting positive responses from interlocutors.[100]

3.3.2 The Soviet Union

The 1949 negotiations took place as the Cold War entered a deep freeze: the Truman Doctrine had been set out in March 1947, primarily out of concern over Soviet interference in Greece and Turkey; the Soviet Union had declined Marshall Aid in July 1947; the Berlin Airlift had commenced in mid-1948 (to run until May 1949); and April 1949 saw the signing of the North Atlantic Treaty. Soviet–ICRC relations were also in an extremely poor state following the end of the Second World War, with Soviet authorities continuing to cast the ICRC as a bourgeois, if not fascist, organisation.[101] The Soviet Union had, moreover, not been particularly active in League circles, nor had it sent delegates to any of the preparatory sessions since 1946. Indeed, Soviet intentions with respect to attendance at Geneva in 1949 were evidently unknown until the Soviet

99 Indeed, in an internal delegation note of 9 May 1949, Mr Alexander of the UK delegation referred to the 'Greater Powers (including Monaco)' (UK Foreign and Commonwealth Office, 'United Kingdom Delegation Circular No. 24 – Liaison with Other Delegations' (1949)). As Best notes, 'Monaco mattered partly because *he* [de Geouffre de La Pradelle] mattered . . . he was a weighty spokesman for that most persistent of pressure-groups, the International Committee of Military Medicine and Pharmacy, from which, based in Monaco before the war, had flowed a stream of humanitarian proposals' (*War and Law since 1945*, 97).

100 Best refers to Albert Lamarle, deputy head of delegation, as effecting a 'French revolution', overcoming 'legal niceties' in the negotiation of Common Article 2 (*War and Law since 1945*, 177–8). Underlining M. Lamarle's humanitarian (and 'Liberated') credentials, Fritz Kalshoven (commenting on Lamarle's role in developing a later abandoned preamble for the draft Civilians Convention) recalls that he: 'was told by René-Jean Wilhelm, who was already with the ICRC at the time of the Stockholm Conference, one of the French delegates, Mr Albert Lamarle, at the time of the Second World War had been involved with the resistance in France. That experience and his ensuing interest in human rights may well have prompted his proposing a text which clearly reflected the ideas on human rights that were being developed at the time' (Kalshoven, 'The Undertaking to Respect and Ensure Respect in All Circumstances: From Tiny Seed to Ripening Fruit', 17, at note 42).

101 Best, *War and Law since 1945*, 83.

delegation turned up, all but unannounced – and accompanied by satellite delegations – at the opening of the conference.[102]

Given the prominent role of the Soviet Union in the post-1945 world, there was general support for Soviet participation at Geneva in 1949 to ensure that any conference outputs would have the broadest possible base of support and legitimacy.[103] This was a particular source of concern for American and French negotiators. Soviet views of the draft Conventions were, however, all but unknown at the start of the conference: commentators and observers in other delegations had been able to do little more than infer from statements by Soviet-allied delegations during the preparatory meetings.[104]

That said, once the conference got underway, observers were struck by the progressive 'humanitarian' approach adopted by the Soviets[105] – including with respect to what was to become Common Article 3. Some Western delegations initially struggled to make sense of this approach given that, as a great power with overseas involvements, the Soviet Union might have been expected to adopt a realpolitik-based approach.[106] Over the course of the conference, however, it became apparent that the Soviet Union had adopted an anti-colonialist, nominally pro-peace, progressive humanitarian agenda to engender support amongst the developing-world beneficiaries of decolonisation, and to require the Western powers to defend morally problematic positions, including in respect of internal armed conflict.[107] As one

[102] Best, *War and Law since 1945*, 85; Mantilla, 'Forum Isolation: Social Opprobrium and the Origins of the International Law of Internal Conflict', 332; Steinacher, *Humanitarians at War: The Red Cross in the Shadow of the Holocaust*, 226–7.

[103] Best, *War and Law since 1945*, 87, 109–10. As Barsalou observes, 'the Soviet absence from the negotiating table at the two previous conferences of 1947 and 1948 greatly increased, in the opinion of U.S. legal advisors, Soviet bargaining power at the Geneva conference of 1949 "by putting a premium on their mere attendance and sharpening up the necessity of their concurrence in the final drafts"' ('Making Humanitarian Law in the Cold: The Cold War, the United State and the Genesis of the Geneva Conventions of 1949', 24, quoting US Department of State, 'Albert Clattenburg Jr., Chairman of the American Delegation, to the Secretary of State', 11).

[104] Best, *War and Law since 1945*, 85–6.

[105] Ibid., 109–10. Also Mantilla, 'The Protagonism of the USSR and Socialist States in the Revision of International Humanitarian Law'.

[106] See e.g. Canadian observations cited in: Best, *War and Law since 1945*, 110. The Americans appear to have anticipated the likely 'humanitarian' Soviet tack rather better than the French or British. Ultimately, however, this proved of little assistance in combating this gambit. See Barsalou, 'Making Humanitarian Law in the Cold: The Cold War, the United State and the Genesis of the Geneva Conventions of 1949', 24.

[107] See also responses to Soviet attempts at the diplomatic conference to prohibit the use of nuclear weapons, discussed in: F. Bugnion, 'The International Committee of the Red

commentator has put it, '[m]eeting the Soviet bloc's well-contrived humanitarian offensive put the US and UK on the defensive and in a dilemma', in particular as the Western allies had a strong interest in ensuring that the Soviets did not simply walk out of the Geneva talks.[108]

Soviet support for a robust form of Common Article 3 at Geneva is accordingly best explained as a rational manoeuvre, of a piece with similar behaviour elsewhere during proceedings at Geneva, and reflecting (Realist) Soviet dominance of its bloc. This approach may have been attractive in part as it increased the likelihood of Western states endorsing provisions that might later prove disadvantageous in armed conflict. More fundamentally, though, this agenda appears to have been designed to embarrass and marginalise the Western allies, and to bolster Soviet great power status and moral credibility internationally, by making the former appear fundamentally *illiberal*: 'highlighting the inconsistency between their professed liberal-democratic worldview and their conservative stance toward progressive international law'.[109]

Given Soviet approaches in this and comparable instances to treaty drafting and observance, there was evidently also little concern on the part of Soviet negotiators about potential domestic costs of translating rhetoric into practice – consistent with the Regime Type hypothesis.[110] Accordingly, the Soviet position may be understood as reflecting a set of

Cross and Nuclear Weapons: From Hiroshima to the Dawn of the 21st Century', 515–16. Also: Best, *War and Law since 1945*, 110–14; Steinacher, *Humanitarians at War: The Red Cross in the Shadow of the Holocaust*, 226–7. For another example of Soviet positioning vis à vis decolonisation, see e.g. Soviet arguments with respect to 'improved public health for Africa through immediate de-colonization' in Osakwe, *The Participation of the Soviet Union in Universal International Organizations: A Political and Legal Analysis of Soviet Strategies and Aspirations Inside ILO, Unesco and WHO*, 117. More generally, as Mantilla observes, 'even before the decolonized world gained sufficient strength of its own (after 1955), the USSR used anticolonial rhetoric to pillory European powers and with them the broader liberal democratic West in an international propaganda war for "hearts and minds"' ('Forum Isolation: Social Opprobrium and the Origins of the International Law of Internal Conflict', 329, citing Roberts, *The Contentious History of the International Bill of Human Rights*). See also Mantilla, 'The Protagonism of the USSR and Socialist States in the Revision of International Humanitarian Law', *Journal of the History of International Law* 21 (2019), 181–211, p. 185, 187–188.

108 Best, *War and Law since 1945*, 111.

109 Mantilla, 'The Origins and Evolution of the 1949 Geneva Conventions and the 1977 Additional Protocols', 42–3, citing Gaiduk, *Divided Together: The United States and the Soviet Union in the United Nations, 1945–1965*; see also Mantilla, 'Forum Isolation: Social Opprobrium and the Origins of the International Law of Internal Conflict', 327–8.

110 Indeed, as John Simon, UK Attorney-General, observed at the time, the Soviets had 'taken pretty good care (that in the Eastern bloc) . . . civil war could never occur' (UK Foreign and Commonwealth Office, 'Letter from M. Reed, Law Officers' Dept., to

rational considerations, enabled by an authoritarian domestic regime. That said, it is particularly important to note the manner in which Soviet behaviour at Geneva also affected the prevalent humanitarian discourse in negotiations, including in respect of internal armed, ensuring that – consistent with the Logic of Argument hypothesis – any proposals emanating from the West would need to be framed in suitably progressive, 'humanitarian' terms to have a chance of broader endorsement.

3.3.3 *Other National Delegations*

To a large extent, support for (and concern about) Common Article 3 ran along pre-decolonisation Cold War and regional lines. That is to say, Western European, Latin American and Antipodean views largely – though not always or entirely – reflected the views put forward by the USA, the UK and France.[111] Greece was perhaps the most vocal such delegation, opposing the inclusion of Common Article 3 against the background of the 1946 to October 1949 civil war.[112] The Netherlands, however, did not evince particular concerns about the regulation of civil war, despite being a colonial power.[113]

The Mexican and Scandinavian delegations took rather more progressive positions regarding civil war (and more generally). The Scandinavians were potentially motivated by home-grown (or Swedish-inspired) 'League-ist' humanitarianism and/or by Soviet proximity, while

Kemball, Foreign Office, "Question of the Application of the Red Cross Conventions to Civil War"', quoted in: Best, *War and Law since 1945*, 173). See also Diplomatic Conference for the Establishment of International Conventions for the Protection of Victims of War, *Final Record* Vol. II (Section B), 14). More generally, see also the discussion of Soviet rhetoric and practice with respect to the 1972 Convention on the Prohibition of the Development, Production and Stockpiling of Bacteriological (Biological) and Toxin Weapons and on Their Destruction in Feldbrugge, Van den Berg and Simons, *Encyclopedia of Soviet Law*, 345.

111 Illustrating the degree of fluidity involved, the UK delegation at one point observed that the New Zealand position in respect of civil war was 'obviously coloured by recent Indonesian history . . . [and consequently] was fixed broadly on humanitarian grounds' (UK Foreign and Commonwealth Office, 'Civilian Convention – Note of an interview with the New Zealand Delegate', 2).

112 See International Committee of the Red Cross, *Seventeenth International Red Cross Conference, Stockholm, August 1948: Report*, 71–2. Diplomatic Conference for the Establishment of International Conventions for the Protection of Victims of War, *Final Record*, Vol. II (Section B), 10–11, 16.

113 By 1949 the post-war Netherlands government were, however, under significant political pressure to come to a negotiated settlement in their principal colony. See van Dijk, 'The American Political Intervention in the Conflict in the Dutch East Indies 1945–1949'.

Mexico was to stick to a doggedly neutral position throughout the Cold War. However, there is little on record to suggest that the views of these delegations proved especially influential in the drafting of Common Article 3, save possibly to temper US views somewhat and with respect to technical drafting interventions.

In similar fashion, Eastern European views reflected Soviet preferences, though with fewer outliers. As to other significant geostrategic players, China was represented at Geneva by the nationalist Republic of China, whose delegates, despite being heavily embroiled in a losing civil war, did not feature significantly in the negotiations over Common Article 3; there was no German state capable of attending until May 1949, and Japan remained under US occupation.

Large clusters of African and Asian delegates remained mute during these negotiations. It has been suggested that the newly independent India may have adopted a pro-Soviet line out of fear of Soviet intervention in that state.[114] Equally, though, other newly independent Commonwealth states, notably including Pakistan, adhered more closely to mainstream Western positions.

There was, however, one prominent dissenting Asian voice during the proceedings: General Oung of Burma, which had also just gained its independence from the UK, but which, unlike India and Pakistan, did not join the Commonwealth. The Burmese government was, indeed, in a difficult position domestically in 1949, facing Karen and communist insurgencies which had broken out immediately on independence in 1948. Nevertheless, General Oung was not altogether without support: eleven other delegations joined in voting against the inclusion of Common Article 3 in the final text. The final vote was held anonymously at Oung's request, to avoid causing embarrassment to his 'friends': he was evidently understood, though, as speaking on Common Article 3 not just for Burma but for 'Eastern' and 'Asiatic' states generally.[115]

While the great powers and their respective allies argued about the optimal content of what was to become Common Article 3, General Oung objected to the inclusion of internal armed conflict within the scope of the Conventions at all. The gist of his argument, nicely capturing the centrality of both Realist factors and of the Logic of Argument hypothesis to the drafting of Common Article 3, was that requiring

[114] Best, *War and Law since 1945*, 96.

[115] See Diplomatic Conference for the Establishment of International Conventions for the Protection of Victims of War, *Final Record*, Vol. II (Section B), 78, 102, 337.

governments to conduct themselves domestically in a particular fashion was essentially an affront to sovereignty, and that the provision of conventional protections to insurgents would encourage insurgency.[116] As Best observes, Oung was essentially observing that: '[t]he bigger, older States had taken great pains ... to exclude from the Conventions all human rights recognitions that might endanger their security during international wars. Why ... should smaller, newer States be put to security risks during internal wars?'[117]

In the event, General Oung's concerns were marginalised, out of step with the humanitarian Zeitgeist of the conference and overlooked as the Western great powers squabbled with the Soviet Union and its allies, seeking to demonstrate humanitarian concern without tying their hands too tightly in future conflicts. As Chapter 4 demonstrates, however, General Oung's views nevertheless foreshadowed many of the concerns that shaped the 1977 Additional Protocols.

3.3.4 The ICRC

Though notionally government-convened, the 1949 conference was largely a creature of the ICRC.[118] The Committee was, moreover, by some margin the most prominent civil society body contributing to the negotiations and, as discussed in Chapter 2, had a longstanding ambition, dating from before 1939, to extend humanitarian protection in civil wars.[119] Consequently, its role in the drafting of Common Article 3 merits particular examination.

Perhaps most importantly, ICRC support appears to have been critical in enabling the conference as a whole to adopt the French compromise: in particular, the ICRC's humanitarian 'blessing' for the eventual

116 See e.g. on 28 July: '[i]f you adopt [Common Article 3] you will not only be embarrassing the *de jure* government, but you will also seriously endanger its sovereignty, as you will be taking away from it its own legal machinery to maintain the security of its population and the prosperity of its State' (Diplomatic Conference for the Establishment of International Conventions for the Protection of Victims of War, *Final Record,* Vol. II (Section B), 329).

117 Best, *War and Law since 1945*, 175.

118 Rey-Schyrr, for example, portrays Jean Pictet of the Committee as the 'chief architect of the 1949 Conventions' (*From Yalta to Dien Bien Phu: The History of the International Committee of the Red Cross 1945 to 1955,* 214, at note 15).

119 See Best, *War and Law since 1945*, 168–9. On the evolution in the run-up to the 1949 conference of the ICRC's approach to the regulation of internal armed conflict (including Pictet's awareness of colonial sensitivities), see van Dijk, 'Human Rights in War: On the Entangled Foundations of the 1949 Geneva Conventions', 567–70.

compromise appears to have been a distinct factor in its adoption. The ICRC also opened the debate on Common Article 3, framing this primarily as a matter of bringing 'into conformity' the wording of the four draft Conventions.[120] Committee representatives were also asked by delegates to comment on proposed wording on several occasions during the debates over Common Article 3, the Committee providing the last word in a number of instances. Indeed, the ultimately adopted French proposal was the only form of wording regulating internal armed conflicts – other than its own post-Stockholm drafting – that the ICRC supported.

The manner in which the ICRC shaped debates and outcomes at Geneva, including in respect of Common Article 3 – 'simultaneously assess[ing] and shap[ing] the attitudes of key actors toward ideas for new law' – suggests that it acted as an effective norm entrepreneur in this regard.[121] Indeed, consistent with the implications of the Agent Characteristics hypothesis, the ICRC's expert authority in respect of the Conventions appears to have been critical to this role. In fairness, this was not always explicitly recognised – though the conference record contains in some places extensive tributes to the ICRC's activities and contributions to the drafting process, the extent to which these were genuine may be debated.[122]

There was, however, evidently widespread respect for the ICRC's technical expertise. While critical of the Committee in a number of respects, for example, Albert Clattenburg of the US delegation 'remained impressed by the excellent work of the international committee in preparing the drafts of the new conventions'.[123] In similar fashion, even the British and (at least publicly) Soviet delegations appear to have found little to complain about in the ICRC's stewardship of the debates over the drafting of Common Article 3. Taken together, this suggests that in the course of these debates the ICRC was indeed

120 Diplomatic Conference for the Establishment of International Conventions for the Protection of Victims of War, *Final Record*, Vol. II (Section B), 10.

121 Mantilla, 'The Origins and Evolution of the 1949 Geneva Conventions and the 1977 Additional Protocols', 38. As Best notes, the Committee 'retained practical control over the shaping process through the new Conventions' three years' development. It persisted in using its own judgment and pressing for its own ideas, without necessarily consulting States beforehand' (*War and Law since 1945*, 93).

122 See e.g. Diplomatic Conference for the Establishment of International Conventions for the Protection of Victims of War, *Final Record*, Vol. II (Section B), 515–18.

123 Cited in: Steinacher, *Humanitarians at War: The Red Cross in the Shadow of the Holocaust*, 228.

viewed generally as 'more the expert drafting secretariat than the vociferous advocate prepared to duel publicly with states to the final day of a diplomatic conference'.[124]

The Committee itself was also evidently aware that its wartime record had done it few favours in the eyes of the Allied powers, compounding the longstanding friction between the 'bourgeois' Committee and Soviet authorities as well as rendering its bona fides suspect in the UK and at least open to question in the USA. In consequence, rather than attempting to rely on moral authority (an area where the ICRC was impaired in the eyes of a significant number of state interlocutors) to promote its agenda at Geneva, the Committee appears instead to have viewed the process of treaty revision in part as a means to rebuild its battered credibility and leadership of the Red Cross movement after a problematic, bruising wartime experience.[125]

In short, recourse to the Committee's technical expertise in humanitarian law provided a valuable opportunity to improve its reputation in the eyes of key governments and emphasise its ongoing relevance.[126] Adopting the role of a politically neutral, expert broker at Geneva also provided the ICRC with a chance to improve its relationships with the major powers, the Committee recognising

124 Forsythe, *The Humanitarians: The International Committee of the Red Cross*, 261.

125 See e.g. discussions in: Junod, *The Imperiled Red Cross and the Palestine–Eretz-Yisrael Conflict, 1945–1952: The Influence of Institutional Concerns on a Humanitarian Operation*, 13–49; Steinacher, *Humanitarians at War: The Red Cross in the Shadow of the Holocaust*, 84–136, 190–233. The ICRC's wartime experience is the subject of an extensive literature in its own right. The ICRC moreover, recognised how critical 'moral support' was to its ability to function: 'The International Committee may not command material power. Its work is based on an act of faith. It depends above all on the moral support of the invisible legions' (P. Ruegger, 'Radio Address' (1948), quoted in Steinacher, *Humanitarians at War: The Red Cross in the Shadow of the Holocaust*, 215).

126 A sense of the centrality of the post-war treaty revision process to the ICRC can be gleaned from a 1948 Foreign Affairs article by Max Huber: 'Ever since 1864, the International Committee of the Red Cross has felt that it had the duty, in conjunction with national Red Cross Societies and, whenever possible, with governmental experts, to put forward proposals for the improvement of existing international conventions and the conclusion of new agreements on matters not sufficiently covered or not covered at all; and it submits carefully considered drafts of such agreements' (Huber, 'The Principles of the Red Cross', 726). Rey-Schyrr's account of the ICRC's creation of a dedicated legal division in the run-up to the conference, with staff working full-time on the process of revising the 1929 Conventions (alongside the ICRC's report on its wartime activities), similarly suggests that the Committee viewed this exercise as critical to its future prospects (*From Yalta to Dien Bien Phu: The History of the International Committee of the Red Cross 1945 to 1955*, 214).

early on – consistent with the Realist hypothesis – that without the participation of the 'Big Five' the revision exercise 'would have little chance of success'.[127]

From this perspective, the ICRC appears to have played its cards well at Geneva, including in respect of the regulation of internal armed conflict.[128] An ICRC member even acknowledged post facto that: 'the Committee was aware from the outset of the work that the original text, even in the Stockholm wording, had no chance of being adopted'.[129] If this position was indeed 'merely a tactical negotiating maneuver',[130] then it only underlines the extent to which the ICRC was alive to the opportunity afforded by the conference to rebuild its battered wartime credibility.[131] This endeavour was, moreover, evidently largely successful, with commentators characterising the Geneva conference as variously a 'big success for the ICRC and its standing in the world', as well as 'both a decided victory over its critics, and something of a surprise, given the Committee's impossible and unhappy position after attacks made on its inaction with regard to the concentration camps'.[132]

[127] Rey-Schyrr, *From Yalta to Dien Bien Phu: The History of the International Committee of the Red Cross 1945 to 1955*, 216.

[128] This is not to say, however, that there was anything preordained about this outcome. As observed by Mantilla, citing confidential internal ICRC records, even the Committee representatives at the Geneva conference had occasion to doubt the prospects of this particular endeavour ('Under (Social) Pressure: The Historical Regulation of Internal Armed Conflicts through International Law', 158). In similar vein, Robert Heinsch laconically notes that: '[w]hen the ICRC presented its ideas on the extension of the scope of application at the Stockholm Conference, it might have not completely taken into account all the political and practical aspects which were then occupying various subcommittees in 1949' ('The International Committee of the Red Cross and the Geneva Conventions of 1949', 43).

[129] Diplomatic Conference for the Establishment of International Conventions for the Protection of Victims of War, *Final Record*, Vol. II (Section B), 336–7.

[130] Elder, 'The Historical Background of Common Article 3 of the Geneva Convention of 1949', 51, note 40.

[131] See Bugnion, 'The Geneva Conventions of 12 August 1949: From the 1949 Diplomatic Conference to the Dawn of the New Millennium', 43. ('With the diplomatic conference, the ICRC's international standing was, to a large extent, restored ... the new Conventions recognized its special status as a neutral intermediary and entrusted it with new tasks for the protection of war victims – a major success indeed, by any reckoning.')

[132] Steinacher, *Humanitarians at War: The Red Cross in the Shadow of the Holocaust*, 234; Moorehead, *Dunant's Dream: War, Switzerland and the History of the Red Cross*, 559, quoted in *Humanitarians at War: The Red Cross in the Shadow of the Holocaust*, 234.

3.4 Explaining Common Article 3

3.4.1 Great Power Preferences

> 'The preferences of great powers are likely to be especially significant in shaping the civil war regime.' (The Realist hypothesis)

Both the preparation for and the conduct of the diplomatic conference were strongly shaped by relations amongst and the preferences of great powers, set against the backdrop of the onset of the Cold War. The importance ascribed by the ICRC to the participation of the 'Big Five' in the revision process is testament to the extent to which it was understood that, to be credible, any revised regime would require great power support. There was also widespread awareness of this necessity amongst governments and their delegations at Geneva – with French anxiety over Soviet attendance particularly marked.

The Cold War, and more specifically US, UK, French and Soviet preferences, also closely shaped conference outcomes more broadly insofar as the conference was to an extent a contest between the 'humanitarian' Soviet bloc and more 'realistic' Western states. This tendency was perhaps most obviously seen in the debate over nuclear weapons, though the debates over Common Article 3 can also be viewed through this lens. Indeed, while the French decision to put forward compromise wording clearly reflected specific concerns about the conduct of colonial conflicts, this initiative was also consistent with France's immediate post-war foreign policy positioning as an inter-bloc arbitrator and concern to ensure Soviet 'buy-in' to any revised treaties.

Material power differentials also help make sense of other aspects of the negotiation of Common Article 3. It is difficult to imagine, for example, an absence of instructions to the Burmese delegation as being sufficient to effect a pause in negotiations. When the Soviet delegation was afflicted by this difficulty, however, the other members of the special committee showed remarkable deference. Equally, not all great powers were equally influential at Geneva: whereas the USA and the Soviet Union dominated their respective blocs, the British experience underlines the extent to which great power status alone was insufficient to materially influence negotiations, even in respect of strongly held preferences.

Moreover, viewing Common Article 3 solely through the lens of great power preferences risks underestimating the extent to which great power views were themselves shaped by the preferences of less powerful states. If the UK delegation was initially dismissive of the contribution of 'small countries' to negotiations, for example, it became apparent over time to the British that delegations from materially less powerful states mattered.[133] Both the USA and the UK came to recognise that 'small delegations' (including those from Mexico and Scandinavian states) could not be ignored with impunity, or taken for granted, indicating frustration at different points with the conduct of their erstwhile allies at Geneva. The French similarly came to share British concerns about the prospect of isolation in respect of civil war regulation, while the Soviet approach was itself reflective of a desire to appeal to the 'hearts and minds' of the newly decolonised. Small country delegations also played influential roles in debates, particularly where they possessed specific technical expertise: Monaco provides one such example in respect of debates over Common Article 3. General Oung's prominence in debate is also testament to the extent to which the voice of smaller delegations could not be ignored.

It is reasonable to view great power politics, and above all the nascent Cold War, as having framed the diplomatic conference, and accordingly to have been an important consideration in the genesis and eventual adoption of the French proposal. In view of the contributions of non-great power delegations to proceedings, however, and the mixed record of great power delegations themselves in advancing their preferred agendas at Geneva, Common Article 3 cannot be attributed entirely to great power preferences. In other words, while there was doubtless a great deal of sensitivity to great power preferences throughout proceedings, the views of the great powers alone were not determinative. Other factors, therefore, must be taken into account in explaining the drafting of Common Article 3.

3.4.2 Rationalist Considerations

> 'The more intrusive or restrictive any proposed set of civil war-regulating treaty provisions, the less likely they are to be supported by governments in the course of treaty negotiations, especially where governments are engaged in or foresee a possibility of a civil war or insurgency. The end of a civil war or insurgency may, however, make a government more likely to support such provisions.' (The Rationalist hypothesis)

[133] See UK Foreign and Commonwealth Office, 'W E Beckett (Foreign Office) to J A C Gutteridge (Delegation to the Conference on War Victims)' (1949); referenced in Nabulsi, *Traditions of War*, 14. And subsequently: UK Foreign and Commonwealth Office, 'United Kingdom Delegation Circular No. 24 – Liaison with Other Delegations' (1949). ('The idea is that we should make a concerted and special effort to get to know the members of these small Delegations.')

It is tempting to view Common Article 3 as simply the least (rationally) problematic option available to delegations collectively at the diplomatic conference in respect of internal armed conflict. The drafting makes minimal demands of governments, yet was a sufficiently progressive step to enable participants to claim a reputation-enhancing humanitarian 'victory'. Certainly, of all the drafting suggestions put forward, the eventual wording adopted was intrusive and restrictive to a relatively minimal degree, albeit more intrusive and restrictive than anything which had gone before: indeed, Common Article 3 provides few tangible benefits to insurrectionists and only a minimal opening to the ICRC. Nevertheless, the final wording does not shed a great deal of light on why it was rational for governments collectively to adopt such a provision in the first place.

The negotiating history indicates that the final wording was not arrived at through a mechanistic balancing of security-related or other strategic or tactical preferences (let alone interests) amongst the various delegations involved.[134] It is true, certainly, that a number of delegations considered any regulation of civil wars to be undesirable owing to security-related considerations. Burma, Greece and the UK could be said to fall into that category given ongoing insurgencies in Burma and the remaining colonial possessions of the UK, and a full-blown civil war in Greece. French preferences would also place them close to, if not in, this category. Accordingly, the first part of this hypothesis appears largely to be borne out with respect to the initial positions of these delegations.

Such considerations appear to have been less critical for other delegations, however, including those of colonial states such as Portugal and the Netherlands, who evidently played little part in the negotiation of Common Article 3.[135] Despite British views to the contrary, moreover, uprisings may also not have been entirely inconceivable in the Soviet bloc

[134] As Mantilla puts it: '[r]ationalist bargaining mechanisms such as side payments and issue linkages might be posited, yet these explanations find no support in the archival evidence' ('Forum Isolation: Social Opprobrium and the Origins of the International Law of Internal Conflict', 340–1).

[135] The Dutch did not participate closely in the debates over Common Article 3, although the 1949 conference coincided with the aftermath of the December 1948 'police action' in Java and Sumatra, by which point the Netherlands government had 'just about lost the battle for what the world was learning to call Indonesia' (Best, *War and Law since 1945*, 172). It bears noting, however, that in contrast to the British and French experiences, Dutch conduct in Indonesia had caused the USA to intervene politically in support of a negotiated settlement, with the prospect of withdrawal of Marshall Plan aid as a potential sanction. (See discussion in van Dijk, 'The American Political Intervention in the Conflict in the Dutch East Indies 1945–1949', 88–90.)

in 1949: Czechoslovakia had only recently been brought into Moscow's orbit; the Berlin airlift continued until May 1949; and the Hungarian uprising lay only a few years in the future. Even if the anticipated costs of provision support (and subsequent treaty adherence) may not – particularly from a Soviet perspective – have extended to compliance in inconvenient circumstances, it is nevertheless reasonable to conclude that evidence in support of the first part of the Rationalist hypothesis is mixed.

Support for the regulation of internal armed conflict may, of course, have been perceived as a relatively costless humanitarian gesture by a number of governments. Just as Soviet foreign policy utilised humanitarianism as a rhetorical gambit to be overlooked in practice where inconvenient, so the USA may have had little to lose from such regulation, given the minimal risk of armed insurrection in its immediate neighbourhood. Likewise, stable, established democracies such as the Scandinavian states and Switzerland also had little reason to fear the prospect of civil war in their own territories.

There is little to suggest, moreover, that underlying French or British preferences changed in the course of negotiations. Rather, these delegations appear to have come round to supporting the relatively undemanding French proposal only once it became clear that the question before the conference had become that of 'how' rather than 'whether' to regulate civil wars in revised Conventions. The British and French can accordingly be viewed as having responded rationally to an inability to secure higher-ranked preferences for no or discretionary regulation, compounded by concerns that it would look bad for the democratic war-time Allies to publicly show themselves resistant to principled humanitarianism (especially once the Soviet bloc had picked up the humanitarian gauntlet), by electing to put forward a progressive, but ultimately relatively undemanding, form of words.

This observation merely begs a further question, though. Even if Common Article 3 was adopted by some as a humanitarian fig leaf, why were so many delegations – including those of France and the UK, but also other states involved in or potentially facing internal armed conflict – ready to entertain the adoption of such a fig leaf in the first place?

3.4.3 Agent Characteristics

'The greater their perceived moral authority and their ability to leverage subject area expertise, the more likely governments and non-state actors are to be able to elicit the support of other governments for demanding civil war-regulating provisions in the course of treaty negotiations.' (The Agent Characteristics hypothesis)

One possible answer to the question just posed is that governments were persuaded to countenance such regulation by other governments or civil society.[136] The prominent roles of the ICRC, League and legal experts in the debates leading up to and at the 1949 conference, moreover, lend support to the view that non-coercive norm entrepreneurship was central to the inclusion of Common Article 3 in the revised Conventions.

The ICRC provides the most prominent example of civil society norm entrepreneurship at and prior to the Geneva meeting. In the aftermath of the Second World War, the ICRC's moral authority in the eyes of key states was severely weakened: poor relations with the Soviet Union persisted, while relations with the Western allies were also in many cases problematic. The ICRC reinforced its leading position in the Red Cross movement at Stockholm in 1948, however, and managed the preparation of texts for the 1949 Conference, burnishing its technical expertise and bolstering its position as the principal agent for the 'progressive development' of international humanitarian law. The ICRC then utilised its technical expertise to reinforce its frayed moral authority in the eyes of many governments, including intervening with both technical and principled arguments in the debates over Common Article 3. The role of the ICRC in the development of Common Article 3 is particularly evident in the manner in which the Committee's imprimatur effectively sealed the conclusion of the special committee debate in favour of the French proposal.

That said, technical expertise alone appears to have been insufficient in a number of instances to persuade other delegations of the merits of a case where moral credibility was perceived to be lacking. Soviet interventions in connection with atomic weapons provide one potential such example, though the ineffectiveness of undoubted UK legal expertise in persuading other delegations of the merits of the initial British position on internal armed conflict stands out in respect of Common Article 3. At the same time, the Burmese experience – with a sole delegate evidently accepted as speaking on behalf of 'the Asiatic countries' – suggests that broadly perceived moral authority alone was similarly insufficient to

[136] This is not to say, it should be underlined, that the targets of such normative entrepreneurship need necessarily have internalised the positions advocated. (See discussion in Chapter 1, Section 1.4.3.1.)

enable delegations to make a significant impression on the outcome of proceedings.

More generally, delegations where technical expertise was coupled with widely recognised moral authority appear to have been relatively well placed to be influential at the Geneva negotiations. France's status as a formerly occupied state, for example, appears to have lent the French delegation at the conference a degree of moral authority in the eyes of the delegates of other 'liberated' states that was simply not available to the other members of the 'Big Five'.[137] It seems doubtful, for example, whether the proposal of 15 June would have been so well received had it been seen to emanate from the UK rather than France.

That said, while great power status may also have lent the French greater 'voice' at the conference than delegations from less powerful states, perceived moral authority and technical expertise could also combine to engender influence even in the absence of material power. Monaco provides an interesting example in this respect, having made significant contributions to the process of negotiating Common Article 3 with a delegation led by a widely respected, technically expert international lawyer, and a foreign policy bound by treaty to align with that of France but no obvious ulterior motive.[138] In contrast, in the eyes of other participants – particularly those representing newly independent states – the bona fides of the colonial states and the American (and likely also Soviet) superpowers would appear to have been more suspect, and their persuasiveness limited accordingly.[139]

3.4.4 *Arguing on the Record*

'Governments will be more likely to support the adoption of civil war-regulating provisions in treaty negotiations when strong, coherent arguments

[137] As noted by the British post facto, 'the countries of Scandinavia and Western Europe, from which support of commonsense solutions would normally be expected, were still under the influence of the horrors experienced under the German occupation' (UK Foreign and Commonwealth Office, 'FO Minute by Mr. Alexander: Geneva Convention-Protection of War Victims. Draft Letter from Mr. Kemball to Mr. W. H. Gardner, War Office, Enclosing Copy of Sir R. Craigie's Final Report on the Geneva Conference on the Protection of War Victims', 3 in attached report).

[138] See British description of Monaco as a 'Greater Power' at note 99. More generally, and presumably rather to British chagrin, as Best observes, there was no correlation between the sizes of delegations at the diplomatic conference and their degree of influence (*War and Law since 1945*, 101).

[139] See discussion at: Best, *War and Law since 1945*, 175.

premised on widely shared values and principles are made in support.' (The Logic of Argument hypothesis)

One of the more striking aspects of the conference proceedings is that, with very few exceptions, delegations appear to have preferred to present arguments which would be publicly palatable to other delegations (and possibly also the historical record generally) and, in the case of Western delegations, domestic opinion. More particularly, delegations vastly preferred to put forward arguments which would be understood and appreciated as strong and principled by other conference participants. This tendency appears, moreover, to have contributed significantly to shaping both the debate around and the final form of Common Article 3.[140]

In general terms, the final record in relation to Common Article 3 consists almost entirely of principled arguments, commonly contrasting conservative 'sovereignty-related' concerns with (prevalent) more progressive 'humanitarian' positions. Moreover, few delegations seem to have been ready to entirely abjure the latter: all delegations involved, including General Oung, paid at least lip service to the importance of promoting humanitarian principles in internal armed conflict.[141]

These tendencies placed certain delegations in a more difficult position than others. With respect to the UK delegation, for example, whereas in Whitehall the practical and principled undesirability of regulating internal armed conflicts in revised treaties was largely taken as given, in Geneva such views were broadly regarded as humanitarian heresy.[142]

140 Indeed, as Mantilla notes: ' . . . none of the sponsoring delegations in the 1940s made instrumental arguments to sponsor [Common Article 3] . . . when instrumental claims were made it was against [Common Article 3] as designed (i.e., without conditions of application) and even those arguments failed' ('Forum Isolation: Social Opprobrium and the Origins of the International Law of Internal Conflict', 340–1).

141 See e.g. General Oung in Diplomatic Conference for the Establishment of International Conventions for the Protection of Victims of War, *Final Record*, Vol. II (Section B), 329: 'no Government of an independent country can, or will ever, be inhuman or cruel in its actions towards its own nationals'.

142 As put by delegation head Sir Robert Craigie in his post-conference report: 'For want of a better term, I have used the adjective "humanitarian" to describe this element in the Conference which persistently took an unrealistic view of what was practicable in time of war and which was exploited by the false humanitarianism of the Iron Curtain countries . . . the Delegation found itself constantly at odds with a foolish idealism' (UK Foreign and Commonwealth Office, 'FO Minute by Mr Alexander: Geneva Convention-Protection of War Victims. Draft Letter from Mr. Kemball to Mr. W. H. Gardner, War Office, Enclosing Copy of Sir R. Craigie's Final Report on the Geneva Conference on the Protection of War Victims', 5). The French were evidently similarly afflicted at times – see e.g. Diplomatic Conference for the Establishment of International Conventions for the Protection of Victims of War, *Final Record*, Vol. II

The UK and, where aligned, other delegations such as those of Australia and the USA, were thus effectively restricted to making arguments based on points of law (which were themselves debatable), or on the practical difficulties of applying any revised Conventions in civil wars.[143] The classic position – that governments had the right to deal with traitors as they saw fit – was conspicuous by its absence: while a principled argument, this view appears to have failed to gain traction principally because it did not sufficiently reflect the dominant humanitarian principles more widely espoused at Geneva.

Rather, the appeal to humanitarian principles with respect to Common Article 3 appears to have been effective largely because it echoed progressive sentiments that were in the ascendancy in the West and in the nascent United Nations system more generally – the humanitarian Zeitgeist of the negotiations. A further factor was that the Soviet bloc set out here, as in other instances at Geneva, to hoist Western delegations with their own rhetorical petard.[144] With the shadow of the Second World War hanging over proceedings, the main Nuremberg Trials having ended only a few years previously, the Universal Declaration of Human Rights and Genocide Convention having been adopted by the UN General Assembly the previous year, and Control Council trials ongoing, the British government – for one – appears to have recognised that it would be in a difficult position domestically and internationally if the UK was seen to be acting inconsistently with the high-sounding principles espoused during and following the war.[145] Against this background, and particularly with the Soviet Union and satellites taking a robust 'humanitarian' line, appeals to states' prerogatives, even where these reflected genuinely principled preferences, were likely to gain relatively little on-the-record support from other delegations.

(Section B), 12–13. ('Mr. LAMARLE (France) wished firstly to dispel a misunderstanding which appeared to have occurred as a result of his remarks on the previous day . . . He had not thought for one moment of placing the State above humanitarian laws, but on the contrary, of conceiving the State as the servant of these laws and of, the common rights.')

143 As Best puts it: 'Whitehall had to argue, and sometimes lost' ('Making the Geneva Conventions of 1949: The View from Whitehall', 11).

144 See e.g. Boyd van Dijk's exposition of the extent to which 'human rights thinking' influenced deliberations at Geneva, including in the drafting of Common Article 3 ('Human Rights in War: On the Entangled Foundations of the 1949 Geneva Conventions').

145 See note 67.

Such dissonance between rhetorically acceptable discourse and real government preferences may have also contributed significantly to making the French proposal so attractive not only to the British, but also to many of the other delegations who were quick to evince support. Indeed, although more substantive obligations have been read into Common Article 3 in the decades since its drafting, the Final Record does not indicate that the proposed wording was thought to impose terribly onerous restrictions.[146] Rather, as noted above, part of its attractiveness was that the drafting allowed delegations to claim to have made significant humanitarian progress, while satisfying many of the qualms of less enthusiastic governments. In other words, Common Article 3 was rhetorically satisfying, but reassuringly undemanding.

Indeed, the wording of Common Article 3 – as the 'humanitarian' emphasis of the French instructions of 4 June suggests – seems to have been designed to be difficult to criticise from a principled, humanitarian point of view, eliciting (for example) an initially muted Soviet response.[147] Armed with the French proposal, not to mention the ICRC's imprimatur, more conservative delegations were thus put in a rather stronger position than previously – rhetorically speaking, at least. This allowed them to face down the eventual Soviet counterproposal without appearing overly lacking in progressive sentiment.

Common Article 3 cannot be explained entirely by the rhetorical context in which it was drafted: the Cold War environment, rationally held government preferences and the extent to which governments were collectively and individually susceptible to persuasion by norm entrepreneurs are also likely to have played a role. Nevertheless, the negotiation of Common Article 3 in the public eye through a discursive process based on commonly shared principles and values seems highly likely to have contributed to the readiness of so many delegations to accede to the inclusion of Common Article 3 in the revised Conventions – underlying 'real' preferences notwithstanding.

[146] See e.g. *Prosecutor v. Duško Tadić aka 'Dule'*, For an indication of sentiment at the time, see e.g. UK views cited at notes 70 and 71.

[147] The British noted – with apparent chagrin – that owing in part to domestic politics, the French delegation had 'found itself pushed into the "humanitarian camp"' (UK Foreign and Commonwealth Office, 'FO Minute by Mr Alexander: Geneva Convention-Protection of War Victims. Draft Letter from Mr. Kemball to Mr. W. H. Gardner, War Office, Enclosing Copy of Sir R. Craigie's Final Report on the Geneva Conference on the Protection of War Victims', 8).

3.4.5 *What about Democracy?*

'Democracies are more likely to support intrusive, restrictive civil war-regulating provisions than non-democracies.' (The Regime Type hypothesis)

Aspects of the Regime Type hypothesis are supported by the negotiation of Common Article 3 – particularly the sensitivity of Western, democratic delegations to being publicly cast as 'un-humanitarian'. This can be seen, for example, in US awareness of the risk of being portrayed in this fashion by the Soviet delegation, more starkly in UK concern at being 'roasted' in 'merely liberal' newspapers, and in the French desire to present their June compromise proposal as reflecting principled 'humanitarian' concerns rather than simple political advantage.

That said, what stands out more generally about the negotiation of Common Article 3 in respect of the Regime Type hypothesis is that the most vocal proponents of robust civil war regulation at Geneva were not democracies, but the delegations of authoritarian Soviet bloc states. Democracies, on the other hand, most prominently the UK, had persistent reservations about too robust a set of provisions.

The above discussion suggests, of course, little commitment on the part of the Soviet bloc to the humanitarian principles its delegations so enthusiastically espoused. Rather, the progressive Soviet stance in the context of internal armed conflict regulation appears to have been used as a ploy to bolster support from post-colonial communities and governments, while embarrassing and scoring rhetorical points against liberal Western governments. Given the greater likelihood of civil unrest in the latter and their colonial outposts than in the Soviet sphere, and the potentially limited impact of international legal commitments on Soviet behaviour in any case, this stance presumably appeared to Moscow to be all but cost-free.[148] In contrast, the reluctance of Western democracies such as the UK and France to embrace a radically progressive form of civil war regulation appears to have been informed by concerns over actually having to live up to any commitments. Delegations of such states may thus have had good reason to tread rather more carefully than non-democracies in this

[148] The logic here reflects that set out in Hollyer and Rosendorff, 'Why Do Authoritarian Regimes Sign the Convention against Torture? Signaling, Domestic Politics and Non-Compliance'. (This is sometimes termed the 'Bad Ass Theory' of human rights treaty ratification: Voeten, 'The Bad Ass Theory of Why Dictators Sign the Convention against Torture'; J. Vreeland, 'Dictatorships, Torture, and Human Rights Treaties: The Bad Ass Theory'.)

regard, especially when a failure to evince sufficient humanitarian enthusiasm may have been rhetorically problematic.

The Regime Type hypothesis – as drafted – has not been borne out in the drafting of Common Article 3. The case does show, though, that there were important differences in the considerations driving democratic and authoritarian state behaviour. Even if these did not result in the behaviour that might be expected, this nevertheless suggests that it is likely to be instructive to consider further the relevance of this hypothesis and underlying assumptions in other, comparable contexts.

3.5 Aftermath

The conclusion of the Geneva conference was a key milestone in re-establishing the ICRC's post-war pre-eminence in the Red Cross movement and as the leading international humanitarian actor, as well as consolidating its continuing 'guardianship' of international humanitarian law.[149] Common Article 3 also constituted a considerable success for the Committee – realising its longstanding post-1936 concern to extend IHL's ambit to civil wars, accompanied by recognition of the ICRC's right of initiative in such conflicts.

The Conventions were also ratified in relatively short order by states, commencing with Switzerland in March 1950, swiftly followed by Monaco, Liechtenstein, Chile and India the same year. France ratified the Conventions in 1951, the Soviet Union in 1954, the USA in 1955, and the UK in 1957, though Myanmar held out until 1992. In total, of the 196 current states parties, 72 had ratified the four Conventions within a decade of the 1949 conference. Indeed, over time, participation in the 1949 Conventions appears to have become almost a signifier of statehood, with the dissolution of the Soviet Union and the collapse of Yugoslavia heralding a sudden upsurge in ratifications. Latvia, Slovenia, Turkmenistan, Kazakhstan, Croatia, Kyrgyzstan and Bosnia and Herzegovina all ratified in 1992, with a further swathe of newly independent states following suit in 1993. It bears underlining, moreover, that in all the years since 1949, not a single reservation has been entered in respect of Common Article 3.[150]

[149] See e.g. views in Steinacher, *Humanitarians at War: The Red Cross in the Shadow of the Holocaust*, at 235.

[150] Reservations provisionally entered by Argentina and Portugal on signature were not confirmed on ratification.

It would be a mistake, however, to deduce from this that Common Article 3 has been enthusiastically embraced by governments. The UK and France, for example, declined to implement Common Article 3 in early conflicts in Malaysia, Kenya, Cyprus and Algeria, in circumstances in which the application of this provision might have been thought reasonably appropriate. Similar difficulties were encountered in post-colonial contexts in the 1960s and subsequently, including in Aden, Congo, and Biafra.[151] Put more generally, it is probably fair to say that compliance with Common Article 3 has consistently disappointed.[152]

Indeed, these difficulties and limitations (amongst others) were evident to the ICRC fairly early on in the post-1949 life of Common Article 3 and the revised Conventions more generally. While the Committee convened a series of meetings and proposed a range of initiatives to more closely constrain the conduct of internal armed conflict over the course of the 1950s and 1960s, it took an initiative from outside the ICRC – principally debates around the 1968 Tehran Conference on Human Rights – to prompt the ICRC and states to commence the discussions that eventually led to the two Additional Protocols of 1977.[153]

Conclusion

Common Article 3 was adopted largely on the basis that 'Half a loaf is better than no bread.'[154] To quote Best: ' . . . it was unthinkable after so many years of seeking and so much humanitarian expectation to fail to

151 See discussions in e.g. Moir, *The Law of Internal Armed Conflict*, 67–82; Klose, *Human Rights in the Shadow of Colonial Violence: The Wars of Independence in Kenya and Algeria*; also several contributions in Evangelista and Tannenwald (eds.), *Do the Geneva Conventions Matter?*, including Mantilla, 'The Origins and Evolution of the 1949 Geneva Conventions and the 1977 Additional Protocols', 51–2; Drohan, *Brutality in an Age of Human Rights: Activism and Counterinsurgency at the End of the British Empire*, 12, 49, 108; Branche, 'The French Army and the Geneva Conventions during the Algerian War of Independence and After' ; Conway-Lanz, 'The Struggle to Fight a Humane War: The United States, the Korean War, and the 1949 Geneva Conventions'; Higgins, *The Approach of International Law to Wars of National Liberation*, 24–26.

152 Mantilla refers, for example, to a practice of 'conflict denial' owing to the (intentionally) indeterminate drafting of Common Article 3. 'Forum Isolation: Social Opprobrium and the Origins of the International Law of Internal Conflict', 342–3.

153 See generally Chapter 4. For an overview of these initiatives, see also Mantilla, 'The Origins and Evolution of the 1949 Geneva Conventions and the 1977 Additional Protocols', 49–55.

154 Plinio Bolla, Head, Swiss Delegation, in Diplomatic Conference for the Establishment of International Conventions for the Protection of Victims of War, *Final Record*, Vol. II (Section B), 335.

do something about civil wars; the new article had enough virtue and novelty in it to constitute a radical breakthrough; and, as has already been observed, the difficulties and problems that could still be found in the French version were nothing compared with those that had absolutely obstructed the road to compromise earlier on'.[155]

This statement belies the complexity of the considerations underlying the drafting of this provision. Indeed, while Mantilla is undoubtedly correct in highlighting the extent to which British and French behaviour represented a rational response to social pressure amid concerns of isolation at the conference, a range of material and social factors and mechanisms evidently had a bearing on the behaviour of these and other delegations and governments in negotiating Common Article 3.

Above all, the process of drafting Common Article 3 was overshadowed by the Cold War, to a large extent comprising negotiations between US- and USSR-led blocks. The latter stages of debate focused on delivering wording that would bridge the gaps between the stated goals and actual preferences of the blocs but that would also be satisfactory to unaligned stakeholders, including the ICRC. The governments of Western powers such as the UK, France, and the USA also appear to have been very aware of their vulnerability to charges of hypocrisy given the inconsistency between the liberal democratic principles espoused in the fight against the Axis and the illiberal measures applied to repress colonial independence movements. As such, it is perhaps unsurprising that the Soviet Union seized on this discursive weak point to discomfit Western delegations given the 'Bad Ass' approach of the former to international commitments.

Western governments also appear to have generally accepted the Stockholm drafts as legitimate starting points for discussion in relation to civil war regulation. Given sensitivity about being cast as unhumanitarian, as well as the drafts' international and Red Cross movement provenance, it would simply not have been acceptable to leave Geneva without *something* to show in regard to civil wars. Accordingly, as much as the UK was initially of the view that it would not be desirable to regulate civil wars, allied governments – including the USA and a number of continental European allies – evidently had different ideas. A fear of Soviet humanitarian-themed propaganda also affected UK decision-makers during the negotiations, to the point where the British retreated from their initial opposition to the regulation of civil war,

155 Best, *War and Law since 1945*, 177.

leaving General Oung to make this case. Even for governments largely sympathetic to the Burmese delegate's position, it was simply unacceptable to openly avow such views at Geneva.

More specifically with respect to the hypotheses set out above, given superpower dominance in a context shaped by the nascent Cold War, civil war regulation in the form of Common Article 3 appears to have resulted principally from the difficulties facing Western states in credibly and publicly countering a principled Soviet position which was largely consistent with the stated preferences of civil society as embodied in the League and ICRC. These difficulties forced Western delegations to make a rational choice to opt for a relatively low-cost humanitarian commitment, which the ICRC was prepared to endorse, and which Soviet-allied delegations were hard-pressed to oppose as insufficient.

While technical expertise and moral authority were relevant to the outcome, neither attribute appears to have alone been sufficient to make a significant impact on the course of debate (witness the UK and Burmese experiences). This was particularly the case where the views presented were not consistent with principled positions put forward by dominant, materially powerful states – in this case the USA and the USSR. Its technical expertise notwithstanding, the ICRC also appears to have utilised the treaty review process as a means of rebuilding its moral authority in the aftermath of the Second World War: it is thus difficult to portray Common Article 3 as having been brought about particularly owing to the ICRC's moral authority. Indeed, the ICRC's endorsement of the French compromise drafting could be viewed as simple recognition of political reality – though this is likely to be an over-simplistic view given that support for the ICRC vis à vis other Red Cross movement bodies and generally varied across delegations in the run-up to and at the 1949 conference.

The present chapter also illuminates particularly well the limitations of the Regime Type hypothesis with regard to the significance of domestic democratic governance in regime development, in the face of Hollyer and Rosendorff's 'Bad Ass' theory of non-democratic behaviour. Hollyer and Rosendorff observe that non-democratic governments can support otherwise demanding regimes with impunity, safe in the knowledge that they are unlikely to be called on to live up to their commitments. In contrast, democratic governments may be likely to tread more carefully before entering into demanding commitments, reflecting a countervailing concern at the rather more likely prospect of being expected to live up to their commitments.

The discussion also casts doubt on the likelihood of liberal states necessarily being willing to endorse a more robust regime: even if the classification of colonial states such as France, the Netherlands or the UK as 'liberal' could be questioned, the US delegation was notably far less progressively minded in this respect than its Soviet counterparts.[156] Rather, the analysis reflects Hathaway's finding in the context of human rights treaties that even in the absence of effective enforcement prospects, democracies with less than stellar records are likely to be more reluctant to make related treaty commitments than their non-democratic counterparts.[157]

Last, the discussion suggests an additional factor relevant to the design of Common Article 3: the extent to which the arguments presented were consistent with what might be termed the humanitarian Zeitgeist of negotiations. This is conceptually perhaps best understood as the international normative context in which negotiations are set and which delimits the bounds of rhetorical acceptability. It is difficult to imagine Common Article 3 – or like provision – emerging from a similar negotiation process in a different normative setting: i.e. without the distinctive international 'humanitarianism' of the immediate post-war context to function as a normative lodestone.

To an extent this concept is implicit in the fifth hypothesis, insofar as this normative 'superstructure' may be considered to form an element of the Habermasian lifeworld underpinning that proposition. At the same time, though, as Risse has acknowledged, a relatively thin lifeworld may be sufficient for a 'logic of argument' to operate.[158] Accordingly, the potential distinct relevance to drafting outcomes of the normative Zeitgeist will be borne in mind in the remaining case studies.

[156] See Slaughter's definition of a 'liberal democracy' in 'International Law in a World of Liberal States', 511.

[157] O. Hathaway, 'Why Do Countries Commit to Human Rights Treaties?'

[158] 'Habermas's theory is rather silent on the question of how much of a common lifeworld people need to share in order to communicate in a reasonable manner' (Risse, '"Let's Argue!": Communicative Action in World Politics', 14).

4

The Additional Protocols of 1977

'But the course is set for more law, and one can only hope that it may serve the cause of humanity.'[1]

Introduction

The 1949 Conventions were negotiated at a conference that spanned a matter of months. In contrast, it took four years of annual sessions – from 1974 to 1977 – to negotiate the two Additional Protocols that followed ('Protocol I' and 'Protocol II', respectively). Many of the measures adopted in these sessions remain controversial, moreover, with neither Protocol attracting the same level of support as their 1949 precursors.

This chapter sets out the background to the negotiations of these instruments and highlights critical turning points in the debates around key provisions relating to the regulation of internal armed conflict – principally Article 1(4) of Protocol I and Article 1 of Protocol II. The former requires states parties to treat 'wars of national liberation' as international armed conflicts for the purposes of that Protocol; the latter sets out the scope and threshold for the remainder of Protocol II, which applies to internal armed conflicts more generally. The chapter then considers the negotiation of these and related provisions from the perspectives of the principal actors involved: conservative and more progressive Western governments, the Soviet Union, delegations from non-aligned developing world governments including Egypt, India and Pakistan, and the ICRC, highlighting causal drivers and mechanisms associated with actor behaviour and negotiation outcomes. The chapter concludes with an assessment of the relevance to these drafting outcomes of the hypotheses set out in Chapter 1.

Once again, the discussion in the chapter largely vindicates the theoretical approach set out in Chapter 1. In this instance, the discussion

[1] Baxter, 'Humanitarian Law or Humanitarian Politics – The 1974 Diplomatic Conference on Humanitarian Law', 26.

highlights the salience of US and Western great power views to drafting outcomes, but also the constraints on the influence of these states when faced with mass opposition from developing world delegations, particularly with Soviet and some Western support. In a similar vein, while Protocol II can broadly be cast as reflecting Rationalist insights set against a 'rhetorically progressive' normative backdrop, Article 1(4) of Protocol I is more perplexing from the former perspective. Key drafting outcomes may also be attributed in part to the limited impact of Western and ICRC technical expertise (and impaired moral authority) in the eyes of developing world negotiating partners. Lastly, the discussion also identifies a potentially important limitation to the Regime Type hypothesis, developing world opposition to an extensive form of Protocol II pointing to (at least notional) support for the regulation of internal armed conflict being more closely related to the domestic prevalence of liberal values than to democratic governance per se.

4.1 Historical Background

4.1.1 Origins of the Treaty Revision Process

In contrast to its 1949 predecessor, the impetus for the 1974–7 diplomatic conference – the 'CDDH'[2] – originated outside the Red Cross movement. In particular, reflecting the increasing prominence in the (by now developing-world-dominated) United Nations system of concerns about the protection of 'human rights in armed conflict', the 1968 Tehran Conference on Human Rights can be seen in retrospect as setting 'the wheels rolling again for further development of jus in bello'.[3]

[2] This acronym, common across much of the commentary on the 1977 Protocols, reflects the French title of the diplomatic conference: the 'Conference diplomatique sur le droit humanitaire'.

[3] Forsythe, *Humanitarian Politics: The International Committee of the Red Cross*, 112. See also International Committee of the Red Cross, *Reaffirmation and Development of the Laws and Customs Applicable in Armed Conflicts, Report Prepared for the XXIst International Conference of the Red Cross, Istanbul, September 1969*, 19–30. Resolution XXIII of the Tehran conference requested the UN Secretary General to study the 'need for additional humanitarian international conventions or for possible revision of existing Conventions to ensure the better protection of civilians, prisoners and combatants in all armed conflicts and the prohibition and limitation of the use of certain methods and means of warfare' (United Nations, *Final Act of the International Conference on Human Rights, Tehran*, 13 May 1968). This resolution was in large part the work of Seán MacBride – briefly IRA Chief of Staff (1936), a member of the Irish Dáil (1947–58) and Irish Minister for External Affairs (1948–51). MacBride was also a founder member of Amnesty International and that organisation's international chairman between 1961 and

The Tehran conference took place amid increasingly strident discourse in the UN General Assembly and its committees on decolonisation and the 'rights of peoples to self-determination'.[4] This resulted in the adoption of a series of General Assembly resolutions and reports following the 1968 conference calling for greater attention to be paid to the protection of human rights in armed conflict generally, as well as to 'the need for protection of the rights of civilians and combatants in conflicts which arise from the struggles of peoples under colonial and foreign rule for liberation and self-determination'.[5] These developments gave rise to concern amongst the governments of more conservative Western powers that revision of the law of armed conflict under UN auspices might result in potentially radical shifts in this body of law, including in respect of internal armed conflicts. As in 1949, this raised the spectre of affording prisoner of war (POW) status to captured insurgents, as well as the risk of implicitly legitimising armed 'national liberation movements'. This was particularly discomfiting to governments then involved in conflicts with such groups, ranging from the UK

1974. In 1968 he was also Secretary General of the International Commission of Jurists and was heavily engaged in campaigning to improve the protection of human rights in armed conflict. (See discussion in: Suter, *An International Law of Guerrilla Warfare: The Global Politics of Law-Making*, 24–33.)

[4] See e.g. *Declaration on Principles of International Law concerning Friendly Relations and Co-operation among States in Accordance with the Charter of the United Nations, 24 October 1970* (Doc. A/RES/25/2625), available at: http://undocs.org/A/RES/2625 (XXV) [accessed 20 November 2018].

[5] UN General Assembly, *Respect for Human Rights in Armed Conflicts*, 16 December 1969 (Doc. A/RES/2597), available at: https://refworld.org/docid/3b00f1d34e.html [accessed 6 December 2018]. See also in similar vein: UN General Assembly, *Respect for Human Rights in Armed Conflicts*, 19 December 1968 (Doc. A/RES/2444), available at: https://refworld.org/docid/3b00f1d558.html [accessed 6 December 2018]; UN General Assembly, *Respect for Human Rights in Armed Conflicts*, 9 December 1970 (Doc. A/RES/2674), available at: https://refworld.org/docid/3b00f04954.html [accessed 6 December 2018]; UN General Assembly, *Respect for Human Rights in Armed Conflicts*, 20 December 1971 (Doc. A/RES/2852), available at: https://refworld.org/docid/3b00f1c010.html [accessed 6 December 2018]. Also associated Secretary General's reports: *Respect for Human Rights in Armed Conflicts: Report of the Secretary-General*, 20 November 1969, A/7720, available at: https://undocs.org/pdf?symbol=en/A/7720 [accessed 6 September 2019]; *Respect for Human Rights in Armed Conflicts: Report of the Secretary-General*, 18 September 1970, A/8052, available at: https://digitallibrary.un.org/record/647214 [accessed 6 September 2019]. Hans Longva of Norway and Georges Abi-Saab of Egypt, subsequently key participants in their national delegations at the CDDH, also participated in the preparation of these reports, informed by earlier ICRC reports. (See Mantilla, 'Under (Social) Pressure: The Historical Regulation of Internal Armed Conflicts through International Law', 228–9.)

in Northern Ireland, to Portuguese engagement in Angola, and US anxiety regarding Indochina.[6]

The ICRC, for its part, was also anxious to retain its traditional prerogative as the leading agent for the 'progressive development' of what was becoming known as international humanitarian law (IHL).[7] The Committee had earlier abandoned a short-lived 1950s initiative to enhance Common Article 3 on meeting robust opposition from both western governments – led by the USA – and the Soviet Union at the 1957 Red Cross Conference in New Delhi.[8] By the late 1960s, however, circumstances had shifted: spurred into action by the Tehran conference, the Committee was now encouraged to act by Western governments keen to steer discussions away from the United Nations to a 'more responsible and expert ICRC forum'.[9]

The Committee thus had both institutional incentives and a political tailwind in writing to UN Secretary General U Thant on 18 September 1968, observing that: 'the studies which the Secretary General is requested to undertake [following the Tehran Conference] concern a sphere very similar to that in which has [sic] been the

[6] As a contemporaneous British legal expert put it: 'The Western states seem to have been slow to appreciate that humanitarian law-making might afford a useful opportunity to offset military reverse and that human rights could be impressed for that purpose' (Draper, 'Humanitarian Law and Human Rights', 195; cited at Alexander, 'A Short History of International Humanitarian Law', 120). On the connections between decolonisation and human rights discourse, see Klose, *Human Rights in the Shadow of Colonial Violence: The Wars of Independence in Kenya and Algeria*, chapter 6, esp. 219–30.

[7] See Baxter, 'Humanitarian Law or Humanitarian Politics – The 1974 Diplomatic Conference on Humanitarian Law', 5–6; also Forsythe, *The Humanitarians: The International Committee of the Red Cross*, 261–2; Suter, *An International Law of Guerrilla Warfare: The Global Politics of Law-Making*, 105–9. On the origins of the term 'international humanitarian law', see Alexander, 'A Short History of International Humanitarian Law'.

[8] Bugnion refers to this initiative as being shut down by an 'unholy alliance'. 'Adoption of the Additional Protocols of 8 June 1977: A Milestone in the Development of International Humanitarian Law', 787. For more detail on this episode, see Suter, *An International Law of Guerrilla Warfare: The Global Politics of Law-Making*, 91–6; Mantilla, 'Under (Social) Pressure: The Historical Regulation of Internal Armed Conflicts through International Law', chapter 4; Mantilla, 'The Origins and Evolution of the 1949 Geneva Conventions and the 1977 Additional Protocols', 50–1.

[9] UK Foreign and Commonwealth Office, 'Letter from K G MacInnes to Mr Parsons, "ICRC Conference on Humanitarian Law Applicable in Armed Conflicts, Geneva 24 May – 12 June"'. As Bugnion put it, from a more ICRC-centric perspective: 'the ICRC had no doubt that if the UN took a leadership role in developing humanitarian law, this would inevitably politicize this branch of law. As a result, the ICRC had to seek to reassert its traditional leadership role in that area' ('Adoption of the Additional Protocols of 8 June 1977: A Milestone in the Development of International Humanitarian Law', 789).

efforts deployed by the International Committee these last few years'. The communication went on to say that the ICRC had 'decided to take all preparatory steps and studies likely to lead to the reaffirmation and the development of laws and customs of a humanitarian character in armed conflicts' – in short, asserting (albeit in impeccably diplomatic language) the Committee's pre-eminence in this field.[10] The ICRC also persuaded the Human Rights Division of the UN Secretariat that the former should take the lead in the process of legal development, with non-Western states assenting variously 'for reasons of tradition, deference to the West, the ICRC's image of expertise, or apathy'.[11] Accordingly, by 1969 the Committee found itself managing what promised to be a major international legislative initiative.

4.1.2 Prelude: The 1971 and 1972 Conferences of Government Experts

In line with its traditional practice, the ICRC's initial step was to convene a small group of 18 government and non-state experts in February 1969 to prepare a report for the International Conference of the Red Cross scheduled to take place in Istanbul later that year.[12] Having received the movement's blessing at Istanbul, the Committee next convened a 'Conference of Government Experts on the Reaffirmation and Development of International Humanitarian Law Applicable in Armed

[10] International Committee of the Red Cross, 'Reaffirmation and Development of the Laws and Customs Applicable in Armed Conflicts, Report Prepared for the XXIst International Conference of the Red Cross, Istanbul, September 1969', 23.

[11] Forsythe, *Humanitarian Politics: The International Committee of the Red Cross*, 112. See also discussions in Aldrich, 'Human Rights in Armed Conflict: Development of the Law'; Baxter, 'Humanitarian Law or Humanitarian Politics – The 1974 Diplomatic Conference on Humanitarian Law'; Best, *War and Law since 1945*, 345. See for background International Committee of the Red Cross, 'Reaffirmation and Development of the Laws and Customs Applicable in Armed Conflicts, Report Prepared for the XXIst International Conference of the Red Cross, Istanbul, September 1969', 26–30. That said, not all Western states supported this move: Sweden in particular, appears to have preferred that discussion continue in a UN context rather than under the ICRC's auspices. (See UK Foreign and Commonwealth Office, 'Record of a Meeting Held in Sir Vincent Evans' Office on Wednesday 10 January at 2.45pm', paras. 4–5.)

[12] See International Committee of the Red Cross, 'Reaffirmation and Development of the Laws and Customs Applicable in Armed Conflicts, Report Prepared for the XXIst International Conference of the Red Cross, Istanbul, September 1969', 25.

Conflicts'.[13] This conference took place over two sessions, in May 1971 and May 1972.[14]

Around 200 participants, drawn from 41 states, attended the first session of this conference, rendering it a good deal more unwieldy than its precursors from the 1949 treaties. The second session, however – to which, following complaints to the ICRC, all states party to the 1949 Conventions were invited – was almost double the size again, with more than 400 participants from 77 states.[15] One effect of this expanded attendance was that the meetings increasingly resembled full-blown diplomatic conferences.[16]

There was some co-ordination amongst Western governments prior to both conferences, with an informal 'Western Working Group' crystallising around the USA, the UK, France, Canada, Belgium and the Netherlands, and the USA and the UK liaising particularly closely. Despite these discussions, though, there was little unity of purpose. Some of these governments, including those of the UK and the USA, indicated a preference for a narrower approach to 'reaffirmation and development', focused on improving implementation of then-existing treaty law. The Americans were also particularly concerned to safeguard prisoner of war rights, with the Vietnam conflict dominating the US agenda. In contrast, Scandinavian governments were supportive of a more expansive agenda, Hans Longva of the Norwegian delegation emerging as a particularly vocal advocate for the categorisation of 'wars of national liberation' as international (rather than internal) armed conflicts.[17]

[13] See Resolutions 13, 17 and 18 in: International Committee of the Red Cross, 'Resolutions Adopted by the XXIst International Conference of the Red Cross'.

[14] See generally discussions in Alexander, 'International Humanitarian Law, Postcolonialism and the 1977 Geneva Protocol I'; Mantilla, 'Under (Social) Pressure: The Historical Regulation of Internal Armed Conflicts through International Law', chapter 4; Suter, *An International Law of Guerrilla Warfare: The Global Politics of Law-Making*, 115–17.

[15] Indeed, this was the 'major human rights event of the year' for the British Foreign and Commonwealth Office (UK Foreign and Commonwealth Office, 'Letter from K G MacInnes to Mr Parsons, "ICRC Conference on Humanitarian Law Applicable in Armed Conflicts, Geneva 24 May–12 June"').

[16] Baxter, 'Humanitarian Law or Humanitarian Politics – The 1974 Diplomatic Conference on Humanitarian Law', 8.

[17] See UK Foreign and Commonwealth Office, 'Letter from I K C Ellison to R G Sheridan, "Norwegian Representation at the ICRC Conference on Humanitarian Law in Armed Conflicts"'.

The practical lead in 1971 in terms of concrete proposals for the regulation of internal armed conflict was taken by the Canadians, who put forward a set of draft clauses proposing, inter alia, that any new provisions regulating non-international armed conflicts should apply in 'all cases of armed conflict occurring in the territory of one of the High Contracting Parties, involving government forces on one side and military forces whether regular or irregular on the other side, and to which Common Article 2 of the Conventions is not applicable'.[18] This position was supported by the Austrian delegation, while the Spanish, British and Italians took a more cautious line, suggesting that some 'belligerency-type' criteria (relating e.g. to the degree of organisation of insurgents) should be satisfied for such provisions to apply. Adopting a rather more radical tack, the Norwegians proposed not only that a single protocol be adopted to cover both international and non-international conflicts, but also that the 1949 Conventions as a whole be deemed to apply in wars of national liberation and 'any other armed conflict where hostilities have reached a level making the application of the Conventions a humanitarian necessity'.[19] Scandinavian radicalism aside, the more conservative Western delegations were also evidently already in a minority regarding the treatment of wars of national liberation, the ICRC report noting drily that 'most of the experts . . . who spoke on the subject considered that wars of liberation were international armed conflicts'.[20]

A rather greater diversity of opinion is reflected in the records of the 1972 meeting, for which the ICRC prepared two complete draft protocols to apply to 'Common Article 2' (i.e. international armed conflicts) and 'Common Article 3' conflicts, respectively.[21] Reflecting renewed efforts

[18] See International Committee of the Red Cross, '*Conference of Government Experts on the Reaffirmation and Development of International Humanitarian Law Applicable in Armed Conflicts (Geneva, 24 May–12 June 1971): Report on the Work of the Conference*', 57.

[19] Ibid., 61–2.

[20] Ibid., 54. See International Committee of the Red Cross, '*Conference of Government Experts on the Reaffirmation and Development of International Humanitarian Law Applicable in Armed Conflicts (Geneva, 24 May–12 June 1971): V - Protection of Victims of Non-International Armed Conflicts*', 33.

[21] See International Committee of the Red Cross, 'Conference of Government Experts on the Reaffirmation and Development of International Humanitarian Law Applicable in Armed Conflicts (Second Session: 3 May–3 June 1972): Report on the Work of the Conference (Volume II – Annexes)', 1–23. The ICRC did acknowledge the strength of critics of the traditional international/non-international division by including in its proposals at this stage a draft set of 'Regulations concerning special cases of armed conflicts not of an international character', which would have rendered the 1949 Conventions as a whole applicable when an insurgent force exercised 'effective power,

to co-ordinate a Western group through NATO, mainstream Western opinion supported this division. Both American and Canadian proposals in this instance, echoed by the Austrians and French, called for the second draft protocol to be applicable in situations where Common Article 3 was engaged, provided that non-state armed groups satisfied a minimal set of 'belligerency-type' criteria.[22]

Slightly more conservative positions were pressed by the Argentine, British, Spanish and Romanian delegations, each of which preferred to restrict the application of any new protocol to situations where additional 'belligerency-type' criteria were satisfied, including – on the part of Argentina and Romania – government recognition of insurgents.[23] However, other delegations again had a more radical agenda: Algeria, Cameroon, Egypt, the Ivory Coast, Libya, Nigeria, Norway, Pakistan and Yugoslavia collectively proposed that the draft protocol regulating *international* armed conflicts include an additional scoping paragraph extending the ambit of that protocol to 'armed struggles waged by peoples for the exercise of their right of self-determination'.[24] In short, by 1972 it was clear that there were likely to be at least two significant internal armed conflict-related areas of controversy at the CDDH: the potential elevation of wars of national liberation to the status of international armed conflict, and the scope and content of any dedicated internal armed conflict-regulating measures.

Following the 1971 and 1972 expert meetings, the ICRC prepared revised drafts of what were to become 'Protocol I' and 'Protocol II', to apply in international and internal armed conflicts, respectively.[25] The former provided for regulation of methods and means of combat – previously the domain of 'Hague' law – as well as greater protection to civilians in armed

by means of its administration and adequately organized armed forces, over a part of the territory', and a 'Draft Declaration on the Application of International Humanitarian Law in Armed Struggles for Self-Determination' which would have required adherents to agree to the application of the 1949 Conventions in such conflicts. (See International Committee of the Red Cross, '*Conference of Government Experts on the Reaffirmation and Development of International Humanitarian Law Applicable in Armed Conflicts (Second Session: 3 May–3 June 1972) Report on the Work of the Conference (Volume II – Annexes)*' 22–3.) These proposals fell by the wayside, however, as the drafting process continued.

22 Ibid., 33–6. In terms of the latter criteria, the USA, for example, referred to 'situations in which hostilities take place between organized armed forces, each of which is under a responsible command' (Ibid., 33).

23 Ibid., 33–6.

24 Ibid., 114.

25 International Committee of the Red Cross, '*Draft Additional Protocols to the Geneva Conventions of August 12, 1949: Commentary*'.

conflict, and the identification and marking of medical and civil defence personnel and equipment. The latter, in contrast, covered in rather more abbreviated form 'humane treatment of persons in the power of parties to the conflict', affording protection and relief for civilians, the wounded, sick, and shipwrecked, and regulating means and methods of combat. Broadly speaking, the ICRC sought to bolster the 1949 regime regulating international armed conflicts while 'filling out' the protections afforded by Common Article 3 in non-international armed conflicts.

The two drafts obtained the blessing of the International Conference of the Red Cross in Tehran in November 1973. With this, the stage was set for the first session of the CDDH, which opened in Geneva in February 1974.

4.2 The Diplomatic Conference (1974–1977)

4.2.1 Round I: Wars of National Liberation (1974)

> The Africans used the occasion for a political drive to promote the Liberation Movements, but strictly in a black/white context and in relation to Southern Africa. The Arabs naturally supported them to promote the Palestinians who initially had been prepared to settle for far less. And the Communists, who anyway are unenthusiastic about the whole negotiation, saw a good occasion to push the claims of the Viet Cong to international recognition and to isolate and embarrass the West over the liberation movement issue. The Americans felt they had to make a major effort to block the invitation to the Viet Cong and by one vote they did so. But the effort diverted their attention from the main issues at the beginning.[26]

> '[L]ittle short of a fiasco . . . '[27]

The diplomatic conference that convened in Geneva on 20 February 1974 was a very different creature from its 1949 predecessor. For one, there were vastly more delegations in attendance: 126 states sent delegations in 1974, in contrast to 64 in 1949.[28] The international context and issues preoccupying delegations in 1974 were also more varied, with a more

[26] UK Foreign and Commonwealth Office, 'Diplomatic Conference on Humanitarian Law in Armed Conflicts - Geneva 20 February/29 March 1974: First Session - Delegation Report', para. 6.

[27] UK Foreign and Commonwealth Office, 'Second Session of the Geneva Diplomatic Conference on Humanitarian Law in Armed Conflict, 3 February–18 April, 1975: Brief for the United Kingdom Delegation, document dated 29 January 1975, p. 3, para. 6.

[28] The numbers of delegations in attendance varied from year to year. Around 135 states sent delegations over the course of the four sessions, though only 109 attended in 1977. See List of Participants *CDDH*, 1978, II:29–350.

pronounced North – South divide complicating the East – West cleavage of 1949.

Despite these differences, the ICRC and the Swiss hosts appear to have approached the 1974 meeting largely as if it were a rerun of 1949. An inflammatory speech by the President of Mauretania at the opening plenary meeting served notice, though, that this was not to be the case.[29] The fact that almost the entirety of the 1974 session was taken up by heavily politicised preliminary organisational discussions, moreover, with only two weeks of the almost-six week meeting devoted to work in committee, underlined that this would not be 'business as usual'.[30]

One such organisational matter – the distribution of conference offices – was eventually settled on the basis of geographic distribution (a pattern familiar from UN practice). A far greater controversy, however, was sparked by the non-invitation to the conference of the Viet Cong-backed 'Provisional Revolutionary Government of the Republic of South Vietnam' (the PRG). To this was swiftly added developing world and Soviet bloc concern over the absence of Guinea-Bissau and 'national liberal movements' from the conference. Facing the massed rhetorical support of these groups, the more conservative Western delegations had little choice but to strike a conciliatory note. In a compromise offer, the Canadian and US delegations took the lead in proposing to allow Guinea-Bissau and national liberation movements to attend (albeit without voting rights), while maintaining a harder line on the PRG, a proposal which eventually won over a majority of the conference.[31]

The conservative West thus won a tactical victory on this issue. The overall tone of the preliminary discussions, however – largely comprising a dialogue of the deaf between legalistic arguments put forward by conservative Western delegations, and moralistic, aggrieved claims from the developing world, supported by like-minded Soviet-bloc and Western participants – highlighted the rhetorical gaps between blocs.[32]

[29] See SR.1 *CDDH*, 1978, V:12–14.

[30] For background on initial 'behind the scenes' discussions see US Department of State, 'Telegram from US Mission in Geneva to Department of State: Laws of War Conference – Current Status'.

[31] The final vote was 38 to 37, with 3 abstentions. For details of US manoeuvring, see e.g. US Department of State, 'Telegram from US Mission in Geneva to State Department: PRG Question at Laws of War Conference'.

[32] The request of Monaco's de Geouffre de La Pradelle for deliberations to be 'free of emotion', for example, was met by claims that the Western powers were making cynical use of legalistic rules to exclude those 'most affected' by the conference. (See SR.3 *CDDH*, 1978,

Committee meetings eventually began in March, with Committee I swiftly becoming bogged down in debate over the scope of Protocol I, which extended over almost the entirety of this committee's 16 meetings during the 1974 session. The most technically adept developing world advocate in these meetings was Georges Abi-Saab of Egypt, who set out at length arguments – based largely on UN General Assembly resolutions – in favour of treating wars of national liberation as international conflicts.[33] Ranged against these, delegations from the UK, the USA and states such as Belgium and France detailed the technical difficulties and impracticability of accommodating national liberation struggles within the framework of the 1949 Conventions. The latter also highlighted the risk of introducing 'just war' concepts relating to 'political motivation or subjective judgment' into what was portrayed as a hitherto purely 'humanitarian' discourse.[34]Given the widespread support for Abi-Saab from delegations of other developing countries, Soviet and other Communist delegations and Scandinavian delegations, these technical and principled counter-arguments met a chilly reception.[35] Even Jean Pictet's impassioned plea that '[i]t would be very dangerous, and against the spirit of humanitarian law, to classify armed conflicts on the basis of non-objective and non-legal criteria',[36] merely spurred a Tanzanian delegate to remark that he 'was astonished that Switzerland was not in favour of defining various categories of conflict, since the ICRC itself had already drawn a distinction between international conflicts and internal conflicts'. The same delegate then stated bluntly that '[s]truggles for national liberation were undeniably international conflicts, and his delegation was not prepared to accept a humanitarian law drawn up solely in the interest of the imperialist powers'.[37]

V:23–4, 28.) Sudan in particular railed against 'those who were trying to drown the issue (of national liberation movement participation) in legal sophistry' (on the grounds that such movements did not represent states) (SR6 *CDDH*, 1978, V:63). Elsewhere a Ugandan delegate interjected that '[l]egal arguments had been advanced . . . but under no circumstances should law be invoked as a barrier to justice' (SR.5 *CDDH*, 1978, V:50).

[33] See e.g. I/SR.2 *CDDH*, 1978, VIII:8. For an illustration of these views as they developed prior to and subsequent to the CDDH, see Abi-Saab, 'Wars of National Liberation and the Laws of War', 1985.

[34] See e.g. I/SR.2 *CDDH*, 1978, VIII:11–14. See also Lysaght, 'The Attitude of Western Countries', 351.

[35] I/SR.2 *CDDH*, 1978, VIII:11–14.

[36] I/SR.3 *CDDH*, VIII:19. Similar sentiments were expressed by Cassese for Italy (I/SR.3 *CDDH*, VIII: 22–3), de Geouffre de La Pradelle on behalf of Monaco (I/SR.4 *CDDH*, VIII:27–8) and Kalshoven on behalf of the Netherlands (I/SR.4 *CDDH*, VIII:31).

[37] I/SR.3 *CDDH*, 1978, VIII:20.

By this point, as a New Zealand delegate noted, it was evident that 'the delegations of the Western minority and of the rest of the world came to Geneva prepared for two quite different conferences'.[38] Indeed, as the session wore on, compromise looked increasingly unlikely, notwithstanding the ICRC's reminder of the 'need to preserve the universality of the Geneva Conventions and to adopt provisions that would be accepted by the greatest possible number of parties'.[39]

A variety of drafting options were canvassed, including an Austrian-introduced proposal adapting the Martens Clause, and a belated Canadian/New Zealand proposal to delay a decision on the topic to allow for intersessional debate.[40] It had become apparent as the weeks wore on, however, that 'the price of the conference's achieving anything at all was going to be the identification of "armed conflicts in which people are fighting against colonial domination and alien occupation and against racist regimes" (i.e. "wars of national liberation") as *international* armed conflicts'.[41] Few participants must have been surprised, therefore, when the committee voted by 70 votes to 21, with 13 abstentions, to expand the scope of draft Protocol I to encompass wars of national liberation, with Communist and developing world delegations, along with a number of Latin American delegations and Finland and Norway, lined up against a vastly outnumbered rump Western vote.[42] The adoption of the proposed wording – to become Article 1(4) of

[38] Quentin-Baxter, 'Report of the New Zealand Delegation to the First Session of the Diplomatic Conference for the Reaffirmation and Development of International Humanitarian Law Applicable in Armed Conflicts', p. 4, para. 11.

[39] I/SR.6 *CDDH*, 1978, VIII:49.

[40] The Austrian-introduced proposal was that: '[i]n cases not included in the present Protocol or in other instruments of conventional law, civilians and combatants remain under the protection and the authority of the principles of international law, as they result from established custom, from the principles of humanity and the dictates of public conscience' (see: *CDDH*/I/12 and Corr. l and *CDDH*/I/12 and Add.l (8 March 1974), in: CDDH, 1978, III:6). This amendment was sponsored by: Argentina, Austria, Belgium, the Federal Republic of Germany, Italy, the Netherlands, Pakistan and the UK. See also: I/SR.13 *CDDH*, 1978, VIII:97–8.

[41] Best, *War and Law since 1945*, 345.

[42] See I/SR.13 *CDDH*, 1978, VIII:99–102. The wording adopted in committee included reference to: 'armed conflicts in which peoples are fighting against colonial [domination] and alien occupation and racist regimes in the exercise of their right of self-determination, as enshrined in the Charter of the United Nations and the Declaration on Principles of International Law concerning Friendly Relations and Co-operation among States'. See *CDDH*/I/71 (20 March 1974), in *CDDH*, 1978, III:8–9 (sponsored by Argentina, Honduras, Mexico, Panama and Peru).

Protocol I – was subsequently welcomed in plenary, with only Western reservations, on 29 March 1974.[43]

4.2.2 *Rounds II and III: Disinterest, Weak Consensus and the Scope of Protocol II (1975 and 1976)*

The acrimony that pervaded the 1974 meetings was largely absent in 1975 and 1976. This can be accounted for by two principal reasons: first, the more conservative Western delegations, principally the UK, the USA, France and Canada – the Western 'inner core' – had learned from the first session. Under US leadership, this group decided – albeit with some difficulty – in intersessional meetings after the 1974 session to aim at seeing both protocols through in workable form, subsequently proving more flexible and cannier in subsequent negotiations with the more demanding developing world delegations.[44] Second, developing world interest in the proceedings declined in the aftermath of the victory of 1974.[45]

In consequence, even potentially contentious issues were handled in a relatively smooth manner in 1975 and 1976.[46] Rather than try to refight the 1974 drafting battle in the ensuing sessions, for example, conservative Western delegations sought instead to ameliorate the implications of Article 1(4) in areas of critical concern. This resulted in ultimately successful pushes to (a) limit the circumstances in which captured national liberation movement fighters would be eligible for POW protections, and (b) limit the ability of national liberation movements to demand the benefits of the protocol during conflicts with governments.[47] Perhaps the most critical debates in respect of internal armed conflicts in the second and third sessions,

[43] SR.22 *CDDH*, 1978, V:227–9. See Forsythe, 'The 1974 Diplomatic Conference on Humanitarian Law: Some Observations', 79–80. As Baxter notes, this wording was primarily produced by a powerful 'Arab and African bloc', seeking to take aim at South Africa, Rhodesia, Portugal and Israel ('Humanitarian Law or Humanitarian Politics – The 1974 Diplomatic Conference on Humanitarian Law', 12).

[44] See discussion and references below re. WEOG co-ordination.

[45] Indeed, a number of developing world delegations that had attended in 1974 did not participate in subsequent sessions. (See lists at: *CDDH*, 1978, II:29–350.)

[46] Though fraught, for example, the 'PRG issue' was handled with relative equanimity in 1975 (at least in comparison to 1974), with the USA again succeeding in having the PRG excluded, over three days of debate at the opening of the session. (See SR.23, 24, 25, 26 and Add. 1, *CDDH*, 1978, V:272–4, 277–311.)

[47] See further discussions below.

however, were the 1975 Committee I discussions on the scope of Protocol II.[48]

These discussions – focused around the drafting of Article 1 of the draft protocol – ran from 14 February until 17 March 1975. As initially prepared by the ICRC, Article 1 provided that the protocol would apply 'to all armed conflicts not covered by Article 2 [of the 1949 Conventions], taking place between armed forces or other organized armed groups under responsible command ... [and] shall not apply to situations of internal disturbances and tensions, *inter alia* riots, isolated and sporadic acts of violence and other acts of similar nature'.[49] In short, from the outset the drafting was rather more restrictive than Common Article 3, including a minimalist 'belligerency-type' requirement for non-governmental groups to be under responsible command, and expressly excluding low-intensity forms of violence ('internal disturbances and tensions').

This wording was unsurprisingly heavily debated in the committee. Despite the controversial subject matter, though, these meetings were far less heated and more conciliatory in tone than their 1974 forebears, as well as featuring a greater diversity of opinions across and within blocs. In this case, the by-now traditional concerns about risks to sovereignty and of opening the way to foreign intervention were voiced in preliminary meetings by Argentina, East Germany, Yugoslavia, Mexico and Algeria.[50] Other delegations from developing world and Soviet bloc states were complimentary about various aspects of the ICRC proposal, however.[51] A Nigerian delegate observed, for example, that: '[s]tate sovereignty was not and could never be an impregnable fortress: slight inroads into it were often necessary to enable mankind to live in a better world', and that 'the ICRC draft of Article 1 represented the views of his delegation to a large extent'.[52] Egypt's Georges Abi-Saab took a similar line, noting risks in seeking to overly narrow the application of Protocol II and describing the ICRC drafting as 'a step in the right direction of gearing the scope of protection to the level of intensity of the conflict rather than to abstract legal categories such as internal and international armed conflict'.[53]

48 See records of opening discussion on this topic at I/SR.22 *CDDH*, 1978, VIII:201–14.

49 Part Three: Draft Additional Protocols to the Geneva Conventions of August 12, 1949, *CDDH*, 1978, I:33.

50 See I/SR.22, I/SR.24 *CDDH*, 1978, VIII:205, 207, 230, 231, 233.

51 See e.g. I/SR.22 *CDDH*, VIII:205–9.

52 I/SR.24 *CDDH*, VIII:232–3.

53 He did add, however, that '[s]everal delegations from the third world had expressed legitimate anxiety ... about the possibility of Protocol II being used as a justification for intervention ... [adding that the Conference] should try to meet that anxiety to a greater

Indonesian, South Vietnamese and Pakistani speakers were also less dismissive of Protocol II in these early exchanges than might have been expected, supporting a higher – but not discretionary – threshold for the application of Protocol II.[54] Norway, 'in a spirit of realism', also agreed to proceed on a two-protocol basis.[55] Indeed, only the Indian delegation was stringently opposed from the outset to the regulation of internal armed conflicts, maintaining in early debates that 'no convincing arguments had been put forward to justify the need for draft Protocol II'.[56]

As with Common Article 3 in 1949, Article 1 was referred to a working group (on this occasion chaired by New Zealand) for recrafting, a subgroup of which recommended the following wording to the working group on 12 March:

> 1. The present Protocol, which develops and supplements Article 3 common to the Geneva Conventions of 12 August 1949 without modifying its existing conditions of application, shall apply to all armed conflicts which are not covered by Article 1 of Protocol I and which take place in the territory of a High Contracting Party between its armed forces and dissident armed forces or other organized armed groups which, under responsible command, exercise such control over a part of its territory as to enable them to carry out sustained and concerted military operations and to implement the present Protocol.
> 2. The present Protocol shall not apply to situations of internal disturbances and tensions, such as riots, isolated and sporadic acts of violence and other acts of a similar nature, as not being armed conflicts.[57]

Featuring a rather higher threshold for the protocol's application than originally proposed by the ICRC, this wording was adopted by the working group, and subsequently by consensus in Committee I on 17 March.[58] Amongst more conservative Western participants this was regarded as a tactical victory after the reverse of 1974: the avoidance of a vote,

extent and should keep it in mind in drafting each of the articles of Protocol II' (I/SR.24 *CDDH*, VIII:234).

54 I/SR.22, I/SR. 23 *CDDH*, VIII:211–12, 225–6.

55 I/SR.23 *CDDH*, VIII:217–18.

56 I/SR.23 *CDDH*, VIII:224.

57 See *CDDH*/219/Rev. l *CDDH*, 1978, X:40 Para. 92.

58 See debate in I/SR.29 *CDDH*, 1978, VIII:285–98. This language was likely based on Pakistani and/or Canadian drafting proposals. (See UK Foreign and Commonwealth Office, 'UK Mission in Geneva to Priority FCO Telno. 35 Saving', p. 2, para. 5.)

however, did not mean that this wording had gained unanimous or uncritical support.[59]

Indeed, at the closing committee debate on 17 March a number of delegations remained unconvinced: Brazil, Romania, India, Iraq, Indonesia, Iran and Burundi all argued that 'explicit recognition of the existence of an armed conflict [by the parties] was a prerequisite for the application of Protocol II to a conflict occurring on the territory of a "High Contracting Party"' – in short, taking the view that the protocol should apply at the discretion of the relevant state party.[60] Nigeria also was more sceptical on this occasion.[61] On the other side, Canada, the USSR, Italy, and Belgium were content with the wording, whereas the Dutch, Swiss, US and East German delegations would have preferred more robust drafting. Hans Longva of Norway in particular – perhaps the most consistently 'progressive' voice at the conference – bemoaned the higher threshold of the redrafted Article 1 as reflecting a 'lack of political readiness on the part of certain delegations' to afford to non-state parties in internal armed conflict the benefits that would accrue to national liberation movements under Article 1(4) of Protocol I.[62]

The fragility of the consensus achieved in committee was underlined when the proposed wording was considered in plenary on 17 April. At this point, the Indian and Philippine delegations indicated significant discomfort, the former stating bluntly that as national liberation movements had been catered for in Protocol I, 'Protocol II would not be necessary, since any other conflict taking place within the territory of a sovereign State would be an internal conflict and any international instrument designed to regulate non-international conflicts might in actual application impede the settlement of the conflict and lead to external interference.'[63] While the draft article remained unaltered in plenary, across-the-board support for a far-reaching Protocol II (or

[59] See e.g. UK Foreign and Commonwealth Office, 'Diplomatic Conference on Humanitarian Law in Armed Conflicts – Geneva 3 February–18 April: Second Session – Delegation Report'; Aldrich, 'Report of the United States Delegation to the Diplomatic Conference on the Reaffirmation and Development of International Humanitarian Law Applicable in Armed Conflicts, Second Session, Geneva, Switzerland, February 3–April 18, 1975'. The British were supportive of the draft given the high threshold language, in light of concerns about Northern Ireland.

[60] See I/SR.29 *CDDH*, 1978, VIII:286, 288, 289, 292, 293.

[61] I/SR.29 *CDDH*, VIII:292.

[62] I/SR.29 *CDDH*, VIII:294. See also other explanations of position at I/SR.29 *CDDH*, VIII:286–94.

[63] SR.29 *CDDH*, 1978, V:345. Re. the Philippines, see SR.29 *CDDH*, V:350–52.

indeed for Protocol II in any form) could evidently not be taken for granted.

4.2.3 Round IV: Protocol II Revisited and the Pakistani Draft (1977)

> The rush with which business was brought to a close in the fourth year was due to general weariness and agreement that enough was enough – not to mention the inabilities of their hosts to go on paying poor States' expenses ad infinitum. One hundred and nine States stuck it out to the end and all but (inimitably) Israel found enough that was acceptable in the final document to enable them to sign it.[64]

When the 1977 session of the diplomatic conference opened on 17 March, initial indications were that this session would continue in the tone of its 1976 predecessor. Indeed, the USA-driven Western effort during this round to lessen the impact of Article 1(4) on the remainder of Protocol I attracted remarkably little concern from developing countries.

Though controversial to this day, drafting brokered by Aldrich to address the conditions under which detainees from national liberation movements would be afforded POW protections – reflecting an approach favoured by Aldrich which he had pressured sceptical Western delegations to support – was adopted in committee with minimal debate on 22 April, garnering cross-bloc support, an outcome repeated in plenary on 26 May.[65] In similar fashion, conservative Western delegations ultimately elected to accommodate wording proposed in 1975 by a mixed group of Eastern bloc and developing world delegations, along with Australia, Finland, New Zealand, Norway, and Syria to permit national liberation movements to 'assume the same rights and obligations' as states parties to Protocol I. In this instance, the British, Canadians and others placed reliance on the drafting requiring states parties to accord such rights only when a national liberation

[64] Best, *War and Law since 1945*, 406–7.

[65] See records of Committee and Plenary votes and – notwithstanding minimal debate – extensive explanations of position at SR.40, SR.41 *CDDH*, 1978, VI:121–55; III/SR.55, III/SR.56 *CDDH*, 1978, XV:155–87. The key to this wording, at the time draft Article 42, emerging as Article 44 in the final version of Protocol I, was that combatants would be entitled to POW protections provided that they carry arms openly during military engagements and 'during such time as [they are] visible to the adversary while . . . engaged in a military deployment preceding the launching of an attack in which [they are] to participate'. (See contrasting requirements of Article 4.A of Geneva Convention III. Also generally discussion in e.g. Aldrich, 'New Life for the Laws of War', 768–75.) These provisions were debated in the 1975 and 1976 sessions, but only concluded in 1977.

movement both 'accepts and applies' the protocol – reasoning that this last requirement was unlikely to be satisfied.[66]

The plenary meeting on 23 May provided a spark of life when Israel proved to be the only delegation to insist on a vote on the inclusion of 'wars of national liberation' within the ambit of Protocol I, notwithstanding a US plea to allow the article to be adopted by consensus.[67] This spark was all but extinguished, however, when Israel lost the vote by 87 to 1, with 11 abstentions.[68]

Internal armed conflicts came to the fore again, though, in the run-up to 2 June, when the conference was to commence discussion of Protocol II in plenary. Until this point, Protocol II had been developed in parallel to Protocol I, a process which had resulted in a draft that closely mirrored the latter, with the Scandinavians particularly strong advocates of robust regulation of internal armed conflict.[69] A number of developing country delegations, however, had reserved their position throughout, resulting in growing concern before the 1977 session amongst supportive governments (including the USA and the UK) and the ICRC as to the viability of delivering Protocol II in any form, given the 'weak consensus' over its provisions.[70]

In an effort to overcome these divisions, Canada and Pakistan had led intersessional work to craft an abbreviated version of Protocol II that would have a better chance of successfully navigating the 1977 session. This more 'sovereignty-friendly' redraft of Protocol II, containing 28 articles instead of the previous draft's 47, was unveiled to the conference on 27 May and tabled as an amendment proposal on 1 June, immediately prior to the scheduled commencement of debate on Protocol II.[71]

[66] See Committee decision and explanations of votes at: I/SR.67, I/SR.68, I/SR.76 *CDDH*, 1978, IX:364–76, 474. Plenary decisions and explanations of position are at: SR.46 *CDDH*, 1978, VI:352–5. For wording of the original proposal, see *CDDH*/I/233 and Add. 1 to 4 (5 March 1975), in *CDDH*, 1978, III:353. This wording was included in draft Article 84, subsequently Article 96 of Protocol I.

[67] See SR.36 *CDDH*, 1978, VI:39–41.

[68] SR.36 *CDDH*, VI:41. Additional Protocol I was subsequently adopted by consensus in plenary on 8 June (SR.56 *CDDH*, 1978, VII:191–4).

[69] See UK Foreign and Commonwealth Office, 'Diplomatic Conference on Humanitarian Law in Armed Conflicts - Geneva 3 February–18 April: Second Session - Delegation Report', pp. 3–4, paras. 5–6.

[70] See e.g. Aldrich, 'Report of the U.S. Delegation to the Diplomatic Conference on the Reaffirmation and Development of International Humanitarian Law Applicable in Armed Conflicts, Third Session, Washington, Geneva, Switzerland, April 21–June 11, 1976', 23. Also: Mantilla, 'Under (Social) Pressure: The Historical Regulation of Internal Armed Conflicts through International Law', 278.

[71] See discussion in Junod, 'Additional Protocol II: History and Scope', 33. Notwithstanding this 1977 'unveiling', Canada had been working behind the scenes on the (re)drafting of Protocol II

The 'Pakistani draft' drew on the earlier Canadian proposal for Protocol II, albeit retaining Article 1 as agreed in committee, and more generally reflected a 'gentlemen's agreement' amongst negotiating blocs reached through 'corridor consultations', with ICRC drafting assistance and Egyptian support.[72] Consequently, there was little opposition to this proposal amongst delegates generally, including both those from more conservative Western delegations and those from developing countries.

Scandinavian delegations, however, were more exercised. Accordingly, despite there being an evident 'general wish to reach agreement on a simplified version', the Swedish delegate called for a rigorous review process, to ensure that 'certain articles in [the committee draft], which were of paramount humanitarian importance, would be retained'.[73] The outcome of this discussion – based on a Soviet proposal – was an agreement to consider the Pakistani draft as a series of amendments to the committee draft.[74]

From this point on, however, the fate of the committee draft was sealed. Indeed, the Pakistani drafting remained controversial for some developing world delegations, with Article 1 adopted in plenary only in the teeth of serious objections: Argentina, Cameroon, Chile, India and Syria voted against its adoption, with another 29 delegations abstaining.[75] India (predictably) again denounced the entire endeavour of Protocol II, while the Argentineans and Syrians cited concerns about the risk of 'subjectivity' in Article 1.[76] Many of the delegations that had abstained – representing primarily Latin American and African states – were similarly unhappy with the wording.[77] The canard of government recognition of insurgents as a condition for the application of Protocol II was even raised, notwithstanding the extended discussion on this issue which had previously taken place in Committee 1.[78]

From a rather different perspective – and signifying the vast gap between the more progressive Scandinavians and others at the

for some time. (See UK Foreign and Commonwealth Office, 'R A Facey (UK Mission in Geneva) to N Jarrold (FCO UN Department): "Humanitarian Law: Protocol II"'.)

72 See SR.49 *CDDH*, 1978, VII:61. Also Forsythe, 'Legal Management of Internal War: The 1977 Protocol on Non-International Armed Conflicts', 278–9.

73 SR.49 *CDDH*, 1978, VII:59, 65.

74 See SR.49 *CDDH*, VII:63–5.

75 SR.49 *CDDH*, VII:70.

76 See variously at e.g.: SR.49 *CDDH*, VII:67, 72–3, 75, 80–1.

77 See generally SR.49 *CDDH*, VII:59–84.

78 See Brazilian and Colombian explanations of vote at: SR.49, *CDDH*, VII: 76–9. Also Philippine comments at: SR.49 *CDDH*, VII:82–3.

conference – Norway also abstained in the vote on Article 1, voicing misgivings about the high threshold of the article. Indeed, the Norwegians were ultimately the only Western delegation at the conference to reserve their position on Protocol II as a whole.[79]

That said, the Pakistani draft largely progressed through plenary without incident, with articles deleted or adopted by consensus in many cases without discussion or comment.[80] Where there were discussions, these were also exceedingly brief. Accordingly, with the USA leading the Western bloc in 'consensus-seeking', the Pakistani draft (with minor amendments) was adopted by consensus on 8 June, albeit with India and a number of other developing world delegations indicating 'sovereigntist' discomfort.[81] To the more 'humanitarian' delegations, however – in particular the Scandinavians – adoption of the watered-down Pakistani draft must have been at best a bittersweet conclusion after almost a decade of work.[82]

4.3 Key Roles and Perspectives

4.3.1 *The 'Conservative' vs. the 'Progressive' West*

> Most of the Western Europeans had the double misfortune of a government which was too harassed to come to grips with their problems, and too sensitive to its own public opinion to allow them much freedom of action ... Positions ran the gamut from Portuguese entrenchment and French detachment to the compulsion of Norway and Australia to fraternise with the enemy. This ragged little army might have responded to wise American generalship; but Mr Aldrich, though alert and articulate, had little experience of, or feeling for, multilateral diplomacy. There was a more

[79] SR.49 *CDDH*, 1978, VII:71.

[80] As noted in a UK telegram of 10 June: 'The Plenary turned to the consideration of Protocol II late in the afternoon of 2 June. During the preceding 24 hours, it had been agreed informally among the regional groups that the non-aligned would make no concerted attempt to block the adoption of a Protocol II based on the simplified text tabled by Pakistan [*CDDH*/427] provided that there was likewise no concerted attempt to force through Articles unacceptable to them and which did not appear in the Pakistani draft, particularly any of those which they regarded as a threat to their national sovereignty'. UK Foreign and Commonwealth Office, 'Saving Telegram from UKMIS Geneva to FCO (Telno 30)', p. 1)

[81] The USA led the way on a number of occasions in reducing the demands of Protocol II where necessary to obtain wider support. See e.g. SR.50, SR.51 *CDDH*, VII:85, 115. While a few delegations expressed 'sovereigntist' concerns about Protocol II, India stands out as the most implacably opposed (see esp. SR.56 *CDDH*, VII:202–4).

[82] See generally discussions at SR.56 *CDDH*, 1978, VII:194–227.

> fundamental, and less excusable weakness in the Western position: although magnificently equipped to campaign in the territory of the laws of war, the Western forces had failed to appreciate that the decisive engagement must take place in the marshes and quicksand of United Nations practice.[83]

The above observation neatly sums up the difficulties faced by Western states in addressing the issues thrown up at the first session of the CDDH: a broad range of views were encompassed, there was little leadership and minimal co-ordination, and many delegations were ill-prepared for the approach taken by developing world counterparts. While this situation improved over time, moreover, the conservative Western delegations remained on the back foot throughout the CDDH – indeed, as the preceding discussion illustrates, much of the final drafting proved acceptable only with difficulty, particularly in relation to Protocol I.

4.3.1.1 The United States

The US approach to the CDDH as a whole was overshadowed by the Vietnam War, which influenced US positions in a number of ways: in general, though, experiences in Vietnam enhanced 'American willingness to participate in, and even to encourage, an international effort to revise and improve the law of combatant warfare'.[84] More particularly, the USA was concerned to bolster the protection of American personnel captured in that conflict, and so to strengthen the protection of detainees in non-international armed conflicts more broadly.[85] Head of delegation Aldrich also evinced a 'desire to prove that [in Vietnam] the armed forces of the United States had acted in accordance with international law – not merely the law of the old *Hague Conventions*, but the law as nations wanted it to be in the 1970s'.[86]

The US approach also reflected détente and concern not to alienate developing world delegations or the Soviet bloc if possible. The associated Realist capacity of superpower co-operation can in particular be glimpsed in the informal US agreement with the USSR to keep nuclear weapons 'off the table', alongside a readiness to discuss other aspects of

83 Quentin-Baxter, 'Report of the New Zealand Delegation to the First Session of the Diplomatic Conference for the Reaffirmation and Development of International Humanitarian Law Applicable in Armed Conflicts', pp. 3–4, para. 9.

84 Aldrich, 'Some Reflections on the Origins of the 1977 Geneva Protocols', 132.

85 See Aldrich, 'Some Reflections on the Origins of the 1977 Geneva Protocols', 131; also Mantilla, 'Under (Social) Pressure: The Historical Regulation of Internal Armed Conflicts through International Law', 201–8.

86 Aldrich, 'Some Reflections on the Origins of the 1977 Geneva Protocols', 132.

weapons usage.[87] That said though, the Americans were also wary of more radical developing world preferences, in particular with respect to the role of national liberation movements (as well as the PRG) at the CDDH and in the ensuing Protocols.

US positions at Geneva also reflected a complex of sometimes competing domestic and transnational factors. These included an at-times highly conservative Pentagon.[88] Israel posed additional complications: almost entirely isolated at the conference, and with obvious concerns about Article 1(4) and its implications, the Israelis appear to have been a persistent thorn in Aldrich's side, at times going behind his back to the Pentagon and White House, seeking to limit Aldrich's leeway to accommodate developing world preferences.[89]

[87] See Forsythe, *Humanitarian Politics: The International Committee of the Red Cross*, 119. Also: Aldrich, 'Some Reflections on the Origins of the 1977 Geneva Protocols', 133 (' . . . as the conference settled into its substantive work, our common interests as major military powers came to the fore, in particular, our common interest in not having the conference adopt by vote provisions either of us could not accept'). See also related discussion in Giovanni Mantilla, 'The Protagonism of the USSR and Socialist States in the Revision of International Humanitarian Law', 195–202.

[88] See e.g. observations in: UK Army Legal Services, 'David Hughes-Morgan (Brigadier Legal Staff) to UK Ministry of Defence (Various), "Humanitarian Law Article 42 of Protocol I – Guerrillas"', 1. Also Israel CDDH delegation member, Interview (author papers). On US domestic background more generally see Mantilla, 'Under (Social) Pressure: The Historical Regulation of Internal Armed Conflicts through International Law', 243–4.

[89] Indeed, Aldrich was characterised by one Israeli delegate as suffering from 'Stockholm Syndrome'. (The Israelis were not alone, though, in utilising such bilateral channels – see e.g. Foreign and Commonwealth Office, 'W. G. Harris (UN Dept.) to E. C. Glover, UK Embassy, Washington, DC, "Humanitarian Law in Armed Conflict"'.) Likewise, the Israelis also intervened directly with UK government figures, on occasion causing irritation – see UK Foreign and Commonwealth Office, 'T A H Solesby (UN Dept.) to M S Weir, "Conference on Humanitarian Law: NLMs" (with 14 March Addendum by M S Weir)'; UK Foreign and Commonwealth Office, 'R A Facey (UK Mission, Geneva) to T A H Solesby (UN Dept.), "Conference on Humanitarian Law: NLMs"'; UK Foreign and Commonwealth Office, 'M S Weir to Maxey (UN Dept.), "Mr Allon's Meeting with the Secretary of State"'. That said, Aldrich equally had significant personal authority within the Department of Defense as well as the Department of State – see Combs, 'Profile: Judge George H. Aldrich', 50. ('Judge Aldrich . . . was entrusted with unusual control over the American negotiating posture. He had gained the trust of the United States Defense Department during the time he was employed there in the early 1960s and, because he was viewed as Dr. Kissinger's lawyer, few were willing to challenge the position papers he drafted, figuring that he would prevail in any event.') As Aldrich himself noted in respect of his own disposition, moreover: '[g]rowing up during the Second World War and the years in which the post-war world was formed . . . it seemed natural that my goals looked towards the new world order of the United Nations and the promotion of international law as a means to make a Third World War less likely' (Aldrich, 'Notes

Aldrich, in consequence, generally adopted a cautious, pragmatic approach at the CDDH, holding out doggedly on key points such as PRG participation, but otherwise seeking to be as conciliatory as he was able to Soviet bloc and developing country delegations.[90] In particular, he preferred to work by consensus, with a persistent eye to the US–Soviet relationship: as he later put it (by way of illustration), the USA 'negotiated the best article on protecting powers that the Soviets could accept, rather than press for a vote'.[91] As the preceding history relates, however, a focus on pragmatic compromise was not uniformly shared amongst delegations – prompting Aldrich to complain that some delegations had failed to grasp that 'the adoption of rules one favors is of little value if those rules will not be accepted and respected by the countries at which they are aimed'.[92]

The negotiation of Article 1(4) of Protocol I exemplified all of these tendencies. Aldrich appears to have recognised fairly early on that with developing world and Soviet bloc support for the inclusion of wars of national liberation in the first Article of draft Protocol I, the more conservative Western delegations would likely be unable to effect the removal of the offending language from the final drafts, especially given that the West itself was not of one voice (Australia and Norway had co-sponsored the proposal to include such conflicts in the ambit of Article 1).[93] The USA had also achieved a significant victory at the 1974 meeting in preventing PRG participation, and Aldrich may have perceived little value in

from the Vietnam Peace Negotiations'; quoted in Combs, 'Profile: Judge George H. Aldrich', 48–9).

90 Re. co-operation with other delegations on this issue, see US Department of State, 'US Department of State Telegram – PRG Issue at Law of War Conference: Supporting Countries'. Also Aldrich, 'Some Reflections on the Origins of the 1977 Geneva Protocols', 134. Underlining the nature of Aldrich's approach, UK archival materials include reference to a 'mutual admiration society' in Committee III between Aldrich and Dr Van Luu of North Vietnam (see UK Foreign and Commonwealth Office, 'M R Eaton to Bowie (UN Dept.), "Diplomatic Conference on Humanitarian Law in Armed Conflicts – Delegation Report" (Attaching Draft Committee III Report)', p. 3, para. 5 in attached draft report).

91 Aldrich, 'Some Reflections on the Origins of the 1977 Geneva Protocols', 133.

92 Ibid.

93 See Aldrich, 'Classified Report of the United States Delegation to the Diplomatic Conference on the Reaffirmation and Development of International Humanitarian Law Applicable in Armed Conflicts, Geneva, Switzerland, February 20–March 29 1974', p. 5, para. 1. ('It will also be necessary to think what impact the concept of wars of national liberation may have on other articles of Protocol I and of the Geneva Conventions of 1949 in general, and to avoid any formulation which Permits unequal application of the Protocols and the Convention to different Parties to a conflict.')

expending further political capital at that session or subsequently in an endeavour that was unlikely to succeed.[94]

In line with this view, and again illustrating the ability of the USA to leverage its superpower status, Aldrich subsequently exerted significant pressure on fellow Western delegations in intersessional debates, arguing that there was little point in continuing to challenge the drafting of Article 1(4) in future negotiations. Instead, he (rationally) focused conservative Western efforts on ameliorating the implications of the 1974 Committee decision, an approach underpinned by a view that Article 1(4) was primarily a political nuisance, capable of a restrictive interpretation allaying Western concerns.[95]

With respect to the scope of Protocol II, the 1975 discussions led Aldrich to expect this agreement to be stillborn: the USA, along with other Western states, had supported the ICRC's draft Article 1, as presented in 1974, as a logical choice to align the threshold of draft Protocol II with that of Common Article 3 of the 1949 Conventions. Once the draft came up for discussion in Committee I in 1975, though, it became apparent that the views of developing countries were going to prevent the adoption of this article as originally drafted.

The USA therefore again focused on damage limitation, Aldrich's subsequent report noting that 'as a price for raising the threshold [of this Article], we were able to exact a formulation which we hope will lend itself less readily to subjective interpretation by a state which is involved in an internal armed conflict'.[96] As the drafting progressed, however, Aldrich became increasingly resigned to the prospect of Protocol II being a dead letter given the (pre-Pakistani draft) combination of a high materiality threshold and relatively demanding substantive individual articles.[97] As

[94] Ibid., 2.

[95] See e.g. UK Foreign and Commonwealth Office, 'Report of Washington Meeting on 13 and 14 January 1975 on Humanitarian Law in Armed Conflict' (Undated, Received in Registry 28 January 1975), paras. 2, 8–11; UK Foreign and Commonwealth Office, 'P M Maxey (UN Dept) to Coles (Scored out, Replaced in Manuscript – Illegible), "Humanitarian Law: Reception for Delegates to London Meeting of Western Group" (Appending Briefing Note)', paras. 4, 8 in Briefing Note. See also US Department of State, 'Telegram from US Mission in Geneva to Department of State: Laws of War Conference – Liberation Movement Problem'. Also observations in Neuerbourg, 'Ninety-Seven Nations and Three Liberation Movements Signed a Document Friday Completing Four Years of Work on How to Improve Humanitarian Rules of Welfare'.

[96] Aldrich, 'Report of the United States Delegation to the Diplomatic Conference on the Reaffirmation and Development of International Humanitarian Law Applicable in Armed Conflicts, Second Session, Geneva, Switzerland, February 3–April 18, 1975', 8.

[97] Ibid.

with other conservative Western delegations, the USA accordingly ultimately welcomed the Pakistani-proposed 1977 redraft as a pragmatic step forward.[98]

In theoretical terms, the US experience at the CDDH is instructive in a number of key respects. For one, lending credence to the Realist hypothesis, when working with the USSR delegation, Aldrich was able to manage the conference's agenda to a degree. Moreover, the USA evidently also overawed its Western allies on occasion at Geneva – the process through which the 'conservative West' was persuaded to back Aldrich's strategy in respect of Article 1(4), despite in some cases strong misgivings, being a case in point.[99]

At the same time, Aldrich's appraisal of the slim chance of convincing developing world counterparts to compromise on their 1974 gains in this respect, and the adoption of a 'second-best' strategy to ameliorate concerns about Article 1(4), point strongly to the operation of a Rationalist calculus. In similar fashion, US – and Aldrich's – sensitivity to domestic and international perceptions of American positioning during the CDDH, alongside constraints imposed by domestic actors and constituencies, also suggest a distinctly 'Liberal' aspect to US behaviour at the CDDH, highlighting the relevance of factors highlighted in the Regime Type hypothesis.[100]

4.3.1.2 The UK

The British approach to negotiating the Additional Protocols had much in common with that adopted by the USA, but with persistent concern about potential implications for Northern Ireland rather than Vietnam, anxiety with respect to the former closely shaping UK policy-making regarding the CDDH.[101] The UK also encountered difficulties stemming,

[98] See observations in US Department of State, 'U.S. Participation in the UN: Report by the President to the Congress for the Year 1977', 279.

[99] As Mantilla notes of the 1974 intersessional meetings: 'in the end the weight of the American presence within the Western group locked in the approach suggested by Aldrich' ('Under (Social) Pressure: The Historical Regulation of Internal Armed Conflicts through International Law', 270). The US evidently also exerted similar influence over Latin American states in some instances. See e.g. a Cuban delegate's 1974 observation that a proposed amendment 'had not been supported by all Latin-American countries because they were reluctant to vote against the United States Government' (I/SR.14 *CDDH*, 1978, VIII:105).

[100] See e.g. discussions in Alexander, 'International Humanitarian Law, Postcolonialism and the 1977 Geneva Protocol I', 30–4; Mantilla, 'Under (Social) Pressure: The Historical Regulation of Internal Armed Conflicts through International Law', 211–12.

[101] See e.g. UK Foreign and Commonwealth Office, 'M R Eaton to Sir Vincent Evans: "Diplomatic Conference on Human Rights in Armed Conflict February/March 1974"',

as in 1949, from a lack of preparedness for the (in this case UN-style) political context of negotiations. The British once again came prepared primarily for technical, legal discussions, an approach that swiftly foundered in the face of developing world polemics at Geneva. Lastly, domestic politics may also have affected the UK, with the two general elections of 1974 presenting challenges to the settling of policy preferences.

The early debates over Article 1(4) of Protocol I reveal two linked strands of British doctrinal and practical concern about this provision. First, the British delegation was concerned about the technical practicability of implementing the whole of international humanitarian law in wars of national liberation, including the prisoner-of-war and protecting power aspects of the 1949 Conventions. A second concern was that carving out 'wars of national liberation' from other non-international armed conflicts imported 'just war' principles (*jus ad bellum*) into the formerly (notionally) 'apolitical' *jus in bello* which the ICRC and likeminded governments had in the past promoted and sustained. Needless to say, the possibility of the IRA claiming that the conflict in Northern Ireland should fall into this category was seldom far from British minds at Geneva and in Whitehall.[102]

That said, as matters progressed in Geneva, a pragmatic approach prevailed, arguably reflecting the International Commission of Jurists' observation that while: 'as a matter of law, it is difficult to accommodate the liberation struggles within the complex network of rights and duties under the Geneva Conventions ... this has ceased to be a legal matter and has become a highly political one in which the UK is at present backing the

para. 12; UK Foreign and Commonwealth Office, 'R C Cox (Northern Ireland Office) to T K C Ellison (UN Dept. FCO): "Draft Protocol to Article 3 to the Geneva Conventions – and the Position of Northern Ireland"'.

102 See e.g. UK Foreign and Commonwealth Office, 'UK Mission in Geneva to Immediate FCO Tel No. 185'; UK Foreign and Commonwealth Office, 'Diplomatic Conference on Humanitarian Law in Armed Conflicts – Fourth and Final Session: Geneva 17 March–10 June 1977. Interim Delegation Report', para. 7; UK Foreign and Commonwealth Office, 'Fourth Session of the Diplomatic Conference on Humanitarian Law in Armed Conflict: Geneva, 17 March–10 June 1977: Brief for the UK Delegation', p. 6, para. 23; UK Foreign and Commonwealth Office, 'Draft Report to Ministers on Signature of the Two Additional Protocols of 1977 to the Geneva Conventions of 1949' (Appended to 11 October 1977 Note from M R Eaton to Freeland), paras. 18–22 and annexed note on 'Protocol II – Internal Conflicts – Article 1 – Material Field of Application', paras. 6–9, including draft Statement in Parliament. See also related points in: Mantilla, 'Under (Social) Pressure: The Historical Regulation of Internal Armed Conflicts through International Law', 262; Mantilla, 'The Origins and Evolution of the 1949 Geneva Conventions and the 1977 Additional Protocols', 55, 63.

losing horse and is attracting unnecessary odium in the process'.[103] Bowing to political reality, and under US pressure, a more flexible approach to Article 1(4) was consequently adopted in subsequent sessions, though not without persistent doubts as to the wisdom of following Aldrich's lead.[104]

With respect to Article 1 of Protocol II, and again with Northern Ireland in mind, the UK took a more conservative view throughout than the USA, concerned to be seen as progressive, but not at any cost.[105] The 1975 delegation report accordingly recorded that '[p]rogress on Protocol II was slow but also gave cause for some satisfaction. The threshold provided by Article 1 appears to be high enough to meet all of the United Kingdom's particular concerns ... but not to the extent that the instrument will inevitably become a dead letter.' Like the USA, though, having grown comfortable with the prospect of a 'high-threshold' Protocol II, the UK delegation recognised that 'a major threat ... is the persistence of some delegations, especially those of Norway, Sweden and Finland, in seeking to overburden the Protocol with detailed and high-level obligations ... which would ... greatly reduce the Protocol's chances of wide acceptance and application'.[106]

103 UK Foreign and Commonwealth Office, 'Niall MacDermot, International Commission of Jurists, to David Ennals, Minister of State', para. 4 of attached memo.

104 See e.g. discussion in UK Foreign and Commonwealth Office, 'Diplomatic Conference on Humanitarian Law in Armed Conflicts - Geneva 21 April–11 June: Third Session - Delegation Report', para. 12 (' ... in the view of several Western delegations his [i.e. Aldrich's] personal involvement in negotiations backstage with advocates of liberal treatment for "freedom fighters" (Democratic Republic of Vietnam, PLO, Norway, etc.) led to greater concessions to this viewpoint than were either desirable or justified'). Elsewhere on British doubts as to the US-supported drafting of Art. 42, the UK delegation observed that: 'although Canada and FRG have voiced similar reservations [as the UK] the US has not shown any intention to change their view' (UK Foreign and Commonwealth Office, 'Fourth Session of the Diplomatic Conference on Humanitarian Law in Armed Conflict: Geneva, 17 March–10 June 1977: Brief for the UK Delegation'), p. 11, para. 40. See also: UK Army Legal Services, 'David Hughes-Morgan (Brigadier Legal Staff) to UK Ministry of Defence (Various), "Humanitarian Law Article 42 of Protocol I - Guerrillas"', para. 11. Ultimately, the UK elected not to vote against Art. 42 (rather abstaining) to mitigate the risk of the provision being declared non-reservable by the conference. (See UK Foreign and Commonwealth Office, 'Immediate FCO Telno 277: "Our Tels Nos 224 and 225: Article 42 - Guerillas"'.)

105 See e.g. UK Foreign and Commonwealth Office, 'R J A Martin (UN Dept, FCO) to R C Cox (Northern Ireland Office): "Humanitarian Law in Armed Conflict"', para. 2(a) ('Threshold'); UK Foreign and Commonwealth Office, 'Fourth Session of the Diplomatic Conference on Humanitarian Law in Armed Conflict: Geneva, 17 March–10 June 1977: Brief for the UK Delegation', p. 16, paras. 60–2.

106 UK Foreign and Commonwealth Office, 'Diplomatic Conference on Humanitarian Law in Armed Conflicts - Geneva 3 February–18 April: Second Session - Delegation Report', p. 3, para. 6 See also: UK Foreign and Commonwealth Office, 'M L Tait (UN

Unsurprisingly, the Pakistani revisions of 1977 were subsequently welcomed by the UK as a means of lessening the risk of Protocol II becoming operationally irrelevant, while protecting the UK's Northern Irish concerns – as well as avoiding the risk of a separate, more demanding 'Western-only' instrument being advanced by more progressive Western states.[107]

As in 1949, the UK experience negotiating civil war-regulating provisions at the CDDH underlined the limitations of continued (notional) British great power status. The internal Western debates over Article 1(4), and the connected discussions over what were to become Articles 44 and 96 of Protocol I, are particularly instructive in this regard, highlighting the extent to which the British recognised the limitations of Western power in the absence of US support.[108] At the same time, though, this recognition also demonstrates the extent to which the British adopted a Rationalist approach to negotiations: with the first-ranked preference of redrafting Article 1(4) ruled out, delegation and policymakers reluctantly agreed to follow the US line, with strategies developed to mitigate the risks posed by Article 1(4) in respect of Northern Ireland.[109] A similar approach was in evidence in respect of Protocol II, where, once initial concerns over Northern Ireland were satisfied, the British were able to adopt a cautiously progressive position.

Dept, FCO) to Mr Weir, "Brief for the UK Delegation to the Third Session of the Diplomatic Conference on Humanitarian Law in Armed Conflict"', paras. 8–9; UK Foreign and Commonwealth Office, 'Diplomatic Conference on Humanitarian Law in Armed Conflicts – Geneva 21 April–11 June: Third Session – Delegation Report', para. 3(a).

107 UK Foreign and Commonwealth Office, 'Diplomatic Conference on Humanitarian Law in Armed Conflicts – Fourth and Final Session: Geneva 17 March–10 June 1977. Interim Delegation Report', para. 9. See also: UK Foreign and Commonwealth Office, 'Diplomatic Conference on Humanitarian Law in Armed Conflicts – Geneva 3 February–18 April: Second Session – Delegation Report', pp. 3–4, para. 6.

108 See UK Foreign and Commonwealth Office, 'M K O Simpson-Orlebar (UN Dept., FCO) to Mr Mansfield: "Brief for the UK Delegation to the Fourth Session of the Diplomatic Conference on Humanitarian Law in Armed Conflict"', para. 6(b)('Guerillas: Article 42 of Protocol I'); UK Foreign and Commonwealth Office, 'Humanitarian Law in Armed Conflict: Inner Core Meeting, 14 March 1977 at the US Mission, Geneva', paras. 3–7.

109 See UK Foreign and Commonwealth Office, 'Draft Sections of Report to Ministers on Signature of the Two Additional Protocols of 1977' to the Geneva Conventions of 1949' (Appended to 11 October 1977 Note from M R Eaton to Freeland), especially paras. 18–24; UK Foreign and Commonwealth Office, 'Fourth Session of the Diplomatic Conference on Humanitarian Law in Armed Conflict: Geneva, 17 March–10 June 1977: Brief for the UK Delegation', pp. 5–8, paras. 22–9.

While US positioning was an important determinant of UK behaviour at the CDDH, the British preference – all else being equal – to be seen to be in principle as supportive of the 'progressive development' of IHL also reflected the broader international climate of the 1970s. As the transcript of a broadcast by historian Geoffrey Best – included in FCO archives – notes, '[a]ll the terms of participation in the management of the world's affairs have changed. Countries like ours, if they wish to continue to play a part in the moral side of that management, now have to swallow some of their pride and join in with the rest, even if this sometimes means being lectured to by some of our former dependents.'[110] In other words, in contrast to the immediate post-war world of 1949, by the 1970s UK policymakers appear to have been aware – if perhaps not entirely to have accepted – that 'the world had changed', and that the British would need to adapt their approach in Geneva if the UK was to 'continue to play a part in the moral side' of the development of IHL.

In terms of the provisions regulating internal armed conflict, and pointing to the relevance of the 'Agent Characteristics' hypothesis, this awareness appears to have informed the readiness of the British to remain at the negotiations despite the losses of the 1974 session, as well as to support a 'progressive' Protocol II once threshold concerns were satisfied. Highlighting Regime Type concerns, the British delegation were also evidently sufficiently aware of the need to avoid being perceived negatively both by negotiating counterparts and the public at home to prefer, for example, to rely on Israeli obstinacy to avoid having to call for votes themselves on controversial issues.[111]

[110] Best, 'Updating the Geneva Conventions (Transcript)', para. 5.

[111] See UK Foreign and Commonwealth Office, 'Immediate FCO Telno 277: "Our Tels Nos 224 and 225: Article 42 – Guerillas"', para. 3. ('It is probable that the Israelis will again ask for a vote, but as in the Committee, we should be prepared to do so ourselves if necessary.') On British sensitivity to negative perceptions more generally, see e.g. UK Foreign and Commonwealth Office, 'Diplomatic Conference on Humanitarian Law in Armed Conflicts – Geneva 20 February/29 March 1974: First Session – Delegation Report', para. 8 (referring to: 'great anxiety on all sides not to want to seem unsympathetic to the Africans or to appear racialist'). The British were also uncomfortable with an ICRC initiative to publicise the conference – see UK Foreign and Commonwealth Office, 'J C J Ramsden (UN Dept., FCO) to Mr Freeland', para. 1. ('The ICRC would like to see far more public interest in the work of the Conference .... Colonel Draper and I agreed that the lack of publicity for the work of the Diplomatic Conference was, on the whole, not as bad a thing as the ICRC were suggesting.')

4.3.1.3 Aligned 'Conservative' Western Delegations

The Scandinavian states and Finland, initially along with Australia, consistently took relatively progressive stances throughout the conference: their positions are considered below. The attitudes of most other Western states, though, were broadly aligned – albeit with some important variations – with the positions adopted by the UK and the USA, including through ad hoc meetings of the UN 'Western European and Others Group' (WEOG) and sub-groupings serving as the principal fora for these discussions.

The USA, the UK, Canada, France, and latterly Germany comprised an unofficial WEOG 'inner core', co-ordinating positions through regular intersessional meetings. Even amongst this group though, there were significant differences in opinion, including in respect of Article 1(4) of Protocol I. Here the Americans encountered not just British misgivings, but also Canadian, French, and West German concern, the latter sharing British doubts in respect of the American approach to Article 42 (later Article 44) regulating POW protections for non-state party combatants.[112] Emphasising the importance of US leadership, however, there equally appears to have been widespread awareness that without US support there was little to be gained in labouring these concerns at the CDDH.[113]

Of the conservative Western grouping more generally, Canada was perhaps the most consistently progressive in respect of internal armed conflict, alongside New Zealand.[114] These states' delegations were also

[112] See UK Foreign and Commonwealth Office, 'Fourth Session of the Diplomatic Conference on Humanitarian Law in Armed Conflict: Geneva, 17 March–10 June 1977: Brief for the UK Delegation', p. 3, para. 13. ('WEOG itself is far from cohesive . . . The Delegation should exploit as far as possible the recent tendency towards a harder line by some allies, e.g. FRG, France and Canada, especially on Article 42 of Protocol I.')

[113] See e.g. the eventual French decision not to seek to block consensus on the eventual adoption of Protocol I in plenary (account in: Mantilla, 'Under (Social) Pressure: The Historical Regulation of Internal Armed Conflicts through International Law', 287–8). As noted in the UK delegation report of the 1975 session: 'The United States was at once the most keen advocate of WEOG solidarity and its most flagrant abuser' (UK Foreign and Commonwealth Office, 'Diplomatic Conference on Humanitarian Law in Armed Conflicts – Geneva 3 February–18 April: Second Session – Delegation Report', Annex I, Committee I, pp. 4–5, para. 5).

[114] Though that said, as Charles Lysaght observes, humanitarian motives were also in evidence amongst Western delegations generally in the negotiation of Additional Protocol II: 'There was some disappointment amongst Western delegations that the Protocol was reduced [in 1977]. But most realised that no vital interest of theirs was affected and rested content in the conviction that the Protocol negotiated was the most

the most conciliatory in this respect, attempting to bridge the gaps between their more conservative Western counterparts and developing world delegations, for example, by (unsuccessfully) proposing to establish an intersessional 'Contact Group' to consider the implications and language of Article 1 of Protocol I after the 1974 session. The attitudes of other conservative Western delegations varied with particular issues, with French and Dutch attitudes (along with those of the Portuguese until 1975) as with the British, potentially coloured by colonial concerns, and experiences.[115]

The relatively progressive position adopted by New Zealand, including with respect to wars of national liberation, appears to have reflected a doctrinal view that there was 'no incompatibility between the tradition of the United Nations, which had outgrown the classic concept of war as a conflict among two or more states, and the tradition of the [ICRC], which had regard only to the relief of the suffering entailed in any kind of armed conflict'.[116] For their part, the Canadians also appear to have been wedded to a more progressive, principled position than conservative Western counterparts, in line with a (then-nascent) foreign policy commitment to promoting human rights internationally, and building on Canada's reputation for working constructively on human rights issues in the UN context.[117] Indeed, Canada stands out amongst the more conservative Western group as particularly proactive and effective in promoting an early, home-grown draft of Protocol II imposing basic humanitarian obligations on states with a threshold in line with Common Article 3 of the 1949 Conventions.[118]

extensive that would have any chance of wide acceptance' ('The Attitude of Western Countries', 384).

115 See e.g. British perceptions of Western positions re wars of national liberation in: UK Foreign and Commonwealth Office, 'UK Mission in Geneva to Immediate FCO Tel No. 216'. On French perspectives (and the shadow of French experiences in Algeria generally) see discussion in Alexander, 'International Humanitarian Law, Postcolonialism and the 1977 Geneva Protocol I', 23–30 in particular.

116 Quentin-Baxter, 'Report of the New Zealand Delegation to the First Session of the Diplomatic Conference for the Reaffirmation and Development of International Humanitarian Law Applicable in Armed Conflicts', p. 12, para. 29.

117 See generally Lui, *Why Canada Cares: Human Rights and Foreign Policy in Theory and Practice* . See Forsythe, 'The 1974 Diplomatic Conference on Humanitarian Law: Some Observations', 86–7.

118 See UK Foreign and Commonwealth Office, 'B. M. Mawhinney (First Secretary, Canadian High Commission London) to Michael Arthur (UN Dept., FCO)' and appended telegram; UK Foreign and Commonwealth Office, 'R J A Martin (UN Dept., FCO) to R C Cox (Northern Ireland Office): "Humanitarian Law in Armed Conflict"'; UK Foreign and Commonwealth Office, 'P M Maxey (UN Dept.) to Coles (Scored out,

The Canadians were also influential behind the scenes in corralling Western and delegations to support their preferred approach, at one point noting to an American delegate that it would be 'unfortunate' were an impression to arise that the USA had 'washed its hands' of Protocol II.[119] Head of delegation David Miller evidently also played an important role in assisting the Pakistani delegation in preparing the pared-down 1977 redraft of Protocol II. This suggests that, consistent with the Agent Characteristics hypothesis, and foreshadowing Canada's central role at Rome 1998, the Canadians succeeded in leveraging subject area expertise as well as perceived moral authority to maintain credibility with both the Western and the developing world.[120]

4.3.2 *The 'Progressives': The Nordics (and Australia)*

The delegations of Finland and the Scandinavian states, in particular Norway, were the most consistently 'humanitarian-inclined' at the CDDH. These views manifested in respect of internal armed conflict principally in a preference for regulating both international and non-international armed conflicts through a common set of standards in a single protocol.[121] When it became apparent that such an outcome was unlikely, the Norwegians and allies then shifted approach,

Replaced in Manuscript – Illegible), "Humanitarian Law: Reception for Delegates to London Meeting of Western Group" (Appending Briefing Note)', para. 5 (in appended brief); UK Foreign and Commonwealth Office, 'Report of Washington Meeting on 13 and 14 January 1975 on Humanitarian Law in Armed Conflict' (Undated, Received in Registry 28 January 1975), para. 3.

[119] UK Foreign and Commonwealth Office, 'Report of Washington Meeting 17/18 November 1975 on Humanitarian Law in Armed Conflict (Undated, Received in Registry 28 November 1975)', p. 7, para. 21.

[120] Forsythe, 'Legal Management of Internal War: The 1977 Protocol on Non-International Armed Conflicts', 278. Kalshoven highlights the 'evident blessing' of the head of the Canadian delegation – David Miller – for the simplified 1977 Pakistani draft ('Protocol II, the CDDH and Colombia', 863). Miller's role on behalf of Canada in this regard may also be viewed as foreshadowing the work of Lloyd Axworthy and Philippe Kirsch at Rome in 1998. (See discussion at Chapter 5, Section 5.3.1.) That said, he is also clear that: '[t]here can be little doubt that Justice Hussain's action saved Protocol II from ignominious defeat in the Conference' ('The Diplomatic Conference on Reaffirmation and Development of International Humanitarian Law Applicable in Armed Conflicts, Geneva, 1974–1977', 185).

[121] Sweden, Finland, and to some extent Denmark, largely acted in accord with the Norwegian lead with respect to internal armed conflict. Finland and Denmark feature less heavily in accounts of these negotiations, however, while Sweden focused its efforts more in the area of weapons control rather than the regulation of internal armed conflict.

promoting (again, ultimately unsuccessfully) the inclusion in Protocol II of provisions and standards mirroring those of Protocol I. Norway, initially alongside Australia, also actively supported the developing world initiative to bring wars of national liberation within the ambit of Protocol I.[122]

Highlighting again the importance of domestic political factors, the Australian delegation appears to have been under specific instructions in 1974 not to side with the former colonial powers.[123] This approach was consistent with other developments during the 1972–5 Whitlam government, reflecting a short-lived re-orientation of Australian foreign policy. These included the assertion of an approach to foreign relations that was independent of the USA, the withdrawal of Australian forces from Vietnam and, inter alia, the adoption of public positions in the UN and other contexts supportive of 'the right of peoples, particularly those of Africa, to self-determination and independence'. Australia also recognised 'the important role played by the national liberation movements'.[124] This progressive spirit receded in subsequent sessions, however – again, consistent with the Regime Type hypothesis – following the re-election of the Liberal party in 1975.

Norway, in contrast, took a robust line throughout the CDDH in respect of wars of national liberation and the content of Protocol II. Indeed, the Norwegian delegation went beyond simply supporting the privileging of wars of national liberation, actively advising national liberation movements with respect to attendance at the CDDH.[125] In similar fashion, the Norwegians only reluctantly joined the consensus in the plenary adoption of Protocol II, describing the revised draft as 'a seriously amputated version of the original', and continuing to bemoan the modest ambitions of the revised text and Western hypocrisy even after the fact.[126]

[122] See US Department of State, 'Telegram from US Mission in Geneva to US Mission in Canberra: Laws of War Conference – Wars of Liberation'.

[123] UK Foreign and Commonwealth Office, 'Diplomatic Conference on Humanitarian Law in Armed Conflicts – Geneva 20 February/29 March 1974: First Session – Delegation Report', Annex A (Report on Debates in Plenary and Committees), para. 17.

[124] 'Australian Practice in International Law 1974–1975', 205.

[125] A key figure in this activity was Hans Longva, apparently acting with official sanction. (See UK Foreign and Commonwealth Office, 'R G Britten (British Embassy, Oslo) to T W Keeble (UN Dept., FCO): "Humanitarian Law in Armed Conflict: Liberation Movements"'; also UK Foreign and Commonwealth Office, 'Diplomatic Conference on Humanitarian Law in Armed Conflicts – Geneva 3 February–18 April: Second Session – Delegation Report', Annex I, Committee I, p. 12, para. 12.)

[126] SR.56 *CDDH*, 1978, VII: 205–6. See also generally Eide, 'The New Humanitarian Law in Non-International Armed Conflict'.

Support for the inclusion of wars of national liberation in Protocol I and for a robust Protocol II was of a piece with the strongly human rights-oriented and national liberation movement-supporting foreign policy of Norway and neighbouring states at that time. For example, Sweden, Norway and Finland (the latter 'Nordic' rather than 'Scandinavian') had each provided financial support to such movements in southern Africa since the 1970s. These tendencies were also recognised as reflecting domestic values: as one former national liberation movement representative noted, 'the absence of a colonial tradition, the values and culture of social democracy, the ethics of the Lutheran and Protestant Church were factors influencing sympathy for our case'.[127] The Norwegian policy of engaging with national liberation movements, particularly in Africa, was also underpinned by a unanimous 1973 parliamentary decision 'to endorse a policy of direct, official humanitarian support to the liberation movements'.[128]

Taken together, these observations suggest that – consistent with the Regime Type hypothesis – dominant domestic political values played a significant part in shaping Norwegian (and broader Scandinavian) attitudes regarding the regulation of internal armed conflict. At the same time, however, the 'clean hands' and technical expertise of the Scandinavians evidently remained insufficient for these delegations, whose views were considered beyond the discursive pale by mainstream conservative Western delegations, to generate more widespread Western support for their positions. This potentially suggests a limitation of the Agent Characteristics hypothesis as well as underlining the potential importance of the Logic of Argument hypothesis,

4.3.3 Egypt, India, Pakistan and the Developing World

The decolonisation process that followed the Second World War resulted in a proliferation of newly independent, economically disadvantaged

[127] Sérgio Vieira, 'The Nordic countries and Mozambique: From national liberation to economic liberation', 56; quoted in: Eriksen, *Norway and National Liberation in Southern Africa*, 386. As expressed in similar fashion in an overview of Norwegian relations with Africa: 'Apart from the decisive influence of the UN, the official Norwegian policy towards Africa has been driven by civil society: churches, trade unions and NGOs' (Tostensen, 'Norway's Africa Policy', 35).

[128] Eriksen, *Norway and National Liberation in Southern Africa*, 379.

states, which by the 1970s had begun to coalesce into a 'Global South' in international relations. While this was by no means a coherent assemblage, rather than align explicitly with the USA or the USSR, many such states joined the 'Non-Aligned Movement' (NAM) formally established in 1961 under the leadership of India, Indonesia, Yugoslavia, Egypt. and Ghana. The purposes of the NAM included: preserving 'the national independence, sovereignty, territorial integrity and security of non-aligned countries' and 'support to national liberation movements struggling against colonial and alien domination and foreign occupation'.[129]

Throughout the 1960s, 'non-alignment gradually developed into the dominant concept determining the foreign policy outlook of the majority of Third World states'.[130] Members of this group and developing countries more generally had come to dominate the UN General Assembly by the 1960s. They were also increasingly utilising UN machinery, including the United Nations Conference on Trade and Development and associated groupings (e.g. the 'Group of 77'), to promote these and related ends, including the establishment of a 'New International Economic Order'.[131]

In respect of the CDDH, the demand for IHL to reflect the growing importance of the right of self-determination of peoples (as that concept had emerged in the increasingly 'post-colonial' UN General Assembly) by defining 'wars of national liberation' as international armed conflicts was widely shared amongst non-aligned and developing world delegations.[132] As Best puts it: 'nothing more inflamed Third World opinion against the existing legal order than what were perceived to be the difficulties it unfairly placed in the way of independence and, as they now became generally known, national liberation movements'.[133] Indeed, for some non-aligned and developing world delegations, the CDDH – despite its objective of producing a legally binding treaty as distinct from a hortatory General Assembly declaration – was perceived primarily as an opportunity to promote a broader anticolonial agenda.

[129] Non-Aligned Movement, '*Final Declaration of the Sixth Conference of Heads of State or Government of Non-Aligned Countries, Held at Havana, Cuba, from 3 to 9 September 1979*', 12.

[130] Allison, *The Soviet Union and the Strategy of Non-Alignment in the Third World*, 244.

[131] See for discussion Montbrial, 'For a New World Economic Order'.

[132] For background, see Mantilla, 'Under (Social) Pressure: The Historical Regulation of Internal Armed Conflicts through International Law', 209–11, including citations to: Kay, *The New Nations in the United Nations, 1960-1967*; Henkin, 'The United Nations and Human Rights'.

[133] Best, *War and Law since 1945*, 343.

The British noted, for example, a 'bitter speech' from a delegate from Zaire, declaring that 'his only aim at the Conference was to further the cause of the liberation movements'.[134] While many such delegations were 'anxious to see the new international laws of war protect those who fight for national liberation', they were nevertheless also concerned to avoid providing succour to 'those who take up arms against the post-colonial governments'.[135] The vast majority of non-aligned and developing world delegations were thus keen to support the inclusion of Article 1(4) in Protocol I, but to see only a weak (if any) Protocol II.[136] Accordingly, it is unsurprising that notwithstanding the ICRC's proposals, Norwegian enthusiasm and general Western support, Protocol II encountered a fierce headwind at the CDDH.[137]

In terms of individual non-aligned and developing world contributions, the delegations of Egypt, India and Pakistan stand out as having been particularly influential in respect of the drafting of both Article 1 of Protocol I and Protocol II.

4.3.3.1 Egypt

In the words of a New Zealand delegate, the 'Egyptian delegation was competent at both political and technical levels, and came closest to being the real leader of the Afro-Asian bloc'.[138] This view appears to have reflected enhanced Egyptian status and moral authority under Sadat

[134] UK Foreign and Commonwealth Office, 'M A Arthur (UK Mission in Geneva) to R Facey (UN Department): 'Diplomatic Conference on Humanitarian Law', para. 2. (The author also noted that: '[w]e suspect that if they (the "Third World" [actual phrase used in the letter]) succeed in including wars of national liberation in Protocol I they will not be interested in any Protocol on internal conflicts' As Higgins notes: '[t]o all intents and purposes, the result of the Diplomatic Conference was very positive for national liberation movements and for those involved in wars of national liberation. It could be said, in fact, that a victory of this magnitude with such political and legal implications was even more than national liberation movements or Third World Countries had hoped for' (*The Approach of International Law to Wars of National Liberation*, 40).

[135] Aldrich, 'Some Reflections on the Origins of the 1977 Geneva Protocols', 135.

[136] See inter alia discussions in Moir, *The Law of Internal Armed Conflict*, 89–92; Perna, *The Formation of the Treaty Law of Non-International Armed Conflicts*, 102. Also Higgins, *The Approach of International Law to Wars of National Liberation*, 40–1; citing Suter, *An International Law of Guerrilla Warfare: The Global Politics of Law-Making.*

[137] Forsythe, *The Humanitarians: The International Committee of the Red Cross*, 261–2. See also Cullen, *The Concept of Non-International Armed Conflict in International Humanitarian Law*, 69–73.

[138] Quentin-Baxter, 'Report of the New Zealand Delegation to the First Session of the Diplomatic Conference for the Reaffirmation and Development of International Humanitarian Law Applicable in Armed Conflicts', p. 2, para. 5.

within the Non-Aligned Movement following the October/Yom Kippur War of 1973.[139] Egyptian leadership at the CDDH also reflected the technical ability and personal authority of Georges Abi-Saab, who stands out in the proceedings as a singularly articulate proponent of legal arguments supporting the inclusion of wars of national liberation in Protocol I. Abi-Saab was not only a technically adept specialist, however, he was also an established figure in Western international legal circles, with a prestigious (Western) academic pedigree – Michigan, Harvard, Geneva – who commanded and continues to command respect accordingly.[140] Egypt also adopted a relatively conciliatory, constructive attitude towards conservative Western delegations during the CDDH, contrasting with the more confrontational approach adopted by other developing world states, most notably India. This reflected the post-October/Yom Kippur War re-orientation of Egyptian foreign policy towards closer alignment with and reliance on the USA (underlining again the importance of power relations at the CDDH), as well as Abi-Saab's own background and support from head of delegation Hamid Sultan.[141] Coupled with Egyptian post-October War prestige amongst

[139] As put by one contemporaneous observer, with the October War 'Sadat enhanced his prestige within Egypt and the entire Arab world . . . he has given the Arabs a new sense of self-respect, dignity and prestige' (Rubinstein, 'Egypt's Foreign Policy', 54). See also: Neuberg, 'Sadat to Meet Tito as Soviet Anger Rises'. On Sadat's approach to the Non-Aligned Movement in the context of the Egyptian–Israeli conflict, see Lüthi, 'The Non-Aligned Movement and the Cold War, 1961–1973'. Also more generally on Egypt and the Non-Aligned Movement: Peevers, 'Altering International Law: Nasser, Bandung, and the Suez Crisis'.

[140] In Abi-Saab's own words: ' . . . you have to be rigorous in your legal expertise. When I formulated the case for wars of national liberation as international armed conflicts from a legal perspective, [the West] understood they had to answer; they could not simply push it aside' ('The Third World Intellectual in Praxis: Confrontation, Participation, or Operation behind Enemy Lines?'). Abi-Saab's extensive publications on non-international armed conflict and wars of national liberation include: 'Non-International Armed Conflicts'; 'Wars of National Liberation and the Laws of War', 1985; 'Wars of National Liberation in the Geneva Conventions and Protocols'; 'Wars of National Liberation and the Development of Humanitarian Law'; 'Wars of National Liberation and the Laws of War', 1972.

[141] US diplomatic cables reveal collaboration between the US and Egyptian delegations, including between Aldrich, Abi-Saab and Egyptian head of delegation Prof. Hamid Sultan. (See e.g. US Department of State, 'Telegram from Department of State to US Embassy Cairo: Geneva Conference on Laws of War'.) This relationship placed the USA in a challenging position vis à vis Israel on occasion, including in respect of the drafting of what was to become Art. 96 of Additional Protocol I. (See US Department of State, 'Telegram from US Mission in Geneva to Department of State: Laws of War Conference – Liberation Movement Problem'.) Indeed, Aldrich elsewhere has lauded Sultan Hamid as a 'tower of strength and wisdom' ('Some Reflections on the Origins of

the 'Global South', the Egyptian delegation was thus well-placed in terms of relations with both developing world and Western delegations. The ability of the Egyptian delegation to translate these relations into effective influence, however – consistent with the Agent Characteristics hypothesis – appears in large part to be attributable to the technical fluency and personal authority of Abi-Saab.

4.3.3.2 India

The Indian delegation at the CDDH played the role of antagonistic developing world, post-colonial state par excellence.[142] A keen proponent of a far-reaching Article 1(4) of Protocol I, India was as consistently opposed to Protocol II, its delegates querying the desirability of and need for this protocol from the first session of the Conference onwards – latterly perhaps unsurprisingly, given the 1975–7 national state of emergency.

This approach was moreover of a piece with Indian foreign policy as it developed after the 1962 Sino-Indian war. India remained committed to non-alignment as the centrepiece of its foreign relations, and was a strong supporter of decolonisation, while championing the protection of national autonomy and the safeguarding of newly independent states from great power encroachment. It also relied on an implicit Soviet security guarantee in intervening in the Pakistani civil war in 1971, and had performed a nuclear test of its own in 1974. By 1974, India was accordingly the undisputed major regional power in South Asia, with a stronger relationship with the Soviet Union than with the USA. In 1977, after the state of emergency, the country also had its first non-Congress Party-led government since independence. That said, India was generally unable to translate its military strength into global influence during the 1970s, remaining a marginal presence in global politics during this period.[143]

the 1977 Geneva Protocols', 134). See also generally Shama, *Egyptian Foreign Policy from Mubarak to Morsi: Against the National Interest,* 34–5.

[142] David Forsythe characterises the Indian delegation as 'monkey-wrenchers' in respect of Protocol II (Forsythe, 'Legal Management of Internal War: The 1977 Protocol on Non-International Armed Conflicts', 281).

[143] For an overview of Indian foreign policy during this period, see Mansingh, 'Indira Gandhi's Foreign Policy: Hard Realism?' As observed by Chitalkar and Malone in respect of Indian approaches to multilateral institutions: 'Nehru's death in 1964 marked a watershed for India's foreign policy. India's engagement with multilateralism took a backseat in the latter half of the 1960s, as India focused on regional and domestic challenges . . . The 1970s witnessed more pronounced estrangement between India and

Of a piece with this last, despite its regional power primacy, Indian diplomacy was relatively ineffective in the multilateral setting of the CDDH, particularly compared to Egyptian and Pakistani efforts with respect to internal armed conflicts. Indian delegates were swimming with the tide with respect to Article 1(4) of Protocol I, so this drafting episode provides little insight into the strengths and weaknesses of the Indian approach. During the committee negotiations over Article 1 of Protocol II, however, and in the final discussions over the Pakistani compromise text, Indian misgivings did not obtain the traction that might have been expected given India's regional status as a nuclear power and position as a founder of the Non-Aligned Movement. This suggests limits to Indian Realist capacity as well as highlighting the difficulties encountered by 'monkey-wrenchers' such as India (and 'maximalists' such as Norway) in effecting outcomes via positions that made the 'best' the enemy of the 'good' by failing to reconsider or frame positions and arguments around more broadly prevailing sentiments at the conference.[144]

4.3.3.3 Pakistan

Pakistan emerges as a significant developing world player at the CDDH in 1977. Whereas India was aligned with the Soviet Union by the mid-1970s, Pakistan had become more US-oriented: the left-leaning Bhutto government had succeeded in retaining good ties with the Nixon and Ford administrations in the USA, while at the same time forging stronger relations than previously with the Soviet Union. Pakistan also only joined the Non-Aligned Movement in 1979, formerly having been party to the US-sponsored Baghdad Pact and Manila Pact alliances (until 1979 and 1977, respectively). Like the Egyptians, the Pakistani delegation was thus well-placed to function as a bridge-builder between Western, Soviet bloc and developing world delegations at the CDDH, and particularly to have developed a degree of credibility as a reliable interlocutor in both Western and Soviet eyes, in line with Agent Characteristics expectations.

With respect to internal armed conflict, the head of the Pakistani delegation indicated at the second session of the CDDH that: 'it had

the world' ('India and Global Governance', 584). On Indian relations with the USA and USSR during this period, see helpful chapters in the same volume by Rajan Menon and Ashley J. Tellis.

[144] The characterisation of Norway as 'maximalist' is from Forsythe, 'Legal Management of Internal War: The 1977 Protocol on Non-International Armed Conflicts', 280. The reference to the best as the enemy of the good paraphrases Voltaire (Ratcliffe, *Concise Oxford Dictionary of Quotations*, 389).

been the consistent position of his Government to recognize the imperative necessity to elaborate and extend the application of humanitarian law to armed conflicts of a non-international character ... [and that it] favoured the extension of rules applicable to international conflicts to cover all armed conflicts'.[145] There is, however, no obvious foreign policy-based 'smoking gun' to explain this orientation. The Bhutto government had come to power following the 1971 Bangladesh Liberation War, which had resulted in the loss of East Pakistan, and Pakistan and India had been in dispute since 1948 over Kashmir. These experiences may conceivably have informed Pakistani inclination to strengthen the governance of internal armed conflicts.[146] Alternatively, of course, the Pakistani delegation may simply have seized an opportunity to build East–West and North–South bridges where they were well placed to do so (particularly in contradistinction to India).[147]

Motivation aside, however, contemporaneous records and observers recognise the central role of the Pakistani delegation in preventing the abandonment of Protocol II, and in enabling developing world delegations to support a revised, abbreviated set of proposals.[148] In terms of process, head-of-delegation Mushtaq Hussain and colleagues apparently conducted behind-the-scenes discussions principally with the Canadians, who had previously produced an abbreviated draft 'Protocol II' in 1971, and who (as noted above) were singularly committed to this endeavour.[149] The end result was a draft designed to ameliorate developing world anxieties. Once this had obtained Egyptian approval, moreover, the

[145] I/SR.23 *CDDH*, 1978, VIII:225. That said, it bears underlining that the head of the Pakistani delegation – Mushtaq Hussain, a judge of the Lahore High Court – does not appear to have been a particular supporter of Bhutto (indeed, Judge Hussain was to go on to preside over the 1979 trial of the (then former) prime minister). See Iqbal, 'Judge Harboured Bias against Bhutto, SC Told'. Also: Anwar, *The Terrorist Prince*, 125–7.

[146] Not least as India had also undergone these events, but with a very different result in terms of policy orientation.

[147] Forsythe's observation that: '[t]he head of the Pakistani delegation was strongly committed to securing more law on internal war' suggests that this may equally have been a personal commitment on Mushtaq Hussain's part ('Legal Management of Internal War', 278).

[148] See e.g. Bothe, 'The International Committee of the Red Cross and the Additional Protocols of 1977', 69, note 85; Forsythe, 'Legal Management of Internal War', 278–9.

[149] Forsythe, 'Legal Management of Internal War', 278. The final version of Protocol II has 28 articles, with some overlap in important areas with the 24-article Canadian draft. (See International Committee of the Red Cross, '*Conference of Government Experts on the Reaffirmation and Development of International Humanitarian Law Applicable in Armed Conflicts (Geneva, 24 May–12 June 1971): Report on the Work of the Conference*', 57–61.)

majority of other developing world delegations followed suit, with Western and Soviet bloc delegations also falling into line.[150] As Forsythe has put it: 'It was Pakistan's leadership on this issue that brought along a number of states from the lesser developed ranks, and thus made possible the adoption of [Protocol II].'[151]

4.3.4 *The Soviet Union*

The Soviet Union had sought to build closer ties with non-aligned states since the 1955 Bandung Conference, and taking the view that the Non-Aligned Movement was anti-Western in orientation, encouraged non-aligned states to reject Western overtures.[152] This led to the conclusion of a series of 'friendship and co-operation' treaties between the USSR and a range of developing countries, including India, Iraq and Egypt, Somalia, Angola and Mozambique, with a view to forming a 'contractual basis of a shift in the balance of Third World political loyalties'.[153] Given this orientation, it is unsurprising that the Soviet Union and its associated bloc were – as in 1949, quite rationally – enthusiastic supporters of the developing world effort to include wars of national liberation within Article 1(4) of Protocol I.[154] This alignment was also consistent with longstanding Soviet legal doctrine, though the sincerity of this commitment is debatable, perhaps suggesting a more instrumental form of support for developing world endeavours than the principled humanitarianism of Norway.[155]

150 This episode is described in Forsythe, 'Legal Management of Internal War', 278–9.
151 Forsythe, *The Humanitarians*, 262.
152 Allison, *The Soviet Union and the Strategy of Non-Alignment in the Third World*, 46, 180.
153 Ibid., 224.
154 Re. the composition of the 'Eastern bloc', and the status of outliers such as Romania and Yugoslavia, see Ciobanu, 'The Attitude of the Socialist Countries'.
155 See Neff, *War and the Law of Nations: A General History*, 373. As put by Ciobanu in respect of Soviet bloc support for the drafting of Article 1(4) of Additional Protocol I: '[t]he delegates from the socialist countries appeared rather preoccupied with the elaboration of a reasonable line of reasoning in support of the majority's submission that wars of national liberation were in all fairness to be characterized as international armed conflicts' ('The Attitude of the Socialist Countries', 410). He adds, though, that: 'They (the governments of the socialist countries) see in any genuine war of this kind a bellum justum which deserves the support of all countries attached to the idea of justice' (413). This view is consistent with Boris Mamlyuk's characterisation of the Soviet approach to international law, as: 'a Romantic, humanistic, moral expression of dissatisfaction with the inequitable distribution of material resources on Earth, formally calling

That said, the Soviet Union also supported Canada and other Western states, as well as Egypt and Pakistan, in promoting the adoption of a moderate version of Protocol II,[156] in addition to working closely with the USA in other respects at the CDDH – especially in relation to the treatment of nuclear weapons.[157] It may be presumed that, as in 1949, USSR delegation members were not particularly concerned about expectations of Soviet compliance with the strictures of Protocol II.[158] Perhaps more interestingly, however, this conduct suggests that, contrary to some suggestions, Soviet bloc support for Article 1(4) was unlikely to have been motivated by a simple desire to frustrate the Western powers.[159] Indeed, relations between USSR and Western delegations with respect to Protocol II and elsewhere at the CDDH rather reflected the détente-era alignment of Soviet and US interests in some respects, and a consequent warming in relationship, underlining (this time in line with Realist expectations) the capacity of the superpowers to together dominate and set the direction of negotiations.[160]

4.3.5 The ICRC

> 'The ICRC acted as legal advisers but otherwise could only wring their hands as they watched their work eroded and the very basis of their approach to the Conference washed away.'[161]

Although other non-governmental organisations such as the International Commission of Jurists and Amnesty International took an interest in proceedings at the CDDH, governments continued to accord a privileged status to the Committee, and the conference was, like its 1949 predecessor, very much a creature of the ICRC.[162] As such, once again, the Committee's role at the CDDH merits specific discussion.

for action, but showing disdain for formal constraints in relation to ambiguously defined class interests' ('Decolonization as a Cold War Imperative', 197).

156 Forsythe, 'Legal Management of Internal War', 280.

157 See Greenwood, 'A Critique of the Additional Protocols to the Geneva Conventions', 8–9. See also pp. 159–60 above.

158 See discussion on Common Article 3 in Chapter 3.

159 Forsythe, *The Humanitarians*, 261.

160 See e.g. Aldrich, 'Some Reflections on the Origins of the 1977 Geneva Protocols', 133.

161 UK Foreign and Commonwealth Office, 'Diplomatic Conference on Humanitarian Law in Armed Conflicts – Geneva 20 February/29 March 1974: First Session – Delegation Report', para. 5.

162 See Bothe, 'The International Committee of the Red Cross and the Additional Protocols of 1977', 62–3; Suter, *An International Law of Guerrilla Warfare: The*

The ICRC was drawn into the CDDH reluctantly. As Forsythe notes, the ICRC was 'unsure that the 1970s was the right moment', but it 'could hardly stand aside and refuse to play its historical role for the development of IHL'.[163] Discussions of human rights in armed conflict post-1968, however, and 'UN bodies, a wide range of states, private human rights groups, and associations of lawyers [coming to pay] . . . more attention to humanitarian treaties' led the ICRC to act in order to safeguard its traditional role as the 'guardian' of IHL.[164] Western governments were also keen to see the ICRC retain this role, the idea being that: '[t]he ICRC, being isolated from the pressures that plague the UN Secretariat, could retreat into isolation and, making use of its long experience in armed conflicts, carefully draft new technical specifics . . . .'[165]

To a degree, this approach bore fruit, as (in Aldrich's words) '[i]n introducing each article for debate, and occasionally by a reminder during debate, the representatives of the ICRC helped focus the attention of the delegates on the humanitarian precepts that gave a common and uniting thread to our work'.[166] In general, however, the ICRC appears to have failed to have adjusted its behaviour sufficiently to take into account the post-decolonisation political context and the challenges posed to the Committee's conservative, legalistic approach to the development of IHL. As Forsythe has put it, '[t]he legislative process is inherently a political process, in the sense that conferences to develop humanitarian law entail struggle to make public policy. This simple point, so evident to many observers and participants in the process, has not always been fully appreciated by some elements of the ICRC.'[167]

Global Politics of Law-Making, 134–5. Niall MacDermot of the International Commission of Jurists (a former British Government minister) and Nigel Rodley of Amnesty International would also work closely together (including with M. Cherif Bassiouni) in other instances. (See Sikkink, *The Justice Cascade: How Human Rights Prosecutions Are Changing World Politics*, 101.)

163 Forsythe, *The Humanitarians*, 261–2. As Forsythe has put it: '[i]n the mid-1970s the ICRC was not at all sure that the 1974-77 diplomatic conference would result in the *progressive* development of IHL. But, given the push for such a conference through the UN, not always for humanitarian reasons, the organization had to do the best that it could to see that new codification efforts did not lead to back sliding in humanitarian protection' (Ibid., 268–9).

164 Ibid., 264.

165 Forsythe, 'The 1974 Diplomatic Conference on Humanitarian Law: Some Observations', 84.

166 Aldrich, 'Some Reflections on the Origins of the 1977 Geneva Protocols', 135.

167 Forsythe, *Humanitarian Politics: The International Committee of the Red Cross*, 127. Also Suter, *An International Law of Guerrilla Warfare: The Global Politics of Law-Making*, 119–25. As a reviewer of a draft of this manuscript observed, Jean Pictet 'was a western

By 1974, moreover, the relationships that the ICRC had developed over the preceding century with Western and other governments were insufficient to maintain its pre-eminent status.[168] While developing world delegations showed deference to the Committee on occasion, this could not be taken for granted: the uncertain extent of the Committee's authority in the eyes of these delegations resulted in reluctance on the part of the ICRC to test this point given the risk of alienating this new constituency.[169] The ICRC's ability to put forward robust arguments on politically sensitive issues was consequently affected (as observed by Aldrich) by the need for it to maintain working relations not only with its Western 'allies' but also with developing world and socialist counterparts.[170]

In short, while doubtless effective in debates over a range of issues, the ICRC shied away from expressing itself too forcefully on issues of particular political sensitivity, including in relation to Article 1(4) and the ambit of Protocol II, focusing its energies instead on intervening in less sensitive areas where its technical expertise could more effectively be brought to bear.[171] This, in turn, led some Western delegates to complain that the 'tacit support' of the Committee was welcome, but that it was not

legalist who was not entirely astute about his contemporary international relations'. See in similar vein: Greenwood, 'A Critique of the Additional Protocols to the Geneva Conventions', 7.

168 See Forsythe, *The Humanitarians*, 262: 'In general, the ICRC exerted less influence in the mid-1970s than in 1949, owing to the fact that IHL was no longer so heavily influenced by a western club'.

169 See e.g. discussions at: SR.58 *CDDH*, 1978, IX:223–5; SR.63 *CDDH*, 1978, IX:291–303.

170 See Aldrich, 'Classified Report of the United States Delegation to the Diplomatic Conference on the Reaffirmation and Development of International Humanitarian Law Applicable in Armed Conflicts, Geneva, Switzerland, February 20–March 29 1974', 1–2. See in similar vein on the establishment of a 'Coordinating Committee' prior to the 1974 conference session: UK Foreign and Commonwealth Office, 'L J Evans (British Consulate General Geneva) to Ian K C Ellison (UN Dept., FCO): "ICRC – Humanitarian Law in Armed Conflicts"', p. 1, para. 2). ('ICRC had felt somewhat hesitant to nominate a panel themselves since they felt that they would inevitably be criticised by the smaller and developing countries for having loaded the dice in favour of the Western European and developed countries or vice versa. As you know, ICRC have a complex about being (openly at any rate) associated with any group or groupings of particular Powers or interests.')

171 Forsythe, *The Humanitarians: The International Committee of the Red Cross*, 262. Bothe, for example, acknowledging that '[t]he impact of this [ICRC] participation varied depending on the issues and persons involved', highlights Pictet's contribution to the treatment of air crews descending in distress ('The International Committee of the Red Cross and the Additional Protocols of 1977', 62–3). See also Aldrich, 'Some Reflections on the Origins of the 1977 Geneva Protocols', 135.

'of much use unless they spoke out'.[172] Indeed, the British were complaining as early as 1973 about the ICRC's 'misplaced humanitarianism': '[t]hey claim they are endeavouring to reflect all shades of opinion but they have taken a series of decisions unfavourable to us and in line with the more extreme humanitarians'.[173]

This is not to say, of course, that Committee representatives were not influential in debates: even while complaining about the ICRC's 'highly developed political sensitivity ... manifest[ing] itself in a measure of compensatory bias', UK delegates still acknowledged that 'the advisory statements of its representatives ... inevitably carried considerable weight'.[174] While this may have been the case in some instances, however, the overall impression given by the debates over internal armed conflict is that the ICRC did not play its hand particularly well. Having commenced the negotiations with a degree of Western support and acknowledgement of its technical expertise, and the grudging respect of at least some developing world delegations, over the course of the CDDH the ICRC's stature appears to have diminished rather than grown in the eyes of both groups of states.[175]

Amongst conservative Western states, for example, the Committee's failure to stand up more robustly in the face of radical developing world initiatives (such as Article 1(4)) appears in particular to have sapped its support.[176] At the same time, the ICRC's

[172] UK Foreign and Commonwealth Office, 'Diplomatic Conference on Humanitarian Law in Armed Conflicts - Geneva 20 February/29 March 1974: First Session - Delegation Report', para. 8.

[173] UK Foreign and Commonwealth Office, 'T W Keeble (UN Dept., FCO) to Mr Goodenough, Mr Parsons: "Humanitarian Law Applicable in Armed Conflicts: Preparations for the 1974 Diplomatic Conference"', para. 9.

[174] UK Foreign and Commonwealth Office, 'Diplomatic Conference on Humanitarian Law in Armed Conflicts - Geneva 3 February–18 April: Second Session - Delegation Report', Annex I, Committee I, Page 5, para. 6.

[175] Bothe is broadly sympathetic to the ICRC: '[t]aken as a whole and despite certain problems ... the preparation and negotiation of the two Additional Protocols of 1977 once more demonstrated the crucial role of the ICRC in the sphere of humanitarian law' ('The International Committee of the Red Cross and the Additional Protocols of 1977', 79). Even then, however, he still recognises that the Committee: 'underestimated certain difficulties and left a few loopholes' including in respect of wars of national liberation and non-international armed conflict (66–71).

[176] The British observed, for example, that: 'The ICRC spoke in guarded terms in public but in private were clearly in favour of the legal attitudes advanced by most of WEOG.' (UK Foreign and Commonwealth Office, 'Diplomatic Conference on Humanitarian Law in Armed Conflicts - Geneva 20 February/29 March 1974: First Session - Delegation Report', Annex A (Report on Debates in Plenary and Committees), para. 17.)

failure to anticipate and adapt to the 'UN-style' dynamics of the CDDH, in a world transformed since 1949, left developing world delegations unimpressed. Consistent with this view, the Committee's involvement in the eventual Pakistani redraft of Protocol II appears to have been minimal, with that initiative led by Pakistan and Canada.

In terms of hypothesised factors, therefore, while the ICRC clearly played a role as a 'norm entrepreneur' in managing the process leading up to the CDDH and in a range of areas at the conference, in respect of internal armed conflict its impact appears to have been marginal, reflecting an ebbing away of the Committee's perceived authority amongst the various factions as the conference progressed. While delegates from all sides were complimentary about the Committee at various stages of debate, in general terms, the ICRC seems to have placed itself in an invidious position in respect of internal armed conflict, attempting to 'hold the ring' while the competing blocs wrestled with one another. It appears to have been unable (or unwilling to attempt) to exert a significant influence on proceedings, despite evident concern about the prospects forAdditional Protocol II in particular.[177]

4.4 Why Did the CDDH Adopt Article 1(4) and Protocol II?

As in Chapter 3, the following section of this chapter considers the extent to and manner in which the hypotheses set out in Chapter 1 were more or less salient to the negotiation of Article 1(4) of Protocol I and of Protocol II.

4.4.1 Great Power Preferences

> 'The preferences of great powers are likely to be especially significant in shaping the civil war regime.' (The Realist hypothesis)

While the Cold War certainly contributed to shaping the CDDH, the impact of great power preferences on the conference was on the whole more muted than in 1949: indeed, Article 1(4) of Protocol I and Protocol II generally were shaped more by 'North–South' tensions than 'East–West' friction.

[177] See e.g. I/SR.7 *CDDH*, 1978, VIII:51.

This is not to say, of course, that the preferences of more powerful states were not important at key turning points in the Protocols' development. As in 1949, for example, the ICRC focused its pre-conference efforts on engaging and consulting with its traditional partners and great and middle powers. The USA succeeded, in turn, in having the PRG excluded from the 1974 and 1975 sessions, while the USA and Soviet Union successfully combined forces to exclude nuclear weapons from the scope of discussion.[178]

In contrast to 1949, however, it is striking that the impetus behind the CDDH as a whole lay with the developing world, following the 1968 Tehran conference. As the above discussion makes clear, moreover, the key outcomes of the CDDH with respect to internal armed conflict were driven very largely by developing world preferences and concerns. American pressure, it is true, was critical in marshalling conservative Western assent to the inclusion of Article 1(4) in Protocol I, with the British in particular recognising the weakness of their position in the absence of US support. Even here, though, the American position appears to have reflected less wholehearted support for this endeavour, than pragmatic recognition that there was little to be gained by refighting the battles of 1974 directly, and that it was reasonable to aim instead to ameliorate the worst implications of Article 1(4) through careful drafting of other provisions, principally Articles 44 and 96.

Indeed, even where Western powers were able to celebrate success regarding internal armed conflict – as was the case, for example, with the British in respect of the threshold of Protocol II, or the Scandinavians regarding the inclusion of Article 1(4) of Protocol I – these successes were only possible where preferences coincided with those of a critical mass of developing world delegations.[179] Similarly, even though Soviet bloc support lent an air of inevitability to the inclusion of Article 1(4) in Protocol I, where Soviet and developing world preferences were aligned, Soviet support for Protocol II appears to have been only a secondary factor in the final shape of this protocol, the drafting rather more closely reflecting developing world concerns and preferences.[180] Even amongst developing

[178] See e.g. account in Forsythe and Magat, 'Updating the Rules of War; The Third World Wins Some Symbolic Victories'. In connection with nuclear weapons, see also notes 87 and 157 and accompanying text.

[179] See inter alia in Forsythe and Magat, 'Updating the Rules of War; The Third World Wins Some Symbolic Victories'.

[180] The Chinese attended the 1974 session of the CDDH only. The material surveyed does not indicate, moreover, that Chinese views were particularly key to the adoption of any

world delegations, moreover, strongly held Indian preferences appear to have had negligible impact on the drafting of Protocol II.

In short, while outcomes overall at the CDDH may have broadly reflected superpower preferences and Cold War cleavages and divisions, and while Realist American pressure proved decisive in determining conservative Western approaches to Article 1(4) during negotiations, the provisions on internal armed conflict far more closely reflected the preferences of less powerful, developing world states. It is therefore necessary to look to factors other than great power preferences to explain these drafting outcomes.

4.4.2 Rationalist Considerations

> 'The more intrusive or restrictive any proposed set of civil war-regulating treaty provisions, the less likely they are to be supported by governments in the course of treaty negotiations, especially where governments are engaged in or foresee a possibility of a civil war or insurgency. The end of a civil war or insurgency may, however, make a government more likely to support such provisions.' (The Rationalist hypothesis)

Article 1(4) of Protocol I presents a distinct challenge from a rationalist perspective. For the conservative US-led West, of course, both initial dislike of the 1974 drafting and the subsequent decision to seek means of accommodating this provision within a workable Protocol I can be cast as eminently rational. Israeli discomfort with this drafting equally makes perfect, reasonable sense. From a developing world perspective, however, the extension of international humanitarian law as applicable in *international* armed conflicts to 'armed conflicts in which peoples are fighting against colonial domination and alien occupation and against racist regimes in the exercise of their right of self-determination' also begs important questions. In particular, given that separatist conflicts such as the Eritrean war of independence, the FRETILIN insurgency in East

of the provisions on internal armed conflict, save insofar as their views were aligned with those of the Soviet Union and developing world states. See Farina, 'The Attitudes of the People's Republic of China'; Triggs, 'Traditional Asian Approaches to Victims of Armed Conflict and Their Relationship to Modern International Humanitarian Law – The Chinese View: Commentary', in particular p. 153: 'China believes that all "unjust" wars of aggression are those of the imperialist States determined to impose their domination over other States and to ensure continued exploitation of them. Just wars are fought by those opposed to imperialist interests. For the Chinese, the laws of war must fulfil the twin functions of alleviating the suffering caused by such conflicts and favouring those who oppose aggression.'

Timor and, latterly, the Sudanese civil war could reasonably be viewed as such 'wars of national liberation', the determined support for this initiative from African, Asian and Middle Eastern delegations requires explanation.[181]

It may, of course, be observed that Article 1(4) should properly be understood as primarily a rhetorical device, intended to allow developing world and Soviet bloc delegations to demonstrate commitment to the cause of anti-imperialism, whilst remaining largely toothless in practice, its application restricted to a distinct set of conflicts. This view, though, depends on the range of conflicts encompassed by Article 1(4) being understood as exceedingly narrow, encompassing solely the struggles against apartheid in South Africa, the Palestinian–Israeli conflict, and classically 'anti-colonial' conflicts such as (in 1974) the Angolan and Namibian wars of independence, and the struggle for majority rule in Rhodesia.[182]

These conflicts indeed appear to have largely motivated this provision. Its proponents, however, seemingly failed to take into account that, irrespective of their intentions, the wording could result in other conflicts reasonably being understood as falling within the provision's ambit. Many of these same states, moreover – India being perhaps the most prominent example – were also amongst the most persistent objectors to the regulation of internal armed conflict in Protocol II. It is accordingly difficult to present Article 1(4) as the outcome of entirely rational calculation by its main supporters.[183]

[181] For some of the challenges involved in interpreting Article 1(4), see Sandoz, Swinarski, and Zimmermann, *Commentary on the Additional Protocols of 8 June 1977 to the Geneva Conventions of 12 August 1949*, 41–56, especially paras. 102–13.

[182] Aldrich, consistent with his approach during the CDDH, advanced this view in responding to the failure of the Reagan administration to support ratification of Protocol I. See Aldrich, 'Prospects for United States Ratification of Additional Protocol I to the 1949 Geneva Conventions'. ('Paragraph 4 was designed by its sponsors with certain conflicts in mind, specifically those in Palestine and southern Africa, and was drafted in terms fashioned to exclude its application to civil wars within existing states' (Ibid., 6).) As the authors of the ICRC commentary caution, however: '[d]espite the many instruments and texts available, it should be noted that some discrepancies remain, and that the general character of texts which were unanimously approved does not always lead to undisputed conclusions' (Sandoz, Swinarski, and Zimmermann, *Commentary on the Additional Protocols of 8 June 1977 to the Geneva Conventions of 12 August 1949*, 51, para. 96).

[183] Though equally, opposition to this provision from imperial powers such as France and the UK, and from 'targets' such as South Africa and Israel, is entirely consistent with this hypothesis.

Protocol II, on the other hand, is more persuasively cast as a consequence of rationalist calculation amongst concerned Western, Soviet-bloc and developing world delegations. As with Common Article 3, it can be considered to be sufficiently 'humanitarian' to allow delegations from each of these blocs to congratulate themselves on having made progress in regulating internal armed conflict, yet equally to be sufficiently undemanding as to make only weak demands of governments. More specifically, the negotiating history of Protocol II reflects a balancing of strategic, sovereignty-related concerns and the desire to be seen to be advancing humanitarian principles in non-international armed conflicts amongst key delegations involved.

The former was a concern mainly, but not solely, raised by developing world delegations – reasonably enough given, as one commentator has put it, that 'many such countries may have [had] unstable governments which need consolidation and they appeared worried that Protocol II . . . would entitle other States to interfere in their domestic affairs'.[184] India would fall into this category. For more cautious Western states such as the UK and France, moreover, similar considerations underlay hesitation to support a robust Protocol II, in particular with respect to the threshold set in draft Article 1 of that protocol – Northern Ireland featuring prominently, for example, in British calculations. On the other hand, the chief proponents of a more robust Protocol II were European states, primarily Norway and fellow Scandinavians, supported by Canada and New Zealand, with this strong support being consistent with broader foreign policy orientations.

Reflecting these tensions, the Pakistani proposal seems to have been designed specifically to demonstrate some humanitarian progress, whilst reassuring the delegations of newly independent, post-colonialist – and possibly unstable or fragile – developing world polities. To paraphrase Aldrich, the Pakistanis and their supporters sought to negotiate the most intrusive and restrictive protocol that most developing world countries could accept, rather than one that reflected Norwegian preferences: indeed, the adoption of the final wording by consensus, notwithstanding grumbling from 'sovereigntist' partisans such as India and the determinedly 'humanitarian' Norwegian delegation, suggests that the drafters ultimately succeeded in arriving at a form of words that satisfied the minimum requirements of a broad majority of delegations.

[184] Lupis, *The Law of War*, 237.

That said, if Article 1(4) remains a rationalist puzzle, aspects of Protocol II are similarly difficult to explain in terms of this hypothesis. For one, while the content of Protocol II may reflect a balancing of preferences across delegations, as in 1949, it remains unclear why delegations were willing in the first instance to adopt an instrument that placed any further limitations on their conduct in internal armed conflicts beyond the strictures of Common Article 3. While the willingness of Pakistan to support Protocol II may conceivably be attributable to experiences in the 1971 Bangladesh Liberation War, many of the developing countries that 'succeeded in blunting the edge of the movement for a much more ample protection of the victims of civil wars' had also experienced, or were themselves products of, civil wars. While the hypothesis would suggest that such states would tend to support more intrusive and restrictive provisions, this was simply not the case.[185] Once again, therefore, while some aspects of Protocol II may be explicable by a Rationalist approach, in order to explain the adoption of both Article 1(4) and Protocol II, it is necessary to look further afield.

4.4.3 *Agent Characteristics*

> 'The greater their perceived moral authority and their ability to leverage subject area expertise, the more likely governments and non-state actors are to be able to elicit the support of other governments for demanding civil war-regulating provisions in the course of treaty negotiations.' (The Agent Characteristics hypothesis)

With respect to both Article 1(4) and Protocol II, the delegations of conservative Western, developed countries, which in general possessed stronger technical capacity than their developing world counterparts, were on the losing side. The ICRC, possessed of both a singular degree of technical expertise and a traditionally preeminent humanitarian reputation, similarly largely failed to persuade the majority of developing world delegations to support its more expansive agenda for the regulation of civil war. The internal armed conflict-related outcomes of the CDDH thus present a conundrum with respect to the operation of this hypothesis.

Turning first to the ICRC, there are a number of reasons why the Committee found itself in a weaker position in the 1970s than in 1949 in terms of both moral and expert authority. First, the ICRC (and the Red

[185] Baxter, 'Modernizing the Law of War', 173.

Cross movement generally) had lost its quasi-hegemonic non-governmental expert authority in the course of the intervening decades, reflected in the multiplicity of voices raised with respect to 'human rights in armed conflict' in UN circles since 1968.[186] The failure of the Committee to engage authoritatively with the legally grounded (yet, from the perspective of the ICRC, unconventional) positions with respect to internal armed conflict presented by developing world authorities such as Abi-Saab illustrates how it had failed to establish itself sufficiently as a source of technical expertise in the eyes of developing world governments and representatives more familiar with discourse in the UN arena. Indeed, this relative weakening in the ICRC's expert authority in the eyes of the developing world may well explain why, when attempting to respond to proposals to accord special treatment to 'wars of national liberation', Pictet found himself resorting ineffectively to arguments framed in moral, rather than technical legal terms. It is therefore perhaps unsurprising that the ICRC ultimately opted to focus its efforts at the CDDH on less politically sensitive matters than the regulation of internal armed conflict.

The technical expertise available to more conservative Western governments was also of little benefit in countering (or watering down) the proposed inclusion of Article 1(4) in Protocol I. To some extent, the difficulties that afflicted the ICRC also affected these governments in their dealings with developing world representatives. While UK and US representatives, for example, were aware of the discursive difficulties that might be encountered in negotiations (accordingly preferring to hold discussions under ICRC/Swiss auspices rather than in a UN context), in the event they were little better equipped than ICRC technical experts to combat either Abi-Saab's arguments or the non-technical rhetoric deployed by the representatives, inter alia, of Zaire and Mauretania with respect to wars of national liberation.

Many Western states, moreover, were significantly morally compromised in the eyes of developing, post-colonial world, in some instances to a greater degree than in 1949. The US, for example, was hamstrung by its embroilment in Vietnam, while the UK and France – the foremost

[186] Including, of course, those of Sean MacBride and the International Commission of Jurists, alongside Amnesty International and others. On the development of the ICJ and of NGO activity in the realm of human rights generally, see Korey, *NGOs and the Universal Declaration of Human Rights: A Curious Grapevine*; Tolley, *The International Commission of Jurists*.

former colonial powers – were similarly poorly placed to present themselves as morally authoritative voices to developing world counterparts, particularly with ongoing anti-colonial entanglements in Kenya, Vietnam and Algeria (to name but a few instances).[187] The moral authority of the ICRC in the eyes of developing world delegations at the CDDH was similarly uncertain – indeed, potentially tainted by association with the Western great powers. The Committee appears to have been particularly concerned to avoid alienating developing world delegations after the 'fiasco' of 1974, notwithstanding conservative Western frustration at the ICRC's perceived timorousness.

The field was accordingly left more open at the CDDH than in the 1949 negotiations to actors who were not necessarily inclined to respect the ICRC's expert or traditionally recognised moral authority, or the technical expertise of the conservative Western powers or such moral authority as they might seek to exert. Rather, with respect to wars of national liberation, even though Abi-Saab and aligned Norwegian and New Zealand delegations were able to deploy more or less robust technical arguments in favour of the position preferred by the developing world, the overwhelming sense gleaned is that technical arguments mattered little to the majority of developing world delegations. Rather, for many such delegations, these arguments effectively served as a fig leaf for a politically driven preference to accord preferential treatment to anti-colonial conflicts.

The final form of Protocol II also reflects developing world – primarily Pakistani and Egyptian – preferences, to a greater extent than it does ICRC, Canadian or particularly Norwegian views.[188] Indeed, while Canadian influence is evident in the form of the Pakistani draft, the overall impression given by the last-minute negotiations over Protocol II is that the majority of developing world delegations lined up behind Egypt and Pakistan principally because of these delegations' support for

[187] Indeed, the UK delegation was evidently very aware of the British predicament in this regard. As Mantilla notes: 'Although British and French decolonization had advanced apace, both states still held colonial territories. This kept them vulnerable to international scorn. The British seemed especially sensitive, facing ongoing troubles in Northern Ireland' ('Forum Isolation: Social Opprobrium and the Origins of the International Law of Internal Conflict', 343).

[188] The inability of Norwegian delegates to sway more conservative Western counterparts despite the absence of any obvious ulterior motive and evident subject matter expertise raises the question of whether the views of the former were simply too radical for the latter, highlighting the importance of a shared intra- as well as inter-bloc 'lifeworld' in the conduct of negotiations.

the endeavour, rather than because of Canadian technical assistance or the ICRC's endorsement. Rather, in this instance, the former led the way owing to a combination of moral authority in the eyes of developing world counterparts, bolstered by recognised technical expertise – primarily on Egypt's part – and broadly constructive relationships with the conservative, Western powers.

In short, there is little to suggest that ICRC or Western technical capacity had a significant impact on the outcomes of the CDDH with respect to internal armed conflict. Widely perceived moral authority on the part of some delegations, including Norway, New Zealand and Canada, also appears to have been relatively immaterial to these outcomes. Rather, in the face of entrenched political and rhetorical preferences with respect to wars of national liberation and widely held concerns with respect to domestic stability on the part of developing world delegations, such expertise and authority were of little benefit in respect of Article 1(4) and were of only marginal (if any) benefit in respect of Egyptian and Pakistani efforts to 'rescue' Additional Protocol II in 1977.

4.4.4 *Arguing on the Record*

> 'Governments will be more likely to support the adoption of civil war-regulating provisions in treaty negotiations when strong, coherent arguments premised on widely shared values and principles are made in support.' (The Logic of Argument hypothesis)

> 'Those were of a general character, belonging to the nature of politics itself (the politics in which the making and implementation of IHL is embedded) and to the very history of the age; in bold mood, I might even call it "the Zeitgeist".'[189]

One of the more striking aspects of the CDDH is the absence of shared 'values and principles' across developing world and leading Western delegations: put simply, delegates appeared on many occasions to be speaking past one another. UK and US archival material is replete, for example, with complaints about the lack of technical expertise and familiarity of some developing world delegations with 'non-UN style' negotiations. Equally, a number of the latter considered the 'imperialist powers' to be insufficiently attentive to the

[189] Best, *War and Law since 1945*, 414. (The quotation refers to areas in which Best observes that 'a certain insincerity has latterly infiltrated IHL'.)

concerns of newly independent former colonies, as well as lamentably unfamiliar with the latest (progressive, post-colonial) currents in international legal thought.[190]

This normative context reflects the timing of the CDDH, which took place during what Christopher Greenwood has termed 'the high water mark of an approach to international negotiations which gave rhetoric pride of place over substance'.[191] Moreover, many developing world delegations' primary experience of international negotiations was indeed in a UN context, 'where a premium was placed upon vote getting and coalition diplomacy rather than on attention to legal technicalities'.[192] Indeed, an 'important Third World delegate [observed that] ... many of the delegates in his caucus just did not understand the difference between a UN resolution and a draft treaty'.[193]

It is, of course, possible to overstate the significance of these gaps: the vast majority of arguments presented were framed in principled terms, and differences in approach related mainly to assumptions regarding appropriate frames of reference within which principled arguments could be made.[194] Nevertheless, with respect to internal armed conflict, the absence of a 'cognitive consensus' across blocs – in particular between conservative Western delegations and the majority of developing world delegations – significantly hampered the extent to which the CDDH was capable of generating common positions.

This gap was particularly pronounced in the 1974 negotiations over Article 1(4). Abi-Saab aside, developing world delegates generally, including most notably Indian participants but also Zairean,

190 See e.g. Forsythe, 'The 1974 Diplomatic Conference on Humanitarian Law: Some Observations', 82, 88; Forsythe, 'Three Sessions of Legislating Humanitarian Law: Forward March, Retreat, or Parade Rest', 139. As the 1974 New Zealand report of the CDDH puts it: '[t]he tragedy is that the virtues of objectivity and impartiality should seem to be the property of an obstructive minority, instead of a common heritage' (Quentin-Baxter, 'Report of the New Zealand Delegation to the First Session of the Diplomatic Conference for the Reaffirmation and Development of International Humanitarian Law Applicable in Armed Conflicts', p. 13, para. 30).

191 Greenwood, 'A Critique of the Additional Protocols to the Geneva Conventions', 7.

192 Interestingly, Forsythe suggests that the dispute over PRG participation 'may have led to the loss of influence by the lawyers to the more politically oriented individuals within certain Third World delegations' (Forsythe, 'The 1974 Diplomatic Conference on Humanitarian Law: Some Observations', 82).

193 Ibid., 82.

194 Greenwood refers to a 'liberationist' perspective on the part of 'the Third World and Its First and Second World Sympathizers' (Greenwood, 'A Critique of the Additional Protocols to the Geneva Conventions', 7).

Mauritanian and Tanzanian delegates, 'did not capitalize on the legal arguments available to them regarding the criteria according to which the scope and application of the law was to be decided'.[195] Rather, when challenged by Western counterparts, delegates often fell back on positions which must have grated on the ears of the IHL specialists in attendance.[196] The result of this series of interactions was that the former remained unconvinced that the inclusion of Article 1(4) in Protocol I was merited, UK, Belgian and French delegates continuing to protest ineffectively the practical difficulties of privileging this category of conflict.[197]

This was not the case in all instances, though. By the final round of discussions in 1977 over Protocol II, after four sessions of negotiations, sufficient common understanding across blocs appears to have emerged to enable constructive-minded developing world and Western delegations, with Soviet support, to collaborate in developing a set of provisions capable of satisfying the minimum requirements of all key participants, and which would be consistent with the 'rhetorically progressive' international normative context highlighted by Greenwood and Best.[198] There is no record of the corridor consultations that led to the Pakistani proposal; however, the New Zealand and Canadian delegations seem to have gone to significant lengths to avoid alienating developing world delegations. Equally, some of the latter – most prominently Pakistan, supported by Egypt and the Soviet Union – had already prepared the ground rhetorically in 1975 by conceding that sovereignty was not 'impregnable', facilitating developing world support for the 1977 Pakistani draft.

To a large extent, the Logic of Argument hypothesis thus appears to have been borne out in the negotiation of Article 1(4), with an absence of sufficiently shared values and principles significantly impeding discussions over the drafting of Article 1 of Protocol I. This prevented the two blocs primarily concerned with the treatment of wars of national liberation – the developing world and the 'conservative' West – from engaging

195 Forsythe, 'The 1974 Diplomatic Conference on Humanitarian Law: Some Observations', 83.

196 Ibid., 82.

197 See e.g. Forsythe, expressing much the same sentiment: 'it is difficult to formulate in satisfactory form a summary of the three sessions of the Conference, in part because different parties wanted and expected different things from the Conference. Whether a step is forward or backward depends on the vantage point of the viewer' ('Three Sessions of Legislating Humanitarian Law: Forward March, Retreat, or Parade Rest', 141).

198 See notes 189, 191.

effectively with one another, even when the arguments presented by each side were coherent within their respective frames of reference. By the time of the 1977 negotiations over Protocol II, in contrast, there appears to have been sufficient common discursive ground across key members of these blocs to enable a satisfactory consensus to emerge: key developing world delegations were willing to support Protocol II in some form and key Western delegations elected to support the efforts of more moderate developing country counterparts in negotiating a generally acceptable draft on the basis of arguments presented within a shared, 'rhetorically progressive' frame of reference.

4.4.5 What about Democracy?

> 'Democracies are more likely to support intrusive, restrictive civil war-regulating provisions than non-democracies.' (The Regime Type hypothesis)

Support for more intrusive regulation of internal armed conflict at the CDDH was not a particular hallmark of democracies – either Western or in the developing world. The Soviet Union and associated socialist bloc, on the other hand, were keen supporters of both Article 1(4) and of a more demanding Protocol II – presumably primarily for similar reasons as in 1949, and with a similar absence of Soviet concern about being expected to live up to any commitments made.

With respect to Western democracies, it is striking that only a minority of such delegations supported the inclusion of Article 1(4) in Protocol I, principally the Scandinavian states (Norway foremost amongst these) and Australia. None of these states had any prospect of becoming engaged in violent internal strife, let alone of the kind contemplated by Article 1(4), and each at the time had robust 'humanitarian' foreign policies reflecting domestic political commitments and alignments. In contrast, as in 1949, more conservative Western democracies were extremely hesitant about the inclusion of Article 1(4) in Protocol I. Their reluctance was ostensibly driven by concerns about the implications of this provision for the (notionally) apolitical nature of IHL, but it was also closely informed by first-hand experience in conducting conflicts potentially falling within the scope of this provision.

Misgivings over Article 1(4) notwithstanding, there was widespread support amongst Western democratic states for the completion of Protocol II in some form. In some instances this reflected domestic liberal norms (e.g. the Scandinavian states, Canada, and New Zealand), with public opinion evidently relevant in the UK and US cases.[199] That said, democratic states with particular concerns about actually engaging in internal armed conflict – most notably the UK – equally welcomed the Pakistani initiative to water down the committee draft of Protocol II, a development that could conveniently be attributed to developing world obduracy.

While some features of democratic governance (or its absence) appear to have been relevant to Western and socialist bloc views with respect to the regulation of internal armed conflict, the analysis of developing world positions relative to democracy is rather more complex. The principal challenges here are that developing world delegations – both more and less democratic – strongly supported the inclusion of Article 1(4) in Protocol I, but were generally wary of Protocol II.

With respect to Article 1(4), for example, there was evidently little risk perceived by any of its proponents that this provision could potentially affect their own forces in any conflicts in which they might conceivably be engaged. Rather, the ambit of this provision was understood by its supporters as applying only to a very few, distinct conflicts. This enabled both more democratic developing world states such as India and Pakistan and less democratic states such as Egypt to comfortably support the proposed drafting, consistent with positions previously taken in UN contexts.

At the same time, however, both more and less democratic developing world delegations proved at best ambivalent about Protocol II. Most prominently, India was consistently opposed to the adoption of this protocol throughout the conference – regardless of whether under Congress (including the 1975–7 state of emergency) or Janata leadership (from March 1977). In contrast, Pakistan emerged alongside Egypt as leaders of a (relatively) more pragmatic bloc of developing world delegations with respect to Protocol II in 1977, notwithstanding that neither state had an especially robust tradition of democratic (let alone liberal) governance. It is thus difficult to draw a connection between democratic governance and attitudes to Protocol II in respect of developing world states.

[199] Re. the UK, see e.g. Rodley, 'Human Rights in Armed Conflict'. Also references at note 111. Interestingly, in the UK case, domestic political uncertainty in 1974 appears to have placed significant responsibility in the hands of unelected officials, begging the question of the extent to which democratic *governance* or *government* per se underpinned delegation sensitivities and preferences. Re. the USA, see references at note 100.

In sum, as regards conservative Western democracies, democratic governance does appear to have had a bearing on positions on internal armed conflict at the CDDH. This can principally be seen in relation to Protocol II, where combinations of publicly espoused and socially embedded liberal values made it difficult to abjure the draft treaty, notwithstanding political concerns about practical implications in colonial and comparable contexts. Such concerns do not seem to have been overriding concerns of developing world democracies, however, most notably in the case of India. Interestingly, this difference suggests that democratic governance per se was perhaps less relevant to attitudes towards the regulation of internal armed conflict than the extent to which democratic governance and associated liberal norms were embedded and established domestically – arguably the primary distinction between the Western democracies and their developing world counterparts.

4.5 Aftermath

> The outcome of the Conference on the issue of wars of national liberation is not without paradox. While the recognition of these wars as international conflicts was to all appearances a victory for the supporters of national liberation movements, the conditions imposed on guerrilla fighters if they are to be granted protection under the Conventions and Protocol I make it likely that such recognition will be devoid of great practical significance. Yet, western delegations undoubtedly sustained a political defeat and were made to seem restrictive in extending the protection of humanitarian law.[200]

Perhaps unsurprisingly given their troubled birth, and despite the Protocols being lauded in some quarters as heralding 'new life for the laws of war', in the years following 1977 states were rather more hesitant to embrace the two Additional Protocols than their 1949 forebears.[201] While the 1949 Conventions had garnered 43 ratifications by the end of 1954, Additional Protocol I was ratified by only 26 states during the first five years after its adoption, and Additional Protocol II by only 22 states. These numbers increased with the end of the Cold War, Protocol I reaching 117 ratifications and Protocol II 107 by the end of 1992. Both Protocols remain less widely supported than the 1949 Conventions,

200 Lysaght, 'The Attitude of Western Countries', 360.

201 See Aldrich, 'New Life for the Laws of War'; also: Suter, *An International Law of Guerrilla Warfare: The Global Politics of Law-Making*, 177–84.

however: at the time of writing Additional Protocol I has 174 states parties and Protocol II 168, as contrasted with 197 for the 1949 Conventions.

Unsurprisingly, the states that refuse to ratify the Protocols include many that have encountered or whose governments continue to be concerned about violent internal unrest, including Azerbaijan, Eritrea, India, Indonesia, Iran, Israel, Myanmar, Nepal, Pakistan, Sri Lanka, Somalia and Turkey. Similarly, despite having ratified Additional Protocol I, Angola, the Democratic Republic of Congo, Iraq, North Korea, Syria and Vietnam have declined to ratify Protocol II. Other non-parties to both treaties include Bhutan, Malaysia, Singapore, Thailand and – perhaps most conspicuously – the USA, while France and the UK also only relatively recently ratified the treaties. The former eventually ratified Protocol II in 2001, having ratified Protocol I in 1984, and the UK ratified both Protocols in 1998 – only a few months prior to the signature of the Good Friday Agreement.[202] South Africa, alongside Israel arguably the principal post-colonial 'target' of Article 1(4) of Additional Protocol I, similarly ratified both Protocols only in 1995, after the end of apartheid, while Mozambique ratified Protocol II in 2002 following the end of the Mozambican Civil War. In short, key states – including many which have been at risk of or that have encountered civil unrest – have proven reluctant to accede to these instruments.[203]

Ratification is not, of course, the only means by which states have indicated willingness to observe the internal armed conflict-regulating provisions of the two Protocols: elements that states recognise as customary have also been incorporated into the military manuals and rules of engagement of both ratifying and non-ratifying states.[204] Indeed, in the case of the USA,

[202] On historic US discourse over Protocol I, see Aldrich, 'Prospects for United States Ratification of Additional Protocol I to the 1949 Geneva Conventions'.

[203] This should not be understood as suggesting, however, that the reasons for this necessarily relate closely to implications for the conduct of internal armed conflict. (See observations re. eventual British and French ratification of Additional Protocol I in Mantilla, 'Under (Social) Pressure: The Historical Regulation of Internal Armed Conflicts through International Law', 373–4.)

[204] The 2004 UK Joint Service Manual, for example, contains extensive references to both Protocols, including the observation that: '[i]n the Gulf conflict of 1991, Additional Protocol I was not applicable as Iraq and several coalition powers, including the United Kingdom, were not parties to it. However, coalition rules of engagement were constructed so as to take into account those provisions of the Protocol that embodied rules of customary law' ('Joint Service Manual of the Law of Armed Conflict (Ref. JSP 383, 2004 Edition)', 5 [para. 1.13.2]). The June 2015 US Department of Defense Law of War Manual similarly contains extensive references to elements of both Protocols, notwithstanding American non-ratification (see Office of General Counsel, *Department of Defense Law of War Manual*).

then-Secretary of State George Shultz submitted Protocol II to President Reagan for transmission to the Senate for ratification in 1987 with the observation that – subject to a number of reservations and understandings – 'the obligations contained in Protocol II are no more than a restatement of the rules of conduct with which U.S. military forces would almost certainly comply as a matter of national policy, constitutional and legal protections, and common decency'.[205] In similar vein, the Israeli government has recognised the customary status of elements of both Protocols.[206]

At the same time though, even amongst ratifying states, observance of the Protocols' strictures during internal armed conflict has proven problematic. Lindsay Moir observes, for example, that in internal armed conflicts in El Salvador, Bosnia and Herzegovina and Russia – where Additional Protocol II would reasonably have been viewed as applicable – the governments involved each took the view that the Protocol was not engaged.[207] Put simply, governments remain 'very reluctant to admit the existence of any type of conflict within their borders, preferring to prize their State sovereignty over humanitarian concerns and apply only municipal criminal law to the "terrorists"'.[208] Given this, it is also unsurprising that – again, as noted by Moir – the impact of these treaties on the conduct of internal armed conflict is 'most disheartening'.[209]

[205] Shultz, 'Letter of Submittal from the Secretary of State, 13 December 1986' (United States 'Message from the President Transmitting Protocol II Additional to the 1949 Geneva Conventions, Relating to the Protection of Victims of Noninternational Armed Conflicts, January 29, 1987'), 563. President Reagan's Letter of Transmittal also famously described Protocol I as 'fundamentally and irreconcilably flawed' (Ronald Reagan, Letter of Transmittal from the President to the Senate of the United States, 29 January 1987 (ibid., 562)).

[206] The Israeli government report into the conduct of the 2014 Gaza Conflict contains numerous references to the customary status of elements of both Protocols, noting in addition that: '[a]lthough Israel is also not a party to the 1977 Additional Protocols I and II to the 1949 Geneva Conventions, it abides by their provisions inasmuch as they reflect rules of customary international law' (Government of Israel, *The 2014 Gaza Conflict 7 July–26 August 2014: Factual and Legal Aspects*, 138, at note 397).

[207] See Moir, *The Law of Internal Armed Conflict*, 119–31. The only instances Moir identifies where governments and insurgents agreed – exceptionally – on the applicability of Additional Protocol II in internal armed conflict are the cases of El Salvador and the Philippines (131). See also Mack and Pejic, *Increasing Respect for International Humanitarian Law in Non-International Armed Conflicts*, 17–18).

[208] Higgins, *The Approach of International Law to Wars of National Liberation*, 67.

[209] Moir, *The Law of Internal Armed Conflict*, 131. As expressed in an ICRC publication: '. . . even in cases in which the IHL of international armed conflicts contains no detailed provisions or to which no analogies with that law apply, and even without falling back on customary law, the plight of the victims of contemporary non-international armed conflicts would be incomparably improved if only the basic black-letter provisions of

Reflecting these shortcomings, the development of the 'civil war regime' has not stopped at conventional boundaries. In the absence of significant appetite on the part of states for further treaty 'reaffirmation and[/or] development', non-state actors – principally international lawyers and tribunals as well as NGOs such as the ICRC – have sought to further develop this regime in the period since 1977 by considering the extent to which elements of the two Protocols constitute customary international law.[210] Nevertheless, governments have also sought to rein in these actors on occasion, including (as Chapter 5 illustrates) in the design of the Rome Statute of the International Criminal Court.

Art. 3 common to the Conventions and of Protocol II were respected' (Sassòli, Bouvier and Quintin, *How Does Law Protect in War?*, vol. I, chapter 12, 3–4).

[210] This is an area where the ICRC has invested significant resources, a Committee-published guide to IHL observing in 2006 that: '[t]oday, there is a general tendency to reduce the difference between IHL applicable in international and in non-international armed conflicts. The jurisprudence of international criminal tribunals, the influence of human rights and even some treaty rules adopted by States have moved the law of non-international armed conflicts closer to the law of international armed conflicts, and it has even been suggested in some quarters that the difference be eliminated altogether. In the many fields where the treaty rules still differ, this convergence has been rationalized by claiming that under customary international law the differences between the two categories of conflict have gradually disappeared. The ICRC study on customary International Humanitarian Law comes, after ten years of research, to the conclusion that 136 (and arguably even 141) out of 161 rules of customary humanitarian law, many of which are based on rules of Protocol I applicable as a treaty to international armed conflicts, apply equally to non-international armed conflicts' (Sassòli, Bouvier, and Quintin, *How Does Law Protect in War?*, vol. I, chapter 2, 23–4). (See Henckaerts and Doswald-Beck, *Study on Customary International Humanitarian Law*.) In similar vein, as early as 1984 Antonio Cassese concluded (debatably) that: '[t]he adoption of Art. 1 para. 4 testified to the formation of a rule binding on all the States participating in the Conference (irrespective of whether or not they ratify the Protocol), save for Israel, which consistently rejected the provision' (Cassese, 'Wars of National Liberation and Humanitarian Law', 322).

Unsurprisingly, ICRC findings have generated significant debate. See e.g. Wilmshurst and Breau, *Perspectives on the ICRC Study on Customary International Humanitarian Law*, including Scobbie, 'The Approach to Customary International Law in the Study'. See also Bellinger and Haynes, 'A US Government Response to the International Committee of the Red Cross Study Customary International Humanitarian Law', 444: '[I]t is important to make clear – both to the ICRC and to the greater international community – that, based upon the U.S. review thus far, the United States is concerned about the methodology used to ascertain rules and about whether the authors have proffered sufficient facts and evidence to support those rules'. As Scobbie notes: '[t]he mechanics of custom formation is perhaps one of the most contested, yet fundamental, issues in contemporary international law' ('The Approach to Customary International Law in the Study', 23).

Conclusion

Article 1(4) of Protocol I and the abbreviated form of Protocol II eventually adopted were, above all, products of the 'rise of the Third World' in international relations in the 1970s, and in particular of the increased prominence in international affairs and discourse of the Non-Aligned Movement (and of non-aligned states more generally). Unlike in 1949, the 'smaller states' could not conceivably be ignored or taken for granted by any of the great powers (or superpowers): rather it was clear from the outset that the latter would need to tailor their policy preferences to reflect positions likely to be acceptable to a sufficient number of the former.

Although the negotiation of Article 1(4) was particularly fraught, moreover, the extended negotiating process enabled developing world and Western delegations to conduct less antagonistic negotiations over Protocol II, ultimately arriving at a set of provisions capable of satisfying minimal requirements of key states from Western, Soviet and developing world blocs.

The UK and US delegations, for example, both took a narrow, technical-focused approach to negotiations at the outset, influenced by policy concerns relating principally to Northern Ireland and Vietnam, respectively. After the initial shock of the 1974 negotiations, though, both delegations, in common with other conservative Western powers, reassessed their positions and took a more pragmatic approach, adopting (albeit under some duress) a US-led strategy to 'contain' the fallout in Protocol I from Article 1(4). Interestingly, even middle-power Western delegations not specifically aligned with the developing world with respect to wars of national liberation, including Canada and New Zealand, appear to have been better prepared than the UK and the USA going into the 1974 negotiations, and to have been less surprised by the tack taken by the developing world. Demonstrating more familiarity with human rights discourse in the UN General Assembly context than their great power counterparts, New Zealand and Canada in particular facilitated the subsequent building of discursive bridges between more conservative Western delegations and the developing world in the negotiation of Protocol II, to the discomfiture of the more radical Western delegations – primarily Norway.

Amongst developing world delegations, Egypt and Pakistan stand out as performing key roles in facilitating constructive interaction with the West after the 'dialogue of the deaf' of 1974. Informal alignment with the

USA and technical fluency on the part of Egypt in particular, alongside the post-October/Yom Kippur War moral authority of the latter within the developing world, played a part in enabling these delegations to forge productive relationships with Western counterparts without alienating developing world delegations. This had the effect of marginalising more obdurate delegations amongst the latter, such as India, in the final negotiations over Protocol II. For its part, the ICRC appears to have been unable to exert moral authority consistently in relation to politically sensitive issues encountered in the course of negotiations over both Article 1(4) and Protocol II. This limited the Committee to utilising technical expertise to influence outcomes in less sensitive issue areas, rendering it a less effective norm entrepreneur in respect of civil war regulation than might otherwise have been expected. The Soviet Union similarly played little visible part in the negotiations over Article 1(4) and Protocol II. However, Soviet views certainly informed Western appreciation of the unavoidability of privileging wars of national liberation along the lines preferred by the developing world, and potentially also developing world views regarding the inclusion of Protocol II in some form in the conference products.

These outcomes and the processes that led to them have a number of interesting implications with respect to the hypotheses set out in Chapter 1. The findings with respect to the impact of great power preferences on outcomes are ambiguous – USA, UK and French preferences were frustrated with respect to Article 1(4), unlike Soviet (and in 1974 Chinese) support for developing world preferences. At the same time, though, where Soviet and Western great power preferences were aligned with respect to Protocol II, a sufficient majority of developing world delegations acceded to these views to enable the adoption of this instrument. These dynamics suggest that while support for or opposition to any given position on the part of one or more great powers may not guarantee more widespread adoption of a position, when great power preferences are aligned other delegations are more likely to fall into line.

Additionally, while the drafting of Protocol II speaks broadly (though not without qualification) in favour of the salience of the Rationalist hypothesis to the regulation of internal armed conflict, the negotiations over Article 1(4) also suggest limitations to this hypothesis in respect of developing world supporters of this drafting. This may reflect insufficient awareness of the implications of the measure as drafted, reasons unconnected with the wording in question (i.e. a politically driven understanding that Article 1(4) would apply only to a restricted range of cases in

Southern Africa and the Middle East), or simple disregard for possible future costs that might be associated with this provision.

The negotiation of Article 1(4) and of Protocol II also speaks to the limitations of technical authority, highlighting in particular the difficulties encountered by Western powers in bringing technical resources to bear in politically charged issue areas in the absence of widely recognised moral authority. On the other hand, the prominence of Egypt and Pakistan in negotiations suggests that perceived moral authority may bolster delegation effectiveness (and so the efficacy of technical expertise) in such contexts. However, the traditional moral authority of the ICRC – at least in Western eyes – appears to have been of little assistance to the Committee in the negotiation of these provisions, underlining that moral authority in any objective sense was less critical in the negotiations than perceived moral authority in the eyes of key interlocutors.

That said, taken together, both sets of negotiations strongly support the relevance of the Logic of Argument hypothesis. An absence of sufficiently broadly shared values and principles was a particular challenge in negotiating Article 1(4), contributing to delegations from conservative Western and developing world blocs generally not engaging with one another in these negotiations. The means by which Protocol II was ultimately agreed, however, suggests that discursive bridges can be developed to facilitate more constructive discussion and consensus, again, with drafting outcomes consistent with the prevalent 'rhetorically progressive' international normative Zeitgeist.

The potential implications of the case with respect to the Regime Type hypothesis are also interesting to note, with negotiations over the treatment of wars of national liberation underlining that democracies may be more hesitant than non-democracies to (notionally) closely regulate internal armed conflicts. Similarly, domestic liberal norms appear to have been insufficient to ensure support for a robust form of Protocol II (see e.g. UK conduct), while developing world positions with respect to Protocol II suggest that it may be more accurate to associate principled support for the regulation of internal armed conflict with a narrower range of established or stable (or *liberal*) democracies than with the presence or absence of democratic governance institutions per se.

5

War Crimes and Internal Armed Conflict in the Rome Statute (1998)

Introduction

Paragraphs (c) and (e) of Article 8(2) of the Rome Statute of the International Criminal Court (the 'Rome Statute' and 'ICC', respectively) criminalise war crimes in non-international armed conflict for the first time in treaty form, qualified by threshold provisions at paragraphs (d) and (f), respectively. The present chapter examines the processes leading up to the inclusion of these provisions in Article 8.[1]

Once again, the chapter provides a brief historical background before setting out the key turning points in the negotiation of these clauses. As in preceding chapters, the negotiations are considered from the perspectives of key actors: in this case, the Like-Minded Group, the P5

[1] Paragraph (c) defines as war crimes 'serious violations of article 3 common to the four Geneva Conventions of 12 August 1949'. Paragraph (e) does the same for '[o]ther serious violations of the laws and customs applicable in armed conflicts not of an international character, within the established framework of international law', setting out a closed list of prohibited forms of conduct drawing on (but not identical with) the prohibitions of Additional Protocol II. Paragraphs (2)(d) and (f) then apply thresholds of the type familiar from Common Article 3 and Additional Protocol II, providing that paragraphs (c) and (e) apply to 'armed conflicts not of an international character' and not to 'situations of internal disturbances and tensions, such as riots, isolated and sporadic acts of violence or other acts of a similar nature'. Paragraph (f) then adds, in language reflecting the oft-cited *Tadić* decision of the Appeals Chamber of the International Criminal Tribunal for the Former Yugoslavia (ICTY), that paragraph (e) 'applies to armed conflicts that take place in the territory of a State when there is protracted armed conflict between governmental authorities and organized armed groups or between such groups'. (See *Tadić* paragraph 70.) Paragraph 3 of Article 8 adds that: '[n]othing in paragraph 2(c) and (e) shall affect the responsibility of a Government to maintain or re-establish law and order in the State or to defend the unity and territorial integrity of the State, by all legitimate means'. Paragraphs (c) to (f) of Article 8(2) and precursors during the drafting process are referred to collectively in this chapter as the 'internal armed conflict provisions'.

(particularly the USA, the UK and France), the Non-Aligned Movement, and prominent civil society participants (e.g. Amnesty International, Human Rights Watch), before assessing the implications of the case for the five hypotheses set out in Chapter 1.

As in the previous case studies, Chapter 1's pluralist theoretical perspective provides valuable insight into the factors that shaped the 'internal armed conflict provisions' of the Rome Statute. In this case, the chapter underlines that, while like-minded and NGO moral authority and technical expertise played a large part in persuading wavering delegations, the 'internal armed conflict provisions' of the Rome Statute also closely reflect the preferences of the Western 'P3' as well as the post-Cold War liberal Zeitgeist. The conclusion includes a brief discussion of the ICC's subsequent approach to the internal armed conflict provisions of the Rome Statute, and of the court's impact on the conduct of civil conflicts.

5.1 Background

5.1.1 War Crimes and International Criminal Tribunals in Historical Perspective

The concept of war crimes predates the Nuremberg and Tokyo International Military Tribunals (IMTs) of 1945–8, having historically been associated with breaches of the 'Hague Law' of 1899 and 1907. Early international attempts to punish (or to procure the domestic punishment of) those responsible for breaches of the relevant rules, however, met with less than marked success.[2]

The prospect of international criminal liability for war crimes was subsequently given new life in the aftermath of the Second World War,

[2] For background and overview of some definitional debates, see Schwarz, 'War Crimes'. For the ICRC's position, see: 'Rule 156. Definition of War Crimes' in the ICRC Customary IHL Database, available at: https://ihl-databases.icrc.org/customary-ihl/eng/docs/v1_rul_rule156 [accessed 12 December 2018]. On pre-World War Two approaches to and prosecution (or not) of war crimes, including e.g. the aborted Malta and Leipzig trials and the Allies' post-World War One attempt to obtain the extradition of the Kaiser from the Netherlands, as well as inter-war and earlier attempts to establish a permanent international criminal court, see variously: Schabas, *The International Criminal Court: A Commentary on the Rome Statute* (2nd edn.), 1–4; Bryant, *A World History of War Crimes: From Antiquity to the Present*, chapters 1–5; Crowe, *War Crimes, Genocide, and Justice: A Global History*, chapters 1–4; Hall, 'The First Proposal for a Permanent International Criminal Court'; Ferencz, *An International Criminal Court, a Step toward World Peace: A Documentary History and Analysis*, 1:36–46.

as the victors established the IMTs, the US occupation authorities in Germany convened a series of further military tribunals in Nuremberg, and the British did the same in their zone of occupation.[3] The momentum generated by these trials soon faltered though.

Perhaps most critically, a 1948 UN General Assembly initiative charging the International Law Commission (ILC) with studying 'the desirability and possibility of establishing an international judicial organ for the trial of persons charged with genocide or other crimes' fell foul of the Cold War. The Soviet Union perceived threats to its sovereignty from a standing international criminal court, the USA was 'not prepared to accept the establishment of such a court at the height of the [Cold War], France expressed support for the establishment of a permanent international criminal court but did little otherwise to further this process, and the United Kingdom regarded the idea as politically premature'.[4] In Ferencz's elegant prose: '[t]he chilling winds of the cold war had placed the idea of an International Criminal Court into the deep freeze by the end of 1954'.[5] A similar fate befell the work of the ILC on preparing a 'Draft Code of Offences against the Peace and Security of Mankind'.[6]

[3] For an overview of these and other national and international initiatives to prosecute war crimes during this period, see Crowe, *War Crimes, Genocide, and Justice: A Global History*, 243–82; Heller, *The Nuremberg Military Tribunals and the Origins of International Criminal Law*; Lippman, 'Prosecutions of Nazi War Criminals before Post-World War II Domestic Tribunals'.

[4] Bassiouni, *The Statute of the International Criminal Court: A Documentary History*, 12–13. This initiative reflected the inclusion of a reference in Article 6 of the Genocide Convention to an 'international penal tribunal' with potential jurisdiction over genocide and related conduct. The convention was adopted by the General Assembly on 9 December 1948 in Part A of Resolution 3/260: Part B of the resolution referred to the ILC the question of the 'desirability and possibility of establishing an international judicial organ for the trial of persons charged with genocide or other crimes' (UN Doc. A/RES/3/260, 9 December 1948, available at: http://un-documents.net/a3r260.htm [accessed 12 December 2018]). See also Ferencz, *An International Criminal Court, a Step toward World Peace: A Documentary History and Analysis*, 1:16–48.

[5] Ferencz, *An International Criminal Court, a Step toward World Peace: A Documentary History and Analysis*, 1:478.

[6] The ILC was directed to carry out this work in General Assembly Resolution 177(II) of 21 November 1947 (UN Doc. A/519, 8 January 1948, available at: http://undocs.org/a/519 [accessed 2 December 2018], at 111–12). In respect of Resolution 3/260, the ILC reported to the General Assembly in 1950 that setting up the court envisaged in Article 6 of the Genocide Convention was both desirable and possible. The General Assembly then established two committees in 1951 and 1952 to develop this initiative: the first committee prepared a draft statute, which was circulated for comment to governments and revised by the follow-on '1952' committee. Following this, however, the initiative languished in the General Assembly, consideration being deferred on multiple occasions and (notionally) awaiting progress on developing a suitable definition of aggression. (For the draft statute

Though – as set out in Chapters 3 and 4 – significant progress was made during the Cold War in establishing legal norms for the conduct of combatants in internal armed conflict, the prospect of international war crimes prosecutions commanded little attention during the remainder of the Cold War.[7] Rather, the grave breaches provisions of the 1949 Geneva Conventions were considered to constitute a more 'modern system' for addressing the most serious IHL breaches via domestic criminal law.[8]

The world changed, however, with the end of the Cold War. By the early 1990s, the idea of a permanent international criminal court was receiving renewed attention from governments and civil society, including from members of the 'Nuremberg' generation such as Benjamin Ferencz, and M. Cherif Bassiouni – a prominent academic with strong links to civil society – as well as from organisations such as the Association Internationale de Droit Penal, the International Law Association, and the World Federalist Movement.[9] The development of the Rome Statute was in particular kick-started by General

prepared by the '1951' committee, see 'United Nations: Committee on International Criminal Jurisdiction'.) The ILC's work on the draft code was halted in 1954 for the same reason. The former initiative was not resumed, however, following the 1974 adoption by the General Assembly of a definition of aggression (see Resolution 29/3314 (UN Doc. A/RES/29/3314, 14 December 1974, available at: http://un-documents.net/a29r3314.htm [accessed 25 December 2018])). See discussion below re. the fate of the latter initiative. William Schabas provides an excellent précis of the institutional handling of both initiatives prior to the 1989 adoption of General Assembly Resolution 44/39 (UN Doc. A/RES/44/39, 4 December 1989, available at: http://undocs.org/a/RES/44/39 [accessed 25 December 2018]), including the seldom-discussed activity of the Commission on Human Rights and the ILC's work on the draft 'Code of Offences' (re-titled the draft 'Code of Crimes against the Peace and Security of Mankind' in 1987 (UN Doc. A/42/151, 7 December 1987, available at: http://undocs.org/A/RES/42/151 [accessed 12 December 2018]) between 1981 and 1989. See Schabas, *The International Criminal Court: A Commentary on the Rome Statute* (2nd edn.), 6–11. See also *The Work of the International Law Commission,* I:89–92, 97–121 (on these initiatives and the ILC's subsequent activities in respect of the Rome Statute).

7 See discussion in e.g. Perna, *The Formation of the Treaty Law of Non-International Armed Conflicts*, 140. Also Ferencz, 'International Criminal Courts: The Legacy of Nuremberg'.

8 Draper, 'The Implementation and Enforcement of the Geneva Conventions of 1949 and of the Two Additional Protocols of 1978', 37 cited in Öberg, 'The Absorption of Grave Breaches into War Crimes Law', 164 at note 1. See also: Sandoz, 'The History of the Grave Breaches Regime'.

9 See: Glasius, 'Expertise in the Cause of Justice: Global Civil Society Influence on the Statute for an International Criminal Court', 139. See more generally Glasius, *The International Criminal Court: A Global Civil Society Achievement*, 8–12. US and a range of Western European government ministers also entertained the prospect of an international trial of Saddam Hussein following the Iraqi invasion of Kuwait. (See Schabas, *The International Criminal Court: A Commentary on the Rome Statute* (2nd edn.), 13–14.)

Assembly Resolution 44/39 of December 1989, based on a proposal by Arthur Robinson, then prime minister of Trinidad and Tobago, requesting the ILC: 'to address the question of establishing an international criminal court or other international criminal trial mechanism with jurisdiction over persons alleged to have committed crimes which may be covered under such a code, including persons engaged in illicit trafficking in narcotic drugs . . .'.[10]

The ILC's work on this topic was swiftly overtaken by events, however. On 6 October 1992, with French, German and US support, the Security Council established a Bassiouni-led 'Commission of Experts to Investigate Violations of International Humanitarian law in the former Yugoslavia' (the '780 Commission').[11] The work of Bassiouni's Commission and that of the ILC then proceeded in parallel: the ILC had reported to the General Assembly in 1991 with a version of the now-retitled draft 'Code of Crimes' that – in respect of war crimes – drew no distinction between international and non-international armed conflicts, while UN Secretary General Boutros Boutros-Ghali presented an interim report from the 780 Commission to the Security Council on 10 February 1993, which included the observation that the establishment of an ad hoc international criminal tribunal would be 'consistent with the direction of

[10] UN Doc. A/RES/44/39 (4 December 1989), available at: http://un.org/documents/ga/res/44/a44r039.htm [accessed 25 December 2018], at para. 1. See also discussion at Schiff, *Building the International Criminal Court*, 37. Robinson, similarly to Bassiouni and Ferencz, had a track record as a civil society activist who had long supported the establishment of a permanent international criminal court, having been executive director of the Foundation for the Establishment of the International Criminal Court between 1972 and 1987. He acted, moreover, in close concert with Bassiouni and Ferencz, as well as with Robert Woetzel, another longstanding ICC advocate (and legal scholar) of note, founder and president of the Foundation of which Robinson was executive director, and whose doctoral dissertation (published in 1960) had addressed the legality of the IMT in international law. (On the relationship between Woetzel and Robinson, see Samaroo, 'ANR Robinson's Long Road to the International Criminal Court (ICC)'. See also Woetzel, *The Nuremberg Trials in International Law*.) Robinson was also assisted in drafting the December 1989 motion by Walter Hoffman of the World Federalist Movement – which was later to play a significant role in the NGO Coalition for the ICC. (See Robinson, 'Extemporaneous Statement Made by His Excellency Arthur N.R. Robinson President of the Republic of Trinidad and Tobago on April 11, 2002 at the Plenary Session of the Special Treaty Event'.)

[11] This body was known as the '780 Commission' after its founding resolution (UN Doc. S/RES 780, 6 October 1992), available at: https://documents-dds-ny.un.org/doc/UNDOC/GEN/N92/484/40/IMG/N9248440.pdf?OpenElement [accessed 13 December 2018]). For an interesting discussion of this process, see Rajkovic, *The Politics of International Law and Compliance: Serbia, Croatia and The Hague Tribunal*, 42–6.

[the Commission's] work'.[12] The Security Council subsequently adopted Resolution 808 on 22 February 1993, establishing an international tribunal 'for the prosecution of persons responsible for serious violations of humanitarian law committed in the territory of the former Yugoslavia since 1991', and calling on the Secretary General to submit 'a report on all aspects of this matter'.[13] Having consulted with governments – and NGOs – Boutros-Ghali reported back to the Security Council on 3 May 1993 with a detailed proposal including a draft statute for the ICTY which drew in part on the work of the ILC.[14] This statute was adopted unanimously by the Security Council on 25 May 1993 and, in Bassiouni's words, the 'genie was out of the bottle'.[15]

5.1.2 *Internal Armed Conflict and War Crimes in the ICTY, ICTR and Draft ILC Statutes*

Articles 2 and 3 of the ICTY statute, respectively, give that tribunal jurisdiction over 'grave breaches' of the 1949 Conventions and 'violations of the laws or customs of war' – broadly reflecting the range of provisions set out in the 1949 Conventions as well as the subsequent Protocols. There is, however, no explicit mention of war crimes jurisdiction in non-international settings, and the broadly held (albeit debatable) view at the time appears to have been that internal armed conflicts lay outside the scope of the statute – though this was not the position of the French and US governments.[16] The draft statute

[12] International Law Commission, *Yearbook of the International Law Commission: Report of the Commission to the General Assembly on the Work of Its Forty-Third Session (1991) (A/CN.4/SER.A/1991/Add.l (Part 2))*, II(2):79–107, esp. 105 (Art. 22 commentary, para. 4). Letter dated 9 February 1993 from the Secretary-General addressed to the President of the Security Council (UN Doc. S/25274, 10 February 1993), available at: http://undocs.org/S/25274 [accessed 13 December 2018], at 20, para. 74.

[13] UN Doc. S/RES/808 (22 February 1993), available at: http://refworld.org/docid/3b00f15d30.html [accessed 18 January 2015].

[14] *Report of the Secretary-General Pursuant to Paragraph 2 of Security Council Resolution 808 (1993)* [Contains text of the Statute of the International Tribunal for the Prosecution of Persons Responsible for Serious Violations of International Humanitarian Law Committed in the Territory of the Former Yugoslavia since 1991] (UN Doc. S/25704, 3 May 1993), available at: https://documents-dds-ny.un.org/doc/UNDOC/GEN/N93/248/35/IMG/N9324835.pdf?OpenElement [accessed 13 December 2018].

[15] Bassiouni, *The Legislative History of the International Criminal Court (Volume 3)*, 53. See UN Doc. S/RES/827 (25 May 1993), available at: https://undocs.org/S/RES/827(1993) [accessed 25 December 2018].

[16] See UN Security Council, *Provisional Verbatim Record of the Three Thousand Two Hundred and Seventeenth Meeting*, UN Doc. S/PV.3217, 25 May 1993 (esp. pp. 11, 15),

prepared by the ILC in mid-1994, moreover, did not lend particular support to advocates of a more inclusive approach to war crimes.[17]

The landscape shifted though, with subsequent developments later in 1994 and 1995. The first step was the establishment of the ICTR in November 1994.[18] In contrast to the Yugoslav case, the context here was indisputably non-international, prompting the Secretary General to recommend that the statute of the ICTR should encompass: 'crimes regardless of whether they were considered part of customary international law and whether customary international law entailed individual criminal responsibility with respect to war crimes in non-international armed conflict'.[19] In consequence, Article 4 of the ICTR statute – prepared by the US, New

available at http://icty.org/x/file/Legal%20Library/Statute/930525-unsc-verbatim-record.pdf [accessed 13 December 2018].

17 Draft prepared pursuant to General Assembly Resolution 44/39 (see note 10) and subsequently Resolution 47/33 of 25 November 1992 requesting the ILC to 'continue its work on this question by undertaking the project for the elaboration of a draft statute for an international criminal court as a matter of priority as from its next session . . . ' (UN Doc. A/RES/47/33, 25 November 1992), available at: http://un.org/documents/ga/res/47/a47r033.htm [accessed 13 December 2018]'. See Draft Article 20 ('Crimes within the Jurisdiction of the Court') and commentary at: International Law Commission, *Yearbook of the International Law Commission: Report of the Commission to the General Assembly on the Work of Its Forty-Third Session (1994) (A/CN.4/SER.A/1994/Add.l (Part 2))*, II (2):38–41, 67–69. Article 20(c) of the draft states simply that the crimes within the jurisdiction of the court will include 'serious violations of the laws and customs applicable in armed conflict' without further elaboration, while paragraph (e) of that article adds that the court is to have jurisdiction over 'crimes, established under or pursuant to the treaty provisions listed in the Annex, which, having regard to the conduct alleged, constitute exceptionally serious crimes of international concern' (p. 38). The Annex and commentary (pp. 67–9) refers to the grave breaches provisions of the 1949 Conventions and Additional Protocol I but omits mention of either Common Article 3 or Additional Protocol II. The implications of this drafting for the putative court's jurisdiction over war crimes in internal conflict were debated at the time. (See Meron, 'International Criminalization of Internal Atrocities', 574; Greenwood, 'International Humanitarian Law and the Tadic Case Symposium', 281; cited in Moir, *The Law of Internal Armed Conflict*, 164.) Probably the better view is that, as put by Moir: 'the ILC had intended to refer to the customary international law of war crimes in general, whatever it was or would become' (164).

18 This is, of course, another discussion. See e.g. Cisse, 'The International Tribunals for the Former Yugoslavia and Rwanda: Some Elements of Comparison'; Magnarella, 'Expanding the Frontiers of Humanitarian Law: The International Criminal Tribunal for Rwanda'.

19 Schabas, *An Introduction to the International Criminal Court*, 2007 (3rd edn.), 114. See *Report of the Secretary-General pursuant to Paragraph 5 of Security Council Resolution 955 (1994)* (UN Doc. S/1995/134, 13 February 1995), available at: https://documents-dds-ny.un.org/doc/UNDOC/GEN/N95/043/02/PDF/N9504302.pdf?OpenElement [accessed 25 December 2018], para. 12.

Zealand and Rwandan governments – refers to violations of Common Article 3 and Additional Protocol II, providing a precedent for the ICC statute negotiations.[20]

Following swiftly on the heels of the ICTR statute, the Appeals Chamber of the ICTY – led by Antonio Cassese, like Bassiouni a prominent international jurist and activist – took the view in the *Tadić* decision of 2 October 1995 that the phrase 'laws or customs of war' in the ICTY's statute should be understood as including 'acts committed during internal armed conflict', as '[w]hat is inhumane, and consequently proscribed, in international wars, cannot but be inhumane and inadmissible in civil strife'.[21] This was not necessarily dispositive of the (debatable) customary legal position and constituted a broad reading of the ICTY statute. Nevertheless, *Tadić* and the jurisdictional ambit of the ICTR were significant milestones on the road to the drafting of the internal armed conflict provisions of the Rome Statute.[22]

5.2 1996–1998: The UN PrepCom and the Rome Diplomatic Conference

5.2.1 The PrepCom (1996–1998)

Following the Security Council decision to establish the ICTR, the General Assembly established an ad hoc committee in December 1994

[20] UN Doc. S/RES/955, 8 November 1994, available at: https://documents-dds-ny.un.org/doc/UNDOC/GEN/N95/140/97/PDF/N9514097.pdf?OpenElement [accessed 25 December 2018]. See: McGoldrick, Rowe, and Donnelly, *The Permanent International Criminal Court: Legal and Policy Issues*, 36; Perna, *The Formation of the Treaty Law of Non-International Armed Conflicts*, 147.

[21] *Tadić* paragraph 119.

[22] Cassese had form in this area: see e.g. views cited in Chapter 4 on the customary status of Art. 1(4) of Additional Protocol I ('Wars of National Liberation and Humanitarian Law', 322). He similarly claimed in 1984 that: 'at present the customary regulation of non-international armed conflicts is made up of two distinct sets of rules: those arising out of the Hague Convention, which apply to any category of armed conflict, and those exclusively governing large scale civil strife. The latter consist of the rules on civilians which evolved in the 1930's and were confirmed in the 1960's as well as *the detailed rules that took shape in the 1977 Protocol, which arose from the general consent of States*' (Cassese, 'The Geneva Protocols of 1977 on the Humanitarian Law of Armed Conflict and Customary International Law', 112–13. Italics added). See also observations and references in Mantilla, 'Under (Social) Pressure: The Historical Regulation of Internal Armed Conflicts through International Law', 304–8, 311–14 inc. quotation at p. 312 from Verrijn Stuart and Simons, 'The Judge: Interview with Antonio Cassese', 52–3. (' . . . at the ICTY, we said for the first time that war crimes could also be committed in internal armed conflicts. This was breaking new ground. You go beyond the black letter of the law because you look at the spirit of law.')

to review the ILC draft statute, to be chaired by Adriaan Bos of the Netherlands.[23] The work of this committee resulted in the General Assembly establishing a further 'Preparatory Committee on the Establishment of an International Criminal Court' (the 'PrepCom'), with a view to holding a diplomatic conference in 1998.[24]

The PrepCom held six sessions during 1996, 1997 and 1998, with both state and NGO representatives attending.[25] During this period, an umbrella international coalition of non-governmental organisations was also formed under the auspices of the World Federalist Movement to coordinate activities in support of (what was to become) the ICC (the 'NGO Coalition').[26] This was paralleled by the coalescence in spring 1997 of a group of states supportive of a strong court, with Canada, New Zealand, South Africa and Italy featuring prominently – the nucleus of what was to become the Like-Minded Group at Rome in 1998.[27]

The question of whether (and if so how) a permanent court should have jurisdiction over breaches of international humanitarian law in internal armed conflicts proved controversial at the PrepCom. The ad hoc committee report records laconically that 'there were different views' as to whether war crimes jurisdiction should include breaches of Common Article 3 and Additional Protocol II, with (notwithstanding the language of the ICTR statute) some participants expressing 'serious reservations concerning the possibility of covering non-international armed conflicts ... As regards Additional Protocol II, the view was

[23] See General Assembly Resolution 49/53 (UN Doc. A/RES/49/53, 17 February 1995), available at: http://un.org/ga/search/view_doc.asp?symbol=A/RES/49/53 [accessed 14 December 2018]. Cited at: Lee, 'Introduction', 7.

[24] General Assembly Resolution 50/46 (UN Doc. A/RES/50/46, 11 December 1995), available at: http://un.org/documents/ga/res/50/a50r046.htm [accessed 14 December 2018]. See generally Bos, 'From the International Law Commission to the Rome Conference (1994–1998)'. The General Assembly also requested the Secretary General to establish trust funds to finance the attendance of delegates from less developed and developing countries, ultimately facilitating the participation of 52 such states. Lee, 'Introduction', 9.

[25] From 25 March to 12 April and 12 to 30 August 1996; 11 to 21 February, 4 to 15 August and 1 to 12 December 1997, and 16 March to 3 April 1998.

[26] This started out with 25 member organisations and eventually brought together over 1,000 civil society groups. On the NGO Coalition and its activities see *inter alia* Cakmak, 'Transnational Activism in World Politics and Effectiveness of a Loosely Organised Principled Global Network'; Glasius, 'Expertise in the Cause of Justice: Global Civil Society Influence on the Statute for an International Criminal Court'; Glasius, *The International Criminal Court*.

[27] See account in Benedetti, Bonneau, and Washburn, *Negotiating the International Criminal Court*, 79.

expressed that that instrument as a whole had not achieved the status of customary law and therefore was binding only on States parties thereto. The view was also expressed that non-international armed conflicts should not fall within the jurisdiction of the court either with respect to Common Article 3 or Additional Protocol II.'[28] Even following *Tadić,* the 1996 PrepCom report refers obliquely to similarly 'different views' having been expressed on these issues, the bland language masking what were evidently quite serious disagreements.[29]

The issue of war crimes jurisdiction in internal armed conflicts was not settled in the PrepCom. Rather, different formulations were put forward and duly included (in square brackets) in the draft statute prepared by the PrepCom for consideration at Rome (the 'PrepCom Draft').[30] The most extensive formulation included in this draft made reference to the putative court having jurisdiction over: 'serious violations' of Common Article 3 ('Section C' – later to emerge as Article 8(2)(c) of the Rome Statute) and 'other serious violations of the laws and customs applicable in armed conflicts not of an international character' ('Section D' – the forerunner to Article 8(2)(e)), the latter with multiple sub-options, though there were also proposals to narrow or remove altogether the war crimes jurisdiction of the court with respect to internal armed conflicts.[31]

[28] Report of the Ad Hoc Committee on the Establishment of an International Criminal Court, 6 September 1995, UN Doc. A/50/22, available at: https://legal-tools.org/doc/b50da8/pdf/ [accessed 14 December 2018], at p. 16 (para. 74). See: Bassiouni, *The Statute of the International Criminal Court*, 627.

[29] Report of the Preparatory Committee on the Establishment of an International Criminal Court: Volume I (Proceedings of the Preparatory Committee during March–April and August 1996), 13 September 1996, UN Doc. A/51/22, available at: https://legal-tools.org/doc/e75432/pdf/ [accessed 14 December 2018], at 20 (para. 78). See also: Bassiouni, 397, 441, 473.

[30] The draft was published in a series of documents (UN Docs. A/AC.249/1998/CRP.6-18 and corrigenda). The draft war crimes clauses were included in: 'Part 2. Jurisdiction, Admissibility and Applicable Law' (UN Doc. A/AC.249/1998/CRP.8, 2 April 1998, available at: https://legal-tools.org/doc/e652fe/pdf/ [accessed 14 December 2018] (the 'PrepCom Draft War Crimes Clauses')).

[31] See PrepCom Draft War Crimes Clauses pp. 12–15. Also excerpts and discussion in: Bassiouni, *The Statute of the International Criminal Court*, 115, 122, 125–27, 231, 233, 367, 374. See also discussion and commentary in Robinson and von Hebel, 'War Crimes in Internal Conflicts: Article 8 of the ICC Statute', 199; von Hebel and Robinson, 'Crimes within the Jurisdiction of the Court', 104–5, 119–22; Zimmerman and Geiß, 'Article 8 War Crimes Para. 2 (c) to (f) and Para. 3: War Crimes Committed in an Armed Conflict Not of an International Character'. The ILC also completed its 'Draft Code of Crimes against the Peace and Security of Mankind' at its 1996 session. (See Report of the International Law Commission on the Work of Its Forty-Eighth Session, 6 May–26 July 1996, Official Records

There is no reliable documentary means of definitively associating all the various elements of the PrepCom Draft with individual states. It seems, however, that there was relatively wide acceptance amongst PrepCom attendees of the idea that conduct in internal armed conflicts should be capable of constituting war crimes. Reluctance – and in some cases outright opposition – hailed mainly from the permanent five members of the Security Council (the 'P5'), India and Pakistan and 'almost any state that had a non-international armed conflict going on'.[32]

Some insight into the divisions amongst delegations can be gleaned from two proposals put forward at the February 1997 PrepCom meeting. The first proposal was prepared by the ICRC, reflecting an earlier Amnesty International paper, and was put forward by New Zealand and Switzerland.[33] This was a maximalist position, containing an extensive, detailed list of war crimes in non-international armed conflicts.[34] A second, less ambitious proposal submitted by the USA, following consultations with France, Japan and the UK, was limited to serious breaches of Common Article 3 committed 'as part of a systematic plan or policy as part of a large-scale commission of such offences'.[35]

To bridge the gaps between NATO allies, Germany (alongside the Netherlands perhaps the foremost 'like-minded' European

of the General Assembly, Fifty-First Session, Supplement No. 10 (UN Doc. A/512/10), available at: http://legal.un.org/ilc/documentation/english/reports/a_51_10.pdf [accessed 14 December 2018].) Article 20(f) of this draft set out a closed list of prohibited 'acts committed in violation of international humanitarian law applicable in armed conflict not of an international character' (54), with the associated commentary linking this drafting to the *Tadić* decision (56, para. 14).

32 UK Rome Conference delegation member, Interview (author papers).

33 Amnesty International, 'The International Criminal Court: Making the Right Choices – Part I'.

34 See International Committee of the Red Cross, 'War Crimes: Working Paper Prepared by the ICRC for the Preparatory Committee for the Establishment of an International Criminal Court, New York'. Also Working paper submitted by the delegations of New Zealand and Switzerland (UN Doc. A/AC.249/1997/WG.1/DP.2), 14 February 1997, available at: https://legal-tools.org/doc/7ba0b8/pdf/ [accessed 14 December 2018]). See also Moir, *The Law of Internal Armed Conflict*, 165, at note 166; Schabas, *The International Criminal Court: A Commentary on the Rome Statute*, 2016, 223.

35 Proposal submitted by the United States (UN Doc. A/AC.249/1997/WG.1/DP.1), 14 February 1997, available at: https://legal-tools.org/doc/c5359c/pdf/ [accessed 14 December 2018]). Cited in Hall, 'The Third and Fourth Sessions of the UN Preparatory Committee on the Establishment of an International Criminal Court', 128. See also von Hebel and Robinson, 'Crimes within the Jurisdiction of the Court', 105–6.

government) convened two intersessional meetings of NATO members in Bonn in June and October 1997. These meetings resulted in a 'Bonn Paper' that was used as a basis for discussion at the December 1997 meeting. Based in part on work by the UK delegation, which had joined the Like-Minded Group in mid-1997, the approach taken in this paper was to narrow the differences by forgoing language drawn directly from Additional Protocol II in favour of identifying a set of 'comparable norms regarded as fundamental in character and therefore clearly applicable in internal armed conflict'.[36]

The division of the PrepCom War Crimes Draft Clauses into four – Sections 'A' to 'D', with non-international armed conflict covered in Sections C and (more controversially) D – was of a piece with the German proposal. In respect of internal armed conflict, moreover, the drafting echoed the approach taken in *Tadić* rather than the 1996 ILC Draft Code of Crimes, insofar as there was no explicit attempt on the face of the draft to link prohibited conduct to specific treaty provisions. At the same time, however, none of the drafting options included in these draft clauses featured an open-ended list of crimes, echoing the ILC's approach, and suggesting a common concern amongst the drafters about the prospects of future judges emulating Cassese's 'innovative' approach to war crimes in non-international armed conflict in *Tadić*.[37]

[36] Robinson and von Hebel, 'War Crimes in Internal Conflicts: Article 8 of the ICC Statute', 199; von Hebel and Robinson, 'Crimes within the Jurisdiction of the Court', 106. For the proposal that emerged from these discussions, see Reference Paper on War Crimes submitted by Germany (UN Doc. A/AC.249/1997/WG.1/DP.23/Rev.1), 12 December 1997, available at: http://legal-tools.org/doc/0c9b1a/ [accessed 14 December 2018]. At the December meeting the US also agreed to a lower threshold for war crimes provisions than the Pentagon had previously preferred, in light of arguments put forward by other governments that including a high threshold would risk prejudicing future enforcement of the 1949 Conventions. (See Scheffer, *All the Missing Souls*, 180.)

[37] Indeed, Cassese himself recognised this concern on the part of states in the drafting of the Rome Statute. ('The draftsmen of the Rome Statute during the negotiating process simply did not trust judges. I was told there was also this fear of the "Cassese approach", namely judges overdoing, becoming dangerous by, say, producing judgments that can be innovative.' (Verrijn Stuart and Simons, 'The Judge: Interview with Antonio Cassese', 52; cited in Mantilla, 'Under (Social) Pressure: The Historical Regulation of Internal Armed Conflicts through International Law', 312).) On the ILC's drafting, see note 31.

5.2.2 *Internal Armed Conflict at Rome: Debates in the Committee of the Whole*

The December 1997 PrepCom meeting saw the designation by the like-minded group of six 'cornerstone positions' for the forthcoming conference, including that the court should have 'inherent jurisdiction over war crimes, genocide, crimes against humanity and aggression, *whether committed during armed conflict between States or internally within nations*'.[38] This determination notwithstanding, however, the internal armed conflict provisions remained 'a major source of contention until very late in the [Rome] Conference' that convened on 15 June 1998.[39] Certainly, there was a preponderance of support for the inclusion in the court's jurisdiction of war crimes committed in internal armed conflicts, with the Like-Minded Group as well as France and the USA in accord on this point.[40] Equally, though, a minority of states, including China and Russia (the remaining P5 members), India, other Asian states, most Middle Eastern states and Turkey were consistently opposed to such inclusion.[41]

The court's jurisdiction over war crimes in internal armed conflicts was discussed in the Committee of the Whole on the 18 June, 8 July and 13 July.[42] The first meeting provided an opportunity for delegations to set out their initial positions, with few surprises: the representatives of the Netherlands, Australia, Costa Rica, Canada, Belgium, New Zealand, the Czech Republic, Ireland, Brazil, the UK, Japan and Norway all spoke in favour of an extensive internal armed conflict war crimes jurisdiction. Sudan, Turkey, India and China responded, speaking against such inclusion with varying degrees of asperity. The Sudanese representative, in particular, made a forceful case against retaining Section D of the PrepCom War Crimes Draft Clauses, arguing that the draft failed to include the threshold language from Additional Protocol II and citing risks of double standards, threats to territorial integrity, and the prospect of impeding national reconciliation after civil wars. The Indian

[38] See: Kirsch and Robinson, 'Reaching Agreement at the Rome Conference', 71. Cited in Fehl, *Living with a Reluctant Hegemon*, 86. Italics added.

[39] von Hebel and Robinson, 'Crimes within the Jurisdiction of the Court', 104.

[40] Washburn, 'The Negotiation of the Rome Statute for the International Criminal Court and International Lawmaking in the 21st Century', 368. von Hebel and Robinson, 'Crimes within the Jurisdiction of the Court', 104–5.

[41] See von Hebel and Robinson, 'Crimes within the Jurisdiction of the Court', 105.

[42] i.e. all delegations meeting as a committee (for purposes of conference proceedings) rather than in plenary.

representative cited similar sovereignty-related concerns, while Turkey and China were rather more abrupt in their dismissals.[43]

On 6 July, following consultation between Philippe Kirsch – the Canadian chairman of the Committee of the Whole – and representatives of major factions and regional groups on a 'non-paper' on 5 July,[44] the Bureau of the Committee of the Whole (Kirsch, Committee officers and working group coordinators) published a proposal for discussion which reduced slightly the scope of Section D of the PrepCom Draft.[45] This prompted further, rather more wide-ranging, discussion in the Committee of the Whole on 8 July.

The extent of the divisions at this stage can be demonstrated by a roll-call of the delegations speaking in favour of and against the revised proposal. Aligned with the like-minded on this occasion, South Africa, Austria, New Zealand, Belgium, Jordan, Norway, Sierra Leone, Trinidad and Tobago, the UK, Germany, Botswana, Croatia, Australia and Senegal all spoke in favour during the first part of the discussion. Representatives from Uganda, Switzerland, Malawi, Lithuania, Brazil, South Korea, Chile, Mali, Italy, Cuba, Portugal, the USA, Ireland, Georgia, Lesotho, Greece, Cameroon, Slovakia, Austria, Uruguay, Colombia, Finland, Nicaragua, Slovenia, Hungary, Israel, Angola, Bosnia and Herzegovina, Denmark, the Czech Republic, Mexico, Poland, Ethiopia, Burkina Faso, Brunei Darussalam, Malta, Romania, France, Spain, Guatemala, the Philippines, Ecuador, Andorra, Guinea Bissau, Venezuela – and the ICRC – subsequently echoed support throughout the course of the day.

Other interjections made clear the depth of the concerns and opposition on the part of others, however. China, Iran, Algeria, Bahrain, Indonesia, the Comoros, Yemen, Vietnam, Pakistan, Thailand, Sudan, Burundi, Qatar, Saudi Arabia and Libya opposed any mention of war crimes in internal armed conflict, while Syria, Azerbaijan, Afghanistan, Egypt (to an extent), Nepal, Sri Lanka, Russia and Oman adopted (slightly) more conciliatory positions.[46]

[43] United Nations, 'Rome Conference, Vol. II', A/CONF.183/C.1/SR.5, pp. 168–9.

[44] See Washburn, 'The Negotiation of the Rome Statute for the International Criminal Court and International Lawmaking in the 21st Century', 370.

[45] Bureau: discussion paper regarding part 2 (A/Conf.183/C.1/L.53), 6 July 1998, available at: https://legal-tools.org/doc/30dcec/pdf/, 204 [accessed 14 December 2018]. Also United Nations, 'Rome Conference, Vol. III', 204–12. On the Bureau, see Brown, 'The Statute of the ICC: Past, Present and Future', 64–6.

[46] See United Nations, 'Rome Conference, Vol. II', A/CONF.183/C.1/SR.25, SR.26, SR.27, SR.28, 267–94.

Importantly, all participants were able to muster more or less principled reasons for their positions. For example, a South African delegate observed that 'most atrocities were now committed in the context of internal armed conflicts', a delegate from Togo adding that failing to include 'Sections C and D on non-international armed conflicts... in the Statute' would impair 'the credibility of the Court'.[47] These arguments were echoed by EU members, other 'Western' states such as New Zealand and Australia, by then-aspirant EU members such as Slovakia, and by democratic and democratising African states including Senegal and Mali. Delegates from Sierra Leone and Croatia cited their countries' experiences of civil war as a basis for support, while ICRC and Swiss representatives highlighted the customary status of war crimes in non-international armed conflicts, and the head of the Brazilian delegation emphasised that 'any solution taking account of concerns about the inclusion of internal armed conflicts must ensure that existing commitments under customary international law were in no way undermined'.[48]

Opponents of a robust regime similarly had technical legal and principled normative points to make: China challenged the grounding of the more extensive provisions in customary law, while Nepal highlighted that including internal armed conflict provisions in the Statute risked putting states that had not ratified Additional Protocol II in a difficult position.[49] There were also, though, indications of possible scope for compromise. Delegates from Syria, Iran, Egypt, Bahrain, the Comoros, Yemen, Sri Lanka and Oman suggested that they could 'live' with provisions echoing Common Article 3 in certain circumstances (i.e. Section C). A US delegate in turn observed that war crimes jurisdiction in internal armed conflicts was 'vital to the integrity and rationale of the Court', hoping 'that the concerns of certain delegations could be accommodated by appropriate wording ... that clearly established the high threshold to be covered by (the relevant provisions)'.[50]

47 United Nations, 'Rome Conference, Vol. II', A/CONF.183/C.1/SR.25, p. 268, para. 10; A/CONF.183/C.1/SR.26, p. 278, para. 72.

48 United Nations, 'Rome Conference, Vol. II', A/CONF.183/C.1/SR.26, p. 277, at para. 51. See also: A/CONF.183/C.1/SR.26, p. 276, at para. 41; A/CONF.183/C.1/SR.28, p. 294, at para. 108.

49 United Nations, 'Rome Conference, Vol. II', A/CONF. 183/C. 1/SR.25, p. 270, at para. 36; A/CONF.183/C.1/SR.27, p. 287, at para. 73.

50 United Nations, 'Rome Conference, Vol. II', A/CONF.183/C.1/SR.26, p. 280, at para. 97.

Following these discussions, the Bureau prepared another discussion paper with revised clauses, which was circulated on 10 July.[51] The new clauses reflected moves to conciliate concerned delegations by including more limiting scope and threshold language. The principal change was a new provision modelled on Article 1(1) of Additional Protocol II stating that Section D 'applies to armed conflicts that take place in the territory of a State Party between its armed forces and dissident armed forces or other organised armed groups which, under responsible command, exercise such control over a part of its territory as to enable them to carry out sustained and concerted military operations'.[52] A rider was also added stating that: 'nothing in sections C (the precursor to Article 8(2)(c)) and D shall affect the responsibility of a Government to maintain or re-establish law and order in the State or to defend the unity and territorial integrity of the State, by all means consistent with international law', echoing Article 3(1) of Additional Protocol II.[53] Other changes made at this stage included omitting 'outrages on personal dignity' from Section D, adding in child conscription to that section, and indicating that the inclusion of 'crimes of sexual violence' 'require[d] further discussion'.[54]

[51] Bureau proposal regarding part 2 (UN Doc. A/CONF-183/C-1/L.59), 10 July 1998: United Nations, 'Rome Conference, Vol. III', 212.

[52] See United Nations, 'Rome Conference, Vol. III', 215. Article 1 ('Material field of application') of Additional Protocol II states that: '1. This Protocol, which develops and supplements Article 3 common to the Geneva Conventions of 12 August 1949 without modifying its existing conditions of application, shall apply to all armed conflicts which are not covered by Article 1 of the Protocol Additional to the Geneva Conventions of 12 August 1949, and relating to the Protection of Victims of International Armed Conflicts (Protocol I) and which take place in the territory of a High Contracting Party between its armed forces and dissident armed forces or other organized armed groups which, under responsible command, exercise such control over a part of its territory as to enable them to carry out sustained and concerted military operations and to implement this Protocol. 2. This Protocol shall not apply to situations of internal disturbances and tensions, such as riots, isolated and sporadic acts of violence and other acts of a similar nature, as not being armed conflicts.'

[53] United Nations, 'Rome Conference, Vol. III', 215. Article 3 of Additional Protocol II ('Non-intervention') states that: '1. Nothing in this Protocol shall be invoked for the purpose of affecting the sovereignty of a State or the responsibility of the government, by all legitimate means, to maintain or re-establish law and order in the State or to defend the national unity and territorial integrity of the State. 2. Nothing in this Protocol shall be invoked as a justification for intervening, directly or indirectly, for any reason whatever, in the armed conflict or in the internal or external affairs of the High Contracting Party in the territory of which that conflict occurs.'

[54] United Nations, 'Rome Conference, Vol. III', 215.

The revised provisions were discussed by the Committee of the Whole on 13 July, meeting with cautious support from many of the delegations that had supported the previous proposal, as well as from some, such as Sudan, who had previously been more equivocal. Austria (for the EU), for example, supported the proposal, though noting that Section D needed to be expanded 'to cover conflicts in which only organized armed groups were engaged, regardless of whether they exercised control over territory'.[55] Switzerland 'regretted ... the raising of the threshold [for Section D], and the inclusion in sections C and D of additional reservations concerning the re-establishment of law and order and the defence of territorial integrity', but indicated that if these formed part of 'the price that must be paid for a system of automatic jurisdiction, inherent and unconditional ... that price would perhaps be worth paying'.[56] The UK similarly warned against the inclusion of 'a threshold so high as to remove from the Court's jurisdiction the very cases that had given rise to such grave concerns'.[57] Positive views were also expressed by Spain, Sweden, South Africa, Jordan, Sudan, Italy, Finland, Canada, Portugal, Hungary, Romania, the Solomon Islands (represented by UK academic Andrew Clapham, formerly a student of Cassese's), Botswana and Norway – though this last with concerns that 'the new chapeau unduly limited the scope of well-established norms of international law'.[58]

The Bureau compromise language was far from uncontroversial amongst those in favour of a more expansive war crimes jurisdiction, however. The USA argued, for example, that 'the change raising the threshold of applicability of Section D to that of Additional Protocol II to the Geneva Conventions ... should be rejected. The bulk of armed conflicts encountered in the real world were non-international, and that change would send the wrong message to civilian victims of internal armed conflicts', while the ICRC representative drily observed that 'with regard to armed conflicts not of an international character ... under the new threshold added to section D, many conflicts, and indeed, most internal armed conflicts, would not be covered, and many atrocities would thus not be triable under the Statute'.[59] Germany, too, could not

55 United Nations, 'Rome Conference, Vol. II', A/CONF.183/C.1/SR.33, 320, at para. 14.
56 Ibid., 321, at paras. 18–19.
57 Ibid., 326, at para. 80.
58 United Nations, 'Rome Conference, Vol. II', A/CONF.183/C.1/SR.36, 344, at para. 2, and more generally debate at A/CONF.183/C.1/SR.34, SR.35, SR.36, and SR.37 (esp. pp. 329–47).
59 United Nations, 'Rome Conference, Vol. II', A/CONF.183/C.1/SR.33, 321, at para. 24; A/CONF.183/C.1/SR.36, 348, at para. 52.

see any justification for the additional threshold for Section D, while the New Zealand and Australian delegations were dissatisfied with the proposal 'which would leave very serious gaps in the Statute'.[60] Trinidad and Tobago, Uganda and Denmark were similarly dissatisfied.[61]

Several delegations previously opposed to the inclusion of internal armed conflicts also remained unmoved by the Bureau's conciliatory drafting. India, Sri Lanka, Oman, Qatar and Pakistan, Egypt and Algeria remained opposed to the inclusion of clauses addressing internal armed conflict save where there had been a total collapse of the state.[62] Turkey 'maintained ... that sections C and D should be deleted', while Syria and Libya opposed even the inclusion of serious breaches of Common Article 3 without a further modified threshold.[63] The Chinese were slightly more amenable, merely stating that 'the safeguards in sections C and D should reproduce the wording of article 3 of Additional Protocol II', while Iran was ambivalent.[64] Russia expressed 'serious concerns' with the proposed wording, while Indonesia indicated some willingness to accept both Sections C and D, subject to a Thai-proposed restriction on application in the event of foreign interference.[65]

Sierra Leone, however, made a key contribution to forging compromise on the issue of threshold language during this debate, proposing alternative chapeau wording for Section D derived from the *Tadić* decision.[66] This proposal involved forgoing the requirement for armed groups to control territory, and including armed conflict between armed groups, not simply between armed groups and

60 United Nations, 'Rome Conference, Vol. II', A/CONF.183/C.1/SR.34, 328, at para. 22.

61 See United Nations, 'Rome Conference, Vol. II', A/CONF.183/C.1/SR.34, SR.35, at pp. 328, 337, 341.

62 See: United Nations, 'Rome Conference, Vol. II', A/CONF.183/C.1/SR.33, SR.35, SR.36 at pp. 323, 335, 337, 339, 340, 345.

63 United Nations, 'Rome Conference, Vol. II', A/CONF.183/C.1/SR.34, 330, at para. 48; A/CONF.183/C.1/SR.33, 322, at para. 33, A/CONF.183/C.1/SR.36, 344, at para. 6.

64 United Nations, 'Rome Conference, Vol. II', A/CONF.183/C.1/SR.33, 323, at para. 40; A/CONF.183/C.1/SR.34, 331, at para. 62.

65 United Nations, 'Rome Conference, Vol. II', A/CONF.183/C.1/SR.34, 332, at para. 82; A/CONF.183/C.1/SR.35, 338, at para. 35. The latter proposal was put forward on the 14th July by Indonesia, the Philippines, Thailand and Vietnam (Document A/CONF.183/C.1/L.74). United Nations, 'Rome Conference, Vol. III', 248.

66 For a more extended discussion on the relationship between the *Tadić* decision and the Sierra Leone proposal, see Cullen, *The Concept of Non-International Armed Conflict in International Humanitarian Law*, 172. Also generally La Haye, *War Crimes in Internal Armed Conflicts*.

governments.[67] Slovenia and Bosnia and Herzegovina also brought their own not-inconsiderable moral weight to bear in support of this proposal.[68]

Consensus was not reached at the Committee of the Whole on whether or how to address internal armed conflicts. The issue thus remained unresolved when the Committee came to the end of its substantive deliberations. The Bureau then worked overnight on a 'package deal' which was presented to the Committee on a take-it-or-leave-it basis on the evening of 16 July.[69] This proposal was subsequently adopted by the Committee on 17 July, and by the Conference in plenary on the night of the 17–18 July.[70]

The language ultimately adopted for Section D contained amended and additional threshold language derived from *Tadić*. It removed the requirements in the 10 July paper for organised armed groups to be 'under responsible command' and to control territory that had been imported from Additional Protocol II. It also broadened the scope of the provision to cover armed conflicts 'in a territory of a State when there is protracted armed conflict between governmental authorities and organized armed groups or between such groups'.[71] Thus, while modelled on the threshold of Additional Protocol II, and similarly designed to provide comfort to concerned delegations, the final product was in fact rather broader in scope than its 1977 precursor.[72]

Otherwise, however, much of the language of Article 8 was carried over verbatim from the Like-Minded Group's preferences as set out in

[67] United Nations, 'Rome Conference, Vol. II', A/CONF.183/C.1/SR.35, 335, at para. 8. The proposal is set out at Document A/CONF.183/C.1/L.62 (United Nations, 'Rome Conference, Vol. III', 247).

[68] United Nations, 'Rome Conference, Vol. II', A/CONF.183/C.1/SR.36, 346, at para. 30; 347, at para. 42.

[69] Kirsch and Robinson, 'Reaching Agreement at the Rome Conference', 75. See also Washburn, 'The Negotiation of the Rome Statute for the International Criminal Court and International Lawmaking in the 21st Century', 370. The text adopted is at Report of the Committee of the Whole (UN Doc. A/CONF.183/8), 17 July 1998: United Nations, 'Rome Conference, Vol. III', 94–132. (The final draft statute circulated comprised a set of documents: UN Doc. A/CONF.183/C.1/L.76 and Add.1, Add.2 and Add.2/Corr.l, Add.3 and 4, Add.5 and Add.5/Corr. 1, Add.6 and Add.6/Corr. 1, Add.7 and 8, Add.9 and Add.9/Corr.l, and Add. 10-14.)

[70] United Nations, 'Rome Conference, Vol. II', A/CONF.183/SR.9, A/CONF.183/C.1/SR.42, 121–9, 360–2.

[71] Para. (f) United Nations, 'Rome Conference, Vol. III', 98.

[72] This difference and its implications have been extensively analysed elsewhere. See e.g. in Cullen, *The Concept of Non-International Armed Conflict in International Humanitarian Law*.

the PrepCom Draft. The substantive crimes in Section D, in particular, did not stray far from the Bonn Paper proposals, including language on sexual violence and child recruitment.[73] The post-PrepCom drafts also did not include provision for prohibited weapons in Section D, with the only remaining changes during the process being the inclusion of wording (in the 10 July draft) adding protection for UN personnel and facilities, and the removal of references to 'outrages on personal dignity' on the grounds that this was already covered by Section C.[74]

5.3 Key Roles and Perspectives

The following section considers the perspectives and roles of key groups of states and non-governmental organisations – again, principally great powers and the delegations and civil society bodies that contributed most notably to proceedings – in the negotiation of the Rome Statute's internal armed conflict provisions.

5.3.1 The Like-Minded Group

There is no straightforward means of identifying the members of the like-minded group at any given point. Membership of this group shifted over time, and no comprehensive contemporaneous lists appear to have been published. Affiliation with the 'like-minded' also seems to have been a matter of degree, with some delegations associated with like-minded positions on some issues but not others. It is reasonable, however, to view the core of this group as being composed of 'middle powers' who were

[73] See Report of the Preparatory Committee on the Establishment of an International Criminal Court (United Nations, 'Rome Conference, Vol. III', A/CONF.183/2), 19. There were some other suggestions for inclusion of provisions, in particular related to famine and indiscriminate attacks, which were supported by the ICRC and raised in the PrepCom, but which were not included in the final text. See Yves Sandoz of the ICRC at United Nations, 'Rome Conference, Vol. II', A/CONF.183/SR.9, 129, at para. 114.

[74] Amongst the notable difference between the provisions relating to war crimes in international armed conflicts and non-international armed conflicts, respectively, is that the former includes language incorporating the long-standing IHL principle of proportionality in Art. 8(2)(b)(iv) ('Intentionally launching an attack in the knowledge that such attack will cause incidental loss of life or injury to civilians or damage to civilian objects or widespread, long-term and severe damage to the natural environment which would be clearly excessive in relation to the concrete and direct overall military advantage anticipated') to which there is no equivalent clause in sub-paragraphs (c) or (e). *Tadić* notwithstanding, as this difference illustrates, there continue to be doctrinal distinctions between the civil war regime and that governing conduct in international armed conflicts.

members of the Western European and Others UN regional group (WEOG), but who were not amongst the permanent five members of the Security Council. Canada, Germany, the Netherlands, Norway, New Zealand and South Africa all feature in various accounts as having been founders of the Like-Minded Group, or as being especially committed to delivering a progressive, well-developed court.[75] Over time, moreover, this group came to include the UK, many Latin American and sub-Saharan African states, as well as smaller developing nations.

Contours of membership aside, the Rome Statute provisions on internal armed conflict can be regarded as a significant success for the governments and delegations leading this group, reflecting the group's 'cornerstone' position in respect of war crimes. Indeed, the internal armed conflict provisions of the Rome Statute reflect remarkably closely the positions taken by leading like-minded delegations at the PrepCom.

As regards the motivation for the drive by these states to include internal armed conflicts within the ambit of the statute's war crimes provision, Herman von Hebel – since appointed ICC Registrar – has stated, with respect to post-Bonn PrepCom discussions, that:

> a clear majority of delegations supported the inclusion of such norms. The need for the inclusion of such norms was underscored by the fact that most of the armed conflicts that have raged over the world since World War II were conflicts of a non-international armed character. It was observed that it was precisely in internal armed conflicts that national criminal justice systems were in all likelihood unable to adequately respond to violations of such norms. It was also noted that the ICTR Statute already contained norms of international humanitarian law expressly relating to internal armed conflicts.[76]

In other words, for a significant proportion of states – many of which had not experienced violent civil unrest for some time – the *stated* (i.e. apparent) motivations for catering for internal armed conflict within the Rome Statute's war crimes provisions were humanitarian and principled, albeit (rationally) underpinned by the absence of significant anticipated domestic costs in states such as Canada, Germany, New Zealand and Italy. For others, principally countries emerging from civil conflict and undergoing domestic governance transitions, the conference

[75] See e.g. account in Benedetti, Bonneau, and Washburn, *Negotiating the International Criminal Court*, 79. Reference is made in this account to the Like-Minded Group being established by way of dialogue amongst key NGOs and PrepCom representatives from *inter alia* New Zealand, Canada, South Africa and Italy.

[76] von Hebel and Robinson, 'Crimes within the Jurisdiction of the Court', 104–5.

records suggest that support for the inclusion of internal armed conflicts was strongly influenced by domestic experience, consistent with Regime Type (as well as Rationalist) expectations of 'new' democracies (see e.g. interventions and positions taken by Sierra Leone and, inter alia, Bosnia and Herzegovina). The common view taken by the Like-Minded Group accordingly reflects a diversity of experience and motivation.

More granular insight into national preferences can also be provided in some instances, drawing on the rationales for positions taken more generally at the Rome Conference and during the prior negotiations. For Canada, for example – the most prominent of the 'middle powers' associated with the Like-Minded Group, the group's original convenor and arguably its leader – the ICC negotiations formed part of a 'human security'-oriented foreign policy adopted after the Cold War and promoted by means of 'soft power', with an emphasis on moral suasion rather than implicit or overt reliance on material power.[77] This policy, closely associated with Foreign Minister Lloyd Axworthy, was pursued in large part through what became known as the 'New Diplomacy' – an approach to developing international regimes led by groups of committed middle powers working closely with international (albeit predominantly Western-based) and national civil society organisations.[78]

Canadian leadership of the Like-Minded Group manifested itself in a number of ways. First, foreign minister Axworthy took a close personal interest in negotiations, directly engaging with national counterparts to engender support for Canadian efforts, and attending the conference in

[77] Re. Canada's status as 'leader' of this group, see e.g. Clarkson and Mildenberger, *Dependent America?*, 206. More generally, Canadian representatives and support for the putative ICC feature heavily in published accounts of the Rome negotiations. As one Canadian participant has observed: 'Canada's fingerprints are over almost all of the statute. To be honest, there is probably not a page of the statute that does not have directly-proposed language from Canada in it' (Clarkson and Mildenberger, 206. Citing Valerie Oosterveld, quoted in Tenove, 'Canada and the ICC. Part One'). See also Bernard, 'Canada and Human Security'. 'When Lloyd Axworthy became foreign minister in January 1996, he advanced an agenda which was unlike those of his predecessors. Axworthy recognized that since the end of the Cold War, Canada's foreign policy had been struggling to find its bearings in the new international system. The foreign minister moved quickly to articulate a bold and ambitious policy agenda to guide Canada's foreign policy in the years to come. Promoting human security became Canada's new international objective' (Bernard, 236).

[78] Literature on the 'New Diplomacy', the Ottawa Process and the associated 'human security' agenda is extensive. There is insufficient space to consider this topic at any length in the present context, but see e.g. Davenport, 'The New Diplomacy'. Also Behringer, *The Human Security Agenda*; Knight, 'Soft Power, Moral Suasion, and Establishing the International Criminal Court: Canadian Contributions'.

person.[79] The appointment of Kirsch, a prominent Canadian government lawyer, to the key role of chair of the Committee of the Whole, accompanied by a Canadian supporting staff, also contributed strongly to the Canadian 'flavour' of the final draft.[80] Third, the Canadian delegation was particularly well-equipped, 'with expertise in many different aspects of international criminal law, at a time when it was a relatively young and under-populated field' as well as an integral civil society presence.[81] Finally, Canada had tremendous credibility and moral authority in the eyes of many in civil society as well as other Western and developing world delegations. This last was a reflection of Axworthy's 'human security'-focused foreign policy and, in particular, Canada's prominent role in the development of the 1997 anti-land mine treaty bringing Western and developing world governments together with NGOs outside the UN Conference on Disarmament.[82]

Within Europe, Germany and the Netherlands were key like-minded states: Dutch commitment to a strong court was manifested most obviously in Adriaan Bos' appointment as chair of the pre-Rome ad hoc committee and PrepCom. Herman von Hebel, a member of the Dutch delegation in Rome (and at the time of writing ICC Registrar), was also coordinator of the working group on war crimes at and prior to Rome, as well as a member of Kirsch's extended Bureau. In terms of

[79] Behringer, *The Human Security Agenda*, 96. See also Bosco, *Rough Justice*, 49.

[80] Benedetti, Bonneau, and Washburn, *Negotiating the International Criminal Court*, 91.

[81] Tenove, 'Canada and the ICC. Part One'.

[82] Axworthy refers, for example, to the Canadian government's work with non-great power and developing world governments during this process as building up: 'confidence, familiarity, and contact and shared outlooks' (*Navigating a New World: Canada's Global Future, 153*). As Kenneth Anderson observes of the Ottawa Process: 'the ban campaign by its end stages was conceived by sympathetic governments, United Nations institutions, and the international NGO movement as being a genuine partnership' ('The Ottawa Convention Banning Landmines, the Role of International Non-Governmental Organizations and the Idea of International Civil Society', 108). The role of Axworthy (and, indeed of Kirsch and other Canadian participants) at Rome may also be seen as building on a tradition of Canadian international 'good-citizenship' – see e.g. the role of Canadian head of delegation David Miller in brokering the 1977 completion of Additional Protocol II (see: Chapter 4, Section 4.3.1). Valerie Kitchen observes in similar vein that: '[t]he Ottawa Process also provided a way for Canada to set itself apart from other states, much as peacekeeping did forty years ago . . . It was [also] in the tradition of Canadian moral foreign policy that goes back at least to the days of Pearson. But, in launching the idea of human security, it gave Canadian foreign policy a new direction that deepened the Canadian commitment to being a 'do-gooder' on the international scene' ('From Rhetoric to Reality: Canada, the United States, and the Ottawa Process to Ban Landmines', 54).

motivation, the Netherlands, like Canada, appears to have been committed to an expansive war crimes jurisdiction on principled grounds. This was also a rational position for both states given the low likelihood of domestic civil strife, though criticism of national policy-makers following the failures of Dutch peacekeepers at Srebrenica in 1995 may also have contributed to Dutch commitment to a robust internal armed conflict regime.[83]

Germany was similarly a leading European advocate of a strong court, with 'the most extensive view of the Court's jurisdiction and powers', consistent with the legacy of the Second World War, the consequent Nuremberg experience and Germany's subsequent long-standing commitment to strong human rights protections domestically, suggesting the operation of factors associated with the Regime Type hypothesis.[84] More broadly, given the importance ascribed by many EU member states during this period to the development of a common security and foreign policy in the post-Maastricht 1990s and the relative absence of violent civil unrest amongst EU members, it would also have been surprising had the EU not endeavoured to present a united face as far as possible at Rome, including with respect to the internal armed conflict provisions.[85]

New Zealand and Australia, alongside South Africa, similarly feature prominently in lists of leading like-minded states.[86] Felicity Wong of New Zealand appears to have been an especially effective proponent of a more robust ICC, with her delegation, alongside Switzerland, a principled advocate of removing the legal distinction between internal and international armed conflicts. South Africa, in turn, led a coherent Southern African Development Community in support of a strong court,

83 For an overview of this episode, see: Bosco, 'When the Blue Helmets Are to Blame'.

84 Benedetti, Bonneau, and Washburn, *Negotiating the International Criminal Court*, 91. For insight into German policy, see Steinke, *Politics of International Criminal Justice*. Germany's PrepCom and Rome delegations were led by Hans-Peter Kaul, then-Head of the Public International Law Division of the German Federal Foreign Office, who was later to become a judge at the ICC. Indeed, for many years Germany was the leading financial contributor to the ICC

85 On the coordination of EU positions with respect to the US in particular, see Fehl, *Living with a Reluctant Hegemon*; Thomas, 'Rejecting the US Challenge to the International Criminal Court: Normative Entrapment and Compromise in EU Policy-Making'.

86 This is despite the (new) government of Australia apparently not viewing 'the International Criminal Court as its highest priority' at the time of the Rome Conference (Benedetti, Bonneau, and Washburn, *Negotiating the International Criminal Court*, 91). On Australian and New Zealand foreign policy more broadly see e.g. Devetak and True, 'Diplomatic Divergence in the Antipodes: Globalisation, Foreign Policy and State Identity in Australia and New Zealand'.

against the backdrop of developing expertise and experience in transitional justice given then-recent experiences under apartheid and the subsequent Truth and Reconciliation Commission – again highlighting the operation of domestic political (i.e. Regime Type) and Rationalist considerations.[87] Argentina and Brazil also feature heavily in lists of members of the Like-Minded Group, though it is more difficult to trace specific motivations with respect to these delegations.

A significant number of smaller and developing states were also aligned with the like-minded with respect to internal armed conflict. In addition to individual experiences of civil war, and in many cases consequent democratic transitions – again suggestive of the operation of Rationalist and Regime Type-associated factors – the delegations of many such states also included international volunteers associated with the NGO Coalition. Where delegations with such international participation represented governments that had not provided comprehensive instructions, moreover, it appears likely that the positions of such states – including, for example, Sierra Leone – were closely influenced by the views of these embedded international advisors.[88]

More generally, the Rome Conference was 'captured' by the like-minded group, led by Canada, to the extent that it would be surprising if the provisions on war crimes did not have a strongly like-minded flavour. The extended Bureau, for example, was dominated by like-minded delegates, with instances cited of Kirsch wielding a 'robust gavel' to the benefit of this group.[89] Perhaps as importantly, though, the Like-Minded Group also appears to have been quite highly organised internally, enabling positions and arguments to be coordinated throughout the negotiations.[90]

[87] See Benedetti, Bonneau, and Washburn, *Negotiating the International Criminal Court*, 95. It bears noting that South Africa has also been a prominent voice amongst African governments more recently disenchanted with the ICC. (See: Boehme, 'We Chose Africa'; Mills and Bloomfield, 'African Resistance to the International Criminal Court'.)

[88] UK Rome Conference delegation member, Interview (author papers). The scale and implications of this tendency are considered below. (See discussion at Section 5.3.4.)

[89] This observation reflects examples mentioned in interviews with the author. See also, though Benedetti, Bonneau, and Washburn, *Negotiating the International Criminal Court*, 104.

[90] Schiff, *Universalism Meets Sovereignty at the International Criminal Court*, 61, Behringer, *The Human Security Agenda*, 95, 166; Bosco, *Rough Justice*, 45–6. See also comments and observations generally in Kirsch and Holmes, 'The Rome Conference on an International Criminal Court: The Negotiating Process'.

Viewed from the perspective of the like-minded, therefore, the inclusion of a robust internal armed conflict regime for war crimes was in retrospect an 'easy win'.[91] In particular, given the supportive positions of three of the five permanent members of the Security Council, it seems to have been relatively straightforward (at least compared with some of the other issues debated at Rome) for the Like-Minded Group to have agreed to compromise threshold language for these provisions framed around the *Tadić* jurisprudence.

5.3.2 *The 'P-5'*

The permanent five members of the UN Security Council represent a special case in terms of groupings at Rome. Unlike the Like-Minded Group (with which there was some overlap with respect to the UK and, latterly, France), the P5 did not seek to coordinate positions across the negotiations.[92] Rather, the P5 adopted a shared position only where there was a clear common interest and appear to have quietly made these instances known to the Bureau. In the few cases where such interventions were known to have taken place, Kirsch evidently took P5 concerns on board, and the prospects of a contradictory position appearing in the text were accordingly extremely low.[93]

The P5 did not only matter at Rome collectively, however. Their status as recognised great powers – recognised, that is, by virtue of their privileged position in the UN system – also rendered the views of China, France, Russia, the UK and the USA especially significant individually, and engendered amongst other delegations and the Bureau a reluctance to antagonise all members of the P5 at once if avoidable. Indeed, the leaders of the Like-Minded Group appear to have been

[91] The internal armed conflict provisions can also be cast as a 'win-win' game for many like-minded states, in the sense of being cost-less given their relative domestic stability.

[92] Though Scheffer's account indicates that there were extensive marginal discussions amongst P5 delegations at Rome (Scheffer, *All the Missing Souls*, 199–226).

[93] This was particularly the case with respect to the proposed criminalisation of the use of nuclear weapons. ('A second group consisted of the permanent members of the Security Council (P5). Their solidarity was clearest on two points: a strong role for the Council vis-à-vis the court, and the exclusion of nuclear weapons from the weapons prohibited by the statute. With the exception of the United Kingdom, which had joined the [like-minded] shortly before the conference, the P5 also wanted the jurisdiction of the court and its exercise to be carefully circumscribed. They paid particular attention to its jurisdiction over armed conflicts, but their main area of concern (international vs. internal conflicts) varied according to their national perspective' (Kirsch and Holmes, 'The Rome Conference on an International Criminal Court: The Negotiating Process', 4).)

particularly conscious of this risk, with the alignment of British, French and US positions with the like-minded enabling robust internal armed conflict provisions to be delivered notwithstanding the concerns of Russia and China.[94]

5.3.2.1 The United States

American conduct in relation to the ICC and Rome Statute prior to, at, and subsequent to the Rome Conference has generated a literature of its own.[95] Much of this material does not bear directly on the US position vis à vis the internal armed conflict provisions, though it is worth noting US concern that the delegation was being excluded from key closed meetings, and delegation awareness of the potential costs to US reputation and credibility of pursuing its mandated positions at Rome.[96] This suggests an interest on the part of Scheffer to align his delegation's views with those of the Like-Minded Group as far as possible. Given that the USA was already in principle in favour of a robust regime in this respect, the internal armed conflict provisions provided Scheffer with an opportunity to demonstrate progressive leadership.

Indeed, in contrast to other issue areas, the apparent absence of *internal* controversy over the US position on internal conflicts suggests that the USA was – like Canada and other like-minded states – committed on

[94] In Scheffer's words, this reflected that 'most [delegations] agreed that customary international law has developed to a more limited extent with respect to internal armed conflicts [than with respect to international armed conflicts]' ('The United States and the International Criminal Court', 16). With respect to internal armed conflict the gap between even the most progressive members of the Like-Minded Group and the views of France, the UK and US (if not those of China and Russia) does not seem to have been especially significant at any point: as the contrasting February 1997 PrepCom submissions on the issue show, even at that stage, the three western P5 members were in favour of including some reference to non-international armed conflicts within the scope of the war crimes provisions of the putative statute. Differences between these three delegations' views and those of the Like-Minded Group were, moreover, largely bridged in the December 1997 Bonn Paper, French negotiator Marc de Brichambaut subsequently indicating in a bilateral meeting with David Scheffer shortly before the conference that France would join the US 'in ensuring that internal conflicts (civil wars) also would be covered by the court's jurisdiction' (Scheffer, *All the Missing Souls*, 189). French, US and UK accord over this point was affirmed again in an informal meeting at the start of July 1998 in Rome (Scheffer, 204–5).

[95] Including Ambassador Scheffer's own cri de coeur: *All the Missing Souls*. The US approach at Rome seems, ultimately, to have been most heavily influenced by the Department of Defense. See esp. Scheffer, 196–7.

[96] Washburn, 'The Negotiation of the Rome Statute for the International Criminal Court and International Lawmaking in the 21st Century', 374. Scheffer, *All the Missing Souls*, 193.

principled grounds (again supported by helpfully aligned Rationalist considerations) to including internal armed conflicts within the ambit of the war crimes provisions of the Rome Statute. Scheffer accordingly used this alignment to position the USA as a constructive broker in these negotiations, facilitating the incorporation of threshold language and gender-related crimes into Article 8.[97] US conduct in the negotiation of the internal armed conflict provisions similarly suggests that Sheffer perceived in these discussions an opportunity to remedy some of the damage to the USA's reputation in the eyes of like-minded counterparts caused by its obdurate conduct with respect to other issue areas at Rome.

5.3.2.2 The United Kingdom

The UK differed from the USA in formally joining the Like-Minded Group in December 1997, consistent with the adoption of an explicitly 'ethical' foreign policy by newly installed Foreign Minister Robin Cook (with overtones of Axworthy's 'human security' agenda). This led to an opening up of Whitehall to UK members of the NGO Coalition, and to a reappraisal of UK priorities and positions to the point where on 10 June 1998, Foreign and Commonwealth Office Legal Adviser Frank Berman advised US negotiator David Scheffer that: '[t]he United Kingdom sees the court as a plank of the new international order'.[98]

The adoption by the UK of the rotating EU presidency in January 1998 and subsequent pressure to develop a common EU position at Rome may also have played a part in the UK's decision to align itself more closely with the Like-Minded Group, given that all other EU members, save for France, were broadly aligned with this group.[99] Indeed, as observed by one US commentator: 'the European Union had also hailed an independent court as the hallmark of its post-Bosnia try at a common foreign and security policy'.[100] The UK thus had principled (Regime Type-derived) as

[97] Scheffer, *All the Missing Souls*, 16. Scheffer, 'The United States and the International Criminal Court', 16–17.

[98] Interview with member of UK NGO Coalition. Scheffer, *All the Missing Souls*, 192–4.

[99] Again, the extent to and manner in which a common EU approach was adopted at Rome has been extensively discussed elsewhere. See e.g. Groenleer and Van Schaik, 'United We Stand?'; Scheipers and Sicurelli, 'Normative Power Europe'; Thomas, 'Rejecting the US Challenge to the International Criminal Court: Normative Entrapment and Compromise in EU Policy-Making'.

[100] Wedgwood, 'Fiddling in Rome', 21. It is worth bearing in mind, though, that even this association was not sufficient to prevent the UK – and other like-minded states – from incurring the public wrath of more progressive NGOs during the conference itself. See

well as broader (Rational) regional political reasons for adopting a robust position on the court generally.

The UK position on war crimes in internal armed conflict appears, like that of the USA, to have been settled around the time of the 1997 Bonn Paper, and to have been reconciled with the views of leading like-minded states, with a February 1998 statement of policy indicating that 'many of the worst conflicts take place within rather than between states. We therefore support the inclusion within the Court's jurisdiction of grave crimes committed in the course of such conflicts.'[101] Illustrating alignment with the USA on this point, the subsequent internal delegation report to the Foreign and Commonwealth Office also states that 'on most of the war crimes provisions we were able to work closely with the US, with whom we shared concerns'.[102]

The UK, like the USA, saw itself as having contributed significantly to the delivery of the internal armed conflict provisions, the delegation report noting that the threshold language at Article 8(2)(d) was 'drawn from a UK proposal at the Prepcom'.[103] One striking aspect of the UK's publicly stated position with respect to internal armed conflict is, moreover, the absence of any explicit or recorded mention of Northern Ireland. In line with UK conduct in 1949 and 1974–7, this may have reflected reluctance to concede publicly that the internal armed conflict provisions could be relevant to violence in Northern Ireland. Perhaps more likely, however, is that with the April 1998 conclusion of the Belfast Agreement – during the 'honeymoon period' of the Blair government – the Northern Irish issue receded in significance in British eyes. This late development notwithstanding, though, it also bears noting that UK support for the inclusion of threshold language at paragraphs (d) and (f) of Article 8(2) would be consistent with this enduring British concern: even if British neuralgia about Northern Ireland had significantly receded by 1998, it had perhaps not dissipated altogether.[104]

e.g. Human Rights Watch, 'Human Rights Watch Disappointed by U.K. Stand on International Court'.

101 UK Foreign and Commonwealth Office, 'International Criminal Court: Statement of Government Policy'.

102 Wilmshurst, 'Report on the Conference for the Establishment of an International Criminal Court 15 June–17 July 1998'.

103 Ibid. This is presumably a reference to the joint US, UK, French proposal.

104 See Garraway, 'Written Evidence'. (Professor Garraway was a member of the UK delegation in Rome.)

5.3.2.3 France

The French approach to the Rome negotiations, like that of the USA, was complicated by bureaucratic infighting, with the Ministry of Defence taking a particularly stringent line on war crimes. A traditional domestic emphasis on victims' rights, however, resonated strongly with the prevalent discourse at the PrepCom and Rome, enabling the Ministries of Justice and Foreign Affairs to push for France to take a more positive stance on issues of concern to many 'like-minded' participants at the conference.[105] Indeed, according to Scheffer, it was evident as early as in April 1998 that the French position was shifting towards the like-minded, and while France ultimately joined this group only once it had obtained a temporary 'opt-out' from the court's war crimes jurisdiction, with respect to war crimes in internal armed conflicts the French had already been associated with the 1997 US submission, alongside the UK.[106]

In terms of motivation, there is no indication that France did not share US and UK normative concerns vis à vis internal armed conflict, and the association of France with the February 1997 US submission suggests that French, US and UK views may have been similarly motivated in this respect. Scheffer has commented somewhat acidly, though, that 'France wanted to come out the leader in Rome and be viewed as such, even if (or perhaps because) it meant sacrificing some of America's sacred cows'.[107] Accordingly, even if France was not necessarily committed to like-minded positions on internal armed conflict on principled grounds, its delegates may still have been relatively amenable to persuasion as the broader normative Zeitgeist became apparent. One might also speculate as to the extent to which, with the UK on board, the French government proved susceptible to pressure from Germany and EU partners to align with like-minded preferences.[108]

[105] The efforts of the 'charismatic and sociable' acting delegation head at Rome – Béatrice Le Fraper du Hellen – also seem to have been key to the like-minded governments receiving the French delegation 'more warmly than they would have based on the position it took on several key issues' (Benedetti, Bonneau, and Washburn, *Negotiating the International Criminal Court*, 111).

[106] See Article 124 of the Rome Statute. The French approach to war crimes was roundly criticised by concerned NGOs throughout the conference, though there is no evidence that this affected the French position. See e.g. Human Rights Watch, 'French Stand on International Court 'Mixed', Says Rights Group'.

[107] Scheffer, *All the Missing Souls*, 189, 192, 221.

[108] On the ICC as a 'success' of the EU CSFP, see McGoldrick, 'Political and Legal Responses to the ICC', 393.

5.3.2.4 China and Russia

China and Russia adopted obdurate positions on a number of aspects of the Rome Statute, including on war crimes in internal armed conflict. Russia, in particular, shared concerns with France with respect to the scope of the war crimes provisions generally, but despite receiving similar guarantees and then voting in favour of and signing the Rome Statute, has not ratified the ICC treaty (and has since unsigned it). Its pre-Crimean failure to ratify is due at least in part to concerns about the potential jurisdiction of the court over the conflict in Chechnya.[109]

China, in contrast, voted against the adoption of the Statute in Rome in 1998. While this decision reflected a range of issues (including broader Chinese discomfort with international adjudication), these included particular concerns relating to the court's jurisdiction in internal armed conflict. Consistent with the Rationalist hypothesis (as with Russia), these primarily reflected perceived risks associated with the PRC–Taiwan relationship and the status of any potential cross-strait conflict. Concerns about tensions in Tibet and Xianjing, and in respect of the Falun Gong movement also contributed to this position.[110]

[109] See account in Bedont and Matas, 'Negotiating for an International Criminal Court'. See also McGoldrick, 'Political and Legal Responses to the ICC', 395. The jurisprudence of the European Court of Human Rights suggests that such concerns may not be entirely misplaced. See e.g. discussions in: Abresch, 'A Human Rights Law of Internal Armed Conflict'; Leach, 'The Chechen Conflict'; Barrett, 'Chechnya's Last Hope – Enforced Disappearances and the European Court of Human Rights'. See also Kaye, 'Some Thoughts on Russia and the International Criminal Court'. Russia's 'unsigning' of the Rome Statute in response to the ICC prosecutor's investigation into Russian conduct in the Crimea since 2014 is also consistent with this approach.

[110] See esp. Guan, 'The ICC's Jurisdiction over War Crimes in Internal Armed Conflicts: An Insurmountable Obstacle for China's Accession', 705–6, 726. 'The Taiwan issue is at the core of China's real concerns behind its official reasons against the extension of the concept of war crimes to internal armed conflicts both under the Rome Statute and under existing customary international law ... To a lesser degree for concerns of war crimes, possible recurrences of separatist/terrorist violence in the Tibet and Xinjiang provinces are also within China's real concerns' (726). This article forms part of a growing literature exploring the dynamics of China's relationship with the ICC. See e.g. Zhu, *China and the International Criminal Court*; Linton, 'India and China before, at, and after Rome'; Zhu, 'China, the International Criminal Court, and International Adjudication'; Jia, 'China and the International Criminal Court: The Current Situation', 92; Jianping and Zhixiang, 'China's Attitude towards the ICC'. More generally, as Jutta Brunnée has observed, 'China and Russia agree on the core features of their desired (world) order ... a thin conception, focused on the UN Charter and emphasizing sovereignty-based principles like non-intervention or state immunity. In a sense, the goal is a return to a law of co-existence,

5.3.3 *The Non-Aligned Movement*

The non-aligned movement (NAM) did not form an entirely coherent group at Rome.[111] Prominent members took similar positions to China and Russia with respect to war crimes in internal armed conflicts: some NAM delegations (principally India and Middle Eastern states) were also particularly outspoken in their concerns.[112]

In general terms, NAM members were suspicious of the motives of the Like-Minded Group and the NGO Coalition, but also concerned to erode the dominance of the P5. This latter tendency manifested itself around a concern to ensure the inclusion of nuclear weapons as prohibited weapons in the war crimes aspects of the Statute, and a general effort to minimise the extent of Security Council control over the court.[113] Thus, while – broadly speaking – these states joined the P5 (originally with the exception of the UK) in seeking a court with a closely constrained role, NAM objectives also differed from P5 preferences in some key respects.

Like the P5, the NAM also fissured in the course of negotiations.[114] Many Middle Eastern states were ultimately willing to extend the internal armed conflict provisions beyond Common Article 3, comforted by the threshold language, mollified by the retention of the crime of aggression within the Statute, and satisfied by amendments to the language relating to child conscription and enlistment to exclude the involvement of young children in the Palestinian Intifada.[115] Iranian opposition was also assuaged by the inclusion of a broad war crimes regime relating to

stripped of liberal internationalism and its emphasis on human rights' ('Challenging International Law: What's New?').

111 It is important to note, however, that the cohesiveness of this bloc was in any case relatively weak (see e.g. the SADC's support for a strong court). See: Maqungo, 'The Establishment of the International Criminal Court'.

112 Wilmshurst, 'Report on the Conference for the Establishment of an International Criminal Court 15 June–17 July 1998'.

113 Kirsch and Holmes, 'The Rome Conference on an International Criminal Court: The Negotiating Process', 4; Benedetti, Bonneau, and Washburn, *Negotiating the International Criminal Court*, 104.

114 The absence of a broader shared programme may have facilitated the 'cherry-picking' of NAM members by the like-minded. See: Kirsch and Holmes, 'The Rome Conference on an International Criminal Court: The Negotiating Process', 11. The efforts of Rolf Fife, an Arabic-speaking Norwegian delegate, may have been critical with respect to discussions with members of delegations of Arab states to resolve 'linguistic' difficulties, and to 'educate' delegation members who were less familiar with the subject matter. See Benedetti, Bonneau and Washburn, *Negotiating the International Criminal Court: New York to Rome, 1994–1998*, 104.

115 Benedetti, Bonneau and Washburn, *Negotiating the International Criminal Court*, 148.

international armed conflict and the retention of the crime of aggression.[116] Not all states were appeased, however: India notably took an extremely hard (albeit ineffectual) line on internal armed conflicts, reflecting (as with China) a broader policy reluctance to cede authority to an extra-territorial judicial body and, in particular, concerns relating to Kashmir and the northeast of the country.[117]

5.3.4 *International Civil Society*

In contrast to the 1949 and 1974–7 negotiations – where the ICRC was by far the most prominent civil society organisation in attendance – the Rome Conference was permeated by a multitude of influential NGOs, many of which took a close interest in the internal armed conflict provisions. Arguably the most prominent of these were Amnesty International, Human Rights Watch and the International Federation for Human Rights, with the NGO Women's Caucus and No Peace Without Justice (NPWJ) also playing important roles.[118] These groups typically sought the most robust regime possible on

[116] Iranian concerns appear to have been motivated in large part by the experience of the Iran-Iraq War. See: Abtahi, 'The Islamic Republic of Iran and the ICC'. It bears noting that Iran held the presidencies of both the Organisation of the Islamic Conference and the Asian grouping at the UN at the time of the Rome Conference, as well as being the coordinator of the NAM.

[117] Ramanathan, 'India and the ICC', 627–8; Linton, 'India and China before, at, and after Rome', 273–4 citing; Lahiri, 'Should India Continue to Stay out of ICC?' In respect of broader Indian hesitance, Linton observes that: '[t]his aversion to international approaches in criminal justice has echoes of the dissenting opinion of Indian Judge Radhabinod Pal at the International Military Tribunal in Tokyo' ('India and China before, at, and after Rome', 267).

[118] The extent to and manner in which civil society was involved in the drafting of the Rome Statute has been examined at length in numerous studies with many authors taking the view that the Rome Statute was in many ways a victory for civil society, demonstrating 'the efficacy of soft power and the "New Diplomacy"' (Behringer, *The Human Security Agenda*, 96). See also discussion in: Benedetti, Bonneau, and Washburn, *Negotiating the International Criminal Court*, 8–86. According to one account, 236 NGOs were accredited at the Rome Conference, involving the attendance of around 450 individuals (Pace and Thieroff, 'Participation of Non-Governmental Organizations', 392. Close to 500 NGOs were represented at Rome, according to another account (Pace and Schense, 'The Coalition for the International Criminal Court at the Preparatory Commission', 707, at note 6, cited in Hill, 'A Case of NGO Participation: International Criminal Court Negotiations', 147). On the presence of NGOs generally, see e.g. Deitelhoff, 'The Discursive Process of Legalization'; Kirsch and Holmes, 'The Rome Conference on an International Criminal Court: The Negotiating Process'; Pace and Thieroff, 'Participation of Non-Governmental Organizations'.

normative grounds.[119] The influence of civil society was limited in important respects, though: ultimately (as with the ICRC in 1949 and at the CDDH) NGOs were only capable of affecting negotiation outcomes insofar as they were able to influence delegation preferences, and indeed, the final product fell short of the preferences of many in civil society.[120]

NGOs used various methods to influence delegations.[121] The technical, legal analysis of Amnesty International and the associated work of Christopher Keith Hall, for example – which included arguments in favour of including war crimes jurisdiction in internal armed conflict as early as 1994 – was evidently extremely well-reasoned, considered by the UK delegation as 'magnificent stuff' that was extremely difficult to rebut.[122] Human Rights Watch (HRW), for their part, issued a series of critical public calls to action on the part of states before and during the Rome Conference, often with principled commentary by Richard Dicker, including with respect to war crimes in internal armed conflict.[123] HRW also played an important role in fostering Southern African Development Community (SADC) support for the Like-Minded Group's vision of a strong court.[124]

With respect to France, the International Federation for Human Rights (FIDH) was key to the formation and development of the domestically influential French branch of the ICC Coalition. The Women's Caucus,

119 Kirsch and Holmes, 'The Rome Conference on an International Criminal Court: The Negotiating Process', 4–5.

120 See e.g. Bedont and Matas, 'Negotiating for an International Criminal Court'.

121 For an overview of such interaction, see esp. Pearson, 'Non-Governmental Organizations and the International Criminal Court: Changing Landscapes of International Law'.

122 UK Rome Conference delegation member, Interview (author papers). See also Struett, *The Politics of Constructing the International Criminal Court*, 91. An earlier article by Hall also describes, interestingly, the early role of the ICRC in advocating for the establishment of an international criminal court (Hall, 'The First Proposal for a Permanent International Criminal Court').

123 See reference in Struett, *The Politics of Constructing the International Criminal Court*, 91. Also: See e.g. Human Rights Watch, 'French Stand on International Court 'Mixed', Says Rights Group'; Human Rights Watch, 'HRW Disappointed at India's Position on International Court'; Human Rights Watch, 'Human Rights Watch Condemns United States' Threat to Sabotage International Criminal Court'; Human Rights Watch, 'Human Rights Watch Disappointed by U.K. Stand on International Court'; Human Rights Watch, 'Human Rights Watch Praises German Stand on International Court'; Human Rights Watch, 'Human Rights Watch Welcomes New Japanese Position on International Court'.

124 Benedetti, Bonneau and Washburn, *Negotiating the International Criminal Court*, 69.

too – albeit primarily a single-issue grouping focused on gender violence – played an important role in ensuring the participation of NGOs from developing countries, as well as in fostering support for the inclusion of gender violence in the Statute (including in Article 8).[125]

NGOs were also able to influence the negotiations through direct participation as delegation members. NPWJ, an Italian NGO, ran a Judicial Assistance Project that embedded volunteers with technical expertise within less well-equipped delegations, primarily from the developing world. This and similar efforts enabled civil society and associated academic experts (and activists) to participate directly in the Rome negotiations to an unprecedented degree.[126] Some like-minded delegations also already featured significant academic and civil society representation, notably Canada and the Netherlands.[127]

An additional effect of the permeation of proceedings by civil society was to render open to NGOs inter-delegation meetings that would formerly have been (at best) only indirectly accessible to such organisations. Delegations were thus negotiating in an unusually open forum, and NGOs were consequently able to rebut and criticise governments far more directly, and to greater effect, than in more traditional settings.[128] Indeed, the Women's Caucus's success in relation to the incorporation of

[125] Benedetti, Bonneau and Washburn, 69–70.

[126] See Benedetti, Bonneau and Washburn, 80–81. A review of the list of delegation members suggests – though authoritative lists are not available of such experts – that civil society and academic experts attended at Rome as members, variously, of the delegations of Australia (Tim McCormack and Gerry Simpson), Bosnia and Herzegovina (Elizabeth Baumgartner and Eve La Haye), Canada (Valerie Oosterveld, Darryl Robinson and David Matas), the Comoros (Monica Feria Tinta and Thomas Graditsky), Congo-Brazzaville (Gabrielle Dellamorte and Ascanio Pensi), Egypt (where M. Cherif Bassiouni was head of delegation), Germany (e.g. Kai Ambos), Guinea-Bissau (Fabio Buonomo and Christophe Lobry), the Netherlands (e.g. Theo van Boven), Samoa (Roger Clark), Sierra Leone (Cynthia Fairweather (particularly associated with the Tadić-derived Sierra Leone proposal on internal armed conflict (UK Rome Conference delegation member, Interview (author papers))), Giorgia Tortora, and Andrea Carlevaris), the Solomon Islands (Andrew Clapham, Harold Fruchtbaum, and Philippe Sands), and Trinidad and Tobago (Stephanie Godart).

[127] See also tables showing individuals wearing multiple 'hats' at Rome at: Glasius, 'Expertise in the Cause of Justice: Global Civil Society Influence on the Statute for an International Criminal Court', 144–5. Also discussion in Benedetti, Bonneau, and Washburn, *Negotiating the International Criminal Court*, 71–72.

[128] UK Rome Conference delegation member, Interview (author papers); Women's Caucus (UK branch) member, Interview (author papers).

sexual violence as a war crime was due in part to close relationships with the Bosnian and Australian delegations.[129]

The NGO Coalition also contributed to the 'open' atmosphere of proceedings, providing a running commentary through three news services on the progress of the negotiations. Reports from these services not only heightened transparency generally, they also featured interviews with delegation members. This facilitated the (in effect) public leaking of statements and positions that might otherwise have remained behind closed doors, as well as binding delegations into particular positions by publicising delegation member comments, including with respect to war crimes in internal armed conflict.[130]

The motivations of civil society participants in the negotiations can generally – though not in all instances – be said to have been based on normative commitments to a robust court with an expansive jurisdiction. Moreover, these organisations variously brought moral authority (the Women's Caucus), technical expertise (NPWJ) or combinations of both (Amnesty International, Human Rights Watch) to bear on proceedings.

It is difficult to provide conclusive evidence of the extent to which civil society activities specifically impacted the internal armed conflict provisions. It is reasonable, for example, to surmise that the Sierra Leone proposal came about owing to the delegation's embedded international legal advisers. It is more difficult, however, to demonstrate that the adoption of this proposal was caused in a meaningful way by civil society effort. That said, the multiple avenues of civil society ingress into the negotiations suggest that NGOs generally influenced outcomes through a combination of perceived moral authority (in the eyes of many, if not all, delegations), additive technical expertise and ensuring that key negotiations were conducted (in effect) in the open rather than behind closed doors. As observed above, NGOs also contributed to debates on the internal armed conflict provisions. As such, it is reasonable to view civil society as having played a not insignificant role in shaping the internal armed conflict provisions.

That said, questions remain as to the extent to which NGOs at Rome 'preached to the choir': by all accounts, NGOs developed very strong relationships with leading like-minded delegations and associated P5

[129] Glasius, 'Expertise in the Cause of Justice: Global Civil Society Influence on the Statute for an International Criminal Court', 156.

[130] See e.g. IPS Inter-Press Service, 'Clamour Rises for Court to Step into Internal Conflicts'. Also more broadly discussion in Benedetti, Bonneau, and Washburn, *Negotiating the International Criminal Court*, 78.

members. Many of these governments, however – including both developing and developed states – had expressly invited NGO engagement, so were to a degree already amenable to civil society pressure. There is very little evidence to indicate, on the other hand, that any NGOs – save possibly the ICRC – had any significant degree of influence over the less amenable amongst the national delegations. Notwithstanding the close participation of civil society in endeavours at Rome, therefore, some caution may be warranted in describing the Rome Statute as necessarily 'civil society's victory'.[131]

5.4 Hypotheses

5.4.1 Great Power Politics

> The history of the negotiation of the Rome Statute reveals that, like the jurisprudence of the ad hoc tribunals and the text of the Geneva Conventions, the war crimes provisions of the Rome Statute largely codify positions advocated by the permanent members of the Security Council – particularly the United States.[132]

> 'The preferences of great powers are likely to be especially significant in shaping the civil war regime.' (The Realist hypothesis)

The Rome Statute is often considered a poster child for constructivist analysis of international relations and the influence of non-governmental organisations in international affairs. As the preceding account shows, however, great power preferences played an important role in shaping the internal armed conflict provisions.

In particular, the USA, the UK and France – the Western P3 – exerted significant influence on the final form of the internal armed conflict provisions. This influence can be traced through drafting initiatives dating from the February 1997 PrepCom meeting, where representatives of these states demonstrated commitment to a robust but tempered set of internal armed conflict provisions, which was what was finally delivered at Rome – despite the more progressive preferences of some like-minded delegations and NGOs.

[131] 'Transcript, "The New Court: Civil Society's Victory"'. On ICRC views on and involvement in negotiating the Rome Statute, see Roberge, 'The New International Criminal Court: A Preliminary Assessment'.

[132] Danner, 'When Courts Make Law', 37.

The recognition by the leadership of the Like-Minded Group and the NGO Coalition that it would be difficult to establish a credible court without the support of at least some P5 members is testament more generally to the significance of the great powers in the negotiation process, with the Like-Minded Group and supporting NGOs putting significant effort put into 'splitting' the P5 to engender 'enough leeway ... to move forward'.[133] P5 positions, including the preferences of Western P3 governments, thus set part of the scene for the Rome negotiations, with post-Cold War 'in-principle' support for some sort of permanent court from the (at the time) progressive governments of France, the UK and the US, as well as previous cross-P5 support for the Yugoslav and Rwandan tribunals, a key factor enabling the group of middle powers led by Canada to pursue the ICC initiative.[134]

It also appears to have been apparent to delegations generally that the participation of the most powerful states in the system was desirable in order for a meaningful institution to emerge and operate. As one participant observed, a court whose membership comprised only states without meaningful armed forces or states with armed forces with only an extremely remote risk of being challenged by the ICC in practice would be extremely unlikely to be relevant.[135] Philippe Kirsch has similarly emphasised that '[the] best Court in the world on paper would be stillborn if it was unable to receive the political support and resources it needed to be viable'.[136]

In terms of individual delegation preferences, US and UK delegation preferences were particularly influential in determining the drafting eventually adopted. In general terms, the Bonn Paper reflected a significant watering down of maximalist like-minded positions to accommodate US, UK and French preferences. Close attention was also evidently paid by drafters to US and UK views during the negotiations over the internal armed conflict provisions.[137]

133 Benedetti, Bonneau, and Washburn, *Negotiating the International Criminal Court*, 66.

134 Tenove, 'Canada and the ICC. Part One'. On the significance of the 'progressive' alignment of the French, UK and US governments, see Gilbert Bitti (interview with David Bosco), quoted in: Bosco, *Rough Justice*, 44. (As put by a French delegate, with the P5 united against a court: 'the ICC was doomed ... you would have had all the P5 skeptical and that would have been the end of the story'.)

135 UK Rome Conference delegation member, Interview (author papers).

136 Kirsch, 'The Development of the Rome Statute', 453.

137 The French delegation appears to have been less active with respect to these particular provisions, but, interestingly, the record also suggests that Russian and Chinese views

It is, of course, entirely possible that the USA and the UK were aided in this by being able to field well-equipped delegations: certainly, complaints were made at the time that negotiations were dominated by materially more powerful states.[138] Canada and Germany, however (by way of example), were at least as well equipped as the UK, while there is no doubt that the Like-Minded Group were similarly – collectively and individually – able to wield extremely impressive subject area expertise. The US delegation, moreover, was famously hamstrung by internal rifts amongst its component agencies – though these were less in evidence with respect to the internal armed conflict provisions. It would thus be difficult to attribute the relatively strong influence of the US and UK delegations solely to their ability to marshal superior resources in negotiations.

Observers and participants have also commented on the manner in which P5 members' room for manoeuvre was limited by their collective commitment to the Yugoslav and Rwandan tribunals, which may partially explain the readiness of the P5 collectively to support (or at least not oppose) Sierra Leone's *Tadić*-inspired threshold proposals. In terms of broader context, P5 members were also doubtless cognisant of the prevailing political and economically liberal international normative backdrop, signified by clamour about the 'End of History' and the rise to prominence of human rights in international political discourse, to which the ending of the Cold War and the establishment of the ad hoc tribunals had contributed.[139] As one commentator has put it: 'The 1990s were a golden era for initiatives promoting human security and for the mobilization of soft power.'[140] To be certain of being on the 'winning side' therefore, consistent with this Zeitgeist, especially once the UK had come on board with the like-minded, the French delegation may have had little choice but to cast its lot in similar fashion.

with respect to war crimes in internal armed conflict were not accorded the same import by the Bureau as US and UK (and French) views, even where shared. (See e.g. re Russian and Chinese views on Bureau proposals: IPS Inter-Press Service, 'Take It or Leave It'.) The discounting of Russian and Chinese concerns by like-minded states may, of course, simply have reflected an appreciation that China and Russia were unlikely to support robust internal armed conflict provisions in any event, and a willingness to proceed regardless having secured US support for the proposed drafting. (See Krauthammer, 'The Unipolar Moment'.)

138 See e.g. IPS Inter-Press Service, 'Yes, Size Does Matter'.

139 Fukuyama, 'The End of History?'

140 Tenove, 'Canada and the ICC. Part One'.

At the same time, the democratic, Western P3 (if not their Chinese and Russian counterparts) were also susceptible to persuasion from NGOs and like-minded governments, with the UK's conversion to the like-minded cause after the 1997 general election perhaps the foremost example of this phenomenon. It is entirely conceivable that such persuasion fed into the formation of the preferences of these governments with respect to internal armed conflict, though this alone does not diminish the importance placed by supporters of a robust internal armed conflict regime on avoiding collective P5 objections to proposals and obtaining support from these delegations where possible.

Yet again though, even though the conduct and preferences of other delegations may have been closely informed by great power preferences, these preferences alone are insufficient to explain the eventual design of the internal armed conflict provisions in the round. As such, we must also look to other factors for further insight into the provisions' final shape.

5.4.2 Rationalist Considerations

> 'The more intrusive or restrictive any proposed set of civil war-regulating treaty provisions, the less likely they are to be supported by governments in the course of treaty negotiations, especially where governments are engaged in or foresee a possibility of a civil war or insurgency. The end of a civil war or insurgency may, however, make a government more likely to support such provisions.' (The Rationalist hypothesis)

As in previous cases, it is relatively straightforward to cast the internal armed conflict provisions of the Rome Statute as the result of rationalist considerations: many of the foremost supporters of a strong internal armed conflict regime were states at low risk of encountering internal armed conflict within their borders, or that were in transition following recent such conflicts. Equally, delegations of states where governments had concerns about domestic unease were amongst the foremost opponents of a robust regime.

The leading like-minded delegations, for example included such stable democracies as Canada, New Zealand, Australia, Switzerland and a range of Western European countries, as well as domestically more stable Latin American states such as Brazil and Argentina. Indeed, in some of the discussions at the PrepCom, delegations that were most supportive of a robust internal armed conflict regime also lacked military representation – suggesting the relative priority accorded to related issues by the governments of these states.[141] This group was also joined by countries in transition from civil conflicts or domestic strife to democracy, including Bosnia and Herzegovina, Croatia, Sierra Leone, Slovenia and South Africa, consistent with the second element of this hypothesis. In contrast, the most vocal opponents – non-aligned delegations including India, Middle Eastern states and Russia and China – were delegations of states where governments were combating or at risk of encountering internal unrest.

This simple cleavage, however, is again insufficient as an explanation of the shape of the final provisions, not least as P5 members and leading like-minded states – particularly NATO members such as Canada and the Netherlands – still faced a higher likelihood of intervening militarily in domestic strife in third countries. The French military, for instance, were concerned by potential liability stemming from French command of UN forces in Bosnia and Herzegovina at the time of the Srebrenica massacre, while the Northern Irish spectre continued to hang over the UK in the run-up to 1998.[142] In the case of the USA, concerns about potential ICC jurisdiction over US military service members abroad led to the adoption of controversial legislation in 2002.[143] Moreover and more generally, as one commentator has noted: '[w]hen States realise they are setting a standard by which they themselves, or their leaders and military personnel, may be judged, they seem to take greater care and insist upon many safeguards'.[144] In short, many of the states that were generally supportive of a strong court also had good reason to ensure that the provisions regulating internal armed conflict were relatively closely circumscribed, at least to a greater degree than was the case for the ad hoc tribunals.

While not definitive, this last suggests that despite their willingness to support the establishment of ad hoc tribunals for conflicts which were relatively remote, delegations, whether generally more or less supportive of some form of permanent court in principle, hesitated slightly more before agreeing provisions where there was a prospect of these being brought to bear on their own officials. This was particularly true with respect to internal armed conflicts where risks of third party intervention were high.[145] That

141 UK Rome Conference delegation member, Interview (author papers).

142 Bosco, *Rough Justice*, 41.

143 US concerns about the then-putative court's jurisdiction even led to adoption of the so-called 'Hague Invasion Law' in 2002 (properly entitled the 'American Service-Members' Protection Act').

144 Schabas, *An Introduction to the International Criminal Court*, 84.

145 As Mantilla observes, the drafting of the threshold language at Article 8(2)(f) can 'be read (without it being express) as a political balance between the humanitarian supporters of the idea and its detractors, detractors that were aware that total deletion was unlikely

being the case, while rationalist considerations may well have informed some of the basic divisions between groups of delegations, these alone do not appear sufficient to explain why the broad majority of governments represented were able to agree a set of relatively demanding provisions. Once again, we must look further afield to explain the language eventually adopted.

5.4.3 Agent Characteristics

> 'The greater their perceived moral authority and their ability to leverage subject area expertise, the more likely governments and non-state actors are to be able to elicit the support of other governments for demanding civil war-regulating provisions in the course of treaty negotiations.' (The Agent Characteristics hypothesis)

A number of analyses have underlined the importance of moral authority and technical expertise, principally on the part of the NGO Coalition and the Like-Minded Group, in the drafting of the Rome Statute.[146] With respect to Canada, for example, the drafting of the Rome Statute is often cited as a success for 'soft power', drawing heavily on Canada's widespread reputation as a 'good international citizen and the desire to be recognized as such'.[147] Similarly, for members of the EU, 'like-mindedness' appears to have been an opportunity to demonstrate the capacity of the EU to advance an autonomous, shared, progressive foreign policy vision.[148] The adoption of senior roles at the later ICC by many of the key participants in the delegations of like-minded states – most notably Canada, the Netherlands and Germany – is also testament to the technical expertise of these delegations.

anyway' ('Under (Social) Pressure: The Historical Regulation of Internal Armed Conflicts through International Law', 322).

146 See e.g. passing references to UN Secretariat and NGO skill and expertise in Washburn, 'The Negotiation of the Rome Statute for the International Criminal Court and International Lawmaking in the 21st Century', 365, 367.

147 Wylie, 'Valuing Reputation and Prestige: Canadian Foreign Policy and the International Criminal Court', 113. Clarkson and Mildenberger, *Dependent America?*, 207. See also: Bernard, 'Canada and the International Criminal Court'.

148 Indeed, more generally the Like-Minded Group members appear to have conceived of their middle-power status as enabling them 'to construct international architecture that would be perceived as fair and legitimate by the rest of the world. (Moreover . . .) [t]he usually unstated corollary of this thesis was clear: powerful states with complex interests had limited ability to advance impartial international justice' (Bosco, *Rough Justice*, 39).

The NGO Coalition similarly advanced a human rights-oriented, progressive agenda by means of normative persuasion – in line with (and sometimes running ahead of) like-minded governments – while simultaneously bringing technical expertise to bear on the negotiations. Indeed, NGO papers were cited in conference debates, while one of the earlier analyses of the impact of NGOs at Rome is titled 'Expertise in the Cause of Justice'.[149]

The expertise and widely perceived moral authority of key like-minded delegations and supporting NGOs operated in a number of fashions to contribute to the development of robust language with regard to the internal armed conflict provisions of the Rome Statute. Arguments for including internal armed conflicts in the ambit of the war crimes provisions of the draft statute, for example, relied largely on authoritative positions about the customary international law status of such inclusion. While the quality of arguments put forward is considered further below, NGOs and like-minded state delegations (using both 'home' and 'contracted-in' resources through the NPWJ programme) were also able to translate the presence of professional expertise into more or less authoritative statements of the (in their view) 'correct' legal position at Rome, utilising such expertise to develop creative solutions to drafting impasses. In contrast, delegations relatively lacking in expertise in the new field of international criminal law (including many of the delegations opposed to a robust regime) struggled to articulate their position in convincing technical terms. While it may have been difficult to identify subject specialists willing and able to put forward the views advanced by these delegations, the relative absence of such expertise nevertheless put these delegations at a disadvantage from the outset at Rome.

Moral authority was also in evidence in the debates, including with respect to the internal armed conflict provisions. 'Good' international citizens such as Canada, Germany, New Zealand and the Netherlands were in the forefront of the drafting process, working in combination with progressive NGOs to advance a human rights-reflective agenda for war crimes jurisdiction in internal armed conflicts with minimal 'political' concessions to the great powers (including the Western P3).[150] The historical experiences with internal armed conflict of states such as Sierra Leone, Croatia and Bosnia and Herzegovina also appears to have functioned as

[149] Glasius, 'Expertise in the Cause of Justice: Global Civil Society Influence on the Statute for an International Criminal Court'. See also Perna, *The Formation of the Treaty Law of Non-International Armed Conflicts*, 154.

[150] See consideration of the Realist hypothesis, above.

a form of 'moral capital', lending the views of these states additional weight and making it more difficult for dissenters to argue convincingly the merits of a more minimal set of internal armed conflict provisions.

It nevertheless remains difficult to explain drafting outcomes with respect to internal armed conflict on the basis of the apparent preponderance of technical and perceived moral authority on the 'like-minded' side in debates, even taking into account great power preferences and rationalist considerations. In particular, even if some delegations possessed greater levels of more broadly perceived moral authority and technical expertise than others, this still does not explain why some previously unconvinced delegations were susceptible to persuasion by the former. The extent to which these delegations succeeded in nesting their arguments in 'widely-shared values and principles' may go some way towards shedding light on this tendency.

5.4.4 Arguing on the Record

> 'Governments will be more likely to support the adoption of civil war-regulating provisions in treaty negotiations when strong, coherent arguments premised on widely shared values and principles are made in support.' (The Logic of Argument hypothesis)

As has been argued elsewhere, the Rome Conference is a strong candidate for the relevance of this hypothesis to international affairs.[151] There are strong grounds, moreover, for viewing this hypothesis as particularly germane to the war crimes provisions regarding internal armed conflict.

Two broad strands of normative and technical argument can be identified as having been advanced by delegations and NGOs in favour of a robust set of internal armed conflict provisions: (a) that it was 'precisely in internal armed conflicts that national criminal justice systems were in all likelihood unable to adequately respond', and (b) that it was appropriate to adopt a robust set of internal armed conflict provisions as this would be consistent with relevant recent legal 'facts', including the drafting of the ICTR statute and the subsequent *Tadić* decision.[152]

[151] See in particular Deitelhoff, 'The Discursive Process of Legalization: Charting Islands of Persuasion in the ICC Case'.

[152] von Hebel and Robinson, 'Crimes within the Jurisdiction of the Court', 104–5. Re. the impact of arguments made by NGOs, see e.g. Struett, *The Politics of Constructing the International Criminal Court: NGOs, Discourse, and Agency.*

Views of this type were expressed by the ICRC, Human Rights Watch and Amnesty International, with the legal analyses of the latter apparently considered particularly impressive. Similar arguments and supportive analyses were also provided by like-minded delegations with strong legal presences, primarily Canada, the Netherlands and Germany. Equally importantly, opponents of a robust regime struggled to marshal persuasive countervailing arguments: despite drawing on such established principles as sovereignty, the positions put forward by states such as Russia, China, Iran and India were limited in impact and the delegations marginalised from the mainstream at the Rome Conference.

Interestingly, one of the more striking aspects of the arguments put forward by the latter delegations is the absence of reference to then recent developments in the fields of human rights and humanitarian law, including the jurisprudence of the ad hoc tribunals. This observation underlines that what mattered at Rome was not simply the logical strength of arguments – the arguments put forward by India, for example, were certainly coherent – but also the extent to which such arguments were embedded within broadly accepted normative settings.[153] It is relatively straightforward to imagine, for instance, appeals to the principle of sovereignty as being more persuasive in a different normative setting. Equally, the principled, legal, humanitarian arguments that prevailed with respect to internal armed conflicts might have been far less cogent were the international setting not predisposed by the end of the Cold War and the prevailing liberal discourse at the time towards the acceptance of arguments predicated on 'human security'.

Thus, while it may be the case that 'alliance between the [NGO Coalition] and the [Like-Minded Group] demonstrated the efficacy of soft power and the "New Diplomacy"', this efficacy itself turns largely on the conduciveness of the broader international setting to the exercise of soft power and the humanitarian norms propagated by like-minded governments and NGOs at Rome.[154] As noted by one commentator: '[b]ecause an ICC seemed to be a natural extension of the ad hoc tribunals . . . skeptical major powers were reluctant to openly oppose the initiative'.[155]

[153] This point is also made generally in Fehl, 'Explaining the International Criminal Court: A "Practice Test" for Rationalist and Constructivist Approaches', 381–2.

[154] Behringer, *The Human Security Agenda: How Middle Power Leadership Defied U.S. Hegemony*, 96.

[155] Bosco, *Rough Justice*, 40.

Indeed, the international normative context may provide the strongest explanation for why the *Tadić* jurisprudence and precedents from the 1977 Additional Protocols emerged as focal points around which broadly acceptable drafting emerged.[156] Moreover, reflecting the rationalist considerations set out above, Cassese's 'creative' approach to war crimes in internal armed conflict in *Tadić* also evidently encouraged governments to delineate the norms relevant in such conflicts more clearly in the Rome Statute than in the statutes of the ICTR or ICTY, leaving less scope for such judicial creativity in the new world of the ICC.[157]

In sum, while great power preferences, rationalist considerations, and moral and expert authority (on the part of both states and civil society) may all have contributed to shaping the internal armed conflict provisions of the Rome Statute, the broader normative context was also a significant factor in determining the shape of these provisions. More specifically, the discussion suggests that the logical coherency of positions was less of a significant factor with respect to drafting outcomes than the extent to which the arguments advanced were consistent with the prevailing normative 'winds'.[158]

5.4.5 *What about Democracy?*

> 'Democracies are more likely to support intrusive, restrictive civil war-regulating provisions than non-democracies.' (The Regime Type hypothesis)

[156] As Danner has put it: 'The United States, France, Japan and the United Kingdom, among others, supported the inclusion of civil wars in the Statute. China, India, Indonesia, Pakistan, Russia and Turkey all opposed the application of war crimes to civil wars. The controversy over the civil war provisions replicated the debate in the earlier Diplomatic Conferences over how to distinguish international conflicts from civil wars. The delegates found their solution in the Tribunal's jurisprudence, particularly the *Tadić* decision' (Danner, 'When Courts Make Law: How the International Criminal Tribunals Recast the Laws of War', 35).

[157] Schabas, *The International Criminal Court: A Commentary on the Rome Statute*, 2010, 116.

[158] Mantilla notes, for example, that governments' evolving perspectives on the ICC were generally 'embedded in broader, interrelated global transformations, among others: 1. the 'third wave' of democratization and the attendant decline of authoritarianism; 2. the demise of formal empire; 3. the end of the Cold War and the ebb of 'proxy warfare'; 4. the endurance of political, economic and security communities in Europe and elsewhere; 5. the rise of human rights in world politics, helped in no small measure by the striking proliferation and interlocking of domestic and international advocacy groups' ('Under (Social) Pressure: The Historical Regulation of Internal Armed Conflicts through International Law', 318–19).

The case study suggests a possible correlation between regime type and views on the internal armed conflict provisions of the Rome Statute, principally as the major proponents of a robust regime were, almost without exception, established liberal democracies (Canada and Western European governments), supported by countries undergoing transitions to democracy. Equally, the more prominent opponents of a robust regime were the less democratic members of the P5 and the NAM, although India, as an established democracy which also opposed a robust regime, again constitutes a potentially significant outlier.

It is tempting to suggest that this support on the part of democracies may be due to a greater sensitivity on the part of the governments of some (Western) democratic states to internal and external pressure from domestic and international civil society actors – bearing in mind that the civil society organisations present at Rome were themselves predominantly based in established liberal democracies. Western governments may also have been particularly susceptible to persuasion by delegations of other democratic governments with shared values – see for example the apparent sensitivity of the UK delegation to civil society views, and German and Dutch normative leadership of an EU-minus-France-and-UK 'mini-bloc'. Another domestic political factor which may also have featured in the shared, more robust preferences of the governments of France, the UK and the USA was the presence of progressive/socialist-inclined governments in each of these states.

Two additional mechanisms may also have operated for such states, however: first, the governments of some states may well have had preferences for a robust internal armed conflict regime motivated by a preference to mitigate future violence either in their own states or (more likely) elsewhere. Second, some of the smaller countries in transition, owing to relatively weaker domestic expertise and resources, may have been more reliant than the established democracies on international civil society organisations for policy formation and presentation. This last alone may go some way towards explaining the strong, expert views of some smaller states with respect to internal armed conflict.

India, however, remains a challenging case. A prominent democracy, India was generally hostile to the ICC project, as was the case with Additional Protocol II and was particularly ill-disposed to the inclusion of internal armed conflict provisions in the Rome Statute. Its position seems to have been motivated strongly by concerns about the conflict in Kashmir, which suggests that democratic characteristics may be 'trumped' by such practical issues. At the same time, though, India was not alone as a democracy facing potentially violent internal unrest – the UK being a case in point, at least until April 1998.[159] It is perhaps more likely, therefore, that Indian opposition to robust internal armed conflict provisions, and indeed to the ICC project generally, was grounded more fundamentally in India's traditional distrust of international institutions and emphasis on protecting sovereignty in its foreign relations – consistent with the Indian approach in 1949 and 1977. As such, the significance of any apparent correlation between support for robust internal armed conflict provisions and democracy should again perhaps not be overstated.[160]

5.5 Aftermath

Reflecting the standing nature of the ICC and the centrality to its jurisdiction of the war crimes provisions, the application and interpretation of Articles 8(2)(c) to (f) of the Rome Statute has formed an important locus of the court's case work.[161] Despite the efforts expended at Rome, moreover, and a significant body of subsequent academic work on this issue, the court appears to have taken the view that there is little substantive difference between the thresholds at paragraphs (d) and (f) for 'Common Article 3' and 'other' war crimes in internal armed conflict, largely due to the higher threshold at (f) effectively being applied in respect of both paragraphs (c) and (e), rendering paragraph (d) redundant.[162]

159 The Good Friday Agreement was signed on 10 April 1998.

160 Mantilla similarly observes that the opponents of including provision in the Rome Statute for war crimes in internal armed conflict included '[f]ormal but "conflicted" democracies such as India, Sri Lanka or Turkey' ('Under (Social) Pressure: The Historical Regulation of Internal Armed Conflicts through International Law', 319).

161 See commentary at Zimmerman and Geiß, 'Article 8 War Crimes Para. 2 (c) to (f) and Para. 3: War Crimes Committed in an Armed Conflict Not of an International Character', 528–79.

162 As Noëlle Quénivet observes: 'recent case-law reverts to the idea that there are two thresholds, clarifying that because of the way "protracted" is defined this criterion is almost always fulfilled when the requirements for (c) are met . . .' ('Article 8(2)(f)'). See esp. Prosecutor v Jean-Pierre Bemba Gombo, *Judgment Pursuant to Article 74 of the Statute (Public with Annexes I, II, and A to F)*, ICC-01/05-01/08 (21 March 2016, available at: https://icc-cpi.int/courtrecords/cr2016_02238.pdf [accessed 26 December 2018]), paras. 127–8, 137–40. ('The Chamber notes that the concept of "protracted conflict" has not been explicitly defined in the jurisprudence of this Court, but has generally been addressed within the framework of assessing the intensity of the conflict.' Para. 139). See also Prosecutor v Jean-Pierre Bemba Gombo, *Decision Pursuant to Article 61(7)(a) and (b) of the Rome Statute on the Charges of the Prosecutor against Jean-Pierre Bemba Gombo*, ICC-01/05-01/08 (15 June 2009, available at:

The application of this higher threshold may be seen as a post facto victory for the more conservative faction at Rome, though the reasoning underlying the court's preference for paragraph (f) over paragraph (d) suggests that in the court's estimation very little in practice rides on this distinction.[163] In contrast, the drafters' post-*Tadić* effort to restrict the scope for judicial creativity appears to have been rather more successful, with broader recognition that: 'not all violations contained in [Additional Protocol II . . .] have been included in subparagraph (e) and whilst the list is exhaustive for ICC jurisdiction purposes it does not provide an exhaustive list of war crimes in non-international armed conflict'.[164]As a growing literature attests, however, international tribunals are established for objectives beyond doctrinal development and the settlement of case law.[165] In the case of the ICC, a number of such objectives have been identified, Yuval Shany's recent study (for example) identifying ten such goals, organised in a taxonomy of four 'ultimate ends' of 'supporting ICL [international criminal law] '; 'dispute resolution and problem solving'; supporting the ICL regime'; and 'legitimizing the application of ICL'.[166] In related fashion, Cryer et al. (drawing on the work of the ICTY) refer to international criminal law generally as principally serving retributive and deterrent ends.[167]

https://icc-cpi.int/CourtRecords/CR2009_04528.PDF [accessed 26 December 2018]), para. 235; Prosecutor v Germain Katanga, *Judgment Pursuant to Article 74 of the Statute*, ICC-01/04-01/07 (7 March 2014, available at: https://icc-cpi.int/CourtRecords/CR2015_04025.PDF [accessed 26 December 2018]), paras. 1183–87, 1231. Quénivet describes paragraph (f) as 'undoubtedly the most discussed Article in academic literature'. See also commentary at Quénivet, 'Article 8(2)(c)'; Quénivet, 'Article 8(2)(e)'; Quénivet, 'Article 8(2)(f)'; Zimmerman and Geiß, 'Article 8 War Crimes Para. 2 (c) to (f) and Para. 3: War Crimes Committed in an Armed Conflict Not of an International Character', 555–76; Schabas, *The International Criminal Court: A Commentary on the Rome Statute* (2nd edn.), 228–35).

163 Quénivet, 'Article 8(2)(f)'.

164 Quénivet, 'Article 8(2)(e)'. See similar acknowledgement in Zimmerman and Geiß, 'Article 8 War Crimes Para. 2 (c) to (f) and Para. 3: War Crimes Committed in an Armed Conflict Not of an International Character', 529–30.

165 See e.g. Alter, *The New Terrain of International Law: Courts, Politics, Rights*; Alvarez, 'What Are International Judges For? The Main Functions of International Adjudication'; Shany, 'Assessing the Effectiveness of International Courts: A Goal-Based Approach'.

166 See Horovitz, Shany, and Noam, 'The International Criminal Court', 227–37; and generally Shany, *Assessing the Effectiveness of International Courts*; Shany, 'Assessing the Effectiveness of International Courts: A Goal-Based Approach'.

167 Other aims they identify include: incapacitation, rehabilitation, denunciation/education, vindicating victims' rights, recording history, and post-conflict reconciliation. See Cryer et al., *An Introduction to International Criminal Law and Procedure*, 29–42.

The wide range of these objectives illustrates the scope for the court to be pulled in multiple directions by varying constellations of political and legal circumstances (and situations). With a view to the central (or at least oft-stated) aim of the drafters of the various components of the civil war regime to ameliorate the worst excesses of internal armed conflict, however, perhaps the most critical of these for present purposes are the roles of the ICC in 'generating deterrence' and 'promoting peace and security'.[168]

Integral to both objectives are the limitation and prevention of atrocities in internal armed conflict. Recent empirical scholarship suggests, though, that the Court's impact in respect of these aims may be more subtle than the more ardent amongst the drafters of the internal armed conflict provisions would have wished.[169] In a study of the relationship between ICC intervention in civil conflict and conflict termination, for example, Alyssa Prorok finds that: 'when risks of domestic punishment are low the ICC's pursuit of justice undermines peace by threatening leaders' political survival and personal freedom'.[170] In other words, while not necessarily encouraging the commission of war crimes in internal armed conflicts, in situations where domestic justice is unlikely to be forthcoming, ICC intervention may actually *prolong* the conflicts in which atrocities are committed.[171]

168 The full set of objectives specified by Shany, Horovitz, and Noam for the ICC comprises: 'ending impunity'; 'generating deterrence'; 'norm internalization'; 'development of international legal norms'; 'promoting peace and security'; 'victim satisfaction'; 'establishing historical records of atrocious events'; 'encouraging domestic proceedings against ICL violators'; 'conveying a message of condemnation'; and 'projecting an image of procedural fairness and legitimacy' ('The International Criminal Court', 226–37).

169 See e.g. Hillebrecht, 'The Deterrent Effects of the International Criminal Court: Evidence from Libya'; McAllister and Meernik, 'Casting a Shadow over War Zones: The International Criminal Court's Impact on Rebel and Government Forces' Use of Violence against Civilians'; Jo and Simmons, 'Can the International Criminal Court Deter Atrocity?'; Meernik, 'The International Criminal Court and the Deterrence of Human Rights Atrocities'; Greig and Meernik, 'To Prosecute or Not to Prosecute: Civil War Mediation and International Criminal Justice'.

170 Prorok, 'The (In)Compatibility of Peace and Justice? The International Criminal Court and Civil Conflict Termination', 215.

171 In similar vein, Dancy and Wiebelhaus-Brahm observe that the relationship between international trials (more generally) and civil conflict termination 'is neither statistically nor substantively significant'. They add, however, that this may be because 'these kinds of trials overlap with other modes of international involvement', leading them to conclude that: '[i]n general, it may be difficult to observe the independent effects of international trials on civil war countries' ('The Impact of Criminal Prosecutions during Intrastate Conflict', 57).

This does not, of course, mean that ICC intervention may not still have a 'humanising' effect on the conduct of such conflicts. Even here, however, Dancy and Montal are able to observe only that: 'ICC involvement has not made lethal violence less likely in situation states, though a few cases have seen declines in violence after the ICC entered the situation'.[172] Indeed, it remains conceivable that – reflecting the tenor of Prorok's findings – such intervention may actually increase the likelihood of abuses occurring.

This does not mean that the ICC does not have more circumscribed, indirect effects on the prevalence of atrocities in civil (and other) conflicts. As Dancy puts it, 'the ICC has been more influential for what it *is* than what it *does*. As a standard-bearer, and as a focal stigmatizer, the ICC influences self-conscious state and rebel leaders. As an intervener, it has a mixed record'.[173] One suspects, though, that the proponents of a robust set of internal armed provisions in the Rome Statute may be less than entirely satisfied with a court the main function of which in respect of civil conflicts is to act as an international 'shamer-in-chief'.[174]

Conclusion

Conventional wisdom is that the Rome Statute was a 'civil society achievement'. The present chapter illustrates, however, that the internal armed conflict provisions of the Rome Statute cannot be explained solely by reference to civil society activity, but rather that a range of factors need to be taken into account in order to glean a rounded picture of the drafting process.

In particular, while the ICC project was driven principally by the political support of committed middle-ranking, Western powers with

[172] Dancy and Montal, 'From Law versus Politics to Law in Politics: A Pragmatist Assessment of the ICCs Impact Celebrating the Twenty Year Anniversary of the War Crimes Research Office', 682. See similarly: Dancy, 'Searching for Deterrence at the International Criminal Court'.

[173] Dancy, 'Searching for Deterrence at the International Criminal Court', 655. In similar vein, and pointing to the relatively constrained circumstances in which the ICC may have a deterrent effect, Jo and Simmons argue that: '[a]ctors who are concerned with their legitimacy in the eyes of domestic publics and/or the international community are much more likely to be deterred by the possibility of ICC prosecution than those who are not' ('Can the International Criminal Court Deter Atrocity?', 446).

[174] Dancy and Montal, 'From Law versus Politics to Law in Politics: A Pragmatist Assessment of the ICCs Impact Celebrating the Twenty Year Anniversary of the War Crimes Research Office', 682.

the support of prominent civil society organisations in the post-Cold War environment, the end product at Rome in respect of war crimes in internal armed conflict closely reflects the positions and preferences of great powers, principally the Western P3. Rationalist considerations also appear to have been important in the drafting of the internal armed conflict provisions, given the low likelihood of internal unrest faced by many of the leading proponents of a robust regime. Similarly, governments of states recovering from civil wars were at the forefront of efforts to establish a strong internal armed conflict regime.

That said, the chapter bears out the view that international normative factors were important in the drafting of the internal armed conflict provisions: moral authority and technical expertise, in particular, aided 'like-minded' delegations and allied civil society groups to make their case in the context of the 'New Diplomacy' of the 1990s. Similarly, the failure of opponents of a robust regime to nest coherent, principled arguments in the prevailing post-Cold War 'liberal' normative discourse limited the appeal of the positions advanced by India and more critical NAM/P5 members. Indeed, perhaps the most striking feature of the negotiations is the extent to which outcomes reflected the post-Cold War liberal, human security- and human rights-oriented international normative Zeitgeist.

Last, and also interestingly, while democracies were certainly in the vanguard with respect to the drafting of the internal armed conflict provisions, the study has not revealed a 'smoking gun' linking democratic governance to support for a robust internal armed conflict regime. India again presents a challenging case, suggesting that in both more and less democratic states, internal security concerns or inflexible and unaccommodating foreign policy stances may have trumped international normative trends with respect to the regulation of internal armed conflict in the negotiation of the Rome Statute.

6

Explaining the Civil War Regime

Introduction

Chapters 3–5 underline the value of theoretically informed, eclectic analysis of the development and design of the civil war regime, identifying material, ideational, social and strategic factors that shaped treaty provisions. These chapters, however, leave two tasks to be conducted: first, the case studies speak only to their respective outcomes from 1949, 1977 and 1998. The present chapter remedies this, identifying the implications of the overall historical record for the five hypotheses and their underlying causal factors, and drawing together and contrasting the extent to and manner in which the hypotheses are borne out in the three case studies.

Second, the individual case studies have not allowed for reconsideration of the overall manner in which the various causal factors have interacted with one another in bringing these outcomes about. These factors have not operated in isolation from one another: rather, they have operated in combination to affect negotiation outcomes. This discussion accordingly assesses the interaction of these factors at an aggregate level and at different junctures, providing a rounded, integrative understanding of regime development.

The first section of the chapter draws together the findings from Chapters 3–5, revisiting Chapter 1's 'straw person' Figure 1 in light of the case studies to produce a more fine-grained portrait of how hypothesised and other factors contributed to shaping the civil war regime. This is followed by a reconsideration of how these factors combined in different instances to produce drafting outputs. The Conclusion that follows sets the preceding chapters and the present discussion in the context of broader bodies of research on the civil war regime and related topics, and considers the implications of *Negotiating Civil War* for understanding of this regime, along with associated theoretical and policy issues.

As the discussion illustrates, great power preferences indeed limited negotiation outcomes in each of the case studies. These preferences were often themselves endogenously produced, though, with outcomes more broadly reflective of the operation of functional, rationalist logic in a social environment in which morally (and to a lesser degree technically) authoritative participants sought to rhetorically nest arguments within the prevailing normative context of negotiations. The impact of domestic governance type is ambiguous, moreover: governments of states undergoing democratic transitions were indeed likely to support a robust regime, and liberal democratic states were in many instances concerned to be seen to support progressive regime development. Authoritarian states, however, also supported (notionally) demanding civil war regime provisions in a number of instances, having discounted potential costs of compliance.

6.1 Taking Stock: Revisiting the Straw Person

The first section of this chapter draws together the findings of the case studies to re-evaluate and develop the 'straw person' diagram of hypothesis interaction set out at Figure 1 in Chapter 1.[1] This then provides the basis for the second part of this chapter, which highlights key instances in which these interactions manifested in the case studies.

6.1.1 The Realist Hypothesis

The first hypothesis states that '[t]he preferences of great powers are likely to be especially significant in shaping the civil war regime'. As set out in Chapter 1, this proposition draws on the central realist insight, reflected in a range of literature, that international legal rules are likely to reflect the preferences of the most powerful states.[2]

[1] See Chapter 1, Section 1.5.2.

[2] See discussion at Chapter 1, Section 1.4.1, and references to e.g. Schweller and Priess, 'A Tale of Two Realisms: Expanding the Institutions Debate'; Wohlforth, *The Elusive Balance: Power and Perceptions during the Cold War*; Krasner, 'Structural Causes and Regime Consequences: Regimes as Intervening Variables'; Morgenthau, *Politics among Nations: The Struggle for Power and Peace.*

This hypothesis is largely borne out in the three case studies. In each case, negotiation outcomes reflected relatively closely the ex ante preferences of one or more great powers, with drafting also tailored during negotiations to accommodate the preferences of powerful states. When examined in more granular detail, though, the negotiating histories indicate that it is also necessary to qualify this observation. While some great power support appears to have been necessary (or at least a common minimal requirement) to effect a given civil war regime drafting outcome, such support was not always sufficient to determine the shape and content of the resultant measures. An important caveat to this is where all great powers (i.e. since 1945, the P5) were aligned in oligopolistic fashion in support of or in opposition to a given proposition. Here these preferences indeed proved sufficient to determine outcomes: however, such instances have been encountered only exceptionally in the case studies.

In the more common case where there was no such alignment, the case studies together suggest that great power support has been a key element in bringing about drafting outcomes because less powerful supporters of one or another form of drafting have preferred to obtain some – and ideally more rather than less – support from the most powerful states in the international system. Equally, great powers – even when otherwise aligned in support of a given proposition – have in instances also accommodated the preferences of materially less powerful states.

The debate over Common Article 3 exemplifies both these tendencies. The former, for example, can be seen in the concern of French and ICRC delegations to satisfy the minimal preferences of both US- and USSR-oriented blocs, more generally in ICRC concern to ensure 'Big Five' participation in the revision process, and in more discrete instances, such as the deferral of committee consideration of the French proposal pending instructions to the Soviet delegation. Viewed from this perspective, the French drafting proposal was adopted ultimately as it struck a mutually acceptable compromise between US and USSR preferences: while the outcome did not directly reflect the stated preferences of either superpower, the principal challenge in 1949 was to find a form of words that would be acceptable to the leading members of Eastern and Western blocs.[3]

Even in 1949, however, delegations of smaller powers could not be taken for granted, and representatives of materially weaker powers were

[3] See discussions at Chapter 3, Sections 3.3.1.3, 3.3.4, 3.4.1.

able to alter the course of negotiations, including by presenting well-tailored, cogent arguments in favour of one or another position.[4] The associated limitations to individual great power influence can be seen in the retreat of the British and French delegations to 'second-best' positions, following (rational) reassessment of the prospects of achieving initially preferred outcomes.[5]

This 'power of the weak' is further highlighted in debates over internal armed conflict regulation at the CDDH, where developing country preferences were critical to outcomes. Indeed, not only does the USSR appear to have 'bandwagoned' with developing world delegations in supporting (rather than leading) the drafting of Article 1(4) of Protocol I; neither Soviet nor conservative Western preferences in respect of Protocol II would have gained sufficient traction without the accommodation of the overall design of this instrument to developing world preferences.[6]

These negotiations generally show, moreover, how great powers have struggled to achieve outcomes in line with even strongly held preferences where opposed by a committed coalition of materially less powerful states – see for example the debates over PRG attendance in 1974.[7] The 1974–7 negotiations also underline that it was only where particularly strongly held US and USSR views were aligned – as in the combined US–Soviet endeavour to avoid discussion of nuclear weapons at the CDDH – that these delegations were able to exert sufficient authority over smaller powers to ensure outputs in line with these preferences.[8] British and French deferral to US leadership in managing the fallout from the 1974 drafting of Article 1(4) of Protocol I also once again illustrates the significance of material power differentials even amongst great powers.

That said, consistent with Danner's observation that the war crimes provisions of the Rome Statute reflect positions 'advocated by the permanent members of the Security Council – particularly the United States', Chapter 5 highlights the extent to which the like-minded were concerned to garner Western P3 support for the civil war provisions.[9] This is not to argue that the views of the latter were not themselves

[4] See Chapter 3, Section 3.4.1.
[5] Ibid., Section 3.4.2.
[6] See Chapter 4, Sections 4.3.3, 4.4.1.
[7] Ibid., Sections 4.2.1, 4.3.1.1.
[8] See Chapter 4, Sections 4.3.1.1, 4.3.4, 4.4.1.
[9] Danner, 'When Courts Make Law: How the International Criminal Tribunals Recast the Laws of War', 37. See: Chapter 5, Sections 5.3.2, 5.4.1.

affected by other considerations. Like-minded concessions in the Bonn Paper over the treatment of war crimes in internal armed conflict, however – and alignment with British, French and (albeit to a lesser extent) US views during negotiations more generally – nevertheless evidently reflected recognition on the part of the like-minded of the desirability of 'splitting the P5' to ensure sufficient great power support to avoid a politically irrelevant or under-resourced institution.[10] A comparable mechanism operated in the drafting of Article 1(4) of Additional Protocol I, where Soviet support enabled developing world delegations to face down the USA and aligned conservative Western delegations.[11] In short, in both of these instances, as in 1949, great power preferences proved significant in shaping drafting outcomes to the extent that other participants were concerned to ensure great power support for treaty outputs.

Building on the above, it may be helpful to revisit the diagram set out at Figure 1 in Chapter 1, as this relates to the impact of great power preferences on negotiation outcomes, to consider how best to reflect this more nuanced understanding of the role of the former in shaping the latter.

In Figure 1, great power preferences were assumed to have a direct impact on the preferences of other governments, independent of the other hypothesised factors. This portrayal failed to take into account, however, the manner in which great power support has functioned primarily as a limiting factor in determining drafting outcomes, rather than in merely shaping the ex ante preferences of other governments. Figure 1 failed to reflect that, as well as great power preferences shaping those of other delegations, so the former have in a number of instances themselves been shaped by other factors, including the positions of other more and less powerful delegations. The latter tendency can be seen particularly clearly in British and French behaviour in the negotiation of Common Article 3 and in conservative Western behaviour in respect of Article 1(4).[12]

Taking these observations into account, it is probably most accurate to view great power support as performing a critical – albeit not unconstrained – 'gatekeeping' function in the drafting and adoption of civil war-regulating treaty provisions. Given that both great power

[10] See Kirsch, 'The Development of the Rome Statute', 453. Also Chapter 5, Section 5.4.1.
[11] See Chapter 4, Section 4.4.1.
[12] See Chapter 3, Sections 3.3.1.1, 3.3.1.3, 3.4.1, Chapter 4, Sections 4.3.1, 4.4.1.

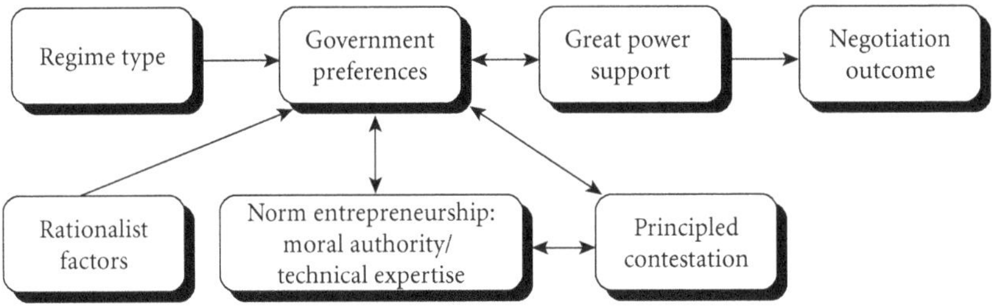

Figure 2: Mapping Interaction (Version 2)

and non-great power preferences may be subject to adjustment to take account of one another in respect of any given proposition, a degree of endogeneity should also be allowed for in the relationship between the former and the latter. Figure 2 accordingly reflects this revised view of the impact of great power preferences on negotiation outcomes, positioning such preferences as limiting drafting outputs, yet recognising that great power positions may also evolve, dependent on the views of other negotiation participants.

Interestingly, the effective need for some degree of great power support for a 'successful' treaty outcome is reminiscent of aspects of hegemonic stability theory.[13] This is not necessarily surprising, rather reflecting appreciation on the part of norm entrepreneurs and treaty drafters that (to paraphrase Krasner) '[t]he potentially dominant state has symbolic, economic, and military capabilities that can be used to entice or compel others to accept [a specific vision of the civil war regime]'.[14] In other words, French and Canadian enthusiasm to broaden the extent of great power support in 1949 and 1998, and developing world reliance on Soviet support in the CDDH, would appear to have reflected awareness of the importance of developing and maintaining the broadest possible great power support for regime viability, both in terms of providing material resources to facilitate regime operation and of enhancing the legitimacy of negotiation outputs. While great power preferences were indeed significant in shaping the civil war regime, therefore, in the final reckoning this appears to have been less by virtue of the ability of great powers to dictate terms to less powerful states in

[13] At the heart of this approach to thinking about international politics is Kindleberger's observation (reflecting on the Great Depression) that: 'for the world economy to be stabilized, there has to be a stabilizer – one stabilizer' (*The World in Depression, 1929–1939*, 304).

[14] Krasner, 'State Power and the Structure of International Trade', 322.

reliance on recognised power primacy, and more a reflection of other negotiation participants' awareness of the value of great power support in terms of material and (to use Krasner's terminology) 'symbolic' advantage.

6.1.2 The Rationalist Hypothesis

Reflecting the functionalist logic underlying rationalist approaches to IR, this proposition recognises that support for civil war regime development may be motivated by a number of benefits, potentially including the accrual of domestic and international reputation and legitimacy, and a reduced likelihood of cross-border spillover of civil wars into neighbouring states. Despite this, though, costs – particularly potential domestic political and security costs – are likely to limit the appeal of such factors. The latter are captured in the first element of the second hypothesis set out in Chapter 1, which states: '[t]he more intrusive or restrictive any proposed set of civil war-regulating treaty provisions, the less likely they are to be supported by governments in the course of treaty negotiations, especially when governments are engaged in or foresee a possibility of a civil war or insurgency.' In other words, governments can be expected to prefer a civil war regime which would not require them to make any significantly costly behavioural changes.

This first part of the Rationalist hypothesis draws on the work of authors such as Keohane and Koremenos on the design of international institutions, but privileges domestic costs, given the traditional sensitivity of governments to international regulation of internal armed conflict. This is assumed to be the default position, moreover, in respect of the civil war regime, where the domestic balance of costs and benefits of a robust regime will always be ranged asymmetrically against governments and in favour of non-government forces.[15]

[15] Granting additional protection to the latter will (at least notionally) restrict governments' discretion to treat members of these groups as they see fit. Such costs may also be incurred even if governments do not sign up to any resultant treaty requirements, as the prospect remains of even unratified treaty provisions subsequently being argued to have customary status. (In the case of the Rome Statute, moreover, Article 8 may also have potentially significant implications for third-party states, given the Statute's jurisdictional arrangements.) See generally discussion in Chapter 1, Section 1.4.2, also variously Koremenos, *The Continent of International Law: Explaining Agreement Design;* Keohane and Martin, 'Institutional Theory as a Research Program'; Dunoff and Trachtman, 'The Law and Economics of Humanitarian Law Violations in Internal Conflict'; Martin, 'An

The second element of the hypothesis recognises, however, that there may also be domestic circumstances conducive to support for a robust civil war regime, in particular that '[t]he end of a civil war or insurgency may . . . make a government more likely to support such provisions'. This expands on the work of Ropp and Sikkink, Moravcsik, and Simmons and Danner, to propose that governments of states recovering from civil internal armed conflict may perceive a particularly valuable benefit in supporting a demanding civil war regime to decrease the likelihood of a return to violence and to lock-in associated domestic reforms (which may include enhanced human rights protections).[16]

With respect to the operation of the functionalist logic underpinning this hypothesis generally, outcomes in all cases save for Article 1(4) can indeed be viewed as 'rational' in the broad sense of striking compromise positions between the preferences of key groups of delegations, approximating an aggregate cost/benefit balance across negotiation participants. Nevertheless, when considered at a more granular level, aspects of behaviour emerge that are less obviously consistent with the expectations of this hypothesis.

While prominent Western democracies, including great powers, were reluctant to support a demanding regime in each of the three instances, for example – consistent with the expectations of the more narrowly drafted hypothesis – the most outspoken supporters of a robust civil war regime in 1949 and of a robust regime for 'wars of national liberation' in 1974 – Soviet bloc and developing world delegations, respectively – appear to have discounted (or failed to recognise) the potential costs of the regime being crafted. (In respect of authoritarian governments, this approach is consistent with Hollyer and Rosendorff's 'Bad Ass' explanation of the tendency of such governments to sign up to human rights regimes.)[17] That said, with respect to the second aspect of this hypothesis, there does seem to be some association between the termination of severe

Institutionalist View: International Institutions and State Strategies'; Keohane, *After Hegemony. Cooperation and Discord in the World Political Economy.*

[16] See Chapter 1, Section 1.4.2. Also Simmons and Danner, 'Credible Commitments and the International Criminal Court'; Moravcsik, 'The Origins of Human Rights Regimes: Democratic Delegation in Postwar Europe'; Ropp and Sikkink, 'International Norms and Domestic Politics in Chile and Guatemala'.

[17] Hollyer and Rosendorff, 'Why Do Authoritarian Regimes Sign the Convention against Torture? Signaling, Domestic Politics and Non-Compliance'. In a similar vein, see Hathaway, 'Why Do Countries Commit to Human Rights Treaties?' Again, though these may be increased in the event of ratification, non-negligible costs may nevertheless still arise for a government even in the absence of ratification.

domestic unrest and support for a robust civil war regime, particularly where a democratic transition is underway. Such a relationship is suggested in particular by the support of such states for intrusive internal armed conflict provisions at Rome in 1998.[18]

Regarding the operation of this hypothesis in the context of the negotiation of Common Article 3, as in other instances, it is possible to cast this provision as a 'rational' outcome of negotiations: minimally intrusive or restrictive, yet still constituting sufficient regime development to enable negotiators to claim humanitarian progress.[19] It is also worth noting that the delegations most concerned at different points in the negotiations to minimise regime constraints – Burma, France, Greece and the UK – represented governments that were also countering violent domestic (including in the French and British cases, colonial) unrest.

That said, Soviet bloc behaviour in 1949 equally underlines the salience of the 'Bad Ass' proposition that delegations may express support for an ostensibly demanding civil war regime, having apparently discounted potential domestic costs.[20] In other words, for governments with little intention of complying with costly injunctions, there is little reason not to lend rhetorical support to notionally far-reaching civil war regime measures where there are countervailing benefits – for example in order to discomfit other delegations (as seems to have been the case with respect to Soviet bloc behaviour in 1949). Moreover, other – including colonial – states, such as Portugal and the Netherlands, whose delegations might have been expected to share British, French, Greek and Burmese misgivings in 1949, did not evince such concerns to the same extent. This again suggests limits to the extent to which this hypothesis should be understood as solely (or even primarily) determinative of government positions without qualification.[21]

Similar dynamics can be identified in the negotiating histories of Article 1(4) of Protocol I and of Protocol II. While mainstream conservative Western attitudes to Article 1(4) in negotiations were broadly consistent with the first element of this hypothesis, Soviet and developing world behaviour again presents a challenge from this perspective, not least as some of the prime movers behind this provision represented relatively unstable polities.[22] It is possible, of course, to view

[18] See Chapter 5, Sections 5.3.1, 5.4.2, 5.4.5.

[19] See Chapter 3, Section 3.4.2.

[20] Ibid., Section 3.4.5.

[21] Ibid., Section 3.4.2.

[22] See, respectively, Chapter 4, Sections 4.3.1, 4.3.3, 4.3.4, 4.4.2.

Scandinavian support for this provision as reflecting the very low likelihood of the governments of these states facing significant violent domestic unrest. In similar fashion to 1949, it is also reasonable to cast Soviet bloc support for this measure as cynical, insofar as rhetorical commitment to Article 1(4) appears unlikely to have been accompanied by an intention to comply with its terms should this prove inconvenient.[23] Developing world support for Article 1(4), in contrast, can be viewed as rational only when an exceedingly narrow interpretation is adopted of this provision's wording. While this may have been the drafters' intention, though, there is little in the drafting to preclude the application of this provision to a wider set of conflicts than anticipated by its proponents, begging the question of the extent to which developing world support for this wording can be cast as entirely consistent with the first part of this hypothesis.[24]

In contrast, the negotiation of Protocol II presents a stronger case for the Rationalist hypothesis. As per Common Article 3, in a general sense this treaty can be viewed as broadly 'rational' insofar as the language ultimately adopted enabled the majority of delegations to laud the instrument's 'humanitarian progress' but was also sufficiently unintrusive and unrestrictive as to be non-threatening to most delegations. Indeed, the relatively high threshold and undemanding content of this Protocol appear to be the prime explanation for both broad conservative Western (certainly UK) and developing world support for the Pakistani draft. At the same time, the dissatisfaction of more progressive delegations such as those of Norway (where a more robust set of measures would have had little domestic cost) and of more conservative delegations such as India (for whom any potential restrictions on domestic room for manoeuvre would have been problematic) can also be explained in terms of the relative costs and benefits of these measures for the governments concerned.[25]

The 1974–7 negotiations shed little light on the second element of this hypothesis. Pakistani support for some form of Protocol II may be understood in terms of the aftermath of experiences related to Bangladeshi independence.[26] Equally, however, while a number of developing world states critical of this endeavour had experienced internal armed conflict (including in both anti- and post-colonial contexts), these

[23] See Chapter 4, Sections 4.3.2, 4.3.4.
[24] Ibid., Section 4.4.2.
[25] Ibid.
[26] Ibid., Section 4.3.3.3.

episodes were not always succeeded by the human rights improvements or transitions to democratic governance highlighted by Ropp and Sikkink and Moravcsik.[27] Indeed, in a number of such cases, internal unrest in one form or another continued during the CDDH.[28]

That said, the second element of the hypothesis was largely borne out in the negotiation of the internal armed conflict provisions of the Rome Statute. Like-minded states undergoing democratic transitions in the wake of civil wars – including Bosnia and Herzegovina and Sierra Leone – were amongst the most prominent supporters of a robust civil war regime.[29] In similar fashion to Scandinavian countries at the CDDH, moreover, key like-minded states were at little risk of encountering violent domestic unrest (e.g. Canada, Germany). The principal opponents of a more robust set of provisions, on the other hand, which on this occasion included (a post-Cold War weakened) Russia and China, as well as developing world opponents such as India and Middle Eastern states, harboured significant concerns about potential costs.[30] Delegations supporting more demanding language to a more qualified degree – including but not limited to the Western P3 – were also concerned to restrict the scope for future Cassese-esque judicial creativity in respect of war crimes in internal armed conflict at the ICC. This was an eminently rational approach given the potentially broad reach of the court's jurisdiction, resulting in both the Bonn paper and the final 'package deal' falling short of the preferences of PrepCom 'maximalists' in this respect.[31]

In sum, the impact of the factors identified in the first part of this hypothesis on negotiation outcomes was mixed. Concerns over provision restrictiveness and intrusiveness were evidently germane to government preferences where governments were concerned about potential costs of being required to live up to their commitments. Equally, there is some support – primarily drawn from the Rome Statute – for the proposition that governments in states undergoing democratic transitions will be inclined to support robust civil war provisions. On the other hand, experiences in 1949 and 1974–7 also lend qualified support to the view that authoritarian governments are less likely to hesitate to endorse restrictive or intrusive provisions than those of democracies.

27 See references at note 16.

28 Algeria, Iraq, Indonesia, and the Philippines would fall into this category, for example.

29 See Chapter 5, Sections 5.2.2, 5.3.1, 5.4.2.

30 Ibid., Sections 5.3.2.4, 5.3.3, 5.4.2.

31 Ibid., Section 5.4.2.

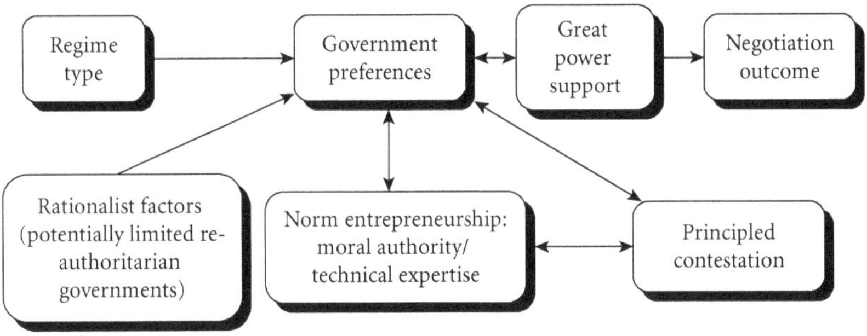

Figure 3: Mapping Interaction (Version 3)

With the above in mind, it may be useful to revisit Figure 2 to consider how best to factor in the impact of Rationalist considerations on treaty outputs. As conceived in Chapter 1, such factors were assumed to have a bearing on the preferences of governments unaffected by the other hypothesised factors. This would largely appear to be borne out.

Moreover, Rationalist factors appear to have had little direct bearing on the operation of the remaining four hypotheses, rather serving to condition individual (and to the extent that this hypothesis captures the operation of a broader functionalist logic, collective) government preferences on an ongoing basis. The first two case studies also strongly suggest that it would be appropriate to qualify the expected operation of the Rationalist hypothesis in respect of authoritarian states, particularly where these are also materially powerful – such as the Cold War-era USSR – where domestic costs and incentives may (albeit not necessarily) be configured very differently from those prevailing in more democratic contexts. These considerations are accordingly reflected in Figure 3.

As with its Realist counterpart, the Rationalist hypothesis provides important insights into delegation behaviour, as well as reflecting generally the prevalence of strategic behaviour in treaty negotiations. That said, neither hypothesis provides more than minimal insight into why governments generally have agreed to progressively more intrusive regulation of internal armed conflict in successive rounds of treaty negotiation. Additional factors need to be taken into account to explain the shape of the civil war regime.

6.1.3 The Agent Characteristics Hypothesis

The third hypothesis set out in Chapter 1 states: '[t]he greater their perceived moral authority and their ability to leverage subject area expertise, the more likely governments and non-state actors are to be able to elicit the support of other governments for demanding civil war-regulating provisions in the course of treaty negotiations.' This insight draws on constructivist insights regarding the role of norm entrepreneurs in regime development, and the use of persuasion – understood broadly – in teaching states about appropriate behaviour.[32]

To capture important nuances, the hypothesis distinguishes two characteristics of norm entrepreneurs which may have bearings on their efficacy. First is an actor's 'decisional power': their ability to bring expert, policy-relevant knowledge to bear on other actors. Second is 'discursive power': the ability to leverage moral authority in the eyes of counterparts. In short, when considering the ability of an actor to persuade others of the appropriateness of a course of action, the extent to which that actor is perceived by counterparts as having 'clean hands' is likely to be relevant, alongside their technical adeptness.[33]

In general terms, the case studies lend credence to both elements of this hypothesis. The roles of the Egyptian and Pakistani delegations in CDDH debates over the treatment of internal armed conflict illustrate particularly well the relevance of combined technical and perceived moral authority with respect to Article 1(4) and Protocol II. These experiences can also be contrasted with the retreat of the ICRC during these debates to less politically sensitive issues, reflecting diminished technical and qualified moral authority, primarily in the eyes of developing world participants.[34] Chapter 5 also illustrates the salience of both aspects of this hypothesis to treaty outcomes, with the moral and technical authority of like-minded states such as Canada as well as of leading members of the NGO coalition playing a critical role in bringing about drafting outcomes.[35] The French contribution to the shaping of Common Article 3 similarly demonstrates the capacity of states to leverage moral authority alongside technical expertise to affect drafting outcomes.[36]

[32] See discussion at Chapter 1, Section 1.4.3.1, including references to Fehl, 'Explaining the International Criminal Court: A "Practice Test" for Rationalist and Constructivist Approaches'; Finnemore and Sikkink, 'International Norm Dynamics and Political Change.'

[33] See discussion at Chapter 1, Section 1.4.3.1, inc. references to Forsythe, *Human Rights in International Relations*; Arts, 'Non-State Actors in Global Governance'; Finnemore, *National Interests in International Society*.

[34] See Chapter 4, Sections 4.3.3.1, 4.3.3.3, 4.3.5, 4.4.3.

[35] See Chapter 5, Sections 5.3.1, 5.3.4, 5.4.3.

[36] See Chapter 3, Sections 3.3.1.3, 3.4.3.

The case studies also illustrate how actors can utilise strengths in either moral authority or technical capacity to compensate for relative weaknesses in the other. Chapter 3 shows, for example, how the ICRC leveraged technical expertise to reinforce its moral authority in the eyes of the Western allies at the diplomatic conference.[37] In similar fashion, developing world delegates at the 1974–7 CDDH negotiations relied primarily on moral rather than on technical, legal arguments in making the case for the privileging of wars of national liberation in Article 1(4). Delegations representing countries recovering from civil wars – Bosnia and Herzegovina and Sierra Leone perhaps being the most prominent examples – exerted related moral authority in debates over the internal armed conflict provisions at the Rome Conference in 1998.[38]

Interestingly, the three cases also suggest that agent moral authority may have been a more fundamental determinant of drafting outcomes than technical expertise. While there are a number of instances in which reliance on technical expertise prejudiced the effectiveness of delegations, there are only a few occasions where moral authority failed to prevail over technically robust arguments put forward by morally compromised opponents. The handicap under which the technically well-equipped UK delegation laboured in 1949 is a prominent case in point. In this instance, the decision of the UK government to adopt a narrow, legalistic approach hindered rather than assisted the UK delegation.[39] US, French and British experiences at the CDDH are also illustrative of this tendency, the ability of these delegations to deploy their formidable technical resources handicapped by their compromised moral authority in the eyes of developing world delegations.[40] The difficulties encountered by the ICRC at the CDDH in convincing developing world delegations of the appropriateness of its preferred courses of action may also be associated with the Committee's moral authority having been compromised by its traditionally close alignment with the conservative West, as well as a lack of familiarity (or comfort) with more radical developing world-led discussions and doctrinal debates that had been conducted primarily outside its traditional sphere of expertise.[41]

The cases of Article 1(4) and of Protocol II are also interesting for additional reasons. In particular, the experience of more conservative

[37] Ibid., Sections 3.3.4, 3.4.3.
[38] See Chapter 4, Sections 4.2.1, 4.3.3, 4.4.3; Chapter 5, Sections 5.2.2, 5.4.3.
[39] See Chapter 3, Section 3.3.1.1.
[40] See Chapter 4, Section 4.4.3.
[41] Ibid., Sections 4.3.5, 4.4.3.

Western powers and the ICRC in respect of Article 1(4), and of the Egyptian, Indian and Pakistani delegations in relation to Protocol II suggest that the ability to leverage perceived moral authority or technical expertise might be limited or enhanced dependent on how effectively arguments are nested within broader normative narratives.[42]

It is conceivable, of course, that the developing world would have remained – especially given Soviet backing – insensitive to conservative Western and ICRC arguments in respect of Article 1(4), even had the latter reframed their arguments in terms familiar to the former from UN debates, for instance by reference to the language of 'human rights in armed conflict'. It is also plausible, however, that had this course been adopted, the conservative West and ICRC might have succeeded in watering down some of the most problematic aspects of Article 1(4). Indian failure to marshal greater support behind its opposition to Protocol II in 1977 in the face of a growing cross-bloc 'cognitive consensus' may also be contrasted with Egyptian and Pakistani success in facilitating the adoption of Protocol II with developing world support.[43] The lack of traction obtained by General Oung in 1949 and the Indian experience at Rome in 1998 additionally bolster the view that the ability of delegations to deploy moral authority or technical expertise effectively can be hindered where arguments are not framed within a shared, dominant discourse.[44]

Presenting the above findings in diagrammatic form is challenging given that delegations relied on various combinations of perceived moral authority and/or technical expertise, and that strengths in one area can compensate in some instances for weaknesses in the other. That said, a potentially critical distinction supported by the case studies is that impaired moral authority in the eyes of negotiating counterparts is likely to be more difficult to remedy than weaknesses in technical expertise: the latter can be 'bought in' (or, as at Rome even provided cost-free by international civil society) in short order, whereas the former will generally need to be rebuilt over time. Regardless of the technical adeptness or moral standing of a delegation, moreover, and as observed above, any arguments presented are likely to be less effective if they are not framed in terms of widely shared values and principles. It should also be borne in mind that the broader normative context in which negotiations are

[42] See Chapter 4, Conclusion. Also related discussion below at Section 6.I.4.
[43] See Chapter 4, Sections 4.3.3, 4.4.3.
[44] See Chapter 3, Section 3.3.3; Chapter 5, Section 5.3.3, 5.4.4.

conducted is unlikely to be significantly affected by a narrower debate over the regulation of internal armed conflict: as such, it is reasonable to view the values and principles comprising this normative context as effectively exogenously given for present purposes.

Figure 4 captures these dynamics, with the secondary nature of technical expertise relative to moral authority represented by a dotted rather than a solid arrow. The filtering role of the broader normative context – the 'Zeitgeist' of negotiations – may be understood for the time being as subsumed within the processes of 'principled contestation' reflecting the operation of the Logic of Argument hypothesis, examined below.

Viewed alongside the Realist and Rationalist factors considered above, Agent Characteristics appear to shed significant light on the shaping of the civil war regime in treaty negotiations in 1949, 1974–7 and 1998 – that is to say, by way of (largely) moral authority-dependent norm entrepreneurship, enabling actors perceived by key interlocutors to have 'clean hands' to deploy technical expertise. The discussion suggests, moreover, that the success or failure of norm entrepreneurship has also depended on how successfully competing positions have been rhetorically nested within the broader normative and ideational context of

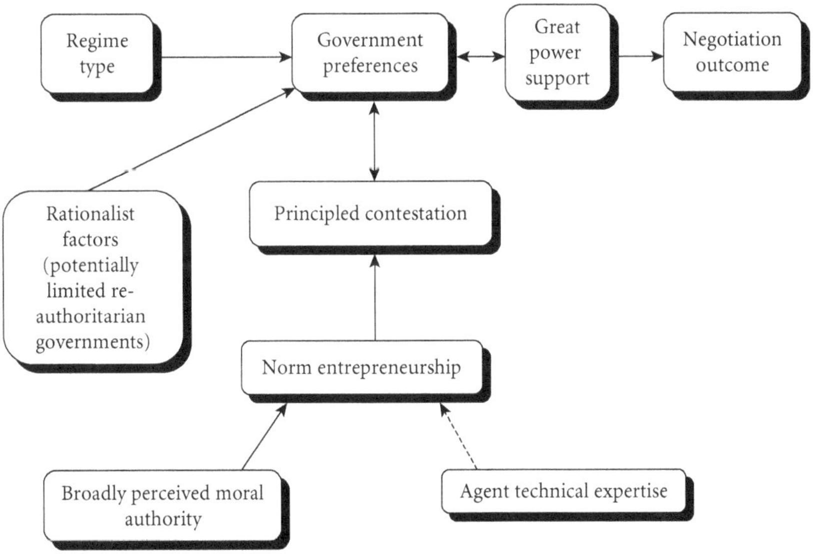

Figure 4: Mapping Interaction (Version 4)

negotiations. This last observation is considered further in the following section of this chapter.

6.1.4 The Logic of Argument Hypothesis

The fourth hypothesis set out in Chapter 1 proposes that '[g]overnments will be more likely to support the adoption of civil war-regulating provisions in treaty negotiations when strong, coherent arguments premised on widely shared values and principles are made in support.' This proposition entails two elements: first that logically coherent arguments should – all else being equal – be more likely to prevail over more incoherent arguments, and second that arguments are likely to be more persuasive where grounded rhetorically in values and principles that reflect the broader normative and ideational context.

In terms of theoretical basis, this hypothesis draws closely on the work of a range of predominantly European scholars on the role of 'communicative action' in international relations. A key postulate of this body of work is that where negotiations take the form of reasoned, scrutinised debate within the context of a shared 'lifeworld', a 'logic of argument' is likely to apply, such that arguments premised on widely shared understandings will be more likely to prevail over arguments less well grounded in shared understandings.[45]

The concept of 'lifeworld' bears unpacking: while this term has a lengthy pedigree in German philosophy,[46] as used by Habermas (insofar as relevant to the current context) it refers primarily to 'the background resources, contexts, and dimensions of social action that enable actors to cooperate on the basis of mutual understanding', including 'shared cultural systems of meaning ... [and] institutional orders that stabilize patterns of action'.[47] Conceptually then, what has been referred to in previous chapters as the broader normative context

[45] See discussion at Chapter 1, Section 1.4.3.2, including references to Deitelhoff, 'The Discursive Process of Legalization: Charting Islands of Persuasion in the ICC Case'; Deitelhoff and Müller, 'Theoretical Paradise – Empirically Lost? Arguing with Habermas'; Risse, '"Let's Argue!": Communicative Action in World Politics'.

[46] As used by Husserl, it may be understood as: 'considering a single community of subjects ... the system of senses or meanings constituting their common language' (Beyer, 'Edmund Husserl'). See also: Husserl, *Die Lebenswelt: Auslegungen der vorgegebenen Welt und ihrer Konstitution*; Carr, 'Husserl's Problematic Concept of the Life-World'.

[47] Bohman and Rehg, 'Jürgen Habermas'. The lifeworld has been termed elsewhere 'the social background to communicative action' (Baxter, 'System and Life-World in Habermas's Theory of Communicative Action', 39).

in which negotiations take place – the Zeitgeist – can be subsumed within this term. In turn, the reference in the hypothesis to 'widely shared values and principles' attempts to capture the means by which key lifeworld elements – the 'shared cultural systems of meanings' – are manifested in the course of debate.

Simply put, it is suggested that the ability of a delegation to present coherent arguments justified in terms of or embedded within a commonly shared normative framework is likely to have a significant impact on the ability of that delegation to elicit support from negotiating counterparts for its preferred course of action. The three empirical chapters, moreover, suggest that this insight helpfully captures important aspects of regime development.

With respect to Common Article 3, for instance, Chapter 3 suggests that arguments premised on humanitarian principles were effective in large part as these reflected broader sentiments that had been rhetorically supported by both Western and Soviet bloc governments, as well as in the UN context. The negotiation of the internal armed conflict provisions of the Rome Statute similarly reinforces the importance of grounding arguments in broadly shared values: in this context, both NGOs and state delegations were more persuasive when the arguments presented were framed as consistent with the dominant post-Cold War 'liberal' normative setting.[48]

The importance of effective normative nesting of arguments is similarly illustrated in the treatment of wars of national liberation at the 1974–7 CDDH. In this instance, the case study suggests that the negotiations over Article 1(4) were so difficult in part precisely because of limitations in the extent to which there was a shared lifeworld between mainstream, conservative Western delegations and the majority of developing world delegations. In other words, the absence of 'cognitive consensus' prevented each set of protagonists from nesting their arguments within a shared normative frame of reference: delegations appeared on occasion to be 'talking past one another'.[49]

Similar difficulties afflicted the UK and Burmese delegations in 1949, where the technical, legalistic tack taken by the former and the appeal of the latter to the traditional international legal principle of sovereignty failed to gain traction with other delegations.[50] That the same dynamic

[48] See Chapter 3, Section 3.4.4; Chapter 5, Section 5.4.4.
[49] See Chapter 4, Section 4.4.4.
[50] See Chapter 3, Sections 3.3.1.1, 3.3.3, 3.4.4.

appears to have been in play with respect to (for example) Indian views in 1998 – where the views presented were clear and logically coherent, yet failed to convince the majority of other delegations – suggests, moreover, that the first aspect of the hypothesis has been of less importance to civil war-regulating outcomes than the second.[51] That is to say, the clarity and coherence of arguments appear to have had less bearing on their effectiveness than the extent to which arguments are consistent with and discursively nested in the prevailing normative context in any given instance.

That said, 'cognitive consensus' with respect to a proposed course of action may also develop over time where not previously present. The success of the Pakistani-led effort to arrive at an agreed form of Protocol II, for example, suggests that between 1974 and 1977 sufficient common ground had developed across negotiating blocs to enable productive, principled discussion. In this instance, the combination of Western, Pakistani and Egyptian arguments (and Soviet support) proved sufficient to tip the outcome in favour of the modest form of Protocol II eventually adopted – with the whole broadly consistent with the prevalent 'rhetorically progressive' international normative Zeitgeist.[52]

Chapters 3 and 5 also suggest that, where there are sufficiently commonly shared values and principles to allow for reasoned debate, a 'logic of argument' is indeed likely to apply. In Chapter 3, for example, reluctant Western delegations were driven by principled Soviet bloc arguments to accept a more humanitarian position than they would otherwise have preferred, being unable to disown the high-sounding principles espoused during the Second World War. In a sense, the Soviet Union 'rhetorically entrapped' the Western allies by deploying arguments that the Western allies perceived themselves as having no choice but to endorse.[53]

The extent to which the Rome Statute reflects a 'logic of argument' has been considered in detail elsewhere, Nicole Deitelhoff in particular making the case that in key turning points in these negotiations 'arguments were taken into consideration only if they related to the effectiveness of the court'.[54] It bears adding, though, that a comparable dynamic is also evident in the negotiations over the internal armed conflict provisions of

[51] See Chapter 5, Sections 5.3.3, 5.4.4.
[52] See Chapter 4, Section 4.4.4.
[53] See Chapter 3, Section 3.4.4.
[54] Deitelhoff, 'The Discursive Process of Legalization: Charting Islands of Persuasion in the ICC Case', 59.

this treaty. Here opponents of a robust regime failed to rebut effectively principled arguments put forward by like-minded delegations and NGOs predicated on the greater likelihood of atrocities being committed in internal (rather than international) armed conflicts, and on post-Cold War legal developments consistent with criminalisation of war crimes in such conflicts.[55]

Chapter 5 also underlines the authoritative nature of supportive civil society legal analysis, suggesting that, where sufficiently robust, such views were likely to be endorsed by leading like-minded states and thus to have a bearing on drafting outcomes, albeit tempered by Realist and Rationalist considerations.[56] Last, it is also testament to the importance of argument that where P5 members were not of one voice in negotiations it was not sufficient merely to rely on their great power status to carry the day. Rather, for the US, UK and French delegations to garner support for their preferred positions, they also needed to engage in principled argument to persuade unconvinced delegations from materially less powerful states.[57]

In presenting the operation of this hypothesis in diagrammatic form it may be helpful to separate the proposition into two elements, given that the better argument seems likely to 'win out' only where there is a sufficiently broadly shared prior consensus amongst delegations as to the appropriate normative frame of reference. Figure 5 accordingly captures this dynamic by ascribing a prior, 'filtering' role to the extent to which arguments are nested in the broader normative setting – the Zeitgeist of negotiations.

In this revised diagram, the distinct contributions of moral authority and technical expertise to norm entrepreneurship are retained. In contrast to Figure 4, though, processes of 'principled contestation' have been disaggregated, distinguishing the extent to which arguments are nested in the Zeitgeist of negotiations from the process of principled contestation in which, all else being equal, the logically more compelling argument should 'win'. The key shift here is to highlight the filtering role of what might be termed 'Zeitgeist-consistency', to emphasise that even otherwise logically compelling arguments are unlikely to be effective, even when made by authoritative or technically expert agents, unless discursively nested within the broader normative context of negotiations.

[55] See Chapter 5, Section 5.4.4.
[56] Ibid., Sections 5.3.4, 5.4.3, 5.4.4.
[57] See e.g. the 'Bonn' debates prior to the Rome Conference (Chapter 5, Section 5.2.1). See also Chapter 5, Sections 5.3.2, 5.4.4.

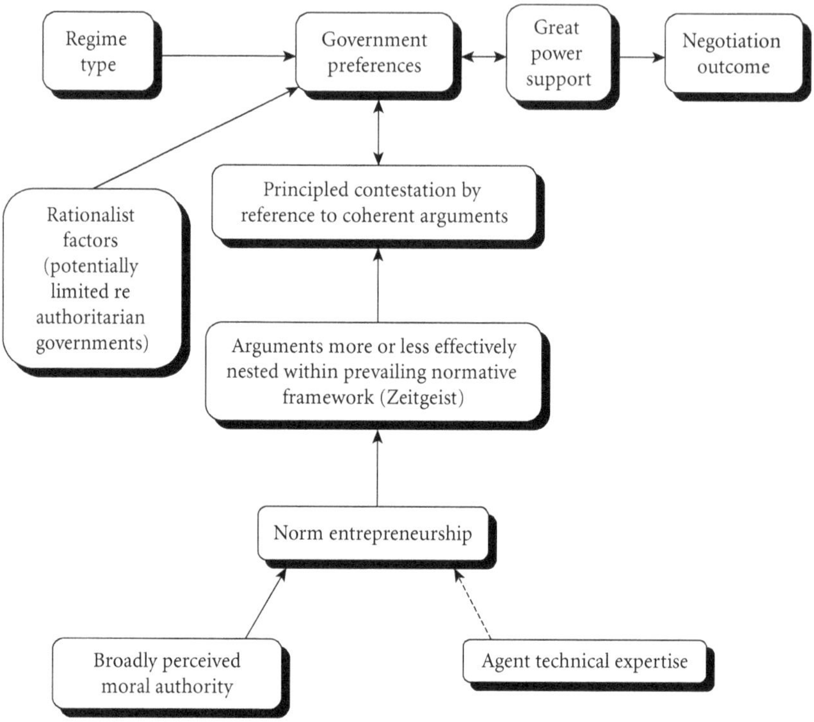

Figure 5: Mapping Interaction (Version 5)

6.1.5 The Regime Type Hypothesis

The fifth hypothesis set out in Chapter 1 is: 'democracies are more likely to support intrusive, restrictive civil war-regulating provisions than non-democracies'. This draws on liberal IR theory, itself reflecting a broader range of scholarship on the 'democratic peace', as well as the empirical observation that democracies have been in the forefront of other international humanitarian and human rights regimes.[58]

The current study reinforces the view that democracy per se is generally less salient to support for a robust civil war regime than a liberal political predisposition. That said, the case studies also suggest that even liberal democracy need not correlate particularly closely with support for

[58] See discussion at Chapter 1, Sections 1.1, 1.4.4, inc. references to Simmons, *Mobilizing for Human Rights: International Law in Domestic Politics;* Moravcsik, 'The New Liberalism'; Doyle, 'Three Pillars of the Liberal Peace'; Bass, *Stay the Hand of Vengeance: The Politics of War Crimes Tribunals;* Slaughter, 'International Law in a World of Liberal States'; Moravcsik, 'Liberalism and International Relations Theory'.

a more robust regime. On the contrary, the negotiation of Common Article 3 and the CDDH show that support for an ostensibly robust regime may be most forthcoming from non-democracies.

In the case of Common Article 3, for example, Western democracies such as the UK and the USA were more reluctant than Soviet bloc counterparts to endorse far-reaching provisions – informed by an assumption that the latter were embracing such provisions primarily to discomfit and discredit the former.[59] A similar dynamic appears to have been in play with respect to the drafting of Article 1(4) of Protocol I, where Western, liberal democracies were the principal opponents of the effort to accord wars of national liberation privileged status, ranged against both developing world and Soviet bloc support for this proposal. It also bears noting that not all democracies were of similar mind in this instance: Norway and India, for example, were prominent supporters of privileging wars of national liberation. Neither of these delegations seems to have been particularly concerned about the consequences of being required to observe the requirements potentially imposed, however, either domestically or elsewhere. The more conservative Western powers on the other hand, including the USA, UK and France, were rather more exercised by the potential implications of Article 1(4).[60]

In contrast, a relatively extensive form of Protocol II was supported by many of the same states that were reluctant to endorse Article 1(4), including conservative Western democracies, with some indications that this support reflected domestic liberal norms and public opinion. At the same time though, enthusiasm in this respect was tempered for some delegations by concerns over being required to live up to any commitments.[61] The analysis with respect to the drafting of the internal armed conflict provisions of the Rome Statute is similar in this regard, with stable, liberal democratic middle powers amongst the most progressive in the Like-Minded Group in respect of the regulation of war crimes in internal armed conflict, and Western great powers adopting a more tempered approach.[62] On this occasion, China and Russia also proved more reluctant to embrace demanding civil war-regulating provisions than might have been expected in light of 'Bad Ass' behaviour in other instances, potentially reflecting perceived compliance costs given the post-Cold War American 'Unipolar Moment' and flux in the systemic

[59] See Chapter 3, Section 3.4.5.

[60] See discussion at Chapter 4, Sections 4.3.1–4, 4.4.2, 4.4.5.

[61] See Chapter 4, Sections 4.3.1.1, 4.3.1.2, 4.4.5.

[62] See Chapter 5, Sections 5.3.1, 5.3.2.1–3.

distribution of power. Consistent with observations in respect of the Rationalist hypothesis, this suggests that while there may in many instances be significant differences in the approach to civil war regulation of more and less democratic states, it cannot be concluded that authoritarian states (even including great powers) will *necessarily* discount Rational implications of a potentially restrictive regime.[63]

The debates over Protocol II and the internal armed conflict provisions of the Rome Statute also highlight a reluctance on the part of some democracies – most notably India – to line up alongside liberal Western democracies in supporting a broadly (if ultimately less radical than some like-minded states might have preferred) progressive internal armed conflict regime.[64] In the former case this may be seen as reflecting a broader reluctance on the part of developing countries generally to support an extensive form of Protocol II.[65] In 1998, however, India appears to have been more marginalised, with other developing world delegations joining Western democracies in supporting a more robust set of provisions.[66] Taken together with the debates over Protocol II at the CDDH, this reinforces the view that democratic governance per se is at most only indirectly related to preferences with respect to the regulation of internal armed conflict.

That said, the case studies *do* lend support to the prevalence of a more fundamental relationship between the extent to which liberal values are embedded domestically (most obviously in stable, Western democracies) and the general readiness of democratic governments to support – albeit hesitantly in some cases, and in particular dependent on the domestic risks highlighted in the Rationalist hypothesis – a more demanding civil war regime. The focus on the 'liberal' rather than the 'democratic' aspects of 'liberal democracy' is, moreover, consistent with the argument put forward by Fareed Zakaria that these two concepts should be treated as distinct, notwithstanding that 'for almost a century in the West, democracy has meant liberal democracy'.[67]

[63] See discussion at Section 6.1.2, above.

[64] See Chapter 4, Section 4.4.5; Chapter 5, Section 5.4.5.

[65] Ibid., Sections 4.2.3, 4.3.3.

[66] See Chapter 5, Sections 5.2.2, 5.3.3, 5.4.5.

[67] See Zakaria, 'The Rise of Illiberal Democracy'. In similar vein, Ní Aoláin and Campbell refer to 'conflicted democracies': states that meet 'minimal requirements of procedural democracy' but that feature 'a deep seated and sharp division in the body politic, whether on ethnic, racial, religious, class, or ideological grounds' which 'must be so acute, and the political circumstances such as to have resulted in or threaten significant political violence' ('The Paradox of Transition in Conflicted Democracies', 176).

Questions still remain, of course, as to how best to conceptualise the essential characteristics of a 'liberal' polity.[68] Slaughter refers to 'liberal democracy', Zakaria juxtaposes illiberal democracy to 'constitutional liberalism', while Schmitter refers to 'real existing democracy'.[69] It is tempting to subject each of these concepts to further examination: for present purposes, though, it is sufficient to observe that socially embedded values – the extent to which liberal values are embedded domestically – appear to have trumped formal democratic governance structures in shaping government attitudes towards international regulation of civil war.[70]

In short, the case studies suggest that socially embedded 'liberal' values may be a better predictor of whether states are likely to be principled supporters of a robust civil war regime than the extent to which a polity might be considered formally more or less 'democratic' – though the views of even liberal states are still likely to be tempered by other considerations, including (as UK experiences in 1949 and 1974–7 highlight) Rationalist concerns.[71] The discussion also reinforces the view that authoritarian governments may lend 'Bad Ass' support to a more robust regime insofar as the potential costs of such support are perceived to be limited. Figure 6 accordingly takes the following form:

Figure 6, as with Figure 1, remains 'shorthand': an approximation of how a range of causal factors have combined and interacted over time in producing the civil war regime. In addition to providing an idealised, abstract representation of hypothesis interaction, however, Figure 6 and the preceding discussion also provide a valuable lens through which to revisit the discussions in Chapters 3, 4 and 5, directing attention to key aspects of the three cases where these factors can be seen to have interacted and combined to produce

[68] See also discussion at Chapter 1, Section 1.4.4.

[69] Slaughter defines 'liberal democracy' as 'some form of representative government secured by the separation of powers, constitutional guarantees of civil and political rights, juridical equality, and a functioning judicial system dedicated to the rule of law' (Slaughter, 'International Law in a World of Liberal States', 511). See also Schmitter, 'The Future of "Real-Existing" Democracy'.

[70] This approach is consistent with John Owen's definition of a 'liberal democracy' (in the context of a discussion of the democratic peace) as 'a state that instantiates liberal ideas, one where liberalism is the dominant ideology and citizens have leverage over war decisions ... those states with a visible liberal presence, and that feature free speech and regular competitive elections of the officials empowered to declare war'. In this view both liberal ideology and formally democratic institutions contribute to state behaviour ('How Liberalism Produces Democratic Peace', 89).

[71] See discussions in Chapter 3, Sections 3.3.1.1, 3.4.2; Chapter 4, Sections 4.3.1.2, 4.4.2.

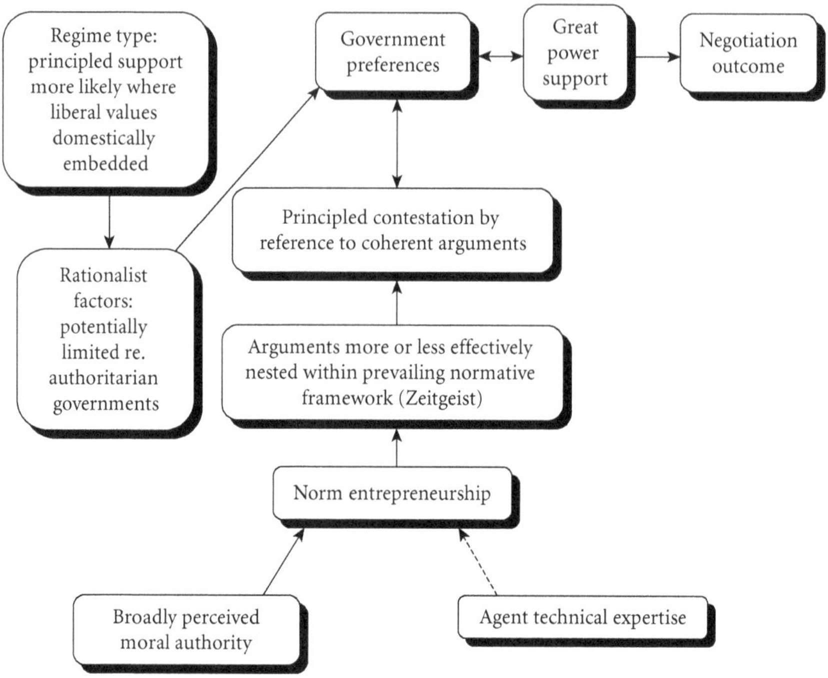

Figure 6: Mapping Interaction (Version 6)

drafting outcomes. The following section highlights and considers such interaction in the three cases.

6.2 Illustrating Interaction: Key Junctures Revisited

6.2.1 Common Article 3

Perhaps the most striking aspect of the drafting of Common Article 3 is the manner in which, against the backdrop of a progressive, humanitarian Zeitgeist, and facing 'Bad Ass' Soviet bloc opposition and a pragmatically inclined USA, the British and French delegations were forced to abandon their initially preferred positions in favour of a more measured, pragmatic stance. In this instance, neither the technical expertise of the colonial great powers, nor their 'P5' status proved sufficient to elicit significant support amongst negotiating partners for these initial positions, which ran against the grain of the prevailing normative backdrop.

Regime type also gave rise to a risk of the Western powers being hoisted by their own (liberal) petards, with concern in Whitehall about the UK being cast publicly as 'inhumane', and British moral authority further undermined at Geneva as observers highlighted inconsistencies between the sentiments and principles espoused by the Western Allies during the war and the rather less progressive British position at the diplomatic conference. Eventually recognising the shortcomings of such intransigence given the prevailing Zeitgeist, and the very strong likelihood of 'progressive development' of the law of internal armed conflict at Geneva, the British (and French) developed a compromise position capable of eliciting broader support from the 'smaller powers' and that would not alienate either the Soviet Union or the USA, belatedly evincing sufficient tactical awareness to build on French moral authority to promote a more humanitarian-flavoured form of drafting in the form of the French proposal of 15 June. Having in the meantime obtained the endorsement of the ICRC and widespread support from delegations of less powerful non-Soviet states, the Franco-British proposal subsequently saw off the more radical Soviet proposal of 8 July (and Burmese pleading) in the closing debates.

In short, consistent with Figure 6, having been 'outflanked' by Soviet humanitarianism and handicapped by domestic/liberal sensitivities (and limited British moral authority at Geneva), the French and British rationally retreated to a less intransigent position, more defensible on principled grounds and capable of eliciting broader support at the conference given the prevailing 'humanitarian' Zeitgeist. This 'discursively reassuring, but reassuringly undemanding' position subsequently proved capable of garnering broader (rational) support as a *texte de conciliation.*

6.2.2 *Additional Protocol I: Article 1(4)*

Critical aspects of the drafting of Article 1(4) of Additional Protocol I can equally be understood in terms of the interaction of the causal factors set out above. In 1974, as in 1949, the conservative West was on the defensive from the outset, with negotiations over what was to emerge as Article 1(4) largely shaped by the strongly held political preferences of developing world delegations in an international normative context where post-colonial rhetoric took precedence over legal substance. The latter group was also supported in this endeavour by the (again, rationally 'Bad Ass') Soviet bloc, and a small number of progressive Western democracies – Norway in the vanguard – with robustly 'humanitarian' foreign policies and minimal prospect of encountering internal armed conflict at home or abroad, including in colonial settings.

The British, with (again rational) concerns about the implications of drafting for Northern Ireland, were left fulminating on the sidelines about the failure of developing world counterparts to recognise the traditional distinction between *jus in bello* and *jus ad bellum*, unable to translate technical legal expertise into favourable outcomes given (once again) its impaired moral authority amongst the latter group reflecting the UK's former imperial pre-eminence and ongoing colonial entanglements. The US and French delegations laboured under similar challenges, in the former case primarily as a result of US embroilment in Vietnam. The UK, along with other conservative Western delegations, also failed to anticipate and frame arguments around the (perceived) radically 'rhetorically progressive' post-colonial expectations of developing world delegations. The ICRC – the traditional 'guardian' of the law of armed conflict – was similarly sidelined, poorly attuned to the heavily politicised atmosphere of the 1974 session of the CDDH and failing to engage effectively with the arguments of leading developing world delegations.

In contrast, the technical capacity of Georges Abi-Saab, coupled with Egyptian prestige and moral authority within the Non-Aligned Movement, and promoting a position closely aligned with the prevailing post-colonial normative environment, lent a tailwind to the initiative to treat 'wars of national liberation' as international armed conflicts for the purposes of Protocol I. With Aldrich's US delegation ultimately unwilling to die in the ditch of Article 1(4) in subsequent sessions, moreover, the UK and aligned WEOG delegations eventually had little (rational) choice but to accommodate the pragmatic American position – underlining the weakness of the former without superpower support. While this approach resulted in the inclusion within Protocol I of a range of drafting mitigants, Article 1(4) of Protocol I nevertheless still represented a significant diplomatic loss for the conservative West.

One of the abiding puzzles surrounding the drafting of Article 1(4) remains the question of why developing world delegations were so anxious to promote language that could potentially benefit future rebel movements in these states. The most plausible answer is that this provision was understood by its proponents as applying to only an exceedingly narrow range of cases. Indeed, this position appears to have underpinned the accommodating approach adopted by the US delegation to the drafting of Article 1(4) in subsequent sessions, with Aldrich continuing to advance this view after the conference. If this is indeed the case, then the potentially broader implications of the drafting aside, there is little to suggest that supportive delegations did not perceive themselves to be acting anything other than rationally in promoting Article 1(4). Indeed, the general sense gleaned from the drafting process is that the Zairean position, viewing the CDDH primarily as a means for 'further[ing] the cause of the liberation movements', is likely to have been widely, if not universally, shared amongst developing world delegations.

6.2.3 *Additional Protocol II: Threshold and Content*

If Article 1(4) characterised the general tenor of the 1974 session of the CDDH as a 'dialogue of the deaf' between the conservative West and the developing world, a more nuanced portrait emerges in the negotiation of Protocol II. Figure 6 again captures key dynamics in this process.

In contrast to the negotiation of Article 1(4), many developing world delegations were less supportive of an ambitious – or indeed, in some cases, any – form of Protocol II, reflecting discomfort with the prospect of enhanced protections for rebels, consistent with the Rationalist hypothesis. WEOG and Soviet bloc delegations, however, with little to fear domestically from the prospect of such regulation, proved generally more comfortable with this prospect. A small number of critical developing world delegations, principally Egypt and Pakistan, were also in the vanguard of this endeavour. Indeed, even the more conservative British were wary of being seen as opposed to strengthening the regulation of internal armed conflict, with concerns about Northern Irish tensions assuaged by the inclusion of a high threshold of application in draft Article 1 in 1975. The 1977 Pakistani draft was particularly welcome to the UK as it lessened the risk of a freestanding Western instrument being proposed that might have been less accommodating of British concerns about Northern Ireland.

The principal opponents of strengthening regulation of (traditionally conceived) internal armed conflict at the CDDH accordingly comprised developing world delegations. Nevertheless, the concerns of these delegations eventually proved susceptible to Egyptian and Pakistani 'norm entrepreneurship', underpinned by the technical and moral authority of these delegations being brought to bear in support of the revised Pakistan draft. The whole endeavour was also set in the same broadly 'rhetorically progressive' normative context that had fostered Article 1(4). Accordingly, with support from both superpower blocs, as well as more progressive Western delegations (notably Canada), Egypt and Pakistan ultimately persuaded the bulk of this group to endorse a form of Protocol II that would also be palatable to (most) WEOG and Soviet bloc counterparts, in the process sidelining 'monkey wrenchers' such as India. As with Common Article 3 before it, and again unsurprisingly, the end result of this process was the adoption of a form of Protocol II that was, while notionally progressive in humanitarian terms, equally reassuringly undemanding.

6.2.4 The Rome Statute: Shaping the Internal Armed Conflict Provisions

As noted above, the negotiation of the Rome Statute is commonly cited as a 'civil society victory' and as emblematic of the 'new diplomacy' of the 1990s. As Chapter 5 shows, though, civil society norm entrepreneurship provides at most a partial explanation for the final shape of the internal armed conflict provisions. Rather, a more rounded account of the drafting of these provisions can be obtained by considering how the relevant elements of Article 8 were produced by the interaction of a more diverse set of causal factors.

In this case, perhaps the most critical driver of drafting outcomes was the adoption by the Like-Minded Group of a robust 'cornerstone' position in respect of war crimes in internal armed conflict. Whereas this reflected a stated, principled commitment on the part of such states (and in many cases also dominant domestic norms as well as engagement with members of the NGO Coalition), for many of the governments concerned this was also a rational position given either low prospects of domestic unrest or democratic transition following civil conflict. The alignment of the domestically liberal Western P3 with the like-minded on this issue once the path was clear (post-Bonn) to a 'Cassese-proof' form of drafting, lent a further tailwind to the inclusion of a robust set of internal armed conflict provisions in the statute, especially set against the liberal post-Cold War normative Zeitgeist.

That said, the role of civil society should not be underestimated: the permeation of the conference (and, indeed, a number of national delegations) by such groups in the context of the 'new diplomacy' lent significant weight to the activities of NGOs in shaping the internal armed conflict provisions of the Rome Statute. Indeed, the combination of expert and morally authoritative non-governmental and like-minded state norm entrepreneurship closely aligned with the prevailing Zeitgeist leaves the impression that the inclusion in the final instrument of a relatively robust – if not as demanding as some would have preferred – set of internal armed conflict provisions was not particularly in doubt at any time during negotiations. Indeed, those delegations particularly opposed to such a regime were marginalised discursively in negotiations, reflecting both the technical skills and moral weight of like-minded delegations and aligned civil society groups, and the challenges encountered by their opponents in rhetorically nesting their positions within the prevailing liberal, 'human security' oriented Zeitgeist.

Conclusion

The discussion above rounds out the three case studies presented in the preceding chapters. Figure 6 presents in schematic form the relationships between the various causal factors highlighted in these chapters as contributing to the design of the civil war regime, revisiting Figure 1 from Chapter 1 in light of the case studies to provide a more nuanced representation of hypothesis interaction. 6.2 then illustrates how the patterns of interaction set out in Figure 6 can be seen in the negotiation of Common Article 3, Article 1(4) of Protocol I, the threshold and scope of Protocol II, and the internal armed conflict provisions of the Rome Statute.

It bears underlining that the schema set out in Figure 6 is necessarily simplified: whereas the portrait above suggests a range of relationships between factors, in practice each of the factors identified has been more and less evident at a range of points in time throughout drafting processes. Equally, each of these factors could be further broken down to provide yet more detailed, albeit also potentially more complex, portrayals and analyses of different aspects of these negotiations.

That said, in bringing together the findings from the case studies, the discussion nevertheless presents a strong case for the relevance of the factors identified in together shaping the civil war regime. Great power preferences, as we have seen, have played an important part in – effectively – limiting the range of possible drafting outcomes in each instance. The 'filtering' role of the Zeitgeist of negotiations – the broader international normative backdrop – also performs a similar, indeed arguably more fundamental constraining function, dramatically lowering the likelihood of drafting outcomes that are not consistent with broader international legal and discursive trends.

We have also seen how state preferences – both going into negotiations and as these have evolved during debates – have been shaped by a range of both exogenous and endogenous factors. Indeed, even when some national preferences – as with Article 1(4) – may not initially appear to reflect Rationalist considerations, on closer examination rational drivers of both initial and revised preferences become evident for all governments considered. The behaviour of liberal democratic states has also been affected by domestic ideational considerations making it difficult for the delegations of such states to entirely disown a broadly 'progressive' approach to regime design, even where – as with the British and French in 1949 – pressing security concerns militate in favour of a more conservative vision.

In contrast, powerful authoritarian states – particularly the USSR during the Cold War – have shown a greater tendency to discount potential compliance costs of a notionally more demanding regime, rather favouring a 'Bad Ass' approach to regime design where support for a more progressive set of rules serves more critical interests, including in the Soviet case strengthening relationships with 'non-aligned' developing world governments. More broadly moreover, overall design outcomes in each case can also be viewed as 'rational', reflecting a balance of the preferences of more and less progressively inclined governments as these have emerged during the negotiation process: indeed, this dynamic can even be seen in respect of Article 1(4), where more conservative Western delegations succeeded in inserting a range of amelioratory measures elsewhere in Protocol I.

At the same time, delegation preferences – including those of great powers – have also been shaped endogenously by and during the process of negotiations. All three cases illustrate how actors perceived by interlocutors as possessing strong moral authority and/or specialist technical expertise have been able to shape the course of diplomatic debates, with the former arguably the more critical of these attributes, enabling 'norm entrepreneurs' to persuade other delegations to accept one or another favoured position, framing arguments by reference to broadly accepted principles and values, themselves reflecting the broader Zeitgeist of negotiations.

More generally, the preceding discussion illustrates the benefits of the eclectic, problem-driven perspective adopted in *Negotiating Civil War*. This approach has enabled a broad-ranging yet also detailed examination of factors and processes that have shaped the civil war regime. It has sought to strike a balance between emphasising a minimal number of (potentially under-specified) material, ideational, social, and/or strategic factors, and a more granular, but potentially narrower, focus on more finely distinguished factors and micro-processes.

This is not, of course, to claim that either the theoretical perspective adopted, or the empirical portrayal provided, necessarily provides the last word on the design of the civil war regime: further investigation into the design and operation (or not) of these provisions remains critical. With this last in mind, the following, concluding discussion accordingly highlights the key arguments and findings of the present study, sets this examination in the context of related, ongoing debates, and identifies potential implications and lessons for international law and IR scholars and practitioners.

Conclusion

The Puzzling Civil War Regime

What explains the measures that states have collectively designed to set appropriate standards of behaviour in internal armed conflict? While the broad contours of the historical record are relatively clear, on closer examination it rapidly becomes evident that the design of the civil war regime cannot be explained satisfactorily by reference solely to presumed determinants of self-interested, rational behaviour, disparities in material power amongst states, domestic politics or culture, normative context, or social processes and/or characteristics of participating actors alone – or, indeed, by a subset of one or two such factors. Seeking to explain the overall shape of the civil war regime in this manner is highly unlikely to render a satisfying account, even where some aspects of negotiations might reflect the operation of one or another of these factors.

This need not mean, though, that the civil war regime is not susceptible to theoretically informed analysis: indeed, IR theory has an impressive record of shedding light on the shape and significance of international legal regimes. The multiplicity of theoretical perspectives represented in contemporary International Relations (and International Law) scholarship, however underlines both the advantages of adopting a pluralist theoretical lens in examining the civil war regime, as well as the need to exercise caution in constructing such a lens. *Negotiating Civil War* has accordingly sought to provide a rounded, nuanced, portrait of the emergence of this regime, leveraging the explanatory capacity of carefully selected theoretical propositions derived from mainstream IR research traditions.

The following discussion assesses the extent to which this endeavour has been successful, and identifies wider lessons that can be derived. The first section sets out the key findings from the case studies and the examination overall. The second section sets *Negotiating Civil War* in the context of related bodies of research and considers scholarly and practical implications. The final section draws the volume to a close.

Findings and Implications

Theoretical Pluralism and the Civil War Regime

The development of the civil war regime can be perceived differently through different theoretical lenses. It is possible to imagine, for example, a variety of distinct realist, rationalist (including neo-liberal institutionalist), liberal and constructivist analyses of this phenomenon, each undertaken by reference to paradigm-specific concepts, logics and mechanisms. As observed above, however, the analytic payoff from such a narrow approach is likely to be limited. Adopting what might be termed a 'conservatively eclectic' theoretical approach, therefore, *Negotiating Civil War* has sought to navigate – and demonstrate the value of – a reasoned middle way between the Scylla of blinkered adherence to a single research tradition, and the Charybdis of 'everything goes' kitchen-sink theorising.

With a view to pragmatically maximising analytic leverage, moreover, this approach has remained open-ended: bounded ex ante by concepts and mechanisms developed in the relevant theoretical schools, yet permitting the identification in the empirical record of other factors that have contributed to regime development. This has enabled *Negotiating Civil War* to examine the impact on drafting outcomes, respectively, of great power preferences; rational cost/benefit analysis; norm entrepreneur characteristics; the extent to which arguments made in negotiations reflect widely shared values and principles – as well as the filtering role of the broader international normative Zeitgeist – and domestic governance. It has also permitted interaction amongst these factors in shaping outcomes to be mapped in individual instances and in aggregate.

The fundamental argument made in this volume is that adopting Chapter 1's tailored, 'conservatively eclectic' approach to theorising about the design of the civil war regime should generate a balanced, nuanced – and ultimately persuasive – account of the design of the civil war regime. The extent to which *Negotiating Civil War* is persuasive remains a matter of opinion: the previous chapters, however, demonstrate the capacity of this theoretical lens to help make sense of the contours of the civil war regime – as a means, in other words, of 'ordering the facts of the world'.[1] This can be seen in the extent to which *Negotiating Civil War* sheds light on each of the individual case studies as well as on the overall development of the civil war regime.

Pluralism in Practice I: 1949, 1974–7, 1998

With respect to the negotiation of Common Article 3, Chapters 3 and 6 together illustrate the manner in which the emergence of this provision during the 1949 diplomatic conference can be rendered comprehensible by reference to the factors underlying the five hypotheses presented in Chapter 1, and to processes of interaction amongst these.

In particular, these chapters highlight how the impact of initial, rationally derived UK and French preferences on drafting outcomes was limited in a discursive and political environment where these views were significantly out of step with the prevalent international humanitarian Zeitgeist, with strong countervailing support from the Soviet bloc for a more progressive vision of civil war regulation, and only limited backing from the USA. The former delegations were also constrained by the liberal rhetorical legacy of the Second World War, with the positive reception of the final French-proposed form of drafting (arrived at after rational re-evaluation by the French and British) reflecting French post-1945 moral authority – an area in which the technically specialist British were more handicapped – and recognition on the part of the French and British of the need to elicit broader support from 'smaller powers'. Chapter 3 also illustrates how the ICRC was able to utilise its technical expertise to reinforce its post-war moral authority during the drafting process of the 1949 Conventions, with the Committee ultimately also putting its weight behind the French proposal.

The interaction of these factors can be seen again in the processes of drafting Article 1(4) of Additional Protocol I and Additional Protocol II. As Chapter 4 and the related discussions in Chapter 6 illustrate, the

[1] As Jackson puts it: '[i]t is immaterial whether those analytical narratives are based in rational-choice, social-mechanistic, or discursive practice ideal-typifications of social action; in all of these cases, what researchers do is to order analytically the empirical data in accord with a model the worth of which lies not in its correspondence to the world, but in its pragmatic consequences for ordering the facts of the world' (*The Conduct of Inquiry in International Relations: Philosophy of Science and Its Implications for the Study of World Politics*, 115).

former provision primarily reflects the views of developing world delegations, with Egyptian technical leadership and moral authority bolstered by Soviet bloc support and a broader progressive international 'normative tailwind'. The US-led, conservative West was in contrast marginalised in the 1974 debates, with impaired moral authority in the eyes of developing world counterparts, and (along with the ICRC) delegations that were poorly equipped to address the developing world effort to categorise wars of national liberation as international armed conflicts.

The negotiation of Protocol II, in contrast, reflects a clearer confluence of rational interests. In this instance, the majority of developing world delegations (led by Pakistan), the Soviet bloc and the conservative West found common ground in a high threshold provision (Article 1) and, in 1977, a minimally demanding set of provisions for the remainder of the Protocol, with the overall endeavour set in the same international normative context as in 1974. In contrast to 1974, however, the identification of discursive middle ground between the various blocs marginalised more radical developing world and Western delegations, enabling the delivery of an instrument that was both satisfyingly progressive, yet reassuringly undemanding.

In similar fashion, the internal armed conflict provisions of the Rome Statute can be explained by a combination of principled support from technically and morally authoritative like-minded and civil society delegations for a demanding war crimes regime, tempered in Bonn and Rome by Western P3 preferences, but also shaped by the interventions of delegations of states in democratic transition following civil wars. This endeavour was also, again, lent a normative tailwind by a liberal post-Cold War normative Zeitgeist, marginalising dissenting delegations.

These examples shed valuable light on the circumstances surrounding the emergence of the civil war regime, helping to make sense both of the doctrinal features of these measures, as well as the subsequent manner in which governments and civil society have sought to operationalise them (or not). They each also, moreover, highlight the principal virtue of the 'conservatively eclectic' theoretical lens applied in *Negotiating Civil War*: the ability to generate a nuanced yet rounded account of the development of the civil war regime, not merely highlighting the manner in which drafting outcomes were shaped by the various factors considered but also illustrating in individual cases and in aggregate how these factors interacted in producing these outcomes.

Pluralism in Practice II: 'Hypothetical' Implications

The case studies and Chapter 6 also enable a range of observations to be made about the contributions of the various factors identified in shaping the civil war regime.

With respect to the role of great powers in producing treaty outcomes, the case studies suggest that while outcomes may rarely have directly reflected great power preferences alone, some measure of great power support has been – in effect – a necessary condition for the adoption of treaty provisions. This has put great powers at an advantage compared to delegations from materially less powerful states in negotiations, but within constraints, particularly as other factors have had distinct bearings on individual and collective preference formation. Perhaps most importantly, the emergence of the civil war regime through multiple rounds of treaty negotiation illustrates that smaller states could not be taken for granted in these negotiations – and that great powers have proven best able to promote their preferences when they have recognised this.

In a similar vein, while the functionalist logic underlying the Rationalist hypothesis can be seen in operation in aspects of each of the case studies, this logic has not applied in a uniform manner across the cases. The bestowal of asymmetric benefits on would-be rebels does appear to have caused particular concern – consistent with the Rationalist proposition – amongst conservative Western delegations in both 1949 and 1974–7, and amongst developing world delegations in 1977 (if not 1974). Consistent with the second element of the hypothesis, delegations of states in democratic transition were also particularly strong supporters of more robust civil war regulation, most obviously in the 1998 Rome Statute negotiations. In all three case studies, moreover – albeit less obviously in respect of Article 1(4) (see below) – outcomes can generally be viewed as striking broadly 'rational' balances amongst the various tendencies represented in negotiations.

However, the Rationalist hypothesis provides only limited substantive insight, into delegation behaviour in a number of instances. Reconciling developing world promotion of Article 1(4) of Protocol I with this logic presents a challenge. Similarly, the behaviour of Soviet bloc delegations in 1949 and at the CDDH can be viewed as rational only insofar as these states discounted compliance costs. The extent to which drafting is relatively more or less restrictive or intrusive, moreover, also provides only minimal insight into the drivers of attitudes towards civil war regulation, particularly for more progressive Western ('Nordic'-type) states with very low likelihoods of domestic unrest.

Form of domestic governance – regime type – alone has also proven a relatively poor predictor of delegation preferences. As noted above, liberal democracies and democracies-in-transition were in many cases – that is, subject to the concerns set out in the 'Rationalist' hypothesis – strong advocates of robust provision. Less democratic states were also prime movers behind many provisions, however, with the Soviet bloc strongly supportive of demanding language for Common Article 3, joined by developing country delegations with respect to Article 1(4) of Protocol I. India was also a prominent democratic outlier with respect to Protocol II and the Rome Statute.

Given Slaughter's explicit focus on 'liberal democracy', this finding is not necessarily indicative of any deep-seated issues with her vision of 'international law in a world of liberal states'.[2] It is nonetheless potentially telling that basic domestic normative orientations (such as a commitment to liberal values) proved a better predictor of behaviour in respect of civil war regulation than formal democratic governance, and that even Western democracies ultimately behaved 'rationally' in terms of giving priority to fundamental domestic concerns in negotiations.

In contrast, the moral authority of norm entrepreneurs has been rather more salient to negotiation outcomes, the case studies suggesting that the extent to which norm entrepreneurs were perceived by negotiating interlocutors as possessing moral authority mattered more in the negotiation of the civil war regime than the ability of these actors to deploy technical expertise in a given issue area. Nevertheless, as the case of Article 1(4) illustrates, even delegations of bodies widely considered to wield significant moral authority – such as the ICRC – still struggled to persuade representatives of other states to adopt a preferred course of action where their arguments were not nested effectively in the normative Zeitgeist of negotiations.

Lastly, however, even where an argument is compelling from a principled perspective, norm entrepreneurs have still needed to take into account (and on occasion to temper positions to accommodate) great power preferences in order to ensure (preferably more rather than less) great power support for drafting proposals. This is not to claim that great powers have been able to rely solely on their preponderance of material power to ensure their preferences prevail in respect of civil war-

[2] 'International Law in a World of Liberal States'.

regulating treaty provisions – though this has been the case where all great powers have been aligned and committed to a given position. Rather it is to recognise that, in common with representatives of other states, delegations of great powers have needed to engage in processes of principled contestation with those of less materially powerful actors, but that great powers have retained outsized influence on treaty outcomes, reflecting the ability of these states to influence the operational prospects and legitimacy of treaty outputs.

The above observations, both in respect of the form of theoretical pluralism adopted, and in respect of the shaping of the civil war regime, are strictly limited to the particular context of *Negotiating Civil War*. None of these is necessarily generalisable to other contexts, and no attempt has been made to identify or assert universal truths applicable in other instances or issue areas. This said, though, it is possible to identify a number of insights from *Negotiating Civil War* that may helpfully inform future scholarship and practice. The following section accordingly situates this volume in a broader scholarly context, and considers potential practical implications for the conduct of international affairs.

Negotiating Civil War in Theory and Practice

Scholarly Setting and Implications

Negotiating Civil War straddles International Law and International Relations (IR): as such, it sits within and contributes to debates across these fields. Perhaps most critically, however, it broadens and deepens understanding of the political factors that have shaped the civil war regime. This regime has, of course, been extensively examined from doctrinal and historical perspectives, with many of these studies valuably informing *Negotiating Civil War*.[3] It is only relatively recently, though, that IR scholars have begun to focus attention on the politics of the design and operation of the civil war regime.[4]

[3] See discussion in Introduction.

[4] See e.g. Hyeran Jo, *Compliant Rebels: Rebel Groups and International Law in World Politics*; various contributions to Matthew Evangelista and Nina Tannenwald (eds.), *Do the Geneva Conventions Matter?* More generally, Jason Lyall has observed a 'meteoric rise of research on civil war' ('Process Tracing, Causal Inference, and Civil War', 187.) Though, for an earlier precursor, see Abbott, 'International Relations Theory, International Law, and the Regime Governing Atrocities in Internal Conflicts', 361–79.

The exemplary work of Giovanni Mantilla arguably leads the way in respect of the design of the civil war regime. While providing a rich account of the design of key elements of the regime (primarily Common Article 3 and the 1977 Additional Protocols), Mantilla nevertheless recognises that the micro-mechanisms he highlights – (social) forum isolation and (rational) covert pushback – are insufficient to explain the overall shape of civil war-regulating treaty measures.[5] *Negotiating Civil War*, in contrast, seeks to provide a more comprehensive, yet still detailed, account of the civil war regime, examining the role in regime design of a broader set of factors derived from mainstream IR research traditions, navigating a '*via media* between overly macro- and micro-conceptualisations of causal mechanisms'.[6]

Negotiating Civil War also forms part of a growing interdisciplinary literature on the design and operation of international legal regimes and institutions more generally. Prominent studies have considered, for example, the design and operation of international human rights and humanitarian law and trade regimes.[7] Another body of literature focuses on the design and operation of international courts.[8] Reflecting the

[5] See discussion at 'Forum Isolation: Social Opprobrium and the Origins of the International Law of Internal Conflict', 330–1 ('[N]ot all states are equally vulnerable to opprobrium on all issues at all times, and not all that are isolated in negotiations cave to social pressure'). See also generally Mantilla, 'Conforming Instrumentalists: Why the USA and the United Kingdom Joined the 1949 Geneva Conventions', 483–511; Mantilla, 'Under (Social) Pressure: The Historical Regulation of Internal Armed Conflicts through International Law'.

[6] See Chapter 1, Section 1.6.

[7] See e.g. Bower, *Norms without the Great Powers: International Law and Changing Social Standards in World Politics*; Koremenos, *The Continent of International Law: Explaining Agreement Design*; Cho, *The Social Foundations of World Trade: Norms, Community, and Constitution*; Dill, *Legitimate Targets? Social Construction, International Law and US Bombing*; Hillebrecht, *Domestic Politics and International Human Rights Tribunals: The Problem of Compliance*; Morrow, *Order within Anarchy: The Laws of War as an International Institution*; Risse, Ropp and Sikkink (eds.), *The Persistent Power of Human Rights: From Commitment to Compliance*; Sikkink, *The Justice Cascade: How Human Rights Prosecutions Are Changing World Politics*; Simmons, *Mobilizing for Human Rights: International Law in Domestic Politics*; Risse, Ropp and Sikkink (eds.), *The Power of Human Rights*.

[8] See e.g. Rudolph, *Power and Principle: The Politics of International Criminal Courts*; Alter, *The New Terrain of International Law: Courts, Politics, Rights*; Bosco, *Rough Justice: The International Criminal Court's Battle to Fix the World, One Prosecution at a Time*; Simmons and Danner, 'Credible Commitments and the International Criminal Court', 225–56; Deitelhoff, 'The Discursive Process of Legalization: Charting Islands of Persuasion in the ICC Case', 33–65; Schiff, *Building the International Criminal Court*; Bass, *Stay the Hand of Vengeance: The Politics of War Crimes Tribunals*.

diverse subject matter, the authors of these studies have also embraced a variety of methodologies and theoretical approaches. Barbara Koremenos' 'Continent of International Law', for example, highlights the extent to which treaty provisions across issue areas can be viewed as reflecting rationalist insights.[9] In contrast, Adam Bower examines the capacity of a (constructivist) 'social theory of treaty influence' in respect of the operation of the Ottawa Mine Ban Treaty and the International Criminal Court, while Gary Bass and Courtney Hillebrecht have examined the role of domestic politics in shaping the design of international criminal courts, and government compliance with international human rights tribunals.

Work in this vein is not limited to applying elements of IR theory to international legal puzzles. Karen Alter's 'New Terrain of International Law' is a 'theory-generating exercise' informed by a wide-ranging body of empirical and theoretical work on international courts, while Yuval Shany draws on organisational studies literature in setting out a 'goal-based approach' to assessing international tribunal effectiveness.[10] Literature on the broader 'politics' and 'political economy' of international law similarly abounds within that discipline, including in respect of international humanitarian law.[11]

Despite this flourishing literature, however, IR-theory derived pluralist accounts of the creation and operation of international legal regimes and institutions remain rare.[12] Accordingly, in embracing a range of theoretically derived potential explanantia of international legal regime design,

[9] See in similar vein James Morrow's work on international humanitarian law: Morrow, *Order within Anarchy: The Laws of War as an International Institution.*

[10] See Alter, *The New Terrain of International Law:* Courts, Politics, Rights; Shany, *Assessing the Effectiveness of International Courts.* There is, in addition, a broad literature considering sociological approaches to (and implications of) international law and courts. See e.g. Hirsch and Lang (eds.), *Research Handbook on the Sociology of International Law.*

[11] See e.g Benvenisti and Lustig, 'Taming Democracy: Codifying the Laws of War to Restore the European Order, 1856–1874'; Kennedy, *Of War and Law*; Mégret, 'From "Savages" to "Unlawful Combatants": A Postcolonial Look at International Humanitarian Law's "Other"', 265–317.

[12] Dunoff and Pollack, in the introductory chapter to their eponymous interdisciplinary volume, recognise that: "[i]ncreasingly ... IR and IL scholars have called for approaches that are more problem-driven, less theory-driven, and more open to considering that the realities of international law and international politics may reflect power-politics considerations associated with realism, functional concerns associated with institutionalism, domestic/international interactions associated with liberalism, and normative or ideational processes emphasized by constructivists' (Dunoff and Pollack, 'International Law and International Relations: Introducing an Interdisciplinary Dialogue', 12). Though the volume provides a singularly impressive overview of the interdisciplinary 'state of the art',

starting from the presumption that each of these is likely to assist in understanding important elements of treaty negotiation processes, *Negotiating Civil War* provides a potentially valuable 'conservatively eclectic' template for analysis of the design and operation of other legal regimes and institutions.

Avenues for Further Research

While empirically rich, the account of civil war regime development presented in *Negotiating Civil War* is also inevitably partial. Empirically, the account is constrained by the availability of primary and secondary material from only a limited range of sources (and, accordingly, perspectives), as well as by the temporal focus on the conduct of negotiations, with only limited consideration of post-negotiation ratification, adherence and compliance behaviour. That said, even the limited picture provided of regime development gives rise to a number of avenues for potential further investigation.

One such area is the extent to which civil war-regulating treaty outcomes (or, indeed, such outcomes in other contexts) might reflect potentially more fundamental relationships and dependencies amongst hypothesised factors: for instance whether particular constellations of domestic political factors, such as a 'liberal' character, may tend to contribute to or constrain governments' perceived moral authority, or the extent to which governments foster technical expertise. Similarly, the most technically adept civil society organisations mentioned in the study – Amnesty International, Human Rights Watch, the ICRC – continue to be based in and have close affiliations with governments of Western, politically liberal, economically developed states. Building on existing work on the operation and efficacy of transnational civil society – and with an eye in particular to the experience of the ICRC at the CDDH – it may be valuable to explore further how the efficacy of such organisations and networks is affected by the extent to which participating governments view civil society interlocutors as politically or culturally 'home-grown'.[13]

each of the chapters in the section on 'Theorising International Law' focuses – in traditional fashion – on IR's main 'theoretical camps' (at pp. 59–172).

[13] The scope for such fundamental relationships is consistent with the characterisation of the various hypotheses as underlain by 'causal factors' rather than (IR's more traditionally conceived) 'independent variables'.

It may also be valuable to consider further how best to conceptualise and operationalise what has been referred to in *Negotiating Civil War* as the broader normative 'Zeitgeist' of negotiations. This concept has been understood in the present study as effectively subsumed within the Habermasian concept of the 'lifeworld' of negotiations: it is possible, however, to conceive of this concept and its operation from multiple perspectives. A distinction might be drawn, for example, between dominant sets of fundamental ideas and beliefs constituting relatively fixed normative backdrops to negotiations amongst different groups of delegations, and the presence or absence of sufficient shared understandings across such groups about the appropriate normative frame of reference for a given discussion.

With respect to the former, it may be plausible to conceive of a systemic 'distribution of norms' – perhaps forming part of the broader ideational structure of international politics as conceived by Alexander Wendt – mirroring Waltz's 'distribution of power' in such a fashion that individual negotiations may be viewed as reflecting the ascent of one set of norms supported by (and constituting) one set of actors and the decline of another set of norms.[14] The Zeitgeist in this conception would be formed by this 'distribution of norms': the success of the Like-Minded Group in embedding progressive norms in the Rome Statute, for example, may be understood as reflecting the dominance of 'liberal' norms in the post-Cold War international system, and the decline of less conducive Cold War-associated norms.

Equally, there are other perspectives from which the development of collective normative understandings may be examined. Chapter 4 highlights, for example, the extent to which negotiations at the CDDH were hampered by the absence of consensus as to the appropriate frame of reference for debates about civil war regulation. With this in mind, it may be interesting to consider what factors are germane to the development over time of such shared understandings. Given, moreover, that 'practices always rest on an engagement with the world inherited from past interactions, and framed by social configurations', this may be an aspect of negotiations particularly well-suited to examination drawing on IR's recent 'practice turn'.[15]

[14] See Wendt, *Social Theory of International Politics*; Waltz, *Theory of International Politics*.

[15] See Pouliot, *International Security in Practice: The Politics of NATO–Russia Diplomacy*, 231. As Pouliot and Cornut observe, in a 'practice theory of diplomacy . . . what diplomats of all stripes do, and the ways in which they perform their trade, is taken to be basis for

The study is also illustrative more generally of the value of providing space in empirical analysis to identify unanticipated factors that have played an important – even if highly context-specific – part in shaping events. An increase in the number of states participating in negotiations, for example, appears to have led to a more complex set of negotiations at the CDDH than in 1949 not only owing to the greater numbers involved, but rather given the 'post-colonial' political predilections of the governments of many of the new states. Indeed, the rise of the 'Third World' and the Non-Aligned Movement in the 1970s and of associated anti-colonialist discourse in the UN context appears to have been a prime explanans of the difficulties encountered by conservative Western powers at the CDDH.

Similarly, the end of the Cold War presaged a dramatic shift in the relative material strength of the (former) Soviet Union and the USA, leading to a period of US dominance and Russian weakness in both material and ideational terms. The associated ascendance of liberal norms – a shift in the systemic 'distribution of norms' – was a significant factor in the negotiation of the Rome Statute, while Soviet collapse in 1989 also likely contributed to Russian hesitation to support robust, ostensibly demanding 'humanitarian' provisions that the Soviet Union in its heyday may well have supported simply to highlight the hesitant nature of Western support.[16]

This is not to attempt to construct universally applicable, covering law-type propositions in respect of the Zeitgeist, or any other factors that have shaped international law on different occasions. Rather, it is to underline the value of a carefully constructed theoretically eclectic lens in generating: 'complex causal stories that . . . lie somewhere between context-sensitive descriptive narratives and universal theories or models . . . [T]he particular attributes of a context influence the specific configuration of mechanisms and logics that generate distinctive processes and outcomes.'[17]

explaining world politics' ('Practice Theory and the Study of Diplomacy: A Research Agenda', 303).

16 The above are, of course, only two of the more apparent sets of background factors that may have had a bearing on negotiation outcomes: other factors, such as cumulative and collective learning processes, may also have contributed to the paths of negotiations at different periods.

17 Sil and Katzenstein, *Beyond Paradigms: Analytic Eclecticism in the Study of World Politics*, 208. This view is, moreover, redolent of Waltz's 1959 observation that: '[the assertion] that all causes may be inter-related, is an argument against assuming that there is a single cause that can be isolated by analysis and eliminated or controlled by wisely constructed

3. *Lessons and Implications for Practice (and Practitioners)*

Negotiating Civil War is a social-scientific endeavour, written in an academic context, with findings that – as noted above – are not necessarily generalisable. This does not mean, however, that practical lessons cannot be derived from the study: two such points in particular bear noting.

The first implication of *Negotiating Civil War* is doctrinal. Practitioners and scholars of international law have puzzled for decades over the meaning and implications of the differing thresholds and content of the treaty regimes governing international and internal armed conflict: indeed, the suggestion in *Tadić* that '[w]hat is inhumane, and consequently proscribed, in international wars, cannot but be inhumane and inadmissible in civil strife' can be considered a judicial attempt to cut through these complex, knotty issues.[18] As *Negotiating Civil War* makes clear, a concern for doctrinal coherence (let alone consistency) was not necessarily uppermost in the minds of those drafting these provisions. This does not obviate the need for civil war-regulating treaty provisions to be interpreted by those seeking to rely on or operationalise them. The negotiating histories do, though, counsel against placing too much reliance on the official *travaux preparatoires* in seeking to discern drafters' intentions.[19] This is not to argue that international law should adhere to doctrinal originalism: it is, rather, to observe that recourse to drafters' intentions to inform the interpretation of international legal instruments is an endeavour to be undertaken with care, and (by corollary) that claims to have discerned such intentions should be treated with caution.

policy. It is also an argument against working with one or several hypotheses without bearing in mind the interrelation of all causes. The prescriptions directly derived from a single image are incomplete because they are based in partial analyses. The partial quality of each image sets up a tension that drives one towards inclusion of the others' (*Man, the State and War*, 229–30).

18 Prosecutor v. Duško Tadić aka 'Dule' (Decision on the Defence Motion for Interlocutory Appeal on Jurisdiction) IT-94-1 (International Criminal Tribunal for the Former Yugoslavia, 2 October 1995). See Danner, 'When Courts Make Law: How the International Criminal Tribunals Recast the Laws of War', 1. See also Zamir, *Classification of Conflicts in International Humanitarian Law: The Legal Impact of Foreign Intervention in Civil Wars*; Cullen, *The Concept of Non-International Armed Conflict in International Humanitarian Law*; La Haye, *War Crimes in Internal Armed Conflicts*.

19 See Vienna Convention on the Law of Treaties (1969, UN Doc. A/Conf.39/27; 1155 UNTS 331), Articles 31(4), 32.

There is also a wider set of lessons that may be derived from *Negotiating Civil War* for government policymakers and officials designing and implementing multilateral negotiating strategies in other contexts. Again, the findings of *Negotiating Civil War* are not designed to be generalisable, and no two sets of intergovernmental or multilateral (let alone multilateral treaty) negotiations are alike. Reflecting the volume's 'conservatively eclectic' theoretical lens, however, if IR's 'mainstream theoretical camps' are indeed together capable of shedding light on important elements of state behaviour in the context of multilateral diplomatic, particularly treaty, negotiations, it may not be unreasonable to suggest that 'Rationalist' and 'Regime-type' factors may be expected to form a relatively fixed de facto set of constraints for policymakers on all sides in such negotiations. In contrast though, policymakers and advising officials are likely to have more leeway in terms of developing and presenting arguments to bolster a preferred position.

In such cases, *Negotiating Civil War* suggests that policymakers will be best served by seeking to maximise and leverage the moral authority of the entities they represent, and by being sensitive to prevailing normative and discursive winds in formulating and presenting views. At the same time, however, whether representing a more or less materially powerful state, delegation members would also be well advised to pay close attention to the preferences and requirements of the most powerful states in the international system.[20]

This is not a deterministic claim: circumstances and negotiation participants will differ widely across fields, and the salience of causal factors is likely to be highly context-dependent. That said, the case studies in the present volume together highlight that delegations have been most effective in shaping civil war regime treaty measures not when they have been technically expert or even when representing great powers, but when exercising moral authority, and when arguments have tacked with prevailing normative winds.

Wrapping up: Making Sense of the Civil War Regime

Negotiating Civil War has sought to explain why the civil war regime developed as it did between 1949 and 1998, applying an eclectic

[20] This is not to say, however, that negotiators need necessarily avoid antagonising great powers: each of the P5 save for France has at one or another time found itself on the losing side of debate in civil war regime design negotiations.

theoretical approach to a structured, focused comparison of three case studies of treaty negotiations from 1949, 1974–7 and 1998. The principal findings are summarised above along with scholarly and practical implications.

These findings constitute a valuable contribution to understanding of the civil war regime. Moreover, whereas emphasising one or another theoretical tradition would have heightened the risk of highlighting certain features of the empirical record but obscuring or downplaying other important features, *Negotiating Civil War* demonstrates how a carefully structured eclectic approach, drawing on mainstream IR theory, can provide an analytically wide-ranging, yet also richly textured, account of the development of this regime.

This is not to say that *Negotiating Civil War* necessarily constitutes the last word in this endeavour: while the theoretical lens adopted in the volume has been designed to assist in identifying elements in the empirical record reflecting mainstream IR's principal theoretical camps, there remains scope to broaden and deepen enquiry into the origins and shaping of the civil war regime. In particular, while the central puzzle motivating the study has distinguished the civil war regime from the international regulation of armed conflict more generally, it is insufficient to view the latter simply as a reciprocity-based regulatory system, inviting consideration of the extent to which the factors contributing to the emergence of the civil war regime can be distinguished from those that have shaped the development of international humanitarian law more generally.[21] Additionally, while *Negotiating Civil War* has focused on the development of the civil war regime, the extent to which the rules and provisions constituting this regime have subsequently impacted (or not) on the behaviour of governments and other actors has been considered only cursorily in the case studies: assessment of the efficacy of this regime will also need to remain to future researchers.

In short, and by way of a final observation, while the present study has built on a vast body of theoretical and empirical material, it has inevitably been impossible to do more than scratch the surface of the potentially relevant material in both domains. That said, just as the research presented here 'stands on the shoulders' of the work of others, it is hoped that *Negotiating Civil War* will also inform future research in this and related fields.

[21] See generally Morrow, *Order within Anarchy: The Laws of War as an International Institution*. Contrast with Finnemore, *National Interests in International Society*, 86.

BIBLIOGRAPHY

Academic Sources

Abbott, Kenneth. International Relations Theory, International Law, and the Regime Governing Atrocities in Internal Conflicts *American Journal of International Law* 93, no. 2 (1999): 361–79.

Abi-Saab, Georges. Wars of National Liberation and the Laws of War. *Annals of International Studies*, Association des Anciens Etudiants de L'Institut Universitaire de Hautes Etudes Internationales, 3 (1972).

Abi-Saab, Georges. Wars of National Liberation and the Development of Humanitarian Law. In Peter J. van Krieken, Robert J. Akkerman and Charles O. Pannenborg (eds.), *Declarations on Principles : A Quest for Universal Peace*, 143–79. Leyden: Sijthoff, 1977.

Abi-Saab, Georges. Wars of National Liberation in the Geneva Conventions and Protocols. In *Recueil Des Cours*, 165:353–445. The Hague: Martinus Nijhoff, 1979.

Abi-Saab, Georges. Wars of National Liberation and the Laws of War. In Friedrich V. Kratochwil and Saul H. Mendlovitz (eds.), *International Law: A Contemporary Perspective*, 2:410–37. Boulder: Westview Press, 1985.

Abi-Saab, Georges. Non-International Armed Conflicts. In *UNESCO International Dimensions of Humanitarian Law*, 217–40. Dordecht: Martinus Nijhoff, 1988.

Abi-Saab, Georges. The Third World Intellectual in Praxis: Confrontation, Participation, or Operation behind Enemy Lines? *Third World Quarterly* 37, no. 11 (2016): 1957–71.

Abi-Saab, Rosemary. *Droit humanitaire et conflits internes – Origines et évolution de la réglementation internationale*. Geneva, Paris: Institut Henry-Dunant, Editions A. Pedone, 1986.

Abi-Saab, Rosemary. Humanitarian Law and Internal Conflicts: The Evolution of Legal Concern. In Astrid J. M. Delissen and Gerard J. Tanja (eds.), *Humanitarian Law of Armed Conflict: Challenges Ahead : Essays in Honour of Frits Kalshoven*, 209–23. Dordrecht: Martinus Nijhoff, 1991.

Abplanalp, Philippe. The International Conferences of the Red Cross as a Factor for the Development of International Humanitarian Law and the Cohesion of the International Red Cross and Red Crescent Movement. *International Review of the Red Cross*, no. 308 (1995): 520–49.

Abresch, William. A Human Rights Law of Internal Armed Conflict: The European Court of Human Rights in Chechnya. *European Journal of International Law* 16, no. 4 (2005): 741–67.

Abtahi, Hirad. The Islamic Republic of Iran and the ICC. *Journal of International Criminal Justice* 3, no. 3 (2005): 635–48.

Adler, Emanuel. Constructivism in International Relations: Sources, Contributions and Debates. In Walter Carlsnaes, Thomas Risse and Beth A. Simmons (eds.), *Handbook of International Relations*. 2nd edn., 112–44. London: Sage, 2013.

Adler, Emanuel, and Peter Haas. Conclusion: Epistemic Communities, World Order, and the Creation of a Reflective Research Program. *International Organization* 46, no. 1 (1992): 367–90.

Akande, Dapo. Classification of Armed Conflicts: Relevant Legal Concepts. In Elizabeth Wilmshurst (ed.), *International Law and the Classification of Conflicts*, 32–79. Oxford: Oxford University Press, 2012.

Albert, Mathias, Oliver Kessler and Stephan Stetter. On Order and Conflict: International Relations and the 'Communicative Turn'. *Review of International Studies* 34, no. S1 (2008): 43–67.

Alderson, Kai. Making Sense of State Socialization. *Review of International Studies* 27, no. 3 (2001): 415–33.

Aldrich, George H. New Life for the Laws of War. *American Journal of International Law* 75, no. 4 (1981): 764–83.

Aldrich, George H. Some Reflections on the Origins of the 1977 Geneva Protocols. In Christophe Swinarski (ed.), *Etudes et Essais Sur Le Droit International Humanitaire et Sur Les Principes de La Croix-Rouge En lhonneur de Jean Pictet = Studies and Essays on International Humanitarian Law and Red Cross Principles in Honour of Jean Pictet*, 129–37. The Hague; Geneva: Martinus Nijhoff; International Committee of the Red Cross, 1984.

Aldrich, George H. Prospects for United States Ratification of Additional Protocol I to the 1949 Geneva Conventions. *American Journal of International Law* 85, no. 1 (1991): 1–20.

Aldrich, George H. Notes from the Vietnam Peace Negotiations. (Unpublished).

Alexander, Amanda. A Short History of International Humanitarian Law. *European Journal of International Law* 26, no. 1 (2015): 109–38.

Alexander, Amanda. International Humanitarian Law, Postcolonialism and the 1977 Geneva Protocol I. *Melbourne Journal of International Law* 17 (2016): 15.

Allen, Rodney G., Martin Cherniack, and George J. Andreopoulos. Refining War: Civil Wars and Humanitarian Controls. *Human Rights Quarterly* 18 (1996): 747.

Allison, Roy. *The Soviet Union and the Strategy of Non-Alignment in the Third World*. Cambridge, UK: Cambridge University Press, 1988.

Alter, Karen J. *The New Terrain of International Law: Courts, Politics, Rights.* Princeton: Princeton University Press, 2014.

Alter, Karen J. The Empire of International Law? *American Journal of International Law* 113, no. 1 (2019): 183–199.

Alvarez, José E. Do Liberal States Behave Better? A Critique of Slaughters Liberal Theory. *European Journal of International Law* 12, no. 2 (2001): 183–246.

Alvarez, José E. What Are International Judges For? The Main Functions of International Adjudication. In Cesare P. R. Romano, Karen Alter and Yuval Shany (eds.), *The Oxford Handbook of International Adjudication*, 158–80. Oxford: Oxford University Press, 2014.

Amnesty International. The International Criminal Court: Making the Right Choices – Part I. Amnesty International, January 1997, available at: http://iccnow.org/documents/ALMakingRightChoises97PartI.pdf [accessed 14 September 2019].

Anderson, Kenneth. The Ottawa Convention Banning Landmines, the Role of International Non-Governmental Organizations and the Idea of International Civil Society. *European Journal of International Law* 11 (2000): 91–120.

Anwar, Raja. *The Terrorist Prince: The Life and Death of Murtaza Bhutto.* London: Verso, 1997.

Aquinas, Thomas. *Summa Theologica.* Westminster, UK: Christian Classics, 1981.

Aristotle. *Politics: Books V and VI.* Translated by David Keyt. Clarendon Aristotle Series. Oxford: Oxford University Press, 1999.

Armitage, David. *Civil Wars: A History in Ideas.* New York: Alfred A. Knopf, 2017.

Arts, Bas. Non-State Actors in Global Governance. Preprints, Bonn: Max-Planck-Projektgruppe Recht Der Gemeinschaftsgueter, 2003, available at: https://econstor.eu/bitstream/10419/85112/1/2003-04_online.pdf [accessed 14 September 2019].

Australian Practice in International Law 1974–1975. *Australian Year Book of International Law* 13 (1975): 325.

Axelrod, Robert, and Robert Keohane, Achieving Cooperation under Anarchy: Strategies and Institutions. *World Politics*, Vol. 38, no. 1 (1985), 226–54.

Axworthy, Lloyd. *Navigating a New World: Canadas Global Future.* Toronto: Vintage, 2004.

Bacino, Leo J. *Reconstructing Russia: U.S. Policy in Revolutionary Russia, 1917–1922.* Kent: Kent State University Press, 1999.

Barnett, Michael, and Raymond Duvall (eds.), *Power in Global Governance.* Cambridge, UK: Cambridge University Press, 2005.

Barnett, Michael, and Raymond Duvall. Power in International Politics. *International Organization* 59, no. 1 (2005): 39–75.

Barnett, Michael, and Martha Finnemore. *Rules for the World: International Organizations in Global Politics.* Ithaca: Cornell University Press, 2004.

Barrett, Joseph. Chechnyas Last Hope – Enforced Disappearances and the European Court of Human Rights. *Harvard Human Rights Journal* 22 (2009): 133.

Barsalou, Olivier. Making Humanitarian Law in the Cold: The Cold War, the United State and the Genesis of the Geneva Conventions of 1949. *IILJ Emerging Scholars Papers*. New York University School of Law, 2008, available at: http://iilj.org/wp-content/uploads/2016/08/Barsalou-Making-Humanitarian-Law-in-the-Cold-2008.pdf [accessed 14 September 2019].

Bartels, Rogier. Timelines, Borderlines and Conflicts. *International Review of the Red Cross* 91, no. 873 (2009): 35–67.

Bartelson, Jens. *A Genealogy of Sovereignty*. Cambridge, UK: Cambridge University Press, 1995.

Bass, Gary. *Stay the Hand of Vengeance: The Politics of War Crimes Tribunals*. Princeton: Princeton University Press, 2001.

Bass, Gary. *Freedom's Battle: The Origins of Humanitarian Intervention*. New York: Knopf, 2008.

Bassiouni, M. Cherif. *The Statute of the International Criminal Court: A Documentary History*. Ardsley: Transnational, 1998.

Bassiouni, M. Cherif. Negotiating the Treaty of Rome on the Establishment of an International Criminal Court. *Cornell International Law Journal* 32 (1999): 443.

Bassiouni, M. Cherif. *The Legislative History of the International Criminal Court*. Vol. 3. 3 vols. Ardsley: Transnational, 2005.

Bates, Elizabeth Stubbins. Sophisticated Constructivism in Human Rights Compliance Theory. *European Journal of International Law* 25, no. 4 (2014): 1169–82.

Baxter, Hugh. System and Life-World in Habermass Theory of Communicative Action. *Theory and Society* 16, no. 1 (1987): 39–86.

Baxter, Richard R. The First Modern Codification of the Law of War – Francis Lieber and General Orders No. 100 (II). *International Review of the Red Cross* 3, no. 26 (1963): 234–50.

Baxter, Richard R. Humanitarian Law or Humanitarian Politics – The 1974 Diplomatic Conference on Humanitarian Law. *Harvard International Law Journal* 16 (1975): 1–26.

Baxter, Richard R. Modernizing the Law of War. *Military Law Review* 78 (1977): 165–183.

Beach, Derek. Process-Tracing Methods in Social Science. *Oxford Research Encyclopedia of Politics,* 2017, available at https://oxfordre.com/politics/view/10.1093/acrefore/9780190228637.001.0001/acrefore-9780190228637-e-176 [accessed 14 September 2019].

Beach, Derek, and Rasmus Brun Pedersen. What Is Process-Tracing Actually Tracing? The Three Variants of Process Tracing Methods and Their Uses and Limitations, 2011, available at: https://ssrn.com/abstract=1902082 [accessed 14 September 2019].

Beach, Derek, and Rasmus Brun Pedersen. *Process-Tracing Methods: Foundations and Guidelines*. Ann Arbor: University of Michigan Press, 2013.

Beach, Derek, and Rasmus Brun Pedersen. *Causal Case Study Methods: Foundations and Guidelines for Comparing, Matching, and Tracing*. Ann Arbor: University of Michigan Press, 2016.

Beach, Derek, and Rasmus Brun Pedersen. How Do I Know Mechanistic Evidence When I See It? A Four-Step Procedure for Tracing Causal Mechanisms in Case Study Research, 2017, available at: https://researchgate.net/publication/320100548_How_do_I_know_mechanistic_evidence_when_I_see_it_A_four-step_procedure_for_tracing_causal_mechanisms_in_case_study_research [accessed 14 September 2019].

Beach, Derek, and Rasmus Brun Pedersen. Selecting Appropriate Cases When Tracing Causal Mechanisms. *Sociological Methods & Research* 47, no. 4 (2018): 837–871.

Beck, Robert J. International Law and International Relations: The Prospects for Interdisciplinary Collaboration. *Journal of International Legal Studies* 1 (1995): 119–50.

Bederman, David J. *International Law in Antiquity*. Cambridge, UK: Cambridge University Press, 2001.

Bedont, Barbara, and David Matas. Negotiating for an International Criminal Court. *Peace Magazine*, Sept.–Oct. 1998: 21.

Behringer, Ronald M. *The Human Security Agenda: How Middle Power Leadership Defied U.S. Hegemony*. New York: Continuum International, 2012.

Bellinger, John B., III, and William J. Haynes II. A US Government Response to the International Committee of the Red Cross Study Customary International Humanitarian Law. *International Review of the Red Cross* 89, no. 866 (2007): 443–71.

Benedetti, Fanny, Karine Bonneau, and John Washburn. *Negotiating the International Criminal Court: New York to Rome, 1994–1998*. The Hague: Martinus Nijhoff, 2013.

Benedetti, Fanny, and John L. Washburn. Drafting the International Criminal Court Treaty: Two Years to Rome and an Afterword on the Rome Diplomatic Conference. *Global Governance* 5, no. 1 (1999): 1–37.

Bennett, Andrew. The Mother of All Isms: Causal Mechanisms and Structured Pluralism in International Relations Theory. *European Journal of International Relations* 19, no. 3 (2013): 459–81.

Bennett, Andrew, and Jeffrey T. Checkel (eds.), *Process Tracing: From Metaphor to Analytic Tool*. Strategies for Social Inquiry. Cambridge, UK: Cambridge University Press, 2015.

Bennett, Andrew, and Jeffrey T. Checkel. Process Tracing: From Philosophical Roots to Best Practice. In Andrew Bennett and Jeffrey T. Checkel (eds.), *Process*

Tracing: From Metaphor to Analytic Tool, 3–38. Strategies for Social Inquiry. Cambridge, UK: Cambridge University Press, 2015.

Bennett, Andrew, and Colin Elman. Case Study Methods. In Christian Reus-Smit and Duncan Snidal (eds.), *The Oxford Handbook of International Relations*, 499–517. Oxford: Oxford University Press, 2008.

Bennett, Andrew, and Alexander George. Process Tracing in Case Study Research, Paper Presented at the MacArthur Foundation Workshop on Case Study Methods, available at: https://uzh.ch/cmsssl/suz/dam/jcr:00000000-5103-bee3-0000-000059b16b9d/05.19.bennett_george.pdf [accessed 14 September 2019].

Benvenisti, Eyal, and Doreen Lustig. Taming Democracy: Codifying the Laws of War to Restore the European Order, 1856–1874. *University of Cambridge Faculty of Law Research Paper* No. 28/2017, available at: https://papers.ssrn.com/sol3/papers.cfm?abstract_id=2985781 [accessed 14 September 2019].

Bernard, Prosper M. Canada and Human Security: From the Axworthy Doctrine to Middle Power Internationalism. *American Review of Canadian Studies* 36, no. 2 (2006): 233–61.

Bernard, Prosper M. Canada and the International Criminal Court: A Case for Renewed Commitment. *Policy Options*, April 2011.

Best, Geoffrey. Making the Geneva Conventions of 1949: The View from Whitehall. In Christophe Swinarski (ed.), *Studies and Essays on International Humanitarian Law and Red Cross Principles in Honour of Jean Pictet*, 5–15. The Hague; Geneva: Martinus Nijhoff; International Committee of the Red Cross, 1984.

Best, Geoffrey. *War and Law since 1945*. Oxford: Clarendon Press, 1994.

Beyer, Christian. Edmund Husserl. In Edward N. Zalta (ed.), *The Stanford Encyclopedia of Philosophy*, Summer 2015. Stanford: Stanford University, 2015, available at: http://plato.stanford.edu/archives/sum2015/entries/husserl/ [accessed 14 September 2019].

Björkdahl, Annika. Swedish Norm Entrepreneurship in the UN. *International Peacekeeping* 14, no. 4 (2007): 538–52.

Bloomfield, Alan. Norm Antipreneurs and Theorising Resistance to Normative Change. *Review of International Studies* 42, no. 2 (2016): 310–33.

Boehme, Franziska. We Chose Africa: South Africa and the Regional Politics of Cooperation with the International Criminal Court. *International Journal of Transitional Justice* 11, no. 1 (2017): 50–70.

Bohman, James, and William Rehg. Jürgen Habermas. In Edward N. Zalta (ed.), *The Stanford Encyclopedia of Philosophy*, Summer 2015. Stanford: Stanford University, 2014, available at: http://plato.stanford.edu/archives/fall2014/entries/habermas/ [accessed 14 September 2019].

Boissier, Pierre. *From Solferino to Tsushima: History of the International Committee of the Red Cross*. Geneva: Henry Dunant Institute, 1985.

Bonner, Michael. *Jihad in Islamic History: Doctrines and Practice*. Princeton: Princeton University Press, 2008.

Bordwell, Percy. *The Law of War between Belligerents: A History and Commentary*. Chicago: Callaghan & Co., 1908.

Bos, Adriaan. From the International Law Commission to the Rome Conference (1994–1998). In Antonio Cassese, Paola Gaeta and John R. W. D. Jones (eds.), *The Rome Statute of the International Criminal Court: A Commentary*, 35–65. Oxford: Oxford University Press, 2002.

Bosco, David. *Rough Justice: The International Criminal Court's Battle to Fix the World, One Prosecution at a Time*. New York: Oxford University Press, 2013.

Bosco, David. When the Blue Helmets Are to Blame. *Foreign Policy*, July 22, 2014.

Bothe, Michael. The International Committee of the Red Cross and the Additional Protocols of 1977. In Andreas Zimmermann, Robin Geiß and Stefanie Haumer (eds.), *Humanizing the Laws of War: The Red Cross and the Development of International Humanitarian Law*, 57–80. Cambridge, UK: Cambridge University Press, 2017.

Bower, Adam. *Norms without the Great Powers: International Law and Changing Social Standards in World Politics*. Oxford: Oxford University Press, 2016.

Branche, Raphaëlle. The French Army and the Geneva Conventions during the Algerian War of Independence and After. In Matthew Evangelista and Nina Tannenwald (eds.), *Do the Geneva Conventions Matter?*, New York: Oxford University Press, 2017.

Bratberg, Øivind. Ideas, Tradition and Norm Entrepreneurs: Retracing Guiding Principles of Foreign Policy in Blair and Chiracs Speeches on Iraq. *Review of International Studies* 37, no. 1 (2011): 327–48.

Brooks, Stephen G. Dueling Realisms. *International Organization* 51, no. 3 (1997): 445–77.

Brooks, Stephen G., and William C. Wohlforth. *World out of Balance: International Relations and the Challenge of American Primacy*. Princeton: Princeton University Press, 2008.

Brown, Bartram S. The Statute of the ICC: Past, Present and Future. In Sarah B. Sewall and Carl Kaysen (eds.), *The United States and the International Criminal Court: National Security and International Law*, 61–84. Oxford: Rowman & Littlefield, 2000.

Brunnée, Jutta. Challenging International Law: What's New? (Essay Based on Keynote Presentation at the Annual Conference of the Canadian Council on International Law in Ottawa, on November 2, 2018). *Opinio Juris* (blog), November 13, 2018, available at: http://opiniojuris.org/2018/11/13/challenging-international-law-whats-new/ [accessed 14 September 2019].

Brunnée, Jutta, and Stephen J. Toope. International Law and Constructivism: Elements of an Interactional Theory of International Law.*Columbia Journal of Transnational Law* 39 (2000): 19–74.

Brunnée, Jutta, and Stephen J. Toope. *Legitimacy and Legality in International Law: An Interactional Account*. Cambridge, UK: Cambridge University Press, 2010.

Bryant, Michael. *A World History of War Crimes: From Antiquity to the Present*. London ; New York: Bloomsbury Academic, 2015.

Bueger, Christian, and Frank Gadinger. The Play of International Practice. *International Studies Quarterly* 59, no. 3 (2015): 449–60.

Bugnion, François. The Geneva Conventions of 12 August 1949: From the 1949 Diplomatic Conference to the Dawn of the New Millennium. *International Affairs* 76, no. 1 (2000): 41–50.

Bugnion, François. *Jus ad Bellum, Jus in Bello* and Non-International Armed Conflicts. *Yearbook of International Humanitarian Law* 6 (2003): 167–98.

Bugnion, François. *The International Committee of the Red Cross and the Protection of War Victims*. London: Macmillan Education, 2003.

Bugnion, François. The International Committee of the Red Cross and Nuclear Weapons: From Hiroshima to the Dawn of the 21st Century. *International Review of the Red Cross* 87, no. 859 (2005): 511–24.

Bugnion, François. Adoption of the Additional Protocols of 8 June 1977: A Milestone in the Development of International Humanitarian Law. *International Review of the Red Cross* 99, no. 905 (2017): 785–96.

Byers, Michael. *Custom, Power and the Power of Rules: International Relations and Customary International Law*. Cambridge, UK: Cambridge University Press, 1999.

Caesar, Julius. *The Civil War*. Translated by J. F. Gardner. London: Penguin Books Ltd, 1967.

Cakmak, Cenap. Transnational Activism in World Politics and Effectiveness of a Loosely Organised Principled Global Network: The Case of the NGO Coalition for an International Criminal Court. *The International Journal of Human Rights* 12, no. 3 (2008): 373–93.

Campbell, Colm, and Fionnuala Ni Aolain. The Paradox of Transition in Conflicted Democracies. *Human Rights Quarterly* 27 (2005): 172–213.

Capoccia, Giovanni. Critical Junctures. In Orfeo Fioretos, Tulia G. Falleti and Adam Sheingate (eds.), *The Oxford Handbook of Historical Institutionalism*, 89–106. Oxford: Oxford University Press, 2016.

Carr, David. Husserls Problematic Concept of the Life-World. *American Philosophical Quarterly* 7, no. 4 (1970): 331–39.

Cassese, Antonio. The Geneva Protocols of 1977 on the Humanitarian Law of Armed Conflict and Customary International Law. *UCLA Pacific Basin Law Journal* 3 (1984): 55–118.

Cassese, Antonio. Wars of National Liberation and Humanitarian Law. In Christophe Swinarski (ed.), *Etudes et Essais Sur Le Droit International Humanitaire et Sur Les Principes de La Croix-Rouge En lhonneur de Jean Pictet / Studies and Essays on International Humanitarian Law and Red Cross*

Principles in Honour of Jean Pictet, 313–24. The Hague; Geneva: Martinus Nijhoff; International Committee of the Red Cross, 1984.

Cassese, Antonio. The Martens Clause: Half a Loaf or Simply Pie in the Sky? *European Journal of International Law* 11, no. 1 (2000): 187–216.

Chayes, Abram, and Antonia Handler Chayes. *The New Sovereignty: Compliance with International Regulatory Agreements*. Cambridge, MA: Harvard University Press, 1998.

Checkel, Jeffrey T. Review: The Constructivist Turn in International Relations Theory. *World Politics* 50, no. 2 (1998): 324–48.

Checkel, Jeffrey T. 'Why Comply? Social Learning and European Identity Change', *International Organization* 55, no. 3 (2001), 553–88.

Checkel, Jeffrey T. Theoretical Pluralism in IR: Possibilities and Limits. In Walter Carlsnaes, Thomas Risse and Beth Simmons (eds.), *Handbook of International Relations*. 2nd edn., 220–41. London: Sage, 2012.

Checkel, Jeffrey T. Transnational Dynamics of Civil War. In Jeffrey T. Checkel (ed.), *Transnational Dynamics of Civil War*, 3–30. Cambridge, UK: Cambridge University Press, 2013.

Checkel, Jeffrey T. Mechanisms, Process and the Study of International Institutions. In Andrew Bennett and Jeffrey T. Checkel (eds.), *Process Tracing: From Metaphor to Analytic Tool*, 74–97. Strategies for Social Inquiry. Cambridge, UK: Cambridge University Press, 2015.

Checkel, Jeffrey T. Methods in Constructivist Approaches. In Alexandra Gheciu and William C. Wohlforth (eds.), *The Oxford Handbook of International Security*, 152–66. Oxford: Oxford University Press, 2018.

Childress, James F. Francis Lieber's Interpretation of the Laws of War: General Orders No. 100 in the Context of His Life and Thought. *American Journal of Jurisprudence* 21 (1976): 34–70.

Chitalkar, Poorvi, and David M. Malone. India and Global Governance. In David M. Malone, C. Raja Mohan and Srinath Raghavan (eds.), *The Oxford Handbook of Indian Foreign Policy*, 581–95. Oxford: Oxford University Press, 2015.

Cho, Sungjoon. *The Social Foundations of World Trade: Norms, Community, and Constitution*. Cambridge, UK: Cambridge University Press, 2014.

Cicero, Marcus Tullius. *Pro Milone*. Translated by N. H. Watts. 5th edn. Cambridge, MA: Harvard University Press, 1972.

Cicero, Marcus Tullius. *The Philippics*. Edited and translated by David R. Shackleton-Bailey. Chapel Hill: University of North Carolina Press, 1986.

Ciobanu, Dan. The Attitude of the Socialist Countries. In Antonio Cassese (ed.), *The New Humanitarian Law of Armed Conflict*, 399–444. Naples: Editoriale Scientifica, 1979.

Cisse, Catherine. The International Tribunals for the Former Yugoslavia and Rwanda: Some Elements of Comparison. *Transnational Law & Contemporary Problems* 7 (1997): 103–118.

Clark, Cal. *Political Science Research Methods: Exploring America at a Crossroads.* Singapore: World Scientific Publishing Company, 2013.

Clarkson, Stephen, and Matto Mildenberger. *Dependent America? How Canada and Mexico Construct US Power.* Toronto: University of Toronto Press, 2011.

Collier, David, Henry Brady, and Jason Seawright. Introduction to the Second Edition: A Sea Change in Political Methodology. In Henry Brady and David Collier (eds.), *Rethinking Social Enquiry: Diverse Tools, Shared Standards.* 2nd edn., 1–10. Lanham: Rowman & Littlefield, 2010.

Combs, Nancy Amoury. Profile: Judge George H. Aldrich. *International Law Forum* 7 (2005): 47–53, available at: https://scholarship.law.wm.edu/facpubs/35/ [accessed 14 September 2019].

Conway-Lanz, Sahr. The Struggle to Fight a Humane War: The United States, the Korean War, and the 1949 Geneva Conventions. In Matthew Evangelista and Nina Tannenwald (eds.), *Do the Geneva Conventions Matter?*, 69–104. New York: Oxford University Press, 2017.

Copeland, Dale. A Realist Critique of the English School. *Review of International Studies* 29, no. 3 (2003): 427–41.

Cornut, Jérémie. Analytic Eclecticism in Practice: A Method for Combining International Relations Theories. *International Studies Perspectives* 16, no. 1 (2015): 50–66.

Cox, Michaelene, and Noha Shawki. *Negotiating Sovereignty and Human Rights: Actors and Issues in Contemporary Human Rights Politics.* Farnham: Ashgate, 2009.

Creveld, Martin Van. *The Transformation of War.* New York: Free Press, 1991.

Crossland, James. *Britain and the International Committee of the Red Cross, 1939–1945.* London: Palgrave Macmillan, 2014.

Crowe, David. *War Crimes, Genocide, and Justice: A Global History.* New York: Palgrave Macmillan US, 2014.

Cryer, Robert, Håkan Friman, Darryl Robinson, and Elizabeth Wilmshurst. *An Introduction to International Criminal Law and Procedure.* Cambridge, UK: Cambridge University Press, 2014.

Cullen, Anthony. *The Concept of Non-International Armed Conflict in International Humanitarian Law.* Cambridge, UK: Cambridge University Press, 2010.

Dancy, Geoff. Searching for Deterrence at the International Criminal Court. *International Criminal Law Review* 17, no. 4 (2017): 625–55.

Dancy, Geoff, and Florencia Montal. From Law versus Politics to Law in Politics: A Pragmatist Assessment of the ICCs Impact. *American University International Law Review* 32, 3 (2017): 645–706.

Dancy, Geoff, and Eric Wiebelhaus-Brahm. The Impact of Criminal Prosecutions during Intrastate Conflict. *Journal of Peace Research* 55, no. 1 (2018): 47–61.

Danner, Allison Marston. When Courts Make Law: How the International Criminal Tribunals Recast the Laws of War. *Vanderbilt Law Review* 59 (2006): 1–65.

Davenport, David. The New Diplomacy. *Policy Review*, no. 116 (December 2002): 17–30.

Davis, George, B. Doctor Francis Lieber's Instructions for the Government of Armies in the Field. *American Journal of International Law*, 1, no. 1 (1907), 13–25.

Dawson, Doyne, and James D. Dawson. *The Origins of Western Warfare: Militarism and Morality in the Ancient World*. Boulder: Westview Press, 1996.

Deighton, Anne. Britain and the Cold War, 1945–1955. In Melvyn P. Leffler and Odd Arne Westad (eds.), *The Cambridge History of the Cold War: Volume 1: Origins*, 112–32. Cambridge, UK: Cambridge University Press, 2010.

Deitelhoff, Nicole. The Discursive Process of Legalization: Charting Islands of Persuasion in the ICC Case. *International Organization* 63, no. 1 (2009): 33–65.

Deitelhoff, Nicole, and Harald Müller. Theoretical Paradise – Empirically Lost? Arguing with Habermas. *Review of International Studies* 31, no. 1 (2005): 167–79.

Detter De Lupis, Ingrid. *The Law of War*. Farnham: Ashgate, 2013.

Devetak, Richard, and Jacqui True. Diplomatic Divergence in the Antipodes: Globalisation, Foreign Policy and State Identity in Australia and New Zealand. *Australian Journal of Political Science* 41, no. 2 (2006): 241–56.

Dijk, Boyd van. Human Rights in War: On the Entangled Foundations of the 1949 Geneva Conventions. *American Journal of International Law* 112, no. 4 (2018): 553–82.

Dijk, Cornelis W. A. J. van. The American Political Intervention in the Conflict in the Dutch East Indies 1945–1949. U.S. Army Command and General Staff College (Masters thesis), 2009, available at: https://apps.dtic.mil/dtic/tr/fulltext/u2/a502059.pdf [accessed 14 September 2019].

Dill, Janina. *Legitimate Targets?: Social Construction, International Law and US Bombing*. Cambridge, UK: Cambridge University Press, 2014.

Dinstein, Yoram. *Non-International Armed Conflicts in International Law*. Cambridge, UK: Cambridge University Press, 2014.

Donnelly, Jack. *Realism and International Relations*. Cambridge, UK: Cambridge University Press, 2000.

Doyle, Michael W. Kant, Liberal Legacies, and Foreign Affairs. *Philosophy & Public Affairs* 12, no. 3 (1983): 205–35.

Doyle, Michael W. Three Pillars of the Liberal Peace. *American Political Science Review* 99, no. 3 (2005): 463–66.

Draper, Gerald I. A. D. Humanitarian Law and Human Rights. *Acta Juridica 1979* (1979): 193–206.

Draper, Gerald I. A. D. The Implementation and Enforcement of the Geneva Conventions of 1949 and of the Two Additional Protocols of 1978. In *Collected Courses of the Hague Academy of International Law* (1979–III), 164: 1–54. Alphen aan den Rijn: Sijthoff and Noordhoff, 1980.

Droege, Cordula. The Interplay between International Humanitarian Law and International Human Rights Law in Situations of Armed Conflict. *Israel Law Review* 40 (2007): 310–355.

Drohan, Brian. *Brutality in an Age of Human Rights: Activism and Counterinsurgency at the End of the British Empire.* Ithaca: Cornell University Press, 2018.

Dunoff, Jeffrey L., and Mark A. Pollack (eds.), *Interdisciplinary Perspectives on International Law and International Relations: The State of the Art.* Cambridge, UK: Cambridge University Press, 2013.

Dunoff, Jeffrey, and Mark Pollack. IL/IR Book Discussion: Beyond the 'Isms War'? *Opinio Juris* (blog), September 16, 2013, available at: http://opiniojuris.org/2013/09/16/ilir-book-discussion-beyond-isms-war/ [accessed 14 September 2019].

Dunoff, Jeffrey, and Mark A. Pollack. International Law and International Relations: Introducing an Interdisciplinary Dialogue. In Jeffrey L. Dunoff and Mark A. Pollack (eds.), *Interdisciplinary Perspectives on International Law and International Relations: The State of the Art*, 3–32. Cambridge, UK: Cambridge University Press, 2013.

Dunoff, Jeffrey, and Joel Trachtman. The Law and Economics of Humanitarian Law Violations in Internal Conflict. *American Journal of International Law* 93, no. 2 (1999): 394–409.

Durand, André. *From Sarajevo to Hiroshima: History of the International Committee of the Red Cross.* Geneva: Henry Dunant Institute, 1984.

Durand, André. Gustave Moynier and the Peace Societies. *International Review of the Red Cross* 36, no. 314 (1996): 532–50.

Edwards, Jill. *The British Government and the Spanish Civil War, 1936–1939.* London: Macmillan, 1979.

Efrat, Asif. Professional Socialization and International Norms: Physicians against Organ Trafficking. *European Journal of International Relations* 21, no. 3 (2015): 647–71.

Eide, Asbjörn. The New Humanitarian Law in Non-International Armed Conflict. In Antonio Cassese (ed.), *The New Humanitarian Law of Armed Conflict*, 277–309. Naples: Editoriale Scientifica, 1979.

Einsiedel, Sebastian von. Civil War Trends and the Changing Nature of Armed Conflict. United Nations University Centre for Policy Research, March 2017, available at: https://i.unu.edu/media/cpr.unu.edu/attachment/2534/OC_10-

CivilWarTrendsandChangingNatureofArmedConflict-05-2017.pdf [accessed 14 September 2019].

Elder, David A. The Historical Background of Common Article 3 of the Geneva Convention of 1949. *Case Western Reserve Journal of International Law* 11 (1979): 37–69.

Elman, Colin. Explanatory Typologies in Qualitative Studies of International Politics. *International Organization* 59, no. 2 (2005): 293–326.

Elman, Colin. Explanatory Typologies in Qualitative Analysis. In David Byrne and Charles Ragin (eds.), *The SAGE Handbook of Case-Based Methods*, 121–31. London: Sage, 2009.

Elman, Colin, John M. Owen, James Mahoney, Nina Tannenwald, Andrew Bennett, and David Waldner. Symposium on Process Tracing. *Security Studies* 248, no. 2 (2015): 199–250.

Eriksen, Tore Linné (ed.), *Norway and National Liberation in Southern Africa*. Uppsala: Nordic Africa Institute, 2000.

Evangelista, Matthew, and Nina Tannenwald (eds.), *Do the Geneva Conventions Matter?* New York: Oxford University Press, 2017.

Fadl, Khaled Abou El. Ahkam Al-Bughat: Irregular Warfare and the Law of Rebellion in Islam. In James Turner Johnson and John Kelsay (eds.), *Cross, Crescent, and Sword: The Justification and Limitation of War in Western and Islamic Tradition*, 149–76. Westport: Greenwood Press, 1990.

Fadl, Khaled Abou El. *Rebellion and Violence in Islamic Law*. Cambridge, UK: Cambridge University Press, 2001.

Faizullaev, Alisher. Diplomatic Interactions and Negotiations. *Negotiation Journal* 30, no. 3 (July 2014): 275–99.

Falk, Richard A. Introduction. In Richard A. Falk (ed.), *The International Law of Civil War*, 1–29. Baltimore and London: Johns Hopkins Press, 1971.

Falk, Richard, A. (ed.), *The International Law of Civil War*. Baltimore and London: Johns Hopkins Press, 1971.

Farina, Niccolo. The Attitudes of the Peoples Republic of China. In Antonio Cassese (ed.),*The New Humanitarian Law of Armed Conflict*, 445–457. Naples: Editoriale Scientifica, 1979.

Fearon, James D. Bargaining, Enforcement, and International Cooperation. *International Organization* 52, no. 2 (1998): 269–305.

Fearon, James, and David Laitin. Ethnicity, Insurgency, and Civil War. *American Political Science Review* 97, no. 1 (2003): 75–90.

Fearon, James, and Alexander Wendt. Rationalism v. Constructivism: A Skeptical View. In Walter Carlsnaes, Thomas Risse and Beth Simmons (eds.), *Handbook of International Relations*, 52–72. London: Sage, 2002.

Feaver, Peter, Gunther Hellmann, Randall Schweller, Jeffrey Taliaferro, William C. Wohlforth, Jeffrey Legro, and Andrew Moravcsik. Brother, Can You Spare a Paradigm? (Or Was Anybody Ever a Realist?) *International Security* 25, no. 1 (2000): 165–93.

Fehl, Caroline. Explaining the International Criminal Court: A 'Practice Test' for Rationalist and Constructivist Approaches. *European Journal of International Relations* 10, no. 3 (2004): 357–94.

Fehl, Caroline. *Living with a Reluctant Hegemon: Explaining European Responses to US Unilateralism*. Oxford: Oxford University Press, 2012.

Feldbrugge, Ferdinand Joseph Maria, Gerard Pieter Van den Berg, and William Bradford Simons. *Encyclopedia of Soviet Law*. Leiden: Brill, 1985.

Ferencz, Benjamin B. *An International Criminal Court, a Step toward World Peace: A Documentary History and Analysis*. Vol. 1. 2 vols. Dobbs Ferry: Oceana, 1980.

Ferencz, Benjamin B. International Criminal Courts: The Legacy of Nuremberg. *Pace International Law Review* 10 (1998): 203–35.

Ferraro, Tristan. The ICRCs Legal Position on the Notion of Armed Conflict Involving Foreign Intervention and on Determining the IHL Applicable to This Type of Conflict. *International Review of the Red Cross* 97, no. 900 (2015): 1227–52.

Festinger, Leon. An Analysis of Compliant Behavior. In Muzafer Sherif, Milbourne Otto Wilson (eds.), *Group Relations at the Crossroads*, 232–56. New York: Harper, 1953.

Finnemore, Martha. *National Interests in International Society*. Ithaca: Cornell University Press, 1996.

Finnemore, Martha. Are Legal Norms Distinctive? *New York University Journal of International Law and Politcs* 32 (2000): 699–706.

Finnemore, Martha. *The Purpose of Intervention: Changing Beliefs about the Use of Force*. Cornell Studies in Security Affairs. Ithaca: Cornell University Press, 2003.

Finnemore, Martha, and Kathryn Sikkink. International Norm Dynamics and Political Change. *International Organization* 52, no. 4 (1998): 887–917.

Finnemore, Martha, and Kathryn Sikkink. Taking Stock: The Constructivist Research Program in International Relations and Comparative Politics. *Annual Review of Political Science* 4, no. 1 (2001): 391–416.

Fleck, Dieter. The Law of Non-International Armed Conflicts. In Dieter Fleck (ed.), *The Handbook of International Humanitarian Law*. 2nd edn., 605–34. Oxford: Oxford University Press, 2009.

Forsythe, David P. The 1974 Diplomatic Conference on Humanitarian Law: Some Observations. *American Journal of International Law* 69 (1975): 77–91.

Forsythe, David P. *Humanitarian Politics: The International Committee of the Red Cross*. Baltimore: Johns Hopkins University Press, 1977.

Forsythe, David P. Three Sessions of Legislating Humanitarian Law: Forward March, Retreat, or Parade Rest. *International Lawyer* 11, no. 1 (1977): 131–142.

Forsythe, David P. Legal Management of Internal War: The 1977 Protocol on Non-International Armed Conflicts. *American Journal of International Law* 72, no. 2 (1978): 272–295.

Forsythe, David P. *The Humanitarians: The International Committee of the Red Cross*. Cambridge, UK: Cambridge University Press, 2005.

Forsythe, David P. *Human Rights in International Relations*. New York: Cambridge University Press, 2006.

Forsythe, David P., and Richard Magat. Updating the Rules of War; The Third World Wins Some Symbolic Victories. *Washington Post*, February 12, 1978, C-3, Col. 1.

Franck, Thomas M. *The Power of Legitimacy among Nations*. Oxford: Oxford University Press, 1990.

Friedlander, Robert A. Great Power Politics and Spains Civil War: The First Phase. *Historian* 28, no. 1 (1965): 72–92.

Friedner Parrat, Charlotta. Bridging the Divide: What the English School Does, and Why. BISA Annual Conference: Research Paper, Bath, 2018. (Author papers).

Friedrichs, Jörg, and Friedrich Kratochwil. On Acting and Knowing: How Pragmatism Can Advance International Relations Research and Methodology. *International Organization* 63, no. 4 (2009): 701–31.

Fukuyama, Francis. The End of History? *The National Interest*, no. 16 (Summer, 1989): 3–18.

Gaiduk, Ilya V. *Divided Together: The United States and the Soviet Union in the United Nations, 1945–1965*. Stanford: Stanford University Press, 2013.

Garfinkel, Alan. *Forms of Explanation: Rethinking the Questions in Social Theory*. New Haven: Yale University Press, 1981.

Garraway, Charles. Written Evidence. House of Commons Defence Select Committee, October 2013, available at: http://publications.parliament.uk/pa/cm201314/cmselect/cmdfence/931/931we05.htm [accessed 14 September 2019].

Gentili, Alberico. *Three Books on the Law of War*. In J. B. Scott (ed.), Classics of International Law. Washington, DC: Carnegie Endowment for International Peace, 1933.

George, Alexander L., and Andrew Bennett. *Case Studies and Theory Development in the Social Sciences*. Cambridge, MA: MIT Press, 2005.

Geouffre de La Pradelle, Paul de. *La conférence diplomatique et les nouvelles Conventions de Genève du 12 août 1949*. Paris: Les Éditions Internationales, 1951.

Giladi, Rotem. Humanity in the Service of Order: Intellectual Roots of the Occupation Category, 2011. Unpublished. (Author papers).

Giladi, Rotem. The Enactment of Irony: Reflections on the Origins of the Martens Clause. *European Journal of International Law* 25, no. 3 (2014): 847–69.

Glasius, Marlies. Expertise in the Cause of Justice: Global Civil Society Influence on the Statute for an International Criminal Court. In Marlies Glasius, Mary Kaldor and Helmut Anheier (eds.), *Global Civil Society 2002*, 137–68. Oxford: Oxford University Press, 2002.

Glasius, Marlies. *The International Criminal Court: A Global Civil Society Achievement.* Abingdon: Routledge, 2006.

Goddard, Stacie E. Brokering Change: Networks and Entrepreneurs in International Politics. *International Theory* 1, no. 2 (2009): 249–81.

Goldsmith, Jack, and Eric Posner. *The Limits of International Law.* Oxford: Oxford University Press, 2005.

Goldsmith, Jack, Eric Posner, John K. Setear, James D. Morrow, Julie Roin, George W. Downs, Michael A. Jones, et al. Rational Choice and International Law (Volume Supplement). *The Journal of Legal Studies* 31, no. S1 (2002).

Goldstein, Judith, Miles Kahler, Robert O. Keohane, and Anne-Marie Slaughter (eds.), *Legalization and World Politics.* International Organization Readers. Cambridge, MA: MIT Press, 2001.

Greenwood, Christopher. International Humanitarian Law and the Tadic Case Symposium: The International Tribunal for Former Yugoslavia Comes to Age. *European Journal of International Law* 7 (1996): 265–83.

Greenwood, Christopher. A Critique of the Additional Protocols to the Geneva Conventions. In Helen Durham and Timothy L. H. McCormack (eds.), *The Changing Face of Conflict and the Efficacy of International Humanitarian Law*, 3–22. Leiden: Martinus Nijhoff, 1999.

Greig, J. Michael, and James D. Meernik. To Prosecute or Not to Prosecute: Civil War Mediation and International Criminal Justice. *International Negotiation* 19, no. 2 (2014): 257–84.

Grieco, Joseph M. The Schools of Thought Problem in International Relations. *International Studies Review* 21, no. 3 (2019): 424–46.

Groenleer, Martijn L. P., and Louise G. Van Schaik. United We Stand? The European Unions International Actorness in the Cases of the International Criminal Court and the Kyoto Protocol. *Journal of Common Market Studies* 45, no. 5 (2007): 969–98.

Grotius, Hugo. *The Rights of War and Peace: Including the Law of Nature and of Nations.* Translated by Archibald Colin Campbell. London: M. Walter Dunne, 1979.

Guan, Jing. The ICCs Jurisdiction over War Crimes in Internal Armed Conflicts: An Insurmountable Obstacle for Chinas Accession. *Penn State International Law Review* 28 (2010): 703–754.

Gutteridge, Joyce A. C. The Geneva Conventions of 1949. *British Year Book of International Law* 26 (1949): 294–326.

Guzman, Andrew. A Compliance-Based Theory of International Law. *California Law Review* 90, no. 6 (2002): 1823–87.

Haas, Peter. Introduction: Epistemic Communities and International Policy Coordination. *International Organization* 46, no. 1 (1992): 1–35.

Haas, Peter, Andrew Bennett, Alice Ba, T. V. Paul, Rudra Sil, and Peter Katzenstein. Symposium: Beyond Paradigms and Research Programs. *Qualitative and Multi-Method Research* 8, no. 2 (Fall 2012): 5–24.

Habermas, Jurgen. *The Divided West.* Edited and translated by Ciaran Cronin. Cambridge, UK: Polity Press, 2006.

Hafner-Burton, Emilie M. *Making Human Rights a Reality.* 1st edn. Princeton: Oxford University Press, 2013.

Hakimi, Monica. Customs Method and Process: Lessons from Humanitarian Law. In Curtis A. Bradley (ed.), *Customs Future: International Law in a Changing World*, 148–71. New York: Cambridge University Press, 2016.

Hall, Christopher Keith. The First Proposal for a Permanent International Criminal Court. *International Review of the Red Cross* 38, no. 322 (1998): 57–74.

Hall, Christopher Keith. The Third and Fourth Sessions of the UN Preparatory Committee on the Establishment of an International Criminal Court. *American Journal of International Law* 92, no. 1 (1998): 124–133.

Halleck, Henry Wager. *International Law: Or, Rules Regulating the Intercourse of States in Peace and War.* New York: D. Van Nostrand, 1861.

Halleck, Henry Wager. *Elements of International Law and Laws of War.* Philadelphia: J. B. Lippincott & Co., 1866.

Halleck, Henry Wager, and George Sherston Baker. *Hallecks International Law: Or, Rules Regulating the Intercourse of States in Peace and War.* 3rd edn. Vol. II. London: Kegan Paul, Trench, Trübner and Co, 1893.

Hamilton, Scott. A Genealogy of Metatheory in IR: How Ontology Emerged from the Inter-Paradigm Debate. *International Theory* 9, no. 1 (2017): 136–70.

Hannikainen, Lauri, Raija Hanski, and Allan Rosas. *Implementing Humanitarian Law Applicable in Armed Conflicts: The Case of Finland.* Dordrecht: Martinus Nijhoff, 1992.

Hathaway, Oona. Do Human Rights Treaties Make a Difference? *Yale Law Journal* 111 (2001): 1935–2042.

Hathaway, Oona. The Cost of Commitment. *Stanford Law Review* 55, no. 5 (2003): 1821–62.

Hathaway, Oona. Why Do Countries Commit to Human Rights Treaties? *Journal of Conflict Resolution* 51, no. 4 (2007): 588–621.

Hayes, Jarrod and Patrick James, Systemism, Analytic Eclecticism, and the Democratic Peace. In Annette Freyberg-Inan, Ewan Harrison and Patrick James (eds.), *Evaluating Progress in International Relations*, 109–25. London: Routledge, 2016.

H-Diplo. Roundtable 6-6 on Reconstructing the Cold War: The Early Years, 1945–1958. ISSF, February 7, 2014, available at: https://issforum.org/roundtables/6-6-reconstructing-cold-war [accessed 14 September 2019].

Hebel, Herman von, and Darryl Robinson. Crimes within the Jurisdiction of the Court. In Roy S. K. Lee (ed.), *The International Criminal Court: The Making of the Rome Statute: Issues, Negotiations and Results*, 79–126. The Hague: Martinus Nijhoff, 1999.

Heinsch, Robert. The International Committee of the Red Cross and the Geneva Conventions of 1949. In Andreas Zimmermann, Robin Geiß and Stefanie Haumer (eds.), *Humanizing the Laws of War: The Red Cross and the Development of International Humanitarian Law*, 27–56. Cambridge, UK: Cambridge University Press, 2017.

Heintschel von Heinegg, Wolf. Blockade. Max Planck Encyclopedia of Public International Law, Oxford University Press, 2015, available at: https://opil.oup law.com/view/10.1093/law:epil/9780199231690/law-9780199231690-e252 [accessed 23 December 2019].

Heller, Kevin Jon. *The Nuremberg Military Tribunals and the Origins of International Criminal Law*. Oxford: Oxford University Press, 2011.

Heller, Regina, Martin Kahl, and Daniela Pisoiu. The Dark' Side of Normative Argumentation – The Case of Counterterrorism Policy. *Global Constitutionalism* 1, no. 2 (2012): 278–312.

Hellmann, Gunther, Helena Rytövuori-Apunen, Jörg Friedrichs, Rudra Sil, Markus Kornprobst, and Patrick Thaddeus Jackson. Pragmatism and International Relations. *International Studies Review* 11, no. 3 (2009): 638–62.

Henckaerts, Jean-Marie, and Louise Doswald-Beck (eds.), *Customary International Humanitarian Law: Volume I – Rules*. 2 vols. Cambridge, UK: Cambridge University Press, 2005.

Henckaerts, Jean-Marie, and Louise Doswald-Beck (eds.), *Customary International Humanitarian Law: Volume II – Practice*. 2 vols. Cambridge, UK: Cambridge University Press, 2005.

Henkin, Louis. The United Nations and Human Rights. *International Organization* 19, no. 3 (1965): 504–17.

Henkin, Louis. *How Nations Behave: Law and Foreign Policy*. 2nd edn. New York: Council on Foreign Relations, Columbia University Press, 1979.

Herodotus. *The Histories, Revised*. Edited by John Marincola. Translated by Aubery de Selincourt. London: Penguin Classics, 2003.

Higgins, Noelle. *The Approach of International Law to Wars of National Liberation*. Moscow: Martin Institute, University of Idaho, 2004, available at: http://doras .dcu.ie/2268/1/monograph.pdf [accessed 14 September 2019].

Higgins, Rosalyn. International Law and Civil Conflict. In Evan Luard (ed.), *The International Regulation of Civil Wars*. London: Thames and Hudson, 1972.

Hill, Gina E. A Case of NGO Participation: International Criminal Court Negotiations. In James W. St G. Walker and Andrew S. Thompson (eds.),

Critical Mass: The Emergence of Global Civil Society, 129–52. Waterloo, ON: Wilfrid Laurier University Press, 2008.

Hillebrecht, Courtney. *Domestic Politics and International Human Rights Tribunals: The Problem of Compliance*. Cambridge, UK: Cambridge University Press, 2014.

Hillebrecht, Courtney. The Deterrent Effects of the International Criminal Court: Evidence from Libya. *International Interactions* 42, no. 4 (2016): 616–43.

Hirsch, Moshe, and Andrew Lang (eds.), *Research Handbook on the Sociology of International Law*. Cheltenham: Edward Elgar Publishing, 2018.

Hitchcock, William I. *France Restored: Cold War Diplomacy and the Quest for Leadership in Europe, 1944–1954*. Chapel Hill: University of North Carolina Press, 1998.

Hitchcock, William I. Human Rights and the Laws of War: The Geneva Conventions of 1949. In Akira Iriye, Petra Goedde and William I. Hitchcock (eds.), *The Human Rights Revolution: An International History*, 93–112. Oxford: Oxford University Press, 2012.

Hollyer, James, and Bryan Rosendorff. Why Do Authoritarian Regimes Sign the Convention against Torture? Signaling, Domestic Politics and Non-Compliance. *Quarterly Journal of Political Science* 6, nos. 3–4 (2011): 275–327.

Hopf, Ted. The Promise of Constructivism in International Relations Theory. *International Security* 23, no. 1 (1998): 171–200.

Hopf, Ted. *Reconstructing the Cold War: The Early Years, 1945–1958*. New York: Oxford University Press, 2012.

Horovitz, Sigall, Yuval Shany, and Gilad Noam. The International Criminal Court. In Yuval Shany (ed.), *Assessing the Effectiveness of International Courts*, 223–52. Oxford: Oxford University Press, 2014.

Huber, Max. The Principles of the Red Cross. *Foreign Affairs* 26, no. 4 (1948): 723–27.

Human Rights Watch. HRW Disappointed at India's Position on International Court. 17 June 1998, available at: http://hrw.org/news/1998/06/16/hrw-disappointed-indias-position-international-court [accessed 14 September 2019].

Human Rights Watch. Human Rights Watch Praises German Stand on International Court. 17 June 1998, available at. http://hrw.org/news/1998/06/16/human-rights-watch-praises-german-stand-international-court [accessed 14 September 2019].

Human Rights Watch. Human Rights Watch Welcomes New Japanese Position on International Court. 27 June 1998, available at: http://hrw.org/news/1998/06/26/human-rights-watch-welcomes-new-japanese-position-international-court [accessed 14 September 2019].

Human Rights Watch. French Stand on International Court 'Mixed', Says Rights Group. 9 July 1998, available at: http://hrw.org/news/1998/07/09/french-stand-international-court-mixed-says-rights-group [accessed 14 September 2019].

Human Rights Watch. Human Rights Watch Condemns United States Threat to Sabotage International Criminal Court. 9 July 1998, available at: https://hrw.org/news/1998/07/09/human-rights-watch-condemns-united-states-threat-sabotage-international-criminal [accessed 14 September 2019].

Human Rights Watch. Human Rights Watch Disappointed by U.K. Stand on International Court. 9 July 1998, available at: http://hrw.org/fr/news/1998/07/09/human-rights-watch-disappointed-uk-stand-international-court [accessed 14 September 2019].

Humphreys, Adam R. C. The Heuristic Explanation of Explanatory Theories in International Relations. *European Journal of International Relations* 17, no. 2 (2011): 257–77

Hurd, Ian. Constructivism. In Christian Reus-Smit and Duncan Snidal (eds.), *Oxford Handbook of International Relations*, 298–313. Oxford: Oxford University Press, 2008.

Husserl, Edmund. *Die Lebenswelt: Auslegungen der vorgegebenen Welt und ihrer Konstitution*. Heidelberg: Springer-Verlag, 2008.

Hutchinson, John. *Champions of Charity: War and the Rise of the Red Cross*. Boulder: Routledge, 1996.

Ingebritsen, Christine. Norm Entrepreneurs: Scandinavias Role in World Politics. *Cooperation and Conflict* 37, no. 1 (2002): 11–23.

Inter-Press Service (IPS). Clamour Rises for Court to Step into Internal Conflicts. *Terraviva Daily Newspaper*, June 19, 1998, available at: https://web.archive.org/web/20081203175209/www.ips.org/icc/tv190601.htm/ [accessed 14 September 2019].

Inter-Press Service (IPS). Yes, Size Does Matter. *Terraviva Daily Newspaper*, June 25, 1998, available at: https://web.archive.org/web/19980624224028/http:/www.ips.org/icc/tv250602.htm [accessed 14 September 2019].

Inter-Press Service (IPS). Take It or Leave It. *Terraviva Daily Newspaper*, July 14, 1998, available at: https://web.archive.org/web/19990504085041/http://ips.org/icc/tv140701.htm [accessed 14 September 2019].

Iqbal, Nasir. Judge Harboured Bias against Bhutto, SC Told. *Dawn*, May 3, 2011, available at: https://dawn.com/news/625920 [accessed 14 September 2019].

Israel CDDH delegation member. Interview, March 2018. (Author papers).

Jackson, Gabriel. *Spanish Republic and the Civil War, 1931–1939*. Princeton: Princeton University Press, 1965.

Jackson, Patrick Thaddeus. *The Conduct of Inquiry in International Relations: Philosophy of Science and Its Implications for the Study of World Politics*. London: Routledge, 2010.

Jackson, Patrick Thaddeus. Review. H-Diplo Roundtable 6-6 on *Reconstructing the Cold War: The Early Years, 1945–1958*. 2014, available at: https://issforum.org/roundtables/6-6-reconstructing-cold-war [accessed 14 September 2019].

Jacobs, Alan M., Peter Derek Beach, Rosa W. Runhardt, David Waldner, and Andrew Bennett. Symposium: Causal Mechanisms and Process Tracing. *Qualitative and Multi-Method Research* 14, no. 1/2 (Spring/Fall 2016): 13–39.

Jia, Bing Bing. China and the International Criminal Court: The Current Situation. *Singapore Year Book of International Law* 10 (2006): 87–97.

Jianping, Lu, and Wang Zhixiang. Chinas Attitude towards the ICC. *Journal of International Criminal Justice* 3, no. 3 (2005): 608–20.

Jo, Hyeran. *Compliant Rebels: Rebel Groups and International Law in World Politics*. 1st edn. Cambridge, UK: Cambridge University Press, 2015.

Jo, Hyeran, and Beth A. Simmons. Can the International Criminal Court Deter Atrocity? *International Organization* 70, no. 3 (2016): 443–75.

Johnston, Alastair Iain. *Social States: China in International Institutions, 1980–2000*. Princeton: Princeton University Press, 2014.

Jose, Betcy. Not Completely the New Normal: How Human Rights Watch Tried to Suppress the Targeted Killing Norm. *Contemporary Security Policy* 38, no. 2 (2017): 237–59.

Junod, Dominique-D. *The Imperiled Red Cross and the Palestine-Eretz-Yisrael Conflict, 1945–1952: The Influence of Institutional Concerns on a Humanitarian Operation*. London: Kegan Paul International, Limited, 1996.

Junod, Sylvie. Additional Protocol II: History and Scope. *American University Law Review* 33, no. 1 (1983): 29–40.

Kalshoven, Frits. Protocol II, the CDDH and Colombia. In Frits Kalshoven, *Reflections on the Law of War: Collected Essays*, 861–92. Leiden; Boston: Martinus Nijhoff, 2007.

Kalshoven, Frits. The Undertaking to Respect and Ensure Respect in All Circumstances: From Tiny Seed to Ripening Fruit. *Yearbook of International Humanitarian Law* 2 (1999): 3–61

Kalshoven, Frits. The Diplomatic Conference on Reaffirmation and Development of International Humanitarian Law Applicable in Armed Conflicts, Geneva, 1974–1977. In Frits Kalshoven, *Reflections on the Law of War: Collected Essays*, 181–274. Leiden; Boston: Martinus Nijhoff, 2007.

Katzenstein, Peter J. Introduction: Alternative Perspectives on National Security. In Peter Katzenstein (ed.), *The Culture of National Security: Norms and Identity in World Politics*, 1–32. New York: Columbia University Press, 1996.

Katzenstein, Peter, and Nobuo Okawara. Japan, Asian-Pacific Security, and the Case for Analytical Eclecticism. *International Security* 26, no. 3 (2002): 153–85.

Kay, David A. *The New Nations in the United Nations, 1960–1967*. New York: Columbia University, 1970.

Kay, Hugh. *Salazar and Modern Portugal*. London: Eyre & Spottiswoode, 1970.

Kaye, David. Some Thoughts on Russia and the International Criminal Court. November 2012, available at: http://councilandcourt.org/files/2012/11/Russia-and-ICC.pdf [accessed 14 September 2019].

Keck, Margaret E., and Kathryn Sikkink. *Activists beyond Borders*. Ithaca: Cornell University Press, 1998.

Keith, Linda Camp. Human Rights Instruments. In Peter Cane and Herbert M. Kritzer (eds.), *The Oxford Handbook of Empirical Legal Research*, 353–75. Oxford: Oxford University Press, 2010.

Kennedy, David. *Of War and Law*. Princeton: Princeton University Press, 2006.

Kennedy, David M., and Thomas Bailey. *The American Spirit: United States History as Seen by Contemporaries*. 12th edn. Vol. 1. 2 vols. Boston: Cengage Learning, 2009.

Keohane, Robert. *After Hegemony: Cooperation and Discord in the World Political Economy*. Princeton: Princeton University Press, 1984.

Keohane, Robert. International Institutions: Two Approaches. *International Studies Quarterly* 32, no. 4 (1988): 379–96.

Keohane, Robert. Observations on the Promise and Pitfalls of Historical Institutionalism in International Relations. In Orfeo Fioretos (ed.), *International Politics and Institutions in Time*, 321–336. Oxford: Oxford University Press, 2017.

Keohane, Robert, and Lisa Martin. Institutional Theory as a Research Program. In Colin Elman and Miriam Fendius Elman (eds.), *Progress in International Relations Theory: Appraising the Field*, 71–108. Cambridge, MA: MIT Press, 2003.

Keohane, Robert, and Helen Milner. *Internationalization and Domestic Politics*. Cambridge, UK: Cambridge University Press, 1996.

Khalaf, Roula. Autocrats of the World Benefit from Donald Trumps Win. *Financial Times*, November 9, 2016.

Kincaid, Harold. *Philosophical Foundations of the Social Sciences: Analyzing Controversies in Social Research*. Cambridge, UK: Cambridge University Press, 1995.

Kindleberger, Charles P. *The World in Depression, 1929–1939* (Revised). Berkeley and Los Angeles: University of California Press, 1986.

Kirsch, Philippe. The Development of the Rome Statute. In Roy S. K. Lee (ed.), *The International Criminal Court: The Making of the Rome Statute: Issues, Negotiations and Results*, 451–62. The Hague: Martinus Nijhoff, 1999.

Kirsch, Philippe, and John T. Holmes. The Rome Conference on an International Criminal Court: The Negotiating Process. *American Journal of International Law* 93, no. 1 (1999): 2–12.

Kirsch, Philippe, and Darryl Robinson. Reaching Agreement at the Rome Conference. In Antonio Cassese, Paola Gaeta and John R. W. D. Jones (eds.), *The Rome Statute of the International Criminal Court: A Commentary*, 67–91. Oxford: Oxford University Press, 2002.

Kitchen, Veronica. From Rhetoric to Reality: Canada, the United States, and the Ottawa Process to Ban Landmines. *International Journal* 57, no. 1 (Winter/2001–2002): 37–55.

Kittel, Bernhard, David Kuehn, Joachim Blatter, Derek Beach, Ingo Rohlfing, Peter A. Hall, Dirk Leuffen, et al. Symposium: Reassessing the Methodology of Process Tracing. *European Political Science* 12, no. 1 (March 2013): 1–85.

Klose, Fabian. *Human Rights in the Shadow of Colonial Violence: The Wars of Independence in Kenya and Algeria*. Translated by Dona Geyer. Philadelphia: University of Pennsylvania Press, 2013.

Klotz, Audie. Norms Reconstituting Interests: Global Racial Equality and US Sanctions against South Africa. *International Organization* 49, no. 3 (1995): 451–78.

Knight, W. Andy. Soft Power, Moral Suasion, and Establishing the International Criminal Court: Canadian Contributions. In Rosalind Irwin (ed.), *Ethics and Security in Canadian Foreign Policy*, 113–37. Vancouver: University of British Columbia Press, 2001.

Knox, John. The Right of Revolution in Scotland. In Albert Marrin (ed.), *War and the Christian Conscience: From Augustine to Martin Luther King, Jr.*, 108–11. Chicago: Henry Regnery Company, 1971.

Knox, John. The Debate at the General Assembly, June 1564. In Roger A. Mason (ed.), *On Rebellion*, 182–209. Cambridge, UK: Cambridge University Press, 1994.

Koh, Harold Hongju. The 1998 Frankel Lecture: Bringing International Law Home. *Houston Law Review* 35 (1998): 623–81.

Koh, Harold Hongju. Internalization through Socialization. *Duke Law Journal* 54 (2004): 975–82.

Koremenos, Barbara. *The Continent of International Law: Explaining Agreement Design*. Cambridge, UK: Cambridge University Press, 2016.

Koremenos, Barbara, Charles Lipson, and Duncan Snidal. The Rational Design of International Institutions. *International Organization* 55, no. 4 (2001): 761–99.

Korey, William. *NGOs and the Universal Declaration of Human Rights: A Curious Grapevine*. New York: St. Martins Press, 1998.

Koskenniemi, Martti. *From Apology to Utopia: The Structure of International Legal Argument*. (Reissue) Cambridge, UK: Cambridge University Press, 2005.

Krasner, Stephen D. State Power and the Structure of International Trade. *World Politics* 28, no. 3 (1976): 317–47.

Krasner, Stephen D. Structural Causes and Regime Consequences: Regimes as Intervening Variables. *International Organization* 36, no. 2 (1982): 185–205.

Kratochwil, Friedrich. The Monologue of 'Science'. *International Studies Review* 5, no. 1 (2003): 124–28.

Kratochwil, Friedrich, and John Ruggie. International Organization: A State of the Art on an Art of the State. *International Organization* 40, no. 4 (1986): 753–75.

Krauthammer, Charles. The Unipolar Moment. *Foreign Affairs* 70, no. 1 (1990): 23–33.

Krebs, Ronald R., and Patrick Thaddeus Jackson. Twisting Tongues and Twisting Arms: The Power of Political Rhetoric. *European Journal of International Relations* 13, no. 1 (2007): 35–66.

Kreβ, Claus, and Frédéric Mégret. The Regulation of Non-International Armed Conflicts: Can a Privilege of Belligerency Be Envisioned in the Law of Non-International Armed Conflicts? *International Review of the Red Cross* 96, no. 893 (2014): 29–66.

Krieger, Heike. A Conflict of Norms: The Relationship between Humanitarian Law and Human Rights Law in the ICRC Customary Law Study. *Journal of Conflict and Security Law* 11, no. 2 (Summer 2006): 265–91.

Krisch, Nico. International Law in Times of Hegemony: Unequal Power and the Shaping of the International Legal Order. *European Journal of International Law* 16, no. 3 (2005): 369–408.

Kristensen, Peter Marcus. International Relations at the End: A Sociological Autopsy. *International Studies Quarterly* 62, no. 2 (2018): 245–59.

La Haye, Eve. *War Crimes in Internal Armed Conflicts*. Cambridge, UK: Cambridge University Press, 2008.

Lahiri, Dilip. Should India Continue to Stay out of ICC? ORF (blog), 24 November 2010, available at: https://orfonline.org/research/should-india-continue-to-stay-out-of-icc/ [accessed 14 September 2019].

Lake, David A. Why 'Isms' Are Evil: Theory, Epistemology, and Academic Sects as Impediments to Understanding and Progress. *International Studies Quarterly* 55, no. 2 (2011): 465–80.

Lake, David A. Theory Is Dead, Long Live Theory: The End of the Great Debates and the Rise of Eclecticism in International Relations. *European Journal of International Relations* 19, no. 3 (2013): 567–87.

Lantis, Jeffrey S., and Carmen Wunderlich. Resiliency Dynamics of Norm Clusters: Norm Contestation and International Cooperation. *Review of International Studies* 44, no. 3 (2018): 570–93.

Laudan, Larry. *Progress and Its Problems: Towards a Theory of Scientific Growth*. Berkeley and Los Angeles: University of California Press, 1978.

Lauterpacht, Hersch. *Recognition in International Law*. Cambridge, UK: Cambridge University Press, 1947.

Leach, Philip. The Chechen Conflict: Analysing the Oversight of the European Court of Human Rights. *European Human Rights Law Review*, no. 6 (2008): 732–61.

Lebow, Richard Ned. The Long Peace, the End of the Cold War, and the Failure of Realism. *International Organization* 48, no. 2 (1994): 249–77.

Lee, Roy S. K. Introduction. In Roy S. K. Lee (ed.), *The International Criminal Court: The Making of the Rome Statute: Issues, Negotiations and Results*, 1–39. The Hague: Martinus Nijhoff, 1999.

Legro, Jeffrey. Which Norms Matter? Revisiting the 'Failure' of Internationalism. *International Organization* 51, no. 1 (1997): 31–63.

Legro, Jeffrey, and Andrew Moravcsik. Is Anybody Still a Realist? *International Security* 24, no. 2 (1999): 5–55.

Leitenberg, M. Deaths in Wars and Conflicts between 1945 and 2000, Cornell University Peace Studies Program. *Occasional Paper* 29 (2006).

Levine, Daniel J., and David M. McCourt. Why Does Pluralism Matter When We Study Politics? A View from Contemporary International Relations. *Perspectives on Politics* 16, no. 1 (2018): 92–109.

Linton, Suzannah. India and China before, at, and after Rome. *Journal of International Criminal Justice* 16, no. 2 (2018): 265–94.

Lippman, Matthew. Prosecutions of Nazi War Criminals before Post-World War II Domestic Tribunals. *University of Miami International and Comparative Law Review* 8, no. 1 (2000): 1–114.

Li-Sun, Zhu. Traditional Asian Approaches – The Chinese View. *Australian Year Book of International Law* 9 (1980): 143–50.

Little, Daniel. Exogenous Variable. In Michael S. Lewis-Beck, Alan Bryman and Tim Futing Liao (eds.), *The SAGE Encyclopedia of Social Science Research Methods*, 1: 347. Thousand Oaks: SAGE Publications, Inc., 2004.

Lobell, Steven E., Norrin M. Ripsman, and Jeffrey W. Taliaferro. *Neoclassical Realism, the State, and Foreign Policy*. Cambridge, UK: Cambridge University Press, 2009.

Lowe, Kimberly A. Humanitarianism and National Sovereignty: Red Cross Intervention on Behalf of Political Prisoners in Soviet Russia, 1921–3. *Journal of Contemporary History* 49, no. 4 (2014): 652–74.

Luard, Evan (ed.), *The International Regulation of Civil Wars*. London: Thames and Hudson, 1972.

Lubell, Noam. Parallel Application of International Humanitarian Law and International Human Rights Law: An Examination of the Debate. *Israel Law Review* 40, no. 2 (2007): 648–60.

Lui, Andrew. *Why Canada Cares: Human Rights and Foreign Policy in Theory and Practice*. Kingston: McGill-Queens Press, 2012.

Luther, Martin. An Open Letter on the Harsh Book against the Peasants. In Albert Marrin (ed.), *War and the Christian Conscience: From Augustine to Martin Luther King, Jr.*, 101–7. Chicago: Henry Regnery Company, 1971.

Lüthi, Lorenz M. The Non-Aligned Movement and the Cold War, 1961–1973. *Journal of Cold War Studies* 18, no. 4 (2017): 98–147.

Lyall, Jason. Process Tracing, Causal Inference, and Civil War. In Andrew Bennett and Jeffrey T. Checkel (eds.), *Process Tracing: From Metaphor to Analytic Tool*, 186–207. Strategies for Social Inquiry. Cambridge, UK: Cambridge University Press, 2015.

Lysaght, Charles. The Attitude of Western Countries. In Antonio Cassese (ed.), *The New Humanitarian Law of Armed Conflict*, 350–385. Naples: Editoriale Scientifica, 1979.

Mack, Michelle, and Jelena Pejic. *Increasing Respect for International Humanitarian Law in Non-International Armed Conflicts*. Geneva: International Committee of the Red Cross, 2008.

Magnarella, Paul J. Expanding the Frontiers of Humanitarian Law: The International Criminal Tribunal for Rwanda. *Florida Journal of International Law* 9 (1994): 421–441.

Mahoney, James. The Logic of Process Tracing Tests in the Social Sciences. *Sociological Methods & Research* 41, no. 4 (2012): 570–97.

Mahoney, James, and Gary Goertz. The Possibility Principle: Choosing Negative Cases in Qualitative Research. *American Political Science Review* 98, no. 4 (2004): 653–70.

Makinda, Samuel. Terrorism in International Society: An Eclectic Perspective. *Journal of Asian Security and International Affairs* 3, no. 1 (2016): 90–101.

Mamlyuk, Boris N. Decolonization as a Cold War Imperative. In Luis Eslava, Michael Fakhri and Vasuki Nesiah (eds.), *Bandung, Global History, and International Law: Critical Pasts and Pending Futures*, 196–214. Cambridge, UK: Cambridge University Press, 2017.

Mansingh, Surjit. Indira Gandhis Foreign Policy: Hard Realism? In David M. Malone, C. Raja Mohan and Srinath Raghavan (eds.), *The Oxford Handbook of Indian Foreign Policy*, 104–16. Oxford: Oxford University Press, 2015.

Mantilla, Giovanni. Under (Social) Pressure: The Historical Regulation of Internal Armed Conflicts through International Law (PhD dissertation). University of Minnesota, 2013, available at: https://conservancy.umn.edu/handle/11299/175520 [accessed 19 September 2019].

Mantilla, Giovanni. Conforming Instrumentalists: Why the USA and the United Kingdom Joined the 1949 Geneva Conventions. *European Journal of International Law* 28, no. 2 (2017): 483–511.

Mantilla, Giovanni. The Origins and Evolution of the 1949 Geneva Conventions and the 1977 Additional Protocols. In Matthew Evangelista and

Nina Tannenwald (eds.), *Do the Geneva Conventions Matter?*, 35–66. Oxford: Oxford University Press, 2017.

Mantilla, Giovanni. Forum Isolation: Social Opprobrium and the Origins of the International Law of Internal Conflict. *International Organization* 72, no. 2 (2018): 317–49.

Mantilla, Giovanni. The Protagonism of the USSR and Socialist States in the Revision of International Humanitarian Law. *Journal of the History of International Law* 21 (2019): 181–211.

Maqungo, Sivu. The Establishment of the International Criminal Court: SADCs Participation in the Negotiations. *African Security Review* 9, no. 1 (2000): 42–53.

March, James, and Johan Olsen. The Institutional Dynamics of International Political Orders. *International Organization* 52, no. 4 (1998): 943–69.

March, James, and Johan Olsen. The Logic of Appropriateness. In Robert E. Goodin (ed.), *The Oxford Handbook of Political Science*, 478–97. Oxford: Oxford University Press, 2011.

Marsh, David, Selen A. Ercan, and Paul Furlong. A Skin Not a Sweater: Ontology and Epistemology in Political Science. In Vivien Lowndes, David Marsh and Gerry Stoker (eds.), *Theory and Methods in Political Science*. 4th edn., 177–98. Basingstoke: Palgrave, 2017.

Martin, Lisa. An Institutionalist View: International Institutions and State Strategies. In T. V. Paul and John A. Hall (eds.), *International Order and the Future of World Politics*, 78–98. Cambridge, UK: Cambridge University Press, 1999.

Martin, Lisa. The President and International Commitments: Treaties as Signaling Devices. *Presidential Studies Quarterly* 35, no. 3 (2005): 440–65.

McAllister, Jacqueline, and James Meernik. Casting a Shadow over War Zones: The International Criminal Courts Impact on Rebel and Government Forces Use of Violence against Civilians. Ljubljana, 2016, available at: http://web.isanet.org/Web/Conferences/CEEISA-ISA-LBJ2016/Archive/a7a5720e-fe27-48a6-8144-b816c183957d.pdf [accessed 14 September 2019].

McCourt, David M. Practice Theory and Relationalism as the New Constructivism. *International Studies Quarterly* 60, no. 3 (2016): 475–85.

McGoldrick, Dominic. Political and Legal Responses to the ICC. In Dominic McGoldrick, Peter J. Rowe and Eric Donnelly (eds.), *The Permanent International Criminal Court: Legal and Policy Issues*, 389–449. Oxford; Portland: Hart Publishing, 2004.

McGoldrick, Dominic, Peter J. Rowe, and Eric Donnelly (eds.), *The Permanent International Criminal Court: Legal and Policy Issues*. Oxford; Portland: Hart, 2004.

Mearsheimer, John. The False Promise of International Institutions. *International Security* 19, no. 3 (1994): 5–49.

Mearsheimer, John. *The Tragedy of Great Power Politics*. New York: WW Norton & Company, 2003.

Mearsheimer, John. Structural Realism. In Timothy Dunne, Milja Kurki and Steve Smith (eds.), *International Relations Theories: Discipline and Diversity*, 51–67. 4th edn. Oxford: Oxford University Press, 2016.

Meernik, James. The International Criminal Court and the Deterrence of Human Rights Atrocities. *Civil Wars* 17, no. 3 (2015): 318–39.

Mégret, Frédéric. From 'Savages' to 'Unlawful Combatants': A Postcolonial Look at International Humanitarian Laws 'Other'. In Anne Orford (ed.), *International Law and Its Others*, 265–317. Cambridge, UK: Cambridge University Press, 2006.

Melander, Erik, Therése Pettersson and Lotta Themnér. Organized Violence, 1989–2015. *Journal of Peace Research* 53, no. 5 (2016): 727–42.

Meron, Theodor. International Criminalization of Internal Atrocities. *American Journal of International Law* 89, no. 3 (1995): 554–77.

Meron, Theodor. The Martens Clause, Principles of Humanity, and Dictates of Public Conscience. *American Journal of International Law* 94, no. 1 (2000): 78–89.

Mills, Kurt, and Alan Bloomfield. African Resistance to the International Criminal Court: Halting the Advance of the Anti-Impunity Norm. *Review of International Studies* 44, no. 1 (2018): 101–27.

Moir, Lindsay. The Historical Development of the Application of Humanitarian Law in Non-International Armed Conflicts to 1949. *International & Comparative Law Quarterly* 47, no. 2 (1998): 337–61.

Moir, Lindsay. *The Law of Internal Armed Conflict*. Cambridge, UK: Cambridge University Press, 2002.

Montbrial, Thierry de. For a New World Economic Order. *Foreign Affairs* 54, no. 1 (1975): 61–78.

Moorehead, Caroline. *Dunants Dream: War, Switzerland and the History of the Red Cross*. New York: Carroll & Graf, 1999.

Moravcsik, Andrew. Liberal International Relations Theory: A Scientific Assessment. In Colin Elman and Miriam Fendius Elman (eds.), *Progress in International Relations Theory: Appraising the Field*, 159–204. Cambridge, MA: MIT Press, 2003.

Moravcsik, Andrew. *Liberalism and International Relations Theory*. Center for International Affairs, Harvard University, Working Paper No. 92-6, 1992.

Moravcsik, Andrew. Taking Preferences Seriously: A Liberal Theory of International Politics. *International Organization* 51, no. 4 (1997): 513–53.

Moravcsik, Andrew. The New Liberalism. In Christian Reus-Smit and Duncan Snidal (eds.), *The Oxford Handbook of International Relations*, 234–54. Oxford: Oxford University Press, 2008.

Moravcsik, Andrew. The Origins of Human Rights Regimes: Democratic Delegation in Postwar Europe. *International Organization* 54, no. 2 (2000): 217–52.

Moravcsik, Andrew. Theory Synthesis in International Relations: Real Not Metaphysical. *International Studies Review* 5, no. 1 (2003): 131–36.

Morgenthau, Hans J. Another 'Great Debate': The National Interest of the United States. *The American Political Science Review* 46, no. 4 (1952): 961–88.

Morgenthau, Hans J. *Politics among Nations: The Struggle for Power and Peace*. 4th edn. New York: Knopf, 1967.

Morrow, James D. *Order within Anarchy: The Laws of War as an International Institution*. Cambridge, UK: Cambridge University Press, 2014.

Morrow, James D. The Laws of War, Common Conjectures, and Legal Systems in International Politics. *The Journal of Legal Studies* 31, no. S1 (2002): S41–60.

Müller, Harald. Arguing, Bargaining and All That: Communicative Action, Rationalist Theory and the Logic of Appropriateness in International Relations. *European Journal of International Relations* 10, no. 3 (2004): 395–435.

Müller, Harald, and Carmen Wunderlich. Not Lost in Contestation: How Norm Entrepreneurs Frame Norm Development in the Nuclear Nonproliferation Regime. *Contemporary Security Policy* 39, no. 3 (2018): 341–66.

Murray, Daragh. *Practitioners Guide to Human Rights Law in Armed Conflict*. Oxford: Oxford University Press, 2016.

Nabulsi, Karma. *Traditions of War*. Oxford: Oxford University Press, 1999.

Neack, Laura (ed.), Forum: Pluralism in IR Theory. *International Studies Perspectives* 16, no. 1 (2015).

Neff, Stephen C. *Justice in Blue and Gray: A Legal History of the Civil War*. Cambridge, MA: Harvard University Press, 2010.

Neff, Stephen C. *War and the Law of Nations: A General History*. Cambridge, UK: Cambridge University Press, 2005.

Neuberg, Paul. Sadat to Meet Tito as Soviet Anger Rises. *The Guardian*, March 27, 1974.

Neuerbourg, Hanns. Ninety-Seven Nations and Three Liberation Movements Signed a Document Friday Completing Four Years of Work on How to Improve Humanitarian Rules of Welfare. Associated Press, June 10, 1977.

Nexon, Daniel, Ted Hopf, Stacie Goddard, Alexander Montgomery, Oliver Kessler, Christian Bueger, Cecelia Lynch, Ty Solomon, Swati Srivastava, and David M. McCourt. Seizing Constructivist Ground? Practice and Relational Theories: Symposium. 3 April 2017, available at: https://isanet.org/Publications/ISQ/Posts/ID/5473/Seizing-Constructivist-Ground-Practice-and-Relational-Theories [accessed 14 September 2019].

Nye, Joseph S. *Soft Power: The Means to Success in World Politics*. New York: Public Affairs, 2004.

Öberg, Marko Divac. The Absorption of Grave Breaches into War Crimes Law. *International Review of the Red Cross* 91, no. 873 (2009): 163–83.

Oberleitner, Gerd. *Human Rights in Armed Conflict: Law, Practice, Policy*. Cambridge, UK: Cambridge University Press, 2015.

Oeter, Stefan. Civil War, Humanitarian Law and the United Nations. In Jochen Frowein and Rüdiger Wolfrum (eds.), *Max Planck Yearbook of United Nations Law*, 1: 195–229. Hague: Kluwer Law International, 1997.

Oglesby, Roscoe Ralph. *Internal War and the Search for Normative Order*. The Hague: Martinus Nijhoff, 1971.

O'Keefe, Roger. The Grave Breaches Regime and Universal Jurisdiction. *Journal of International Criminal Justice* 7, no. 4 (2009): 811–31.

Oppenheim, Lassa. *International Law: A Treatise*. Vol. II. London: Longmans, Green and Co., 1906.

O'Rourke, Vernon A. Recognition of Belligerency and the Spanish War. *American Journal of International Law* 31, no. 3 (1937): 398–413.

Osakwe, C. O. *The Participation of the Soviet Union in Universal International Organizations: A Political and Legal Analysis of Soviet Strategies and Aspirations Inside ILO, Unesco and WHO*. Leiden: Brill, 1972.

Owen, John M. How Liberalism Produces Democratic Peace. *International Security* 19, no. 2 (1994): 87–125.

Pace, William R., and Jennifer Schense. The Coalition for the International Criminal Court at the Preparatory Commission. In Roy S. Lee (ed.), *The International Criminal Court: Elements of Crimes and Rules of Procedure and Evidence*, 705–34. Ardsley: Transnational, 2001.

Pace, William R., and Mark Thieroff. Participation of Non-Governmental Organizations. In Roy S. K. Lee (ed.), *The International Criminal Court: The Making of the Rome Statute: Issues, Negotiations and Results*, 391–8. The Hague: Martinus Nijhoff, 1999.

Parsons, Craig. Before Eclecticism: Competing Alternatives in Constructivist Research. *International Theory* 7, no. 3 (2015): 501–38.

Parsons, Craig. *How to Map Arguments in Political Science*. Oxford: Oxford University Press, 2007.

Paul, T. V., Deborah Welch Larson, and William C. Wohlforth (eds.), *Status in World Politics*. Cambridge, UK: Cambridge University Press, 2014.

Pearson, Zoe. Non-Governmental Organizations and the International Criminal Court: Changing Landscapes of International Law. *Cornell International Law Journal* 39, no. 2 (2006): 243–84.

Peevers, Charlotte. Altering International Law: Nasser, Bandung, and the Suez Crisis. In Luis Eslava, Makhri Fakhri and Vasuki Nesiah (eds.), *Bandung, Global History and International Law: Critical Pasts and Pending Futures*, 574–94. Cambridge, UK: Cambridge University Press, 2017.

Perna, Laura. *The Formation of the Treaty Law of Non-International Armed Conflicts*. Leiden: Martinus Nijhoff, 2006.

Petrova, Margarita H. Rhetorical Entrapment and Normative Enticement: How the United Kingdom Turned from Spoiler into Champion of the Cluster Munition Ban. *International Studies Quarterly* 60, no. 3 (2016): 387–99.

Pierson, Paul. *Politics in Time: History, Institutions, and Social Analysis*. Princeton: Princeton University Press, 2011.

Pike, David W. *France Divided: The French and the Civil War in Spain*. London: Sussex Academic Press, 2012.

Plummer, Joni J. France and Portugal in the Spanish Civil War – Domestic and International Policies (MA thesis). Indiana University at Bloomington, 1988, available at: https://apps.dtic.mil/dtic/tr/fulltext/u2/a203120.pdf [accessed 14 September 2019].

Pohl, Benjamin, and Niels van Willigen. Analytic Eclecticism and EU Foreign Policy (In)Action. *Global Society* 29, no. 2 (2015): 175–98.

Pouliot, Vincent. Diplomats as Permanent Representatives: The Practical Logics of the Multilateral Pecking Order. *International Journal* 66, no. 3 (2011): 543–61.

Pouliot, Vincent. *International Pecking Orders: The Politics and Practice of Multilateral Diplomacy*. Cambridge, UK: Cambridge University Press, 2016.

Pouliot, Vincent. *International Security in Practice: The Politics of NATO–Russia Diplomacy*. Cambridge, UK: Cambridge University Press, 2010.

Pouliot, Vincent, and Jérémie Cornut. Practice Theory and the Study of Diplomacy: A Research Agenda. *Cooperation and Conflict* 50, no. 3 (2015): 297–315.

Pratt, Simon Frankel. Pragmatism as Ontology, Not (Just) Epistemology: Exploring the Full Horizon of Pragmatism as an Approach to IR Theory. *International Studies Review* 18, no. 3 (2016): 508–27.

Price, Jonathan J. *Thucydides and Internal War*. Cambridge, UK: Cambridge University Press, 2001.

Price, Richard. Emerging Customary Norms and Anti-Personnel Landmines. In Christian Reus-Smit (ed.), *The Politics of International Law*, 106–30. Cambridge, UK: Cambridge University Press, 2004.

Price, Richard. Reversing the Gun Sights: Transnational Civil Society Targets Land Mines. *International Organization* 52, no. 3 (1998): 613–44.

Price, Richard, and Christian Reus-Smit. Dangerous Liaisons? Critical International Theory and Constructivism. *European Journal of International Relations* 4, no. 3 (1998): 259–94.

Prorok, Alyssa K. The (In)Compatibility of Peace and Justice? The International Criminal Court and Civil Conflict Termination *International Organization* 71, no. 2 (2017): 213–43.

Quénivet, Noëlle. Commentary on the Law of the International Criminal Court: Article 8(2)(c). Edited by Mark Klamberg, 23 March 2017, available at: https://casematrixnetwork.org/cmn-knowledge-hub/icc-commentary-clicc/commentary-rome-statute/commentary-rome-statute-part-2-articles-5-10/#c1938 [accessed 14 September 2019].

Quénivet, Noëlle. Commentary on the Law of the International Criminal Court: Article 8(2)(e). Edited by Mark Klamberg, 23 March 2016, available at: https://casematrixnetwork.org/cmn-knowledge-hub/icc-commentary-clicc/commentary-rome-statute/commentary-rome-statute-part-2-articles-5-10/#c1947 [accessed 14 September 2019].

Quénivet, Noëlle. Commentary on the Law of the International Criminal Court: Article 8(2)(f). Edited by Mark Klamberg, 23 March 2017, available at: https://casematrixnetwork.org/cmn-knowledge-hub/icc-commentary-clicc/commentary-rome-statute/commentary-rome-statute-part-2-articles-5-10/#c1967 [accessed 14 September 2019].

Rajkovic, Nikolas. *The Politics of International Law and Compliance: Serbia, Croatia and The Hague Tribunal*. Abingdon: Routledge, 2011.

Ramanathan, Usha. India and the ICC. *Journal of International Criminal Justice* 3, no. 3 (2005): 627–34.

Rao, Raza Mumtaz. Nasim Hasan Shah: A Controversial Judge. *Daily Capital*. February 4, 2015.

Ratcliffe, Susan (ed.), *Concise Oxford Dictionary of Quotations*. 6th edn. Oxford: Oxford University Press, 2011.

Raymond, Gregory. Problems and Prospects in the Study of International Norms. *Mershon International Studies Review* 41, no. 2 (1997): 205–45.

Reus-Smit, Christian. Beyond Metatheory? *European Journal of International Relations* 19, no. 3 (2013): 589–608.

Reus-Smit, Christian. Constructivism. In Scott Burchill, Andrew Linklater, Richard Devetak, Jack Donnelly, Matthew Paterson, Christian Reus-Smit and Jacqui True (eds.), *Theories of International Relations*. 3rd edn., 188–212. New York: Palgrave Macmillan, 2005.

Reus-Smit, Christian. Imagining Society: Constructivism and the English School. *The British Journal of Politics & International Relations* 4, no. 3 (2002): 487–509.

Reus-Smit, Christian. Society, Power and Ethics. In Christian Reus-Smit (ed.), *The Politics of International Law*, 272–90. Cambridge, UK: Cambridge University Press, 2004.

Reus-Smit, Christian. The Constitutional Structure of International Society and the Nature of Fundamental Institutions. *International Organization* 51, no. 4 (1997): 555–89.

Reus-Smit, Christian. The Contours of Analytical Eclecticism. Einaudi Center for International Studies, Cornell University, 2011, available at: https://web

.archive.org/web/20150613032718/http:/pacs.einaudi.cornell.edu/system/files/ReusSmit-PKFest1.pdf [accessed 14 September 2019].

Reynolds, David. Great Britain. In David Reynolds (ed.), *The Origins of the Cold War in Europe*, 77–95. New Haven: Yale University Press, 1994.

Rey-Schyrr, Catherine. *From Yalta to Dien Bien Phu: The History of the International Committee of the Red Cross 1945 to 1955*. Geneva: International Committee of the Red Cross, 2017.

Ripsman, Norrin M., Jeffrey W. Taliaferro, and Steven E. Lobell. *Neoclassical Realist Theory of International Politics*. Oxford: Oxford University Press, 2016.

Risse, Thomas. Arguing about Arguing: A Comment. *Critical Policy Studies* 7, no. 3 (2013): 339–49.

Risse, Thomas. Global Governance and Communicative Action. *Government and Opposition* 39, no. 2 (2004): 288–313.

Risse, Thomas. 'Lets Argue!': Communicative Action in World Politics. *International Organization* 54, no. 1 (2003): 1–39.

Risse, Thomas, and Stephen Ropp. International Human Rights Norms and Domestic Change: Conclusions. In Thomas Risse, Stephen Ropp and Kathryn Sikkink (eds.), *The Power of Human Rights*, 234–78. Cambridge, UK: Cambridge University Press, 1999.

Risse, Thomas, Stephen C. Ropp, and Kathryn Sikkink (eds.), *The Persistent Power of Human Rights: From Commitment to Compliance*. Cambridge, UK: Cambridge University Press, 2013.

Risse, Thomas, Stephen Ropp, and Kathryn Sikkink (eds.), *The Power of Human Rights*. Cambridge, UK: Cambridge University Press, 1999.

Risse, Thomas, and Kathryn Sikkink. The Socialization of International Human Rights Norms into Domestic Practices: Introduction. In Thomas Risse, Stephen Ropp and Kathryn Sikkink (eds.), *The Power of Human Rights*, 1–38. Cambridge, UK: Cambridge University Press, 1999.

Risse-Kappen, Thomas. Ideas Do Not Float Freely: Transnational Coalitions, Domestic Structures, and the End of the Cold War. *International Organization* 48, no. 2 (1994): 185–214.

Roberge, Marie-Claude. The New International Criminal Court: A Preliminary Assessment. *International Review of the Red Cross* 38, no. 325 (1998): 671–83.

Roberts, Christopher N. J. *The Contentious History of the International Bill of Human Rights*. Cambridge Studies in Law and Society. Cambridge, UK: Cambridge University Press, 2014.

Robinson, Arthur N. R. Extemporaneous Statement Made by His Excellency Arthur N.R. Robinson President of the Republic of Trinidad and Tobago on April 11, 2002 at the Plenary Session of the Special Treaty Event, April 11, 2002, available at: http://iccnow.org/documents/TrinidadRobinsonPlen11Apr02.pdf [accessed 14 September 2019].

Robinson, Darryl, and Herman von Hebel. War Crimes in Internal Conflicts: Article 8 of the ICC Statute. *Yearbook of International Humanitarian Law* 2 (December 1999): 193–209.

Rodley, Nigel. Human Rights in Armed Conflict. *New World*, April 1975.

Rohlfing, Ingo. *Case Studies and Causal Inference*. Research Methods Series. London: Palgrave Macmillan, 2012.

Root, Elihu. Francis Lieber. *Proceedings of the American Society of International Law at Its Annual Meeting* 7 (1913): 8–30.

Ropp, Stephen, and Kathryn Sikkink. International Norms and Domestic Politics in Chile and Guatemala. In Thomas Risse, Stephen Ropp and Kathryn Sikkink (eds.), *The Power of Human Rights*, 172–204. Cambridge, UK: Cambridge University Press, 1999.

Rose, Gideon. Neoclassical Realism and Theories of Foreign Policy. *World Politics* 51, no. 1 (1998): 144–72.

Rubinstein, Alvin Z. Egypts Foreign Policy. *Current History* 66, no. 390 (1974): 53.

Rudolph, Christopher. Constructing an Atrocities Regime: The Politics of War Crimes Tribunals. *International Organization* 55, no. 3 (2001): 655–91.

Rudolph, Christopher. *Power and Principle: The Politics of International Criminal Courts*. Ithaca: Cornell University Press, 2017.

Ruegger, Paul. Radio Address. Zürich, June 1948. Archiv für Zeitgeschichte, ETH Zürich, Nachlass Paul Ruegger dossier 28.3.2.1 Amerikareise Paul Ruegger.

Ruggie, John Gerard. What Makes the World Hang Together? Neo-Utilitarianism and the Social Constructivist Challenge. *International Organization* 52, no. 4 (1998): 855–85.

Russett, Bruce, Christopher Layne, David E. Spiro, and Michael W. Doyle. The Democratic Peace. *International Security* 19, no. 4 (1995): 164–84.

Sadoul, Paul. *De la guerre civile en droit des gens: reconnaissance de belligérance*. Nancy: P. Scheffer, 1905.

Samaroo, Brinsley. ANR Robinsons Long Road to the International Criminal Court (ICC). The University of Trinidad and Tobago, 6 June 2009, available at: http://acuns.org/wp-content/uploads/2012/06/Long-Road-To-ICC-ANR-Robinson-AM-2009.pdf [accessed 14 September 2019].

Sandoz, Yves. The History of the Grave Breaches Regime. *Journal of International Criminal Justice* 7, no. 4 (2009): 657–82.

Sandoz, Yves, Christophe Swinarski, and Bruno Zimmermann (eds.), *Commentary on the Additional Protocols of 8 June 1977 to the Geneva Conventions of 12 August 1949*. Leiden: International Committee of the Red Cross, Martinus Nijhoff, 1987.

Sassòli, Marco, Antoine A. Bouvier, and Anne Quintin. *How Does Law Protect in War?* 3rd edn. Vol. I. Geneva: International Committee of the Red Cross, 2006.

Schabas, William. *An Introduction to the International Criminal Court.* 3rd edn. Cambridge: Cambridge University Press, 2007.

Schabas, William. *The International Criminal Court: A Commentary on the Rome Statute.* Oxford: Oxford University Press, 2010.

Schabas, William. *The International Criminal Court: A Commentary on the Rome Statute.* 2nd edn. Oxford: Oxford University Press, 2016.

Schabas, William. *Unimaginable Atrocities: Justice, Politics, and Rights at the War Crimes Tribunals.* Oxford: Oxford University Press, 2012.

Scheffer, David J. *All the Missing Souls: A Personal History of the War Crimes Tribunals.* Princeton: Princeton University Press, 2011.

Scheffer, David J. The United States and the International Criminal Court. *American Journal of International Law* 93, no. 1 (1999): 12–22.

Scheipers, Sibylle, and Daniela Sicurelli. Normative Power Europe: A Credible Utopia? *Journal of Common Market Studies* 45, no. 2 (2007): 435–57.

Schiff, Benjamin N. *Building the International Criminal Court.* Cambridge, UK: Cambridge University Press, 2008.

Schimmelfennig, Frank. The Community Trap: Liberal Norms, Rhetorical Action, and the Eastern Enlargement of the European Union. *International Organization* 55, no. 1 (2001): 47–80.

Schmitter, Philippe C. The Future of Real-Existing Democracy. *Society and Economy* 33, no. 2 (2011): 399–428.

Schwarz, Alexander. War Crimes. *Max Planck Encyclopedia of Public International Law*, Oxford University Press, 2014, available at: http://opil.ouplaw.com/view/10.1093/law:epil/9780199231690/law-9780199231690-e431 [accessed 14 September 2019].

Schweller, Randall L. *Unanswered Threats: Political Constraints on the Balance of Power.* Princeton: Princeton University Press, 2006.

Schweller, Randall L., and David Priess. A Tale of Two Realisms: Expanding the Institutions Debate. *Mershon International Studies Review* 41, no. 1 (1997): 1–32.

Scobbie, Iain. The Approach to Customary International Law in the Study. In Elizabeth Wilmshurst and Susan Breau (eds.), *Perspectives on the ICRC Study on Customary International Humanitarian Law*, 15–49. Cambridge, UK: Cambridge University Press, 2007.

Shaffer, Gregory, and Tom Ginsburg. The Empirical Turn in International Legal Scholarship. *American Journal of International Law* 106, no. 1 (2012): 1–46.

Shama, Nael. *Egyptian Foreign Policy from Mubarak to Morsi: Against the National Interest.* Abingdon: Routledge, 2013.

Shany, Yuval. *Assessing the Effectiveness of International Courts*. Oxford: Oxford University Press, 2014.

Shany, Yuval. Assessing the Effectiveness of International Courts: A Goal-Based Approach. *American Journal of International Law* 106, no. 2 (2012): 225–70.

Shawki, Noha, and Michaelene Cox. *Negotiating Sovereignty and Human Rights: Actors and Issues in Contemporary Human Rights Politics*. Farnham: Ashgate, 2009.

Shereshevsky, Yahli. Back in the Game: The Reengagement of States in International Humanitarian Law Making. *Berkeley Journal of International Law* 37, no. 1 (2019): 1–63.

Schiff, B. N. Universalism Meets Sovereignty at the International Criminal Court. In Noha Shawki and Michaelene Cox (eds), *Negotiating Sovereignty and Human Rights: Actors and Issues in Contemporary Human Rights Politics*, 59–79. Farnham: Ashgate, 2009.

Sikkink, Kathryn. Human Rights, Principled Issue-Networks, and Sovereignty in Latin America. *International Organization* 47, no. 3 (1993): 411–41.

Sikkink, Kathryn. *The Justice Cascade: How Human Rights Prosecutions Are Changing World Politics*. New York: W. W. Norton, 2011.

Sil, Rudra, and Peter Katzenstein. Analytic Eclecticism in the Study of World Politics: Reconfiguring Problems and Mechanisms across Research Traditions. *Perspectives on Politics* 8, no. 2 (2010): 411–31.

Sil, Rudra, and Peter Katzenstein. *Beyond Paradigms: Analytic Eclecticism in the Study of World Politics*. New York: Palgrave Macmillan, 2010.

Sil, Rudra, and Peter Katzenstein. De-Centering, Not Discarding, the 'Isms': Some Friendly Amendments. *International Studies Quarterly* 55, no. 2 (2011): 481–85.

Simmons, Beth. International Law and International Relations. In Gregory A. Caldeira, R. Daniel Kelemen and Keith E. Whittington (eds.), *The Oxford Handbook of Law and Politics*, 187–208. Oxford: Oxford University Press, 2008.

Simmons, Beth. *Mobilizing for Human Rights: International Law in Domestic Politics*. Cambridge, UK: Cambridge University Press, 2009.

Simmons, Beth. Why Commit? Explaining State Acceptance of International Human Rights Obligations. 1 May 2002, available at: https://wcfia.harvard.edu/publications/why-commit-explaining-state-acceptance-international-human-rights-obligations [accessed 14 September 2019].

Simmons, Beth, and Allison Danner. Credible Commitments and the International Criminal Court. *International Organization* 64, no. 2 (2010): 225–56.

Sivakumaran, Sandesh. *The Law of Non-International Armed Conflict*. Oxford: Oxford University Press, 2012.

Slaughter, Anne-Marie. *A New World Order*. Princeton: Princeton University Press, 2004.

Slaughter, Anne-Marie. Building Global Democracy. *Chicago Journal of International Law* 1, no. 2 (2000): 223–29.

Slaughter, Anne-Marie. International Law in a World of Liberal States. *European Journal of International Law* 6, no. 1 (1995): 503–38.

Small, Melvin, and J. David Singer. The War-Proneness of Democratic Regimes, 1816–1965. *Jerusalem Journal of International Relations* 1, no. 4 (1976): 50–69.

Smith, Courtney B. The Politics of Global Consensus Building: A Comparative Analysis. *Global Governance* 5, no. 2 (1999): 173–201.

Smith, Nicholas Ross. Can Neoclassical Realism Become a Genuine Theory of International Relations? *The Journal of Politics* 80, no. 2 (2018): 742–49.

Soifer, Hillel David. The Causal Logic of Critical Junctures. *Comparative Political Studies* 45, no. 12 (2012): 1572–97.

Solomon, Ty, and Brent J. Steele. Micro-Moves in International Relations Theory. *European Journal of International Relations* 23, no. 2 (2017): 267–91.

Somin, Ilya. *Stillborn Crusade: The Tragic Failure of Western Intervention in the Russian Civil War, 1918–1920*. New Brunswick: Transaction Publishers, 1996.

Soutou, Georges-Henri. France. In David Reynolds (ed.), *The Origins of the Cold War in Europe*, 96–120. New Haven: Yale University Press, 1994.

Steel, Daniel. Social Mechanisms and Causal Inference. *Philosophy of the Social Sciences* 34, no. 1 (2004): 55–78.

Steele, Brent J. Book review: Reconstructing the Cold War: The Early Years, 1945–1958. By Ted Hopf. New York: Oxford University Press, 2012; International Practices. Edited by Emanuel Adler and Vincent Pouliot. New York: Cambridge University Press, 2011. *Perspectives on Politics* 12, no. 1 (2014): 276–78.

Stein, Arthur A. Neoliberal Institutionalism. In Christian Reus-Smit and Duncan Snidal (eds.), *The Oxford Handbook of International Relations*, 201–21. Oxford: Oxford University Press, 2008.

Steinacher, Gerald. *Humanitarians at War: The Red Cross in the Shadow of the Holocaust*. Oxford: Oxford University Press, 2017.

Steinberg, Richard H. Wanted – Dead or Alive. In Jeffrey L. Dunoff and Mark A. Pollack (eds.), *Interdisciplinary Perspectives on International Law and International Relations: The State of the Art*, 146–72. Cambridge, UK: Cambridge University Press, 2012.

Steinke, Ronen. *Politics of International Criminal Justice: German Perspectives from Nuremberg to The Hague*. Oxford; Portland: Hart, 2012.

Stinchcombe, Arthur L. The Conditions of Fruitfulness of Theorizing about Mechanisms in Social Science. *Philosophy of the Social Sciences* 21, no. 3 (1991): 367–88.

Struett, Michael J. *The Politics of Constructing the International Criminal Court: NGOs, Discourse, and Agency*. New York: Palgrave Macmillan, 2008.

Subotic, Jelena. Constructivism as Professional Practice in the US Academy. *PS: Political Science & Politics* 50, no. 1 (2017): 84–8.

Sunderland, Luke. *Rebel Barons: Resisting Royal Power in Medieval Culture*. Oxford: Oxford University Press, 2017.

Suter, Keith. *An International Law of Guerrilla Warfare: The Global Politics of Law-Making*. London: F. Pinter, 1984.

Taylor, Hannis. *Treatise on International Public Law*. Chicago: Callaghan & Co., 1901.

Tenove, Chris. Canada and the ICC. Part One: The Backstory. Liu Institute – Reports from the Field (blog), May 31, 2010, available at: https://blogs.ubc.ca/ligi/2010/05/31/canada-and-the-icc-part-one-the-backstory/ [accessed 14 September 2019].

Thies, Cameron. A Pragmatic Guide to Qualitative Historical Analysis in the Study of International Relations. *International Studies Perspectives* 3, no. 4 (2002): 351–72.

Thomas, Daniel C. Rejecting the US Challenge to the International Criminal Court: Normative Entrapment and Compromise in EU Policy-Making. *International Politics* 46, no. 4 (2009): 376–94.

Ticehurst, Rupert. The Martens Clause and the Laws of Armed Conflict. *International Review of the Red Cross* 37, no. 317 (1997): 125–34.

Tolley, Howard B. *The International Commission of Jurists: Global Advocates for Human Rights*. Philadelphia: University of Pennsylvania Press, 2010.

Tostensen, Arne. Norways Africa Policy. In Lennart Wohlgemuth (ed.), *The Nordic Countries and Africa: Old and New Relations*, 34–41. Uppsala: Nordic Africa Institute, 2002.

Trampusch, Christine, and Bruno Palier. Between X and Y: How Process Tracing Contributes to Opening the Black Box of Causality. *New Political Economy* 21, no. 5 (2016): 437–54.

Transcript, The New Court: Civil Society's Victory. *Common Ground,* October 6, 1998, available at: http://commongroundradio.org/shows/98/9840.html [accessed 14 September 2019].

Triggs, G. Traditional Asian Approaches to the Protection of Victims of Armed Conflict and Their Relationship to Modern International Humanitarian Law – The Chinese View: Commentary, *Australian Year Book of International Law* 9 (1980): 151–7.

Tuchman, Barbara. *The Proud Tower: A Portrait of the World before the War, 1890–1914*. London: Macmillan, 1966.

Tuininga, Matthew. *Calvins Political Theology and the Public Engagement of the Church: Christs Two Kingdoms*. Cambridge, UK: Cambridge University Press, 2017.

UK Rome Conference delegation member. Interview, August 2014. (Author papers).

Ulbert, Cornelia, and Thomas Risse. Deliberately Changing the Discourse: What Does Make Arguing Effective? *Acta Politica* 40, no. 3 (2005): 351–67.

Ulbert, Cornelia, Thomas Risse, and Harald Müller. Arguing and Bargaining in Multilateral Negotiations. Paper presented to Conference on 'Empirical Approaches to Deliberative Politics', European University Institute, Swiss Chair Firenze, 21–22 May 2004, available at: http://polsoz.fu-berlin.de/polwiss/forschung/international/atasp/publikationen/4_artikel_papiere/26/ulbert_risse_mueller_2004.pdf [accessed 14 September 2019].

Vattel, Emerich de. *The Law of Nations or the Principles of Natural Law, Applied to the Conduct and Affairs of Nations and Sovereigns*. Edited by J. B. Scott. Washington, DC: Carnegie Endowment for International Peace, 1916.

Verrijn Stuart, Heikelina, and Marlise Simons. The Judge: Interview with Antonio Cassese. In Heikelina Verrijn Stuart and Marlise Simons, *The Prosecutor and the Judge: Benjamin Ferencz and Antonio Cassese, Interviews and Writings*, 47–92. Amsterdam: Pallas Publications, Amsterdam University Press, 2009.

Vetter, Charles. *Sherman: Merchant of Terror, Advocate of Peace*. Gretna: Pelican Publishing Co., 1992.

Vieira, Sérgio. The Nordic countries and Mozambique: From national liberation to economic liberation' in 'Nordic Solidarity with the Liberation Struggles in Southern Africa, and Challenges for Democratic Partnerships into the 21st Century', Robben Island 11–14 February 1999, Conference Report, 54–65, available at: http://diva-portal.org/smash/get/diva2:287783/FULLTEXT01 [accessed 14 September 2019].

Voeten, Erik. The Bad Ass Theory of Why Dictators Sign the Convention against Torture. The Monkey Cage (blog), February 4, 2010, available at: http://themonkeycage.org/2010/02/the_bad_ass_theory_of_why_dict/ [accessed 14 September 2019].

Vreeland, James. Dictatorships, Torture, and Human Rights Treaties: The Bad Ass Theory. 12 February 2010, available at: http://vreelander.blogspot.com/2010/02/dictatorships-torture-and-human-rights.html [accessed 14 September 2019].

Vucetic, Srdjan. Genealogy as a Research Tool in International Relations. *Review of International Studies* 37, no. 3 (2011): 1295–1312.

Wæver, Ole. The Rise and Fall of the Inter-Paradigm Debate. In Steve Smith, Ken Booth and Marysia Zalewski (eds.), *International Theory: Positivism and Beyond*, 149–85. Cambridge, UK: Cambridge University Press, 1996.

Walt, Stephen M. *Origins of Alliances*. Ithaca: Cornell University Press, 1990.

Walter, Timo. The Road (Not) Taken? How the Indexicality of Practice Could Make or Break the New Constructivism'. *European Journal of International Relations* 25, no. 2 (2019): 538–61.

Waltz, Kenneth Neal. *Man, the State and War*. 2001 edn. New York: Columbia University Press, 1959.

Waltz, Kenneth Neal. *Theory of International Politics*. New York: McGraw-Hill, 1979.

Warner, Geoffrey. France and Non-Intervention in Spain, July–August 1936. *International Affairs* 38, no. 2 (1962): 203–20.

Washburn, John. The Negotiation of the Rome Statute for the International Criminal Court and International Lawmaking in the 21st Century. *Pace International Law Review* 11 (1999): 361–77.

Watkin, Kenneth, and Andrew J. Norris (eds.), *Non-International Armed Conflict in the Twenty-First Century*. Vol. 88. International Law Studies. Newport: US Naval War College, 2012.

Wedgwood, Ruth. Fiddling in Rome: America and the International Criminal Court. *Foreign Affairs* 77, no. 6 (1998): 20–24.

Wendt, Alexander. The Agent-Structure Problem in International Relations Theory. *International Organization* 41, no. 3 (1987): 335–70.

Wendt, Alexander. Anarchy Is What States Make of It: The Social Construction of Power Politics. *International Organization* 46, no. 2 (1992): 391–425.

Wendt, Alexander. *Social Theory of International Politics*. Cambridge, UK: Cambridge University Press, 1999.

Wheatley, Steven. *The Democratic Legitimacy of International Law*. Oxford: Bloomsbury, 2010.

Widmaier, Wesley W., Mark Blyth, and Leonard Seabrooke. Exogenous Shocks or Endogenous Constructions? The Meanings of Wars and Crises. *International Studies Quarterly* 51, no. 4 (2007): 747–59.

Wight, Colin, Tim Dunne, and Lene Hansen (eds.), Special Issue: The End of International Relations Theory? *European Journal of International Relations* 19, no. 3 (2013).

Wilmshurst, Elizabeth. Report on the Conference for the Establishment of an International Criminal Court 15 June–17 July 1998. September 23, 1998. (Author papers).

Wilmshurst, Elizabeth, and Susan Breau (eds.), *Perspectives on the ICRC Study on Customary International Humanitarian Law*. Cambridge, UK: Cambridge University Press, 2007.

Wilson, Page. The Myth of International Humanitarian Law. *International Affairs* 93, no. 3 (2017): 563–79.

Witt, John Fabian. *Lincolns Code: The Laws of War in American History*. New York: Free Press, 2012.

Woetzel, Robert K. *The Nuremberg Trials in International Law*. London: Stevens, 1960.

Wohlforth, William C. *The Elusive Balance: Power and Perceptions during the Cold War*. Ithaca: Cornell University Press, 1993.

Wolfers, Arnold. 'National Security as an Ambiguous Symbol. *Political Science Quarterly* 67, no. 4 (1952): 481–502.

Women's Caucus (UK branch) member. Interview, December 2014. (Author papers).

Woolsey, Theodore Dwight. *Introduction to the Study of International Law*. 4th edn. New York: Scribner, Armstrong, 1875.

Wright, Quincy. International Law and the American Civil War. *Proceedings of the American Society of International Law* 61 (1967): 50–58.

Wright, Quincy. The American Civil War. In Richard A. Falk (ed.), *The International Law of Civil War*, 30–109. Baltimore and London: Johns Hopkins Press, 1971.

Wunderlich, Carmen. A 'Rogue' Gone Norm Entrepreneurial? Iran within the Nuclear Nonproliferation Regime. In Wolfgang Wagner, Wouter Werner and Michal Onderco (eds.), *Deviance in International Relations: 'Rogue States' and International Security*, 83–104. Palgrave Studies in International Relations. London: Palgrave Macmillan, 2014.

Wunderlich, Carmen. Theoretical Approaches in Norm Dynamics. In Carmen Wunderlich and Harald Müller (eds.), *Norm Dynamics in Multilateral Arms Control: Interests, Conflicts, and Justice*, 20–47. Athens: University of Georgia Press, 2013.

Wylie, Lana. Valuing Reputation and Prestige: Canadian Foreign Policy and the International Criminal Court. *American Review of Canadian Studies* 39, no. 2 (2009): 112–30.

Yingling, Raymund T., and Robert W. Ginnane. The Geneva Conventions of 1949. *American Journal of International Law* 46, no. 3 (1952): 393–427.

Young, John W. *France, the Cold War and the Western Alliance, 1944–49: French Foreign Policy and Post-War Europe*. Leicester: Leicester University Press, 1990.

Young, Oran R. Political Leadership and Regime Formation: On the Development of Institutions in International Society. *International Organization* 45, no. 3 (1991): 281–308.

Yung, Walter. Le rôle et laction de la Croix-Rouge en temps de guerre civile. *Revue internationale de La Croix-Rouge et Bulletin international des Sociétés de la Croix-Rouge* 20, no. 230 (1938): 97–113.

Zakaria, Fareed. The Rise of Illiberal Democracy. *Foreign Affairs* 76, no. 6 (1997): 22–43.

Zamir, Noam. *Classification of Conflicts in International Humanitarian Law: The Legal Impact of Foreign Intervention in Civil Wars*. Cheltenham: Edward Elgar Publishing, 2017.

Zhu, Dan. *China and the International Criminal Court*. London: Palgrave Macmillan, 2018.

Zhu, Dan. China, the International Criminal Court, and International Adjudication. *Netherlands International Law Review* 61, no. 1 (2014): 43–67.

Zimmerman, Andreas, and Robin Geiß. Article 8 War Crimes Para. 2 (c) to (f) and Para. 3: War Crimes Committed in an Armed Conflict Not of an International Character. In Otto Triffterer and Kai Ambos (eds.), *The Rome Statute of the International Criminal Court: A Commentary*, 528–79. 3rd edn. Munich, Oxford, Baden-Baden: C.H. Beck, Hart, Nomos, 2016.

Diplomatic Conference Records (1949, 1974–77, 1998)

Diplomatic Conference for the Establishment of International Conventions for the Protection of Victims of War. *Final Record of the Diplomatic Conference of Geneva of 1949*. Vols. I–IV. Berne: Federal Political Department, 1950, available at https://www.loc.gov/rr/frd/Military_Law/RC-Fin-Rec_Dipl-Conf-1949.html [accessed 28 December 2019].

Official Records of the Diplomatic Conference on the Reaffirmation and Development of International Humanitarian Law Applicable in Armed Conflicts, Geneva. (1974–1977). Vols. I–XVI. Berne: Federal Political Department, 1978, available at https://www.loc.gov/rr/frd/Military_Law/RCdipl-conference-records.html. [accessed 17 September 2019].

United Nations. United Nations Diplomatic Conference of Plenipotentiaries on the Establishment of an International Criminal Court Rome, 15 June–17 July 1998 *Official Records* (A/CONF.183/13) Vols. I–III. United Nations, August 2002, available at http://legal.un.org/icc/rome/proceedings/contents.htm [accessed 17 September 2019].

United Nations, International Criminal Court and Tribunal Records

Final Act of the International Conference on Human Rights, Tehran, 13 May 1968 (Doc A/Conf.32/41), available at: http://legal.un.org/avl/pdf/ha/fatchr/Final_Act_of_TehranConf.pdf [accessed 6 December 2018].

International Criminal Court. Prosecutor v. Jean-Pierre Bemba Gombo, *Decision Pursuant to Article 61(7)(a) and (b) of the Rome Statute on the Charges of the Prosecutor against Jean-Pierre Bemba Gombo* (ICC-01/05-01/08, 15 June 2009), available at: https://icc-cpi.int/CourtRecords/CR2009_04528.PDF [accessed 26 December 2018].

International Criminal Court. Prosecutor v Germain Katanga, *Judgment Pursuant to Article 74 of the Statute* (ICC-01/04-01/07, 7 March 2014), available at: https://icc-cpi.int/CourtRecords/CR2015_04025.PDF [accessed 26 December 2018].

International Criminal Court. Prosecutor v Jean-Pierre Bemba Gombo, *Judgment Pursuant to Article 74 of the Statute (Public with Annexes I, II, and A to F)*, ICC-01/05-01/08 (21 March 2016), available at: https://icc-cpi.int/courtrecords/cr2016_02238.pdf [accessed 26 December 2018].

International Criminal Court. States Parties – Chronological List, available at https://asp.icc-cpi.int/en_menus/asp/states%20parties/Pages/states%20parties%20_%20chronological%20list.aspx [accessed 11 August 2019].

International Criminal Tribunal for the Former Yugoslavia. Prosecutor v. Duško Tadić aka 'Dule', *Decision on the Defence Motion for Interlocutory Appeal on*

Jurisdiction (IT-94-1, 2 October 1995), available at: http://icty.org/x/cases/tadic/acdec/en/51002.htm [accessed 14 September 2019].

International Law Commission. *Yearbook of the International Law Commission: Report of the Commission to the General Assembly on the Work of Its Forty-Third Session* (1994) (A/CN.4/SER.A/1994/Add.l (Part 2)), II(2):38–41, 67–69, available at http://legal.un.org/ilc/publications/yearbooks/english/ilc_1994_v2_p2.pdf [accessed 17 September 2019].

International Law Commission. *Report of the International Law Commission on the Work of Its Forty-Eighth Session, 6 May–26 July 1996, Official Records of the General Assembly, Fifty-First Session, Supplement No. 10* (UN Doc. A/512/10), available at: http://legal.un.org/ilc/documentation/english/reports/a_51_10.pdf [accessed 14 December 2018].

Non-Aligned Movement. *Final Declaration of the Sixth Conference of Heads of State or Government of Non-Aligned Countries, Held at Havana, Cuba, from 3 to 9 September 1979* (UN General Assembly, UN Doc. A/34/542, 11 October 1979), available at: https://undocs.org/A/34/542 [accessed 14 September 2019].

Preparatory Committee on the Establishment of an International Criminal Court, Working Group on Definitions of Crime. Working paper submitted by the delegations of New Zealand and Switzerland (UN Doc. A/AC.249/1997/WG.1/DP.2, 14 February 1997), available at: https://legal-tools.org/doc/7ba0b8/pdf/ [accessed 14 December 2018].

Preparatory Committee on the Establishment of an International Criminal Court, Working Group on Definitions of Crime. Proposal submitted by the United States (UN Doc. A/AC.249/1997/WG.1/DP.1, 14 February 1997), available at: https://legal-tools.org/doc/c5359c/pdf/ [accessed 14 December 2018].

Preparatory Committee on the Establishment of an International Criminal Court, Working Group on Definitions and Elements of Crimes. Reference Paper on War Crimes submitted by Germany (UN Doc. A/AC.249/1997/WG.1/DP.23/Rev.1, 12 December 1997), available at: https://legal-tools.org/doc/0c9b1a/pdf/ [accessed 14 December 2018].

Preparatory Committee on the Establishment of an International Criminal Court. Draft Statute for the International Criminal Court, Part 2. Jurisdiction, Admissibility and Applicable Law (UN Doc. A/AC.249/1998/CRP.8, 2 April 1998), available at: https://legal-tools.org/doc/e652fe/pdf/ [accessed 14 December 2018].

Report of the Ad Hoc Committee on the Establishment of an International Criminal Court (UN Doc. A/50/22, 6 September 1995), available at: https://legal-tools.org/doc/b50da8/pdf/ [accessed 14 December 2018].

Report of the Preparatory Committee on the Establishment of an International Criminal Court: Volume I (Proceedings of the Preparatory Committee during March–April and August 1996) (UN Doc. A/51/22, 13 September 1996), available at: https://legal-tools.org/doc/e75432/pdf/ [accessed 14 December 2018].

UN General Assembly Resolution 177(II) of 21 November 1947 (UN Doc. A/519, 8 January 1948, pp. 111–12), available at: http://undocs.org/a/519 [accessed 2 December 2018].
UN General Assembly Resolution *Respect for Human Rights in Armed Conflicts* (UN Doc. A/RES/2444 (XXIII), 19 December 1968), available at: https://refworld.org/docid/3b00f1d558.html [accessed 6 December 2018].
UN General Assembly Resolution *Respect for Human Rights in Armed Conflicts* (UN Doc. A/RES/2597 (XXIV), 16 December 1969), available at: https://refworld.org/docid/3b00f1d34e.html [accessed 6 December 2018].
UN General Assembly Resolution *Declaration on Principles of International Law concerning Friendly Relations and Co-operation among States in Accordance with the Charter of the United Nations* (UN Doc. A/RES/25/2625, 24 October 1970), available at: http://undocs.org/A/RES/2625(XXV) [accessed 14 September 2019].
UN General Assembly Resolution *Respect for Human Rights in Armed Conflicts* (UN Doc. A/RES/2674 (XXV), 9 December 1970), available at: https://refworld.org/docid/3b00f04954.html [accessed 6 December 2018].
UN General Assembly Resolution *Respect for Human Rights in Armed Conflicts* (UN Doc. A/RES/2852 (XXVI), 20 December 1971), available at: https://refworld.org/docid/3b00f1c010.html [accessed 6 December 2018].
UN General Assembly Resolution 29/3314 (UN Doc. A/RES/29/3314, 14 December 1974), available at: http://un-documents.net/a29r3314.htm [accessed 25 December 2018].
UN General Assembly Resolution 42/151 (UN Doc. A/42/151, 7 December 1987), available at: http://undocs.org/A/RES/42/151 [accessed 12 December 2018].
UN General Assembly Resolution 44/39 (UN Doc. A/RES/44/39, 4 December 1989), available at: http://undocs.org/a/RES/44/39 [accessed 25 December 2018].
UN General Assembly Resolution 47/33 (UN Doc. A/RES/47/33, 25 November 1992), available at: http://un.org/documents/ga/res/47/a47r033.htm [accessed 13 December 2018].
UN General Assembly Resolution 49/53 (UN Doc. A/RES/49/53, 17 February 1995), available at: http://un.org/ga/search/view_doc.asp?symbol=A/RES/49/53 [accessed 14 December 2018].
UN General Assembly Resolution 50/46 (UN Doc. A/RES/50/46, 11 December 1995), available at: http://un.org/documents/ga/res/50/a50r046.htm [accessed 14 December 2018].
UN Security Council Resolution 780 (UN Doc. S/RES 780, 6 October 1992), available at: http://unscr.com/en/resolutions/doc/780 [accessed 14 September 2019].
UN Security Council. Letter dated 9 February 1993 from the Secretary-General addressed to the President of the Security Council (UN Doc. S/25274, 10

February 1993), available at: http://undocs.org/S/25274 [accessed 13 December 2018].

UN Security Council Resolution 808 (UN Doc. S/RES/808, 22 February 1993), available at: http://refworld.org/docid/3b00f15d30.html [accessed 18 January 2015].

UN Security Council. Report of the Secretary-General Pursuant to Paragraph 2 of Security Council Resolution 808 (1993) (UN Doc. S/25704, 3 May 1993), available at: https://documents-dds-ny.un.org/doc/UNDOC/GEN/N93/248/35/IMG/N9324835.pdf?OpenElement [accessed 13 December 2018].

UN Security Council. Provisional Verbatim Record of the Three Thousand Two Hundred and Seventeenth Meeting (UN Doc. S/PV.3217, 25 May 1993), available at: https://undocs.org/en/S/PV.3217 [accessed 14 September 2019].

UN Security Council Resolution 827 (UN Doc. S/RES/827, 25 May 1993), available at: https://undocs.org/S/RES/827(1993) [accessed 25 December 2018].

UN Security Council Resolution 955 (UN Doc. S/RES/955, 8 November 1994), available at: http://unscr.com/en/resolutions/doc/955 [accessed 14 September 2019].

UN Security Council. Report of the Secretary-General pursuant to Paragraph 5 of Security Council Resolution 955 (1994) (UN Doc. S/1995/134, 13 February 1995), available at: https://documents-dds-ny.un.org/doc/UNDOC/GEN/N95/043/02/PDF/N9504302.pdf?OpenElement [accessed 25 December 2018].

United Nations. *Respect for Human Rights in Armed Conflicts: Report of the Secretary-General* (UN Doc. A/7720, 20 November 1969), available at: https://undocs.org/pdf?symbol=en/A/7720 [accessed 6 September 2019].

United Nations. *Respect for Human Rights in Armed Conflicts: Report of the Secretary-General* (UN Doc. A/8052, 18 September 1970), available at: https://digitallibrary.un.org/record/647214 [accessed 6 September 2019].

United Nations. *The Work of the International Law Commission*. 8th edn. Vol. I. 2012, available at: http://legal.un.org/avl/ILC/8th_E/Vol_I.pdf [accessed 14 September 2019].

United Nations Committee on International Criminal Jurisdiction. *The American Journal of International Law* 46, no. 1 (Supplement: Official Documents) (1952): 1–11.

Vienna Convention on the Law of Treaties (UN Doc. A/Conf.39/27, 23 May 1969; 1155 UNTS 331).

Red Cross Records

Documentation préliminaire pour la revision et l'établissement de conventions ayant trait à la Croix-Rouge: Mémorandum adressé par le Comité international de la Croix-Rouge aux gouvernements des États parties à la Convention de Genève et aux sociétés nationales de la Croix-Rouge. *Revue Internationale de La Croix-Rouge et Bulletin International Des Societes de La Croix-Rouge* 27, no. 314 (1945): 85–9.

International Committee of the Red Cross. *Report of the Sixteenth International Red Cross Conference, London, June 1938*, available at: https://library.icrc.org/library/docs/CDDH/CI_1938/CI_1938_RAPPORT_ENG.pdf [accessed 14 September 2019].

International Committee of the Red Cross. *Report on the Work of the Preliminary Conference of National Red Cross Societies for the Study of the Conventions and of Various Problems Relative to the Red Cross, Geneva, July 26–August 3, 1946.* Geneva: International Committee of the Red Cross, 1947, available at: https://loc.gov/rr/frd/Military_Law/pdf/RC_report-1946.pdf [accessed 14 September 2019].

International Committee of the Red Cross. *Report on the Work of the Conference of Government Experts for the Study of the Conventions for the Protection of War Victims (Geneva, April 14–26, 1947).* Geneva: International Committee of the Red Cross, 1947, available at: https://loc.gov/rr/frd/Military_Law/pdf/RC_report-1947.pdf [accessed 14 September 2019].

International Committee of the Red Cross. *Draft Revised or New Conventions for the Protection of War Victims Established by the International Committee of the Red Cross with the Assistance of Government Experts, National Red Cross Societies and Other Humanitarian Associations.* Geneva: International Committee of the Red Cross, 1948, available at: http://loc.gov/rr/frd/Military_Law/pdf/RC_Draft-revised.pdf [accessed 14 September 2019].

International Committee of the Red Cross. *Revised and New Draft Conventions for the Protection of War Victims.* Geneva: International Committee of the Red Cross, 1948, available at: https://loc.gov/rr/frd/Military_Law/pdf/RC_Revisednew-draft.pdf [accessed 14 September 2019].

International Committee of the Red Cross. *Seventeenth International Red Cross Conference, Stockholm, August 1948: Report.* Stockholm: 1948, available at: https://loc.gov/rr/frd/Military_Law/pdf/RC_XVIIth-RC-Conference.pdf [accessed 14 September 2019].

International Committee of the Red Cross. *Remarks and Proposals Submitted by the International Committee of the Red Cross: Document for the Consideration of Governments Invited by the Swiss Federal Council to Attend the Diplomatic Conference at Geneva (April 21, 1949).* Geneva: International Committee of the Red Cross, 1949, available at: https://loc.gov/rr/frd/Military_Law/pdf/RC_Remarks-proposals.pdf [accessed 14 September 2019].

International Committee of the Red Cross. *Reaffirmation and Development of the Laws and Customs Applicable in Armed Conflicts, Report Prepared for the XXIst International Conference of the Red Cross, Istanbul, September 1969*, May 1969, available at: http://loc.gov/rr/frd/Military_Law/pdf/RC-Report-reaffirm-development-1969.pdf [accessed 14 September 2019].

International Committee of the Red Cross. *Conference of Government Experts on the Reaffirmation and Development of International Humanitarian Law Applicable in Armed Conflicts (Geneva, 24 May–12 June 1971): 'V - Protection of Victims of Non-International Armed Conflicts'.* January 1971, available at: https://www.loc.gov/rr/frd/Military_Law/pdf/RC-conference_Vol-5.pdf [accessed 9 March 2020].

International Committee of the Red Cross. *Conference of Government Experts on the Reaffirmation and Development of International Humanitarian Law Applicable in Armed Conflicts (Geneva, 24 May–12 June 1971): Report on the Work of the Conference.* August 1971, available at: http://loc.gov/rr/frd/Military_Law/pdf/RC-Report-conf-of-gov-experts-1971.pdf [accessed 14 September 2019].

International Committee of the Red Cross. *Conference of Government Experts on the Reaffirmation and Development of International Humanitarian Law Applicable in Armed Conflicts (Second Session: 3 May–3 June 1972) Report on the Work of the Conference (Volume II – Annexes).* July 1972, available at: http://loc.gov/rr/frd/Military_Law/pdf/RC-Report-conf-of-gov-experts-1972_V-2.pdf [accessed 14 September 2019].

International Committee of the Red Cross. *Draft Additional Protocols to the Geneva Conventions of August 12, 1949: Commentary.* October 1973, available at: http://loc.gov/rr/frd/Military_Law/pdf/RC-Draft-additional-protocols.pdf [accessed 14 September 2019].

International Committee of the Red Cross. War Crimes: Working Paper Prepared by the ICRC for the Preparatory Committee for the Establishment of an International Criminal Court, New York, February 13, 1997, available at: http://iccnow.org/documents/3PretCmtWarCrimesRedCross.pdf [accessed 14 September 2019].

International Committee of the Red Cross. *The Roots of Restraint in War.* June 18, 2018, available at: https://icrc.org/en/publication/roots-restraint-war [accessed 14 September 2019].

International Committee of the Red Cross. State Parties to the Following International Humanitarian Law and Other Related Treaties as of 4-Sep-2019, available at: http://ihl-databases.icrc.org/applic/ihl/ihl.nsf/xsp/.ibmmodres/domino/OpenAttachment/applic/ihl/ihl.nsf/0AB77CE1BF547803C125841003C68AE/%24File/IHL_and_other_related_Treaties.pdf?Open [accessed 14 September 2019].

ICRC Customary IHL Database, Rule 156. Definition of War Crimes, available at: https://ihl-databases.icrc.org/customary-ihl/eng/docs/v1_rul_rule156 [accessed 12 December 2018].

Government Records

Aldrich, George H. Human Rights in Armed Conflict: Development of the Law. *Department of State Bulletin* 68 (June 18, 1973): 876–82.

Aldrich, George H. Classified Report of the United States Delegation to the Diplomatic Conference on the Reaffirmation and Development of International Humanitarian Law Applicable in Armed Conflicts, Geneva,

Switzerland, February 20–March 29, 1974, June 10, 1974. http://static.history.state.gov/frus/frus1969-76ve03/pdf/d235.pdf [accessed 8 March 2020].

Aldrich, George H. Report of the United States Delegation to the Diplomatic Conference on the Reaffirmation and Development of International Humanitarian Law Applicable in Armed Conflicts, Second Session, Geneva, Switzerland, February 3–April 18, 1975, July 18, 1975. TNA: FCO 61/1374 (Doc. 131). National Archives of the UK.

Aldrich, George H. Report of the U.S. Delegation to the Diplomatic Conference on the Reaffirmation and Development of International Humanitarian Law Applicable in Armed Conflicts, Third Session, Washington, Geneva, Switzerland, April 21–June 11, 1976, October 15, 1976. http://static.history.state.gov/frus/frus1969-76ve03/pdf/d261.pdf [accessed 8 March 2020].

Best, Geoffrey. Updating the Geneva Conventions (Transcript). BBC Radio 3, January 13, 1978. TNA: FCO 58/1124 (Doc. 100). National Archives of the UK.

Caffery, Jefferson. The Ambassador in France (Caffery) to the Secretary of State, February 7, 1947, available at: http://images.library.wisc.edu/FRUS/EFacs/1947v02/reference/frus.frus1947v02.i0009.pdf (at pp. 154–5) [accessed 14 September 2019].

Canadian High Commission. B. M. Mawhinney (First Secretary, Canadian High Commission London) to Michael Arthur (UN Dept., FCO). February 15, 1974. TNA: FCO 61/1231 (Doc. 48). National Archives of the UK.

Government of Israel. *The 2014 Gaza Conflict 7 July–26 August 2014: Factual and Legal Aspects*. 2015, available at: https://mfa.gov.il/ProtectiveEdge/Documents/2014GazaConflictFullReport.pdf [accessed 14 September 2019].

International Commission of Jurists. Niall MacDermot, International Commission of Jurists, to David Ennals, Minister of State. March 19, 1974. TNA: FCO 61/1232 (Doc. W105). National Archives of the UK.

McCahon, William H. Revision and Extension of the Geneva Conventions. *Department of State Bulletin* 21, no. 531 (September 5, 1949): 339–40.

McCahon, William H. Toward Revision of the Geneva Convention. *Department of State Bulletin* 19, no. 484 (October 10, 1948): 464–5.

Ministère des Affaires étrangères. La question de la guerre civile: A. Lamarle, French Head Delegate, to Robert Schuman, Minister of Foreign Affairs in Paris, May 13, 1949. Cote 4–17, Unions Internationales 161, Mai 1949 Correspondances Diverses. Archives Diplomatiques de la Courneuve, France.

Ministère des Affaires étrangères. Note Conventions de Genève en cas de guerre civile Sent by Ministry of Foreign Affairs, International Organizations Direction, to French Delegation in Geneva, June 4, 1949. Cote 4–17, Unions Internationales 161, 'Mai 1949 Correspondances Diverses'. Archives Diplomatiques de la Courneuve, France.

Northern Ireland Office. R C Cox to T K C Ellison (UN Dept., FCO): 'Draft Protocol to Article 3 to the Geneva Conventions – and the Position of

Northern Ireland'. March 14, 1973. TNA: FCO 61/1090 (Doc. 84). National Archives of the UK.

Office of General Counsel. *Department of Defense Law of War Manual.* Washington: Department of Defense, 2015, available at: http://jag.navy.mil/distrib/instructions/Law-of-War-Manual-June-2015.pdf [accessed 14 September 2019].

Quentin-Baxter, Robert Q. Report of the New Zealand Delegation to the First Session of the Diplomatic Conference for the Reaffirmation and Development of International Humanitarian Law Applicable in Armed Conflicts. April 10, 1974. TNA: FCO 61/1233 (Doc. 154). National Archives of the UK.

Reagan, Ronald. Letter of Transmittal from the President to the Senate of the United States, 29 January 1987. In United States: 'Message from the President Transmitting Protocol II Additional to the 1949 Geneva Conventions, Relating to the Protection of Victims of Noninternational Armed Conflicts, January 29, 1987', *International Legal Materials* 26, no. 2 (1987): 562.

Shultz, George P. Letter of Submittal from the Secretary of State, 13 December 1986. In United States: 'Message from the President Transmitting Protocol II Additional to the 1949 Geneva Conventions, Relating to the Protection of Victims of Noninternational Armed Conflicts, January 29, 1987', *International Legal Materials* 26, no. 2 (1987): 563–564.

UK Army Legal Services. David Hughes-Morgan (Brigadier Legal Staff) to UK Ministry of Defence (Various), 'Humanitarian Law Article 42 of Protocol I – Guerrillas'. March 4, 1977. TNA: FCO 58/1125 (Doc. 46). National Archives of the UK.

UK Cabinet Office. Memorandum by the Secretary of State for Foreign Affairs, Ministerial Committee for the Revision of the Geneva Conventions on War Victims. November 25, 1949. TNA: CAB 130/46/GEN281. National Archives of the UK.

UK Foreign and Commonwealth Office. Mill Irving, Foreign Office Minute: Revision of the Geneva Conventions. March 31, 1949. FO 369/4147, K.3541. National Archives of the UK.

UK Foreign and Commonwealth Office. United Kingdom Delegation Circular No. 10 – Diplomatic Conference on Protection of War Victims (Note on meeting held in the Attorney-General's Room at the House of Commons on Monday, 11th April, 1949). April 18, 1949. TNA: FO 369/4150, K.4771. National Archives of the UK.

UK Foreign and Commonwealth Office. United Kingdom Delegation Circular No. 11 – Diplomatic Conference on Protection of War Victims (Appending 'Record of Conversations Held in Paris between the Deputy Leader of the French Delegation and Mr. Strutt and Mr. Alexander'). April 18, 1949. TNA: FO 369/4150, K.4772. National Archives of the UK.

UK Foreign and Commonwealth Office. United Kingdom Delegation Circular No. 15 – Diplomatic Conference on Protection of War Victims (Attaching Official Record of Meeting with the Attorney General of 11 April 1949). April 19, 1949. TNA: FO 369/4150, K.4775. National Archives of the UK.

UK Foreign and Commonwealth Office. Civilian Convention – Note of an Interview with the New Zealand Delegate. April 21, 1949. TNA: FO 369/4150, K.4779. National Archives of the UK.

UK Foreign and Commonwealth Office. W E Beckett (Foreign Office) to J A C Gutteridge (Delegation to the Conference on War Victims). April 25, 1949. TNA: FO 369/4149, K.4571. National Archives of the UK.

UK Foreign and Commonwealth Office. Notes of 11th Meeting of the United Kingdom Delegation. May 4, 1949. TNA: FO 369/4150, K.4976. National Archives of the UK.

UK Foreign and Commonwealth Office. United Kingdom Delegation Circular No. 24 – Liaison with Other Delegations. May 9, 1949. TNA: FO 369/4150, K.4903. National Archives of the UK.

UK Foreign and Commonwealth Office. Letter from R. Craigie to H. A. Caccia, Enc. 'Memorandum on Developments in the Conference on the Subject of the Application of the Conventions to Civil War'. May 9, 1949. TNA: FO 369/4149, K.4720. National Archives of the UK.

UK Foreign and Commonwealth Office. Alexander to Kemball (Excerpt). May 10, 1949. TNA: FO 369/4149/K.4555. National Archives of the UK.

UK Foreign and Commonwealth Office. Letter from M. Reed, Law Officers' Dept., to Kemball, Foreign Office, 'Question of the Application of the Red Cross Conventions to Civil War'. May 16, 1949. TNA: FO 369/4150, K.4885. National Archives of the UK.

UK Foreign and Commonwealth Office. FO Minute by Mr. Alexander: Geneva Convention-Protection of War Victims. Draft Letter from Mr. Kemball to Mr. W. H. Gardner, War Office, Enclosing Copy of Sir R. Craigie's Final Report on the Geneva Conference on the Protection of War Victims. November 4, 1949. TNA: FO 369/4164, K.10540. National Archives of the UK.

UK Foreign and Commonwealth Office. Letter from K G MacInnes to Mr Parsons, 'ICRC Conference on Humanitarian Law Applicable in Armed Conflicts, Geneva 24 May–12 June'. March 11, 1971. TNA: FCO 61/808 (Doc. 62). National Archives of the UK.

UK Foreign and Commonwealth Office. Letter from I K C Ellison to R G Sheridan, 'Norwegian Representation at the ICRC Conference on Humanitarian Law in Armed Conflicts'. October 25, 1971. TNA: FCO 61/820 (Doc. 18). National Archives of the UK.

UK Foreign and Commonwealth Office. L J Evans (British Consulate General Geneva) to Ian K C Ellison (UN Dept., FCO): 'ICRC – Humanitarian Law in

Armed Conflicts'. October 11, 1972. TNA: FCO 61/960 (Doc. 4). National Archives of the UK.
UK Foreign and Commonwealth Office. Record of a Meeting Held in Sir Vincent Evans' Office on Wednesday 10 January (1973) at 2.45pm. n.d. TNA: FCO 61/1090 (Doc. 55). National Archives of the UK.
UK Foreign and Commonwealth Office. T W Keeble (UN Dept., FCO) to Mr Goodenough, Mr Parsons: Humanitarian Law Applicable in Armed Conflicts: Preparations for the 1974 Diplomatic Conference'. March 1, 1973. TNA: FCO 61/1090 (Doc. 74). National Archives of the UK.
UK Foreign and Commonwealth Office. M R Eaton to Sir Vincent Evans: 'Diplomatic Conference on Human Rights in Armed Conflict February/March 1974'. June 5, 1973. TNA: FCO 61/1090 (Doc. 100). National Archives of the UK.
UK Foreign and Commonwealth Office. R G Britten (British Embassy, Oslo) to T W Keeble (UN Dept., FCO): 'Humanitarian Law in Armed Conflict: Liberation Movements'. January 14, 1974. TNA: FCO 61/1231 (Doc. 3). National Archives of the UK.
UK Foreign and Commonwealth Office. R J A Martin (UN Dept., FCO) to R C Cox (Northern Ireland Office): 'Humanitarian Law in Armed Conflict'. February 19, 1974. TNA: FCO 61/1237 (Doc. 26). National Archives of the UK.
UK Foreign and Commonwealth Office. UK Mission in Geneva to Immediate FCO Tel No. 185. March 12, 1974. TNA: FCO 61/1232 (Doc. 89). National Archives of the UK.
UK Foreign and Commonwealth Office. M A Arthur (UK Mission in Geneva) to R Facey (UN Department): 'Diplomatic Conference on Humanitarian Law'. March 15, 1974. TNA: FCO 61/1232 (Doc.93). National Archives of the UK.
UK Foreign and Commonwealth Office. UK Mission in Geneva to Immediate FCO Tel No. 216. March 19, 1974. TNA: FCO 61/1232 (Doc. 97). National Archives of the UK.
UK Foreign and Commonwealth Office. Diplomatic Conference on Humanitarian Law in Armed Conflicts - Geneva 20 February-29 March 1974: First Session - Delegation Report. June 17, 1974. TNA: FCO 61/1233 (Doc. 165). National Archives of the UK.
UK Foreign and Commonwealth Office. Report of Washington Meeting on 13 and 14 January 1975 on Humanitarian Law in Armed Conflict. n.d. TNA: FCO 61/1376 (Doc. 14). National Archives of the UK.
UK Foreign and Commonwealth Office. P M Maxey (UN Dept.) to Coles (Scored out, Replaced in Manuscript - Illegible), 'Humanitarian Law: Reception for Delegates to London Meeting of Western Group' (Appending Briefing Note). January 27, 1975. TNA: FCO 61/1376 (Doc. 34). National Archives of the UK.
UK Foreign and Commonwealth Office, 'Second Session of the Geneva Diplomatic Conference on Humanitarian Law in Armed Conflict, 3 February–18 April,

1975: Brief for the United Kingdom Delegation', 29 January 1975. TNA: FCO 61/1375 (Doc. 17). National Archives of the UK.

UK Foreign and Commonwealth Office. R A Facey (UK Mission in Geneva) to N Jarrold (FCO UN Department): 'Humanitarian Law: Protocol II'. February 10, 1975. TNA: FCO 61/1372 (Doc. 26). National Archives of the UK.

UK Foreign and Commonwealth Office. M S Weir to Maxey (UN Dept.), 'Mr Allon's Meeting with the Secretary of State'. March 3, 1975. TNA: FCO 61/1373 (Doc. 55). National Archives of the UK.

UK Foreign and Commonwealth Office. UK Mission in Geneva to Priority FCO Telno. 35 Saving. March 11, 1975. TNA: FCO 61/1373 (Doc. 54). National Archives of the UK.

UK Foreign and Commonwealth Office. T A H Solesby (UN Dept.) to M S Weir, 'Conference on Humanitarian Law: NLMs' (with 14 March Addendum by M S Weir)'. March 12, 1975.TNA: FCO61/1373 (Doc. 55). National Archives of the UK.

UK Foreign and Commonwealth Office. R A Facey (UK Mission, Geneva) to T A H Solesby (UN Dept.), Conference on Humanitarian Law: NLMs'. March 25, 1975. TNA: FCO 61/1373 (Doc. 70). National Archives of the UK.

UK Foreign and Commonwealth Office. Diplomatic Conference on Humanitarian Law in Armed Conflicts – Geneva 3 February–18 April: Second Session – Delegation Report. August 5, 1975. TNA: FCO 61/1374 (Doc. 134). National Archives of the UK.

UK Foreign and Commonwealth Office. Report of Washington Meeting 17/18 November 1975 on Humanitarian Law in Armed Conflict (Undated, Received in Registry 28 November 1975). November 28, 1975. TNA: FCO 61/1376 (Doc. 51). National Archives of the UK.

UK Foreign and Commonwealth Office. J C J Ramsden (UN Dept., FCO) to Mr Freeland. January 22, 1976. TNA: FCO 58/995 (Doc. 13). National Archives of the UK.

UK Foreign and Commonwealth Office. M L Tait (UN Dept., FCO) to Mr Weir, Brief for the UK Delegation to the Third Session of the Diplomatic Conference on Humanitarian Law in Armed Conflict. April 13, 1976. TNA: FCO 58/995 (Doc. 63). National Archives of the UK.

UK Foreign and Commonwealth Office. M R Eaton to Bowie (UN Dept.), 'Diplomatic Conference on Humanitarian Law in Armed Conflicts – Delegation Report' (Attaching Draft Committee III Report), July 19, 1976. TNA: FCO 58/996 (Doc. 65). National Archives of the UK.

UK Foreign and Commonwealth Office. 'Diplomatic Conference on Humanitarian Law in Armed Conflicts – Geneva 21 April–11 June: Third Session – Delegation Report'. September 21, 1976. TNA: FCO 58/997 (Doc. 76). National Archives of the UK.

UK Foreign and Commonwealth Office. M K O Simpson-Orlebar (UN Dept., FCO) to Mr Mansfield: 'Brief for the UK Delegation to the Fourth Session of the Diplomatic Conference on Humanitarian Law in Armed Conflict'. March 11, 1977. TNA: FCO 58/1125 (Doc. 38). National Archives of the UK.

UK Foreign and Commonwealth Office. W. G. Harris (UN Dept.) to E. C. Glover, UK Embassy, Washington, DC: 'Humanitarian Law in Armed Conflict', April 1, 1977. TNA: FCO 58/1127 (Doc. 75). National Archives of the UK.

UK Foreign and Commonwealth Office. 'Humanitarian Law in Armed Conflict: Inner Core Meeting, 14 March 1977 at the US Mission, Geneva'. April 5, 1977. TNA: FCO 58/1127 (Doc. 76). National Archives of the UK.

UK Foreign and Commonwealth Office. 'Fourth Session of the Diplomatic Conference on Humanitarian Law in Armed Conflict: Geneva, 17 March–10 June 1977: Brief for the UK Delegation'. April 7, 1977. TNA: FCO 58/1126 (Doc. 41). National Archives of the UK.

UK Foreign and Commonwealth Office. Immediate FCO Telno 277: Our Tels Nos 224 and 225: Article 42 – Guerillas'. May 24, 1977. TNA: FCO 58/1124 (Doc. 131). National Archives of the UK.

UK Foreign and Commonwealth Office. Saving Telegram from UKMIS Geneva to FCO (Telno 30). June 10, 1977. TNA: FCO 58/1124 (Doc. 164). National Archives of the UK.

UK Foreign and Commonwealth Office. Diplomatic Conference on Humanitarian Law in Armed Conflicts – Fourth and Final Session: Geneva 17 March–10 June 1977. Interim Delegation Report. July 13, 1977. TNA: FCO 58/1124 (Doc. 174). National Archives of the UK.

UK Foreign and Commonwealth Office. 'Draft Sections of Report to Ministers on Signature of the Two Additional Protocols of 1977 to the Geneva Conventions of 1949' (Appended to 11 October 1977 Note from M R Eaton to Freeland). October 11, 1977. TNA: FCO 58/1129 (Doc. 104). National Archives of the UK.

UK Foreign and Commonwealth Office. 'Fourth Session of the Diplomatic Conference on Humanitarian Law in Armed Conflicts: Geneva 17 March–10 June 1977: Annex B'. December 1, 1977. TNA: FCO 58/1128 (Doc. W97). National Archives of the UK.

UK Foreign and Commonwealth Office. International Criminal Court: Statement of Government Policy. February 24, 1998, House of Commons Dep/3 6092 (hard copy only), see: https://parliament.uk/depositedpapers?page=2188&sort=1# [accessed 14 September 2019].

UK Ministry of Defence. *Joint Service Manual of the Law of Armed Conflict* (Ref. JSP 383, 2004 edition). UK, 2004, available at: https://assets.publishing.service.gov.uk/government/uploads/system/uploads/attachment_data/file/27874/JSP3832004Edition.pdf [accessed 14 September 2019].

UK War Office. Army Council Secretariat, Brief for Secretary of State, Cabinet Meeting of Ministers, 'Revision of Geneva Conventions: Application of Geneva

Conventions to Civil War'. March 26, 1949. TNA: WO 321/14041 (Doc. 35B). National Archives of the UK.

US Department of State. Albert Clattenburg Jr., Chairman of the American Delegation, to the Secretary of State. August 26, 1947. US National Archives and Records Administration: RG – 59, Central Decimal File, 1945–1949, 514.2A12/1–145 to 514.2 Geneva/8–2347 (File 514.2A16 International Red Cross Diplomatic Conference, Geneva), Box 2386.

US Department of State. Telegram from US Mission in Geneva to Department of State: Laws of War Conference – Current Status. February 22, 1974. US National Archives and Records Administration: NARA AAD doc. 1974GENEVA01188, available at: https://aad.archives.gov/aad/createpdf?rid=28832&dt=2474&dl=1345 [accessed 15 September 2019].

US Department of State. Telegram from US Mission in Geneva to State Department: PRG Question at Laws of War Conference. February 28, 1974. US National Archives and Records Administration: NARA AAD doc. 1974GENEVA01308, available at: https://aad.archives.gov/aad/createpdf?rid=28765&dt=2474&dl=1345 [accessed 15 September 2019].

US Department of State. Telegram from US Mission in Geneva to US Mission in Canberra: Laws of War Conference – Wars of Liberation. March 11, 1974. US National Archives and Records Administration: NARA AAD doc. 1974GENEVA01591, available at: https://aad.archives.gov/aad/createpdf?rid=55820&dt=2474&dl=1345 [accessed 15 September 2019].

US Department of State. Telegram from Department of State to US Embassy Cairo: Geneva Conference on Laws of War. January 17, 1975. US National Archives and Records Administration: NARA AAD doc. 1975STATE011987, available at: https://aad.archives.gov/aad/createpdf?rid=115936&dt=2476&dl=1345 [accessed 15 September 2019].

US Department of State. US Department of State Telegram – PRG Issue at Law of War Conference: Supporting Countries. February 6, 1975. US National Archives and Records Administration: NARA AAD doc. 1975GENEVA00767, available at: https://aad.archives.gov/aad/createpdf?rid=100748&dt=2476&dl=1345 [accessed 15 September 2019].

US Department of State. Telegram from US Mission in Geneva to Department of State: Laws of War Conference – Liberation Movement Problem. February 28, 1975. US National Archives and Records Administration: NARA AAD doc. 1975GENEVA01397, available at: https://aad.archives.gov/aad/createpdf?rid=94380&dt=2476&dl=1345 [accessed 15 September 2019].

US Department of State. U.S. Participation in the UN: Report by the President to the Congress for the Year 1977. December 1978, available at: https://archive.org/stream/usparticipationi1977unit/usparticipationi1977unit_djvu.txt [accessed 14 September 2019].

INDEX

Lightning Source UK Ltd.
Milton Keynes UK
UKHW021928190720
366821UK00007B/33

9 781108 497275